Thomas Joseph Ndaluka

Religious Discourse, Social Cohesion and Conflict

Interreligious Studies

edited by

Prof. Dr. Frans Wijsen
and
Dr. Jorge E. Castillo Guerra

This series is published by the
Centre for World Christianity
and Interreligious Studies
at Radboud University Nijmegen

Volume 5

LIT

Thomas Joseph Ndaluka

Religious Discourse, Social Cohesion and Conflict

Muslim – Christian Relations in Tanzania

LIT

The publication of this book was made possible by Radboud University Nijmegen.

Gedruckt auf alterungsbeständigem Werkdruckpapier entsprechend
ANSI Z3948   DIN ISO 9706

Bibliographic information published by the Deutsche Nationalbibliothek
The Deutsche Nationalbibliothek lists this publication in the Deutsche Nationalbibliografie; detailed bibliographic data are available in the Internet at http://dnb.d-nb.de.

ISBN 978-3-643-90211-5

A catalogue record for this book is available from the British Library

©LIT VERLAG GmbH & Co. KG Wien,
Zweigniederlassung Zürich 2012
Klosbachstr. 107
CH-8032 Zürich
Tel. +41 (0) 44-251 75 05
Fax +41 (0) 44-251 75 06
e-Mail: zuerich@lit-verlag.ch
http://www.lit-verlag.ch

LIT VERLAG Dr. W. Hopf
Berlin 2012
Fresnostr. 2
D-48159 Münster
Tel. +49 (0) 2 51-620 320
Fax +49 (0) 2 51-23 19 72
e-Mail: lit@lit-verlag.de
http://www.lit-verlag.de

Distribution:
In Germany: LIT Verlag Fresnostr. 2, D-48159 Münster
Tel. +49 (0) 2 51-620 32 22, Fax +49 (0) 2 51-922 60 99, e-mail: vertrieb@lit-verlag.de

In Austria: Medienlogistik Pichler-ÖBZ, e-mail: mlo@medien-logistik.at

In Switzerland: B + M Buch- und Medienvertrieb, e-mail: order@buch-medien.ch

In the UK: Global Book Marketing, e-mail: mo@centralbooks.com

Dedication

To my sons

Octavius MacTojo and Karl Adeodatus,

who should carry on with this endeavour,

and

in memory

of *Hedwings A. Nkalango (Mwl. Samwel)*,

best mother and teacher

who inspired me to search for knowledge

but did not live to see the fruits of her efforts.

Contents

    List of abbreviations. iii

    Foreword v

1. General introduction 1
    1.1. Historical background to religion in Tanzania. 2
    1.2. Conceptual design 23
    1.3. Technical design 38

2. How Muslims speak about Christians 53
    2.1. Analysis of linguistic practice 54
    2.2. Analysis of discursive practice 81
    2.3. Analysis of social practice 95

3. How Christians speak about Muslims 111
    3.1. Analysis of linguistic practice 112
    3.2. Analysis of discursive practice 137
    3.3. Analysis of social practice 154

4. How Muslims and Christians speak to each other. 175
    4.1. Analysis of linguistic practice 176
    4.2. Analysis of discursive practice 200
    4.3. Analysis of social practice 214

5. Muslim-Christian relations in Tanzania 225
    5.1. Conclusions regarding social identity construction 226
    5.2. Conclusions on the theory underlying CDA. 238
    5.3. Conclusions regarding the method of CDA 246

Contents

Epilogue 253

Bibliography 255

Appendix 265

Summary 267

Curriculum Vitae 271

List of abbreviations

AMNUT	All Muslim National Union of Tanganyika
BAKWATA	Baraza Kuu la Waislamu Tanzania
CCM	Chama cha Mapinduzi
CCT	Christian Council of Tanzania
CDA	Critical Discourse Analysis
CE	Common Era
CHADEMA	Chama cha Democrasia na Maendeleo
CMS	Church Missionary Society
EAMWS	East Africa Muslim Welfare Association
FGDs	Focus Group Discussions
IAO	Islamic Action Organisation
MEO	Mtaa Village Executive Officer
MEMKWA	Mpango kwa Elimu Maalum kwa Watoto Waliokosa
MP	Member of Parliament
MASUD	University of Dar es Salaam Muslim Students' Association
OIC	Organisation for Islamic Conference
PCT	Pentecostal Churches of Tanzania
TANU	Tanganyika African National Union
TAMPRO	Tanzania Muslim Professionals' Organisation
TEC	Tanzania Episcopal Conference (Roman Catholic)
TLP	Tanzania Labour Party
TRA	Tanzania Revenue Authority
UDSM	University of Dar es Salaam
UMCA	Universities Mission to Central Africa
UN	United Nations
UNESCO	United Nations Educational, Scientific and Cultural Organisation
URT	United Republic of Tanzania
US	United States
USA	United States of America
RSO	Regional Security Officer.

Foreword

Several individuals and institutions contributed in one way or another to my study that culminated in the production of this book. I would like to thank all of them, but for lack of space can mention only few individuals and institutions.

The first is the Faculty of Religious Studies at Radboud University, Nijmegen for admission, funding and offering a conducive and friendly environment for my study in Nijmegen. Without their support this work could not have been accomplished. Also I thank the College of Arts and Social Sciences, University of Dar es Salaam (UDSM) for giving me time and resources during my studies, which resulted in this book.

I wish to extend my sincere, heartfelt thanks to Prof. Frans Wijsen and Dr Abu Mvungi, whose close and friendly supervision, constant encouragement, guidance and constructive criticism contributed immensely to the completion of this book. Special thanks to Dr Christopher Comoro, my first local supervisor and colleague for his good faith in selecting me for this project.

I am also indebted to my colleagues at the Department of Sociology and Anthropology, UDSM, especially Dr Rosemarie Mwaipopo who read the draft of chapter three. Her constructive criticism helped me to shape the chapter into what it is now. Great appreciation goes to Ms Marcelle Manley and Dr Michael Andindilile who helped by editing the book and polishing the English language. Fr Smith and Fr Riddle allowed me to use their publications and personal copies. I thank Mr Bashiru Ali for lending me his personal copy of R. Mukandala, et al. (eds). 2006. *Justice, rights and worship: religion and politics in Tanzania.*

Profound gratitude to my family: my wife Tertula, my two sons MacTojo and Adeodatus, my brothers and sisters, uncles, aunts, cousins and nephews, for their encouragement, understanding and patience during all these years, especially while I was away in Nijmegen. I also acknowledge with thanks the contribution of my mother, the late Hedwings A. Nkalango (Mwl. Samwel), who despite being a single parent, inspired me to search for knowledge, but unfortunately did not survive to see the fruits of her efforts.

I also wish to thank my research assistants, who tirelessly helped me in the field: Anna Haule, Faraja Shaban, Juliet Shibiriti, Alfred Balole and Magreth

Msomba. Sincere thanks to my participants who willingly agreed to take part in this study. Without their contributions I could not have established a data base for my research into religious discourse, social cohesion and conflict.

Special thanks to Ms Miep Beuving, office manager of the Centre for World Christianity and Interreligious Studies for her kindness, willingness, helpful and timely assistance when things were not going right. She made my stay at Radboud very pleasant. I am also grateful to all the friends and colleagues whom I met at Radboud University: Frans Dokman, Solomon Dejene, Suhadi Cholil, Fr Ambrose Bwangatto and all those with whom I shared the 14th floor of Erasmus building. Their encouragement and constructive discussion were very important. I also thank Jorge Castillo Guerra for his constant encouragement. Thanks to the Nijmegen international students' office, especially Ms Godelief de Jong, for travel and visa arrangements. Heartfelt gratitude to my church, in particular to Fr Joop (who was also my landlord), Fr Anton, Sr Dona, Sr Dr Yosefine, Ms Vanda, Mr Asfaw, Mr Crispino and all members of the English congregation. Their friendly meetings lifted my spirits and gave me a sense of home. I also thank all the inmates of Dominicus and Catharina house for the friendly environment they provided.

Above all, I remain solely responsible and accountable for any shortcomings in this book. May the almighty God, Mungu and Allah be merciful and may all glory and honour be given to him and him alone. Amen.

Chapter 1:
General introduction

"The world is too fragile, handle it with prayer!"
(Mwalimu Julius K. Nyerere)

In his *Islam between globalization and counterterrorism* Ali Mazrui (2006: 224-232) writes that there has been a global convergence of Islam and Christianity. At the local level militant Muslims sometimes confuse anti-Western and anti-Christian sentiments (Mazrui 2006: 224). Mazrui (2006: 218) cites his East African home country, Kenya, as a place where things might go wrong. On the whole, however, never before in world history have Christianity and Islam been so close (Mazrui 2006: 231).

In this thesis we study the relationships between Muslims and Christians in Tanzania, more particularly social identity transformations through interreligious relations at the individual (micro), institutional (mezzo) and societal (macro) levels. This East African country, dubbed a 'haven of peace', has for some decades harboured seeds of Christian-Muslim conflict (Ludwig 2002; Wijsen & Mfumbusa 2002). This study adopts the socio-cognitive approach of discourse analysis (Van Dijk 1987, Blommaert & Verschueren 1998, Fairclough 1992) to examine, at micro level, the socio-religious transformations taking place in Tanzania.

These transformations are placed in the context of globalisation with its consequences of cultural differentiation (Huntington 1992) and cultural diffusion (Hannerz 1992). It is hypothesised that these trends constitute and are constituted by discourses through which Muslims and Christians try to find common ground (convergence), but at the same time reproduce their own religious identity (divergence).

After debates about attacks on pork butcheries and Christian schools in the late 1980s the Tanzanian parliament was once again divided along religious lines in 2008. On the one hand there were members of parliament, mostly Muslims, defending Tanzania's joining the Organisation for Islamic Conference (OIC) and the establishment of *kadhi* courts. On the other hand there were those, mostly Christians, who opposed these moves. This divided stand was also reflected in the opinions of ordinary Muslim and Christian Tanzanians. It epitomises cultural differentiation in the country. Recent Muslim interest and involvement in

Israel-Palestine relations and Muslim-Christian communication also indicate convergence of the local and the global scenario (localisation-globalisation). Mazrui (2006) notes that Israel-Palestine relations influence the East African political and religious discourse.

In this general introduction I first describe the historical background to religions and Muslim-Christian relations in Tanzania. Then I explain and justify the conceptual design of the thesis. Finally I explain and justify its technical design.

1.1. Historical background to religion in Tanzania

The quotation at the beginning of this chapter comes from Tanzania's first president, Mwalimu Julius Kambarage Nyerere. It suggests that religion is important for Tanzanians and plays a major role in their day-to-day activities. Indeed, Tanzanians have generally been depicted as very religious people. The constitution of the United Republic of Tanzania (URT) grants freedom of choice as regards religious worship. It states: "Every person has the right to the freedom to have conscience, or faith, and choice in matters of religion, including the freedom to change his religion or faith" (URT Constitution CAP. 2 of 2005: Article 19 [1]). All official meetings and/or occasions include prayers by religious or government leaders. For example, at the opening of every parliamentary session the speaker of the house prays for the nation and its parliament. All government executive leaders swear a religious oath; this includes the president elect, ministers, members of parliament, judges and other government officials. The national anthem in fact calls on God to bless Africa, Tanzania, its leaders and citizens. All this shows that religion constitutes and is constituted in Tanzanians' daily life.

Tanzania has three main religions: indigenous African religion, Islam and Christianity. According to the 1967 census 32 percent of Tanzanians were Christians, 30 percent Muslims and 37 percent practised traditional African religion (Said 1998: 276). Since 1967 statistics on religious affiliation were dropped from the national census on the grounds that they were politically sensitive and could undermine national unity and security if not handled with care. In 1973 the Tanzanian National Demographic Survey yielded the following statistics: 40 percent Muslims, 38.9 percent Christians and 21.1 percent adherents of indigenous African beliefs (Tanzania National Bureau of Statistics 1973). Since then no reliable statistics have been provided. Those cited by some religious organisations tend to be biased and outdated, hence highly unreliable.

Some Christian denominations have provided statistics to account for their membership. In 1996, for example, the Roman Catholic Church claimed to have

6.93 million believers, and the Anglican Church 0.65 million. Other Christian churches and Muslims do not have such records (Said 1998:277). Nevertheless the two major religions, Islam and Christianity, have witnessed steady growth in their ranks.

All faiths except African indigenous religion are foreign. Islam, for example, is a result of the country's early contact with the East and Middle East. This contact dates as far back as the first millennium CE. Islam was first introduced in the 7th century by Persian and Arab traders, who came to Tanzania to barter clothing, guns, gunpowder, jewellery and other goods for animal skins, minerals and slaves. During their stay in the country some indigenous people converted to Islam, especially those who had direct contact with Arab Muslims.

Available evidence shows that there are two main Muslim denominations in Tanzania, namely Sunni and Shiite. Three quarters of Tanzania's Muslims are said to be Sunni (Westerlund 1980:89-90). Most Tanzanian Muslims adhere to the Shafi judicial tradition. There are also Hanafi and Qadirriya schools of Indo-Pakistani Muslim origin. Then there are Maliki and Hanbali schools from predominantly Yemenite minority groups. The Shiites are a minority group, mainly of Asian origin. Nevertheless they are subdivided into different branches such as Imami, Ismaili and Bohra/Wohra. Some Muslims, especially those of Oman origin, constitute the Ibadiyya group. The Ahmadiyya is another active Muslim group in the country.

Like Islam, Christianity was imported into the country, this time from Europe. Historical evidence shows that Christianity was already established in Tanzania in the 16th century (though with minimal influence) through early contact with the Portuguese, who invaded some East African coastal areas. Major Christian expansion in the country occurred in the 19th century when both Protestant and Catholic missionaries from Europe came to spread Christianity in the country and in Africa generally.

The same century saw a process of colonisation, in which Tanganyika and Zanzibar, which later became the United Republic of Tanzania, respectively came under German and British rule. The German administrators, aware of the effect of religious conflict in Europe, avoided replicating these conflicts in their colony, hence discouraged the establishment of other religions in areas where a particular religion was dominant. Since Islam predominated in the coastal areas (Westerlund 1980:42), the establishment of Christian denominations was encouraged in the mainland regions. Religion remained a sensitive issue even in the post-colonial era (Njozi 2003:ii).

Thus the study of religion, more particularly Muslim-Christian relations, is an interesting but delicate matter. However, both Islam and Christianity have the same point of departure: the salvation of humankind, which can only be achieved through mission/*da'awah*. Each religion wants to convey a religious message of salvation and civilisation to the 'heathen' or 'infidels'. Whereas many Christians claim that there is no salvation outside Jesus Christ (for Protestants) and/or the church (for Catholics), many Muslims maintain that those who have not submitted themselves to the will of Allah have no place in *ahera* and are destined for hell because they are infidels. Mbogoni (2004:2) and Allport (1973:88) add that both religions invite bigotry by claiming exclusive possession of ultimate truth concerning the destiny and end of humankind, as well as sole authority and means of interpreting that end.

Islam in Tanzania

Islam in Tanzania can be traced as far back as the first millennium (600 CE), basically as a result of contact with people from the Middle and the Far East, who initially came for trading purposes even before the birth of Islam in Arabia (Welbourn 1965:54). Mbogoni (2004) points out that Islam may have arrived on the East African coast as early as the time of the prophet Muhammad, basically via the Medina tribe who were the earliest immigrants from the Arabian Peninsula to explore the East African coast. The Medina tribe was converted to Islam when the prophet Muhammad first arrived in Medina, and only stayed there briefly before travelling to East Africa (Mbogoni 2004:7). These immigrants established settlements in Mogadishu, Shungwaya, Kilwa and Sofala, the first trading centres and cities in the early centuries (Mbogoni 2004:7).

This contact was a result of the Indian Ocean trade network, which has been operating for the past 2000 years. Merchants from as far afield as Greece, China, India and Indonesia, Arabs from South Arabia, and Persians from the Persian Gulf started a trading relationship with the East African coast (Welbourn 1965:54-62), which has persisted ever since.

Trade was made possible by the invention of marine technology (i.e. the building of dhows) and know-how regarding the monsoon winds (Welbourn 1965:54; Whitely 1971), which blew in a southerly direction from November to March. The boats and the winds allowed the Arab mariners and others to import their commodities from the Middle and Far East to the East African coast (Welbourn 1965:54; Martin 1977:106). From April to August traders travelled back when the monsoon winds started blowing northwards (Martin 1977:106), carrying with them East African commodities such as ivory, animal skins, minerals and, later on, slaves (Fabian 1986; Welbourn 1965:58; Whitely 1971). From this period onward Islam, via Muslim Arabs and Arabised Africans, began to infiltrate the African continent (see Whitely 1971).

The introduction of Islam in Tanzania illustrates a unique style of Islamic conversion in Africa. Unlike the northern part of Africa where conversion to Islam was by force, in Tanzania and East Africa generally conversion was effected peacefully (Welbourn 1965:56), largely through acculturation and assimilation. Lewis (1980) puts it aptly: "More than for the other Muslim people of Africa, for East African Muslims [Tanzanians in particular], to be a Muslim is to be an Arab. It is this deep assimilation of Islam and identification with Arab culture and society which is expressed in the universal claim to Arab ancestry."

Levtzion and Pouwels (2000) when analysing the history of Islam in Africa observed that Islamization in the Sub-Saharan Africa and East Africa in particular passed through three stages. The first stage involved the acceptance of elements of Islamic culture and practices, such as dressing style and use of religious concepts. The second stage is marked with formal conversion to Islam involving the converts' acceptance of the *ulama* (religio-legal scholars) as representative of God on earth; and the last stage includes recognition and adherence to the principles of Islamic law and acceptance of the five pillars of Islam.

Rigby (1980) also claims that "Islam was established on the coast not primarily by emigration of Arabs but by the Islamisation of African states". The few Arabs who dared to come to the Tanzanian coast were basically merchants, not Muslim missionaries. Their interaction with the locals, first on the coast before moving into the hinterland, influenced some, especially their servants (slaves), assistants (porters) and local traders, to follow their way of life. This is in line with the statement by Lodhi and Westerlund (1999): "Islam was spread mainly through trade activities along the East African coast, not through conquest and territorial expansion as was partly the case in West Africa, but remained an urban littoral phenomenon for a long time." Welbourn (1965:56), too, earlier asserted that religious conversion in this region was a result of economic and social circumstances (Pouwels 1987). However, this does not mean that Muslims did not practice mission/*da'awah*.

The Arab Muslim traders dominated the Indian oceanic trade and penetrated the African continent from the coast of east Africa; in the process they created small states and trading towns (Welbourn 1965:59). For example, by 950 CE or earlier Muslim mariners/sailors, traders and settlers had reached and established settlements in the Lamu archipelago, the island of Zanzibar which includes the islands of Unguja and Pemba, the port of Kilwa and the island of Mafia. These

Islamic settlements have had a significant impact on the progress of Islam and the conversion of locals (Van Bergen 1981; Rigby 1980; Pouwels 1987).

Rigby (1980) claims that by the end of the 7th century large swathes of the East African coast had already been incorporated into the new Muslim world. For example, in the 7th century Arab Muslims conquered and colonised the coastal area from the Red Sea to the Horn of Africa (Burton 1987:3).

During the same century Arab Muslims exerted influence on the coast of Tanzania and Zanzibar. By then Tanzanian Muslims were under the universal Muslim state of the Umayyad caliphate, whose capital was located in Damascus (Rigby 1980:267). The foundation of the Shanga mosque on Pate Island is believed to be the earliest evidence of a Muslim presence in the whole of East Africa, where excavation in 1980 uncovered silver, gold and copper dating to 830 CE

Moreover, the presence of a mosque at Kizimkazi in southern Zanzibar and the chief mosque of Kilwa, which date as far back as 1007 and 1332, are further proof of Muslims' early presence and the spread of Islam in the East African area. It is claimed that by the early 11th century the sultan of Kilwa had already established control and hegemony over the indigenous people in the area, though local conflicts continued. By the 14th century Islam was widespread along the East African coast. In 1332 Ibn Battuta, after visiting the East African coast, reported that the coastal people were largely Muslims.

However, the 'golden age' of Islam was almost brought to an end by the Portuguese invasion in the 16th century (Mbogoni 2004; Welbourn 1965:63). Using their sophisticated weapons and marine vessels, they destroyed every Muslim city along the coast and gained control of the Indian coastal trade for about two centuries (Welbourn 1965:63; Martin 1977:109). They took over the spice traffic (pepper, cloves, etc.), which was by then a flourishing Arab Muslim trade. Spices from east Africa, particularly from Zanzibar, were highly prized in the East and Far East as well as in European countries. The Portuguese era came to an end in the early 18th century when, with the help of the Oman Empire, Arab Muslim traders, joined by some African locals, managed to wage a war that forced the Portuguese to retreat to Mozambique, losing many harbours and ports on the East African coast (Welbourn 1965:63).

By the early 18th century most of the coastal cities were under the control of Arab governors. They included Mombasa, Zanzibar, Kilwa, Saran and Mafia Island (Martin 1977:108). This restored the trade that was destroyed by the Portuguese invasion of the coast and the spread of Islam resumed (Martin 1977:108).

The shift of the Oman capital to Zanzibar in 1840 marked another era of Islamic expansion in Tanzania (Welbourn 1965:58; Martin 1977:109). The sultan of

General introduction

Oman in Zanzibar facilitated the expansion of trade into the interior as the demand for slaves increased in the Middle East, but also on the sultan's clove plantation in Zanzibar. The demand for ivory and other items also escalated and pushed Arab merchants to venture further inland than ever before (Martin 1977:109).

However, Arab Muslim penetration into the hinterland did not have much impact on the region except in a few pockets such as Tabora and Ujiji. In the words of the legendary Arab trader, Tippu Tip (Hamed bin Muhammed el Murjebi), "we took the main road, but our rations had been bought in Usagara – we got no supplies in Ugogo and at every village we passed we were turned away" (quoted in Whitely 1971:33).

Traces of Islamic influence on the rest of the Tanzanian mainland remain limited, perhaps because the Arab Muslims were discouraged by the nature of the terrain, the locals' hostility towards the Arab traders (Welbourn 1965:59; Whitely 1971), and the lack of large centres with a concentration of people, which could have attracted the Arab merchants to establish commercial settlements (Whitely 1971). Moreover, the migratory lifestyle of local communities at that time would not have favoured the economic interests of the Arab merchants (Lewis 1980).

Although the spread of Islam was limited on the mainland, interaction between the Arab traders and the indigenous people resulted in creolization of the Bantu and Arab languages (Bryceson 2009; Pouwels 1987; Hanse & Twaddle 1995:23), and hence the growth of a new lingua franca – KiSwahili (Wijsen & Tanner 2008), which displayed strong Islamic and Bantu influence (Bryceson, 2009; Pouwels 1987). Consequently KiSwahili became the main medium for trade and literature (Bryceson 2009). It became the national language after Tanzania's independence; it is also spoken in other countries such as Kenya, Burundi, Rwanda, Uganda, the DRC, Zambia, Mozambique and Malawi (Fabian 1986; Blommaert 1999; Mazrui & Mazrui 1998).

Such interaction resulted in the growth of a new Swahili culture (mixed coastal culture) (Smith 1993:95; Bryceson 2009; Mazrui & Mazrui 1998), which was more deeply rooted on the coast and the islands than in the hinterland. These areas came to be known as the Swahili community. The coastal Swahili communities flourished during this early time, even though some of the people falling under this umbrella term did not practise Islam. However, having a Muslim name was seen as a source of prestige and was part of Swahili community culture.

According to Mazrui and Mazrui (1998:126) the culture of the Swahili community was infused with the Islamic way of life and was expressed and understood through the medium of KiSwahili (Spear & Kimambo 1999:63). Pouwels (1987:2) noted that "Islamization of the coast and the origins of coastal culture were related phenomena." This suggests that early contact with the Arabs was not only commercial but also cultural, leading to the development of an Afro-Arab culture and the spread of Islam (Spear & Kimambo 1999:63). KiSwahili played a major role in this cultural fusion, to the extent that some communities became known as the Swahili community (De Vere Allen 1993:3). To be a member of coastal society one first had to adapt to Swahili culture and then convert to Islam and acquire an Islamic name (Hansen & Twaddle 1995:23).

Njozi (2006:254) also states that Swahili was strongly influenced by Islam. "This brought about an ideological conflict on the question of language." According to Njozi (2006:256), "the missionaries were, initially, strongly opposed to the use of KiSwahili as a medium of instruction in schools on the ground that KiSwahili promoted Islamic values." And the situation has not changed much since then. "Even today there are very few Islamic publications in KiSwahili" (Njozi 2006:260).

The great Islamic expansion occurred during the abolition of the slave trade and the advent of European colonial rule in the 1880s and 1890s. During this time many indigenous people embraced Islam. Examples were the conversion of African chiefs such as Fundi Kira of Tabora, Kibasila of Kisangire, Mkwawa of the Uhehe, Kabaka Mutesa III of the Baganda and Ujiji chiefs. Such conversion to Islam was a protest against European invasion and the imposition of the European/Christian way of life, which was seen as a disruption of indigenous cultures. Acceptance of Islam was attributed to Islam's harmony with indigenous African religions (Spear & Kimambo 1999:66). Unlike Christianity, Islam did not aim at changing African religious belief systems. Many Islamic customs, such as polygamy and cleanliness, harmonised well with the African traditions of marrying many wives, male circumcision and, for some ethnic groups, circumcision of women, which were prohibited by Christianity (Spear & Kimambo 1999:66). However, this does not mean that no chiefs converted to Christianity. Van Bergen (1981:48) reports that many chiefs did. They included Mirambo of the Unyamwezi and Mutesa of the Buganda. Many of these chiefs converted to Christianity primarily for protection against powerful ethnic rivals (Van Bergen 1981:48).

Arab trade and Islamic expansion in many ways contributed to the opening up of the African continent, and Tanzania in particular (see Whitely 1971); hence it connected the continent and its peoples with other continents. Before the advent of Europeans in Africa, and Tanzania in particular, Islam had already linked Africans, and Tanzanians for that matter, with the rest of the world. The presence of Islam provided an initial stimulus for European nations to advance into the African continent (Mbogoni 2004:21).

The first European colonists in Tanzania were Germans, who found Islam already established, especially in coastal communities and inland trading centres (Whitely 1971; Van Bergen 1981; Welbourn, 1965; Westerlund 1980). During the German colonial era literate Muslims (who could read and write KiSwahili in Arabic script) worked for the German administration as civil servants (Westerlund 1980:42). Notable examples include the Akidas and Jumbes (Spear & Kimambo 1999:66; Smith 1993:96). Others were recruited to work as colonial soldiers and as interpreters and translators for Germans in the interior (Smith 1993:96; Said 1998:xxii). The German rulers preferred literate Muslims to non-literate ones in their administration. This naturally facilitated the spread of Islam in the interior and in areas where Muslims had no earlier contacts (Westerlund 1980:42). Germans employed KiSwahili-speaking people (most of whom happened to be Muslims) in the administration and the army. The German colonial government also established public schools in the coastal area (e.g. in Tanga) and KiSwahili was the medium of instruction (Westerlund 1980:42). Teachers in these schools were literate Muslims (Westerlund 1980:42).

After the First World War Tanzania was put under UN trusteeship and subsequently became a British protectorate. British colonial rule did little to slow the spread of Islam but, unlike Germany, Britain ruled indirectly (Van Bergen 1981:51). Local chiefs were used to rule on behalf of the colonial administrators, thus rendering the roles of Muslim Akidas and Jumbes redundant (Spear & Kimambo 1999; Smith 1993). The British, moreover, put greater emphasis on secular education and encouraged missionary churches to open more schools that offered secular education (Smith 1993:98). The requirement for civil service jobs changed from literacy in KiSwahili to a secular/Western education (Lodhi & Westerlund 1999:99). Thus those who had access to European missionary schools had a better chance of landing paid jobs in the British colonial administration than others (Njozi 2003:14). Muslims, for their part, were reluctant to introduce secular education in their *madras* (Islamic schools), as it was seen as tantamount to adopting Western civilisation, which in many respects was inherently Christian (Smith 1993:99). As a result they lagged behind Christians in secular education. This somewhat reduced the pace of Islamic expansion into the interior.

While these processes were taking place at the level of the colonial administrators, it should be noted that in the community some people, both Christians and Muslims, were dissatisfied with the colonial economic structure and system, which did not fulfil the aspirations of the majority. Many civil servants and peasants in the villages were disenchanted with the oppressive colonial system. Such dissatisfaction led to the emergence of nationalist elements; the Maji Maji war, the Bushiri rebellion and the Mkwawa war were the result of such dissatisfaction. Nationalism intensified, especially after the Second World War.

Christianity in Tanzania

The introduction of Christianity in Tanzania came after Islam (Mbogoni 2004:2). Islam was well established by the time Christianity was introduced, especially along the coast and in trading centres such as Ujiji, Tabora, Kilwa, Bagamoyo, Pangani, Mafia and the Zanzibar isles. As mentioned already, Christianity was introduced in East Africa by missionaries and explorers from Europe (Mazrui & Mazrui 1998), although there are suggestions that Christians from Ethiopia/Abyssinia, Egypt and/or Somalia/Nubia might have established trade contact with the local people of Tanganyika and Zanzibar, because Christianity had existed in those areas since the first century (Van Bergen 1981:40). What is indisputable, however, is that their contact with the locals did not have any significant impact, so much so that it is difficult to trace such influence in East Africa (Van Bergen 1981:40).

Christian expansion, especially along the coast and on the islands, and evangelisation did not start in earnest until 1499 when Portuguese troops and missionaries arrived with Vasco da Gama, who came to the East African coast in his attempt to sail around the African continent to India (Mbogoni 2004:2). On their arrival the Portuguese found Arab Muslims and Swahili people enjoying close ties and a flourishing trade (Van Bergen 1981:41; Martin 1977). Historically the Portuguese had hostile relations with the Arabs. Hence they used their strong arm tactics on the East African coast, where they came into contact with Arab Muslims (Van Bergen 1981:41). The Portuguese raided and invaded all the coastal trading centres, including Zanzibar and the Mafia islands (Martin 1977:109). In fact, the Catholic priests of the Augustinian order, who accompanied Vasco da Gama, could claim the title of being the pioneers of Christianity in East Africa (Van Bergen 1981:41).

Although they stayed for about two centuries (1499-1698), the Portuguese priests did very little by way of converting the locals to Christianity (Van Bergen 1981:42). In most cases they were perceived as invaders because of their close ties and/or association with the Portuguese traders (Van Bergen 1981:43). This hostility threatened the survival of the Portuguese on the coast of East Africa. In 1630 Yusufu bin Hassan, who had converted to Christianity and acquired the name of

Dom Jeronimo Chingulila, was installed as the first Christian king of Mombasa (Welbourn 1965:63). His Christian status lasted only one year. In 1631 he expelled his Portuguese masters and killed Christian converts. To survive, the converts were required to renounce their Christian faith and convert to Islam. Yusufu bin Hassan's reign lasted only eight years, as the Portuguese reclaimed Mombasa in 1639 (Welbourn 1965:63). After that there were many attempts by Arab Muslims and their allies from Oman to expel the Portuguese, but to no avail.

In 1698 the Arabs (especially Muslims in Mombasa) and local traders appealed to Arabia for military assistance in order to get rid of the loathedChristian yoke. Eventually the Portuguese were driven away by a naval force sent by the imam of Muscat, Seyyid Sultan bin Saif, who was considered by his followers to be a religious as well as a political leader, and Arab soldiers and traders were based on the East African coast.

This conquest put a damper on Christian encounters in East Africa and Tanzania in particular until the latter half of the 19th century. Then missionaries from Europe started to come to East Africa, encouraged by the triumph of evangelisation aimed at spreading Christianity, Western civilisation and commerce on the so-called 'dark continent' (Africa) (Spear & Kimambo 1999:4; Welbourn 1965:64; Van Bergen 1981:46). In 1844 Krapf arrived in Zanzibar as an agent of the Lutheran Church Missionary Society and in 1846 another Lutheran, J. Rebmann, joined him (Welbourn 1965:65; Mbogoni 2004:21). Krapf and Rebmann returned to Europe in 1853 and 1875 respectively without managing to convert the locals and/or establish Christianity in the interior (Welbourn 1965:66).

That did not happen until 1863 when the first Catholic Church was established in Zanzibar by the Holy Ghost missionaries, who established a similar congregation in Bagamoyo in 1868 (Mbogoni 2004:23; Van Bergen 1981:47; Welbourn 1965:66; Versteijnen 1991). The Holy Ghost missionaries were soon followed by the White Fathers (1878), who used Zanzibar and Bagamoyo as a stop-over for their mission to Uganda (Nolan 1978). They eventually settled in north-west Tanzania at Tabora on 12 September 1878 (Nolan 1978:12; Kittler 1957) and afterwards some moved to the southern shore of Lake Victoria, where they established Bukumbi mission. Bukumbi mission was launched in 1879 and in 1892 they opened more churches in Buhaya at Kashozi, Katoke, Rubya and Kagondo en route to Buganda. In 1864 the Universities Mission to Central Africa (UMCA) also moved to Zanzibar, shifting from the Shire highlands of Nyasaland, now Malawi (Welbourn 1965:66). At this juncture the early missions were wholly dependent on the goodwill of the sultan of Zanzibar (Welbourn 1965:66; Mbogoni 2004:23).

Early missionary activity was primarily aimed at taking care of freed slaves through ransoming (Welbourn 1965:66) and avoided converting free individuals in Muslim areas (Smith 1993:98-99). The Holy Ghost congregation established ransoming centres at Bagamoyo and Zanzibar (Welbourn 1965:66). In 1875 the UMCA established a ransoming centre at Tanga (Welbourn 1965:66). Ransomed slaves were baptised and trained so that they could evangelise the ethnic groups from which they had come (Welbourn 1965:66). Ransomed slaves became the first Christians during this early mission in the land now known as Tanzania. In 1872 there were 324 freed slaves, 251 of whom were children. The number increased to 340 in 1876 (Versteijnen, 1991:15).

During this period most of the locals on the coast, especially the Wazaramo and the Wadengereko did not convert to Christianity, simply because Christianity was perceived as a religion for slaves and not for the *waungwana*[1] (civilised) in the community (Hansen & Twaddle 1995:23; Van Bergen 1981:25; Versteijnen, 1991:15).

In 1889 the Holy Ghost missionaries were joined by the Benedictines, who moved to the southern highlands of Tanzania in 1894 (Welbourn 1965:69). By 1890 the Holy Ghost mission had reached Kilimanjaro. Protestants such as the German Moravians and Lutherans came to Tanzania in 1891 and established their stations in south-west Tanzania (Welbourn 1965:69). Thus the Moravians established a station at Tukuyu and opened another at Tabora in 1898 (Welbourn 1965:69). In 1893 the Lutherans took over the work already started by the Church Missionary Society (CMS), now Church Mission Society, in Kilimanjaro. This takeover was influenced by the German administration in Tanzania (Welbourn 1965:69). The Lutherans also started another station at Bukoba (Welbourn 1965:69). By 1901 an African Inland Mission was already established in the region around Lake Victoria (locally known as Lake Nyanza) (Welbourn 1965:70).

All in all, before the outbreak of the First World War the whole of mainland Tanzania had already been reached by different Christian denominations. This was made possible, in part, by the presence of a colonial administration since 1885. Green (2003) attests that, although there was no initial plan of a joint project, colonialism created the preconditions for the kind of political and economic context in which foreign missionaries could work unchallenged and thus promoted full

---

[1] Islam tolerated slavery but prohibited slave traders to enslave African Muslims as they were seen as no less civilised than the slave masters themselves, who at first were Arab and Persian; later on, some rich African Muslims joined this group. To avoid being taken into slavery many Africans, especially on the coast, embraced Islam and were known as waungwana (civilised).

evangelisation to proceed unabated. The same argument is advanced by Welbourn (1965:68).

The indigenous people had difficulty distinguishing Christianity from the colonial administration (Welbourn 1965). As a result the missionary societies struggled to attract converts in the beginning. In this regard Nolan (1977:5) suggests that the "the initial association of the missions with colonialism was a source of resentment and distrust and it was only when the missionaries were perceived to be a politically neutral body capable of serving useful purposes within Unyamwezi[2] society that any collaboration was possible".

This attitude changed with time, as thousands of African converted to Christianity and Christian churches were no longer seen as either alien institutions or cultural agents of colonial and capitalist powers (Spears & Kimambo 1999:3). This was not solely because of the missionaries' evangelisation, but also as a result of efforts by African converts who were trained to be catechists, teachers and local priests. These African pioneers played a major role in delivering the gospel message to their fellow Africans using local languages (Spears & Kimambo 1999:3). The churches gave Africans a new perspective on prevailing social conditions as well as the moral control of their lives (Spears & Kimambo 1999).

Van Bergen (1981) advances four reasons for the success of Christianity in the 19th century evangelisation of Tanzania. Firstly, there was less Muslim influenced resistance in the interior, and secondly, there were few strongly organised local states that resisted the introduction of Christianity in their areas. Thirdly, the goodwill of the sultan of Zanzibar, despite being a Muslim, permitted Christian missionaries to conduct their activities in his area of jurisdiction. This promoted the growth of Christianity in the early stages. Fourthly, the work of propagandists and early explorers such as Krapft, Rebmann, Livingstone, Burton, Speke and Grant in Europe encouraged missionaries to come in droves to Africa (the new world) to preach the word of God (Van Bergen 1981:47).

As in the case of Islam, language was a significant factor. Unlike Islam, which relied on KiSwahili to spread their faith, some Christian denominations used ethnic languages for this purpose and the White Fathers tended to encourage this practice (Welbourn 1965:82; Spear & Kimambo 1999:6). Unlike the White Fathers, the Holy Ghost fathers promoted KiSwahili because they were working

---

[2] Unyamwezi was a place in central Tanzania (currently known as Tabora region) where the Nyamwezi ethnic group lives. This place was a stopover for missionaries from the northern or western part of Tanzania who were going back to Zanzibar or vice versa, that is a stopover for missionaries proceeding from Zanzibar to the northern or western part of Tanzania.

among Swahili speaking people. Sacleux's[3] dictionary, for example, dates back to the 1930s. Nevertheless, the use of ethnic languages attracted more Africans to Christianity, as many people in the interior did not speak KiSwahili, an alien tongue for most ethnic groups in mainland Tanzania (Spear & Kimambo 1999:6).

The use of ethnic languages led the missionaries to translate religious doctrines into the vernacular. Spear and Kimambo (1999:6) note: "Vernacular translations of the scriptures also inculturated the faith in indigenous cultural meanings." Thus conversion to Christianity by indigenous people depended on the way the translated messages were filtered and interpreted by the audiences.

Despite being overwhelmed by new converts, these Christian denominations were disunited (Green 2003). They did not exist as the one body of Christ, but were more like a series of separate churches (Spear & Kimambo 1999), each vying for supremacy and hegemony, especially when two missions operated in the same area (Welbourn 1965). Spear and Kimambo (1999) show, for example, that British Anglicans competed with Scottish Presbyterians, American Baptists and Lutherans. The Roman Catholic Church seems to have been free from inter-denominational competition but not from intra-denominational conflict. Thus there were contradictions and competition between the French White Fathers and the German Benedictines; similarly, the French and American Holy Ghost fathers competed with British Mill Hill fathers, and the American Maryknolls competed with Irish Pallottines (Spear & Kimambo 1999; Welbourn 1965).

Nevertheless, between 1905 and 1944 Christianity spread rapidly on the mainland, attracting many converts. Van Bergen (1981:52) notes that in 1938 Christians made up about 8, 10 and 25 percent of the respective populations of Kenya, Tanganyika and Uganda. He adds that Roman Catholic membership increased from about 300 000 in 1914 to over one million and 1.7 million in 1938 and 1946 respectively (Van Bergen 1981:52).

Protestant churches were not far behind. Their numbers swelled rapidly, though they did not match those of the Roman Catholics. By 1914 the Lutheran Church of German societies had converted about 20 000 Africans to Christianity. This figure grew to 92 000 and 150 000 in 1938 and 1946 respectively. The Anglican Church grew from 225 000 in 1914 to 400 000 and 750 000 in 1938 and 1946 respectively (Van Bergen 1981:52).

This tremendous achievement was partly because of the missionaries' strategy of saving both bodies and souls (Welbourn 1965:79; Versteijnen 1991). Thus

---

[3] Sacleux was a Holy Ghost father who was interested in KiSwahili and Arabic. He wrote one of the first KiSwahili dictionaries to help priests from Europe to evangelise the Swahili community (on Zanzibar and along the coast). The first Swahili dictionary was written by Johann Krampf.

they started by ransoming slaves and teaching, giving them a secular education and skills. Missionary schools were also introduced at every mission station on the mainland (Versteijnen 1991). Some pupils at missionary schools were converted to Christianity and became Christian ambassadors in their villages and ethnic groups (Spears & Kimambo 1999). To the missionaries, secular education with a heavy dose of Christian teaching was a sure tool for evangelising and converting Africans to Christianity.

By 1911 there were about 60 000 pupils enrolled at various mission schools throughout Tanganyika. This was a huge number, considering that there were only 6 000 pupils in German government schools that year (Van Bergen 1981:51).

The German government schools were mostly in Muslim communities (Van Bergen 1981:51) such as Tanga, Dar es Salaam and Bukoba. In 1914 there were about 65 government elementary schools run by the German administration (Welbourn 1965:85). The colonial administration felt obliged to provide education for Muslim communities neglected by the Christian missionaries, who set up schools mainly in the interior of Tanganyika (Van Bergen 1981:51). As a result missionaries blamed the German colonial administration for favouring Muslims and encouraging the spread of Islam (Van Bergen 1981:51).

In addition, in 1925 the post-First World War British administration (Van Bergen 1981:53-54) decided to introduce secular education in all schools in the country (Smith 1993:98). The British intention was to get more Africans into missionary schools, regardless of their religious affiliation, including Muslims and so-called pagans. As a result the school curriculum changed from one that emphasised religious dogma to a secular curriculum. Missionaries felt betrayed and were convinced that they had lost their autonomy in teaching and spreading religious sentiments among their pupils (Van Bergen 1981:54).

Furthermore, in 1948 the United Nations Educational, Scientific and Cultural Organisation's (UNESCO) emphasis on public as opposed to mission education minimised the missions' control over school finances (Van Bergen 1981:55). This was not well received by some missionaries, who felt their funds would no longer be under their firm control (Van Bergen 1981:55).

After the Arusha Declaration in 1967 that followed Tanganyika's independence from Britain in 1961 and union with Zanzibar in 1964, mission schools were nationalised by the government and converted into public schools as part of a drive to promote secular and socialist (*Ujamaa*) education (Smith 1993:102; Mbogoni 2004:125). The main purpose was to have equity in education (Mbogoni 2004:127). By turning mission schools into public schools the post-independence Tanzanian government was able to increase enrolment in schools, especially among the Muslim population, who got left behind in secular education (Mbogoni 2004: 127-130).

Nevertheless, the involvement and interference of subsequent governments (starting with the German and British colonial administrations and, later on, Tanzanian governments) in mission education and schools did not entirely deter the missions. Many Africans continued to be converted to Christianity.

Muslim-Christian relations in Tanzania

As mentioned already, Islam was well established in Tanzania long before the advent of Christianity. It was twelve centuries or so after the introduction of Islam to the coast of East Africa (the exact date is not known) that Christianity gained a significant foothold in the area. This makes it a relatively new phenomenon in Tanzania, and its expansion clashed with the triumph of Islam in East Africa.

The first (early) contact between Muslims and Christians was hostile and fraught with suspicion. The early Christian missionary activities were carried out by Portuguese priests, who accompanied Portuguese traders, scientists, mariners and soldiers in 1498 (Mbogoni 2004). This mission was basically aimed at limiting the spread of Islam in the world after its expulsion from southern Europe. The Portuguese had bad relations with Muslims in North Africa, particularly Morocco, and championed a crusade against Islam (Martin 1977:109). On coming to East Africa, apart from commercial interests, the Portuguese also sought to curb the spread of Islam on the coast (Martin 1977:109).

As a result the Portuguese destroyed every city and town that was controlled by Arab Muslims. However, to use Mbogoni's words, "The Portuguese were interested more in plunder than in the propagation of Christianity" (Mbogoni 2004:21). The Muslim cities destroyed included Kilwa, Mafia, Mombasa and Zanzibar. They also controlled the trading centre of the Arab world, the Muscat city (Martin 1977:109). This offended the Arab Muslims and the Swahili community, which had embraced Islam before the Portuguese Christians landed on the coast of East Africa (Martin 1977:109.

In fact, Portuguese brutality earned them limited cooperation from the Swahili peoples, to the extent that when the Arab Muslims rebelled in the 1660s the Swahili community joined forces with them against the Portuguese, who ended up being thrown out of East Africa, signalling a temporary halt in the spread of Christianity in that area (Mbogoni 2004:21).

The next Muslim-Christian contact did not occur until the beginning of the 19th century, when Christian explorers, scientists and missionaries arrived in

Africa and East Africa in particular (Van Bergen 1981; Mbogoni 2004:21; Welbourn 1965; Spear & Kimambo 1999). By then imperialism had reached a peak in Europe, compelling these Europeans to spread to different parts of the world as part of their colonial enterprise.

Christian missionaries came at a time when the British government had signed the Moresby treaty of 1822 with the sultan of Zanzibar aimed at abolishing the slave trade in his territory (Mbogoni 2004:24). Thus, apart from spreading the message of Jesus Christ, missionaries thought it was their responsibility to ransom (Henschel 2000:5) and receive freed slaves. Freed slaves were put in villages near missionary houses. The missionaries taught these freed slaves new skills and gave them a Western education (Henschel 2000:5-6). The freed slave settlements became the first Christian villages; some of the freed slaves became catechists (Spear & Kimambo 1999).

The Arab Muslims, who were benefiting from the slave trade, did not welcome this development. Their hostility was so open that it threatened the missionaries' security. Freetown, a slave village in Mombasa, was attacked by Arab Muslims in 1880. The British East Africa Company intervened by compensating all those Arabs whose slaves had run away and thereby saved the village from destruction.

As noted already, during this time missionary activities in Tanzania were possible only because of the tolerance of the sultan of Zanzibar (a Muslim), who allowed missionaries to conduct activities in his area of jurisdiction. Versteijnen (1991:3) writes that on 22 December 1860, "a French steam-corvette, carrying three priests, six sisters, a surgeon of the French Navy and some craftsmen dropped anchor in the placid waters of Zanzibar. Sultan Seyyid Majid, who was approached by the priests for his permission, gladly offered both his protection and his full support to their charitable work."

After the era of Seyyid Said the sultanate of Zanzibar received missionaries with open arms, but also warned them to carry out their activities without interfering in Zanzibar politics. According to Welbourn (1965) some missionaries disregarded this condition. He noted that "even the gentle Krapft was accused by Seyyid Said [sultan of Zanzibar] of meddling in politics" (Welbourn 1965:63). Nevertheless this did not destroy the good rapport these early missionaries had with the sultans of Zanzibar.

In February 1868, when they shifted their activities to the coast of East Africa, namely to Bagamoyo, the missionaries' aim was not to convert the local people who were already Muslims, but rather the freed and runaway slaves. Their intention was to set up Bagamoyo and Zanzibar stations as launching pads for work on the mainland of Tanzania (Versteijnen 1975:8).

At this time Christian-Muslim relations were relatively good. The Holy Ghost mission in Bagamoyo had maintained good relations with Bushiri bin Salim al Harthi, the Arab Muslim leader of Pangan, so much so that when Bushiri and the *diwans* of Bagamoyo – Makanda, Mbomboma, Pori, Marara, Simbambili and Jehasi – attacked the German colonial administrator at Bagamoyo in 1889, destroying the northern and western parts of Bagamoyo town, the missionaries and their property were spared. This led father Hans Meyer to declare that "this was a favor, for which we owe gratitude to Bushiri" (quoted in Versteijnen 1975:26). Henschel (2000) quotes the same person (Hans Meyer), who asserted: "You have to recognize that Bushiri and his fanatical supporters respected the mission as a neutral place and never attacked it" (in Henschel 2000:28). Bushiri's attitude towards the Germans was justified by father Gomminger, who saw it as defence against foreign invasion: "You may call the East Africans rebels, but they are not! They only did what every one in every nation would have done, what we would have done. They fight for their freedom and their rights!" (Henschel 2000:27).

However, this was not the case with other mission stations. Although the Holy Ghost fathers of Bagamoyo were spared by the Bushiri Muslim troops, their counterparts, the Benedictines of Pugu, were not. In 1889 the troops of Seleman (a Dar es Salaam chief and Bushiri's ally) destroyed, plundered and killed almost everyone around Pugu mission, leaving the village in ruins (Rupper 1988:31-47).

After the First World War Tanzania became a British protectorate under the trusteeship of the United Nations. The British administrator did not change the German system of handling religious conflict. Unlike the Germans, secular education was emphasised and became the qualification for employment in the colonial administration. This meant a shift in employment privileges from the Muslim Swahili, who were regarded by the Germans as literate (Westerlund 1980:51; Lodhi & Westerlund 1999:99), to the Christians, who under the British administration had acquired secular education through mission schools (Smith 1993:98; Njozi 2003:15).

After the Second World War, Africa and Tanzania in particular witnessed the emergence of nationalist struggles for independence (Said 1998). In Tanzania Muslims and Christians joined forces against the British administration (Said 1998; Smith 1993:100-101). A nonreligious political party was established, the Tanganyika National Union (TANU). It united all Tanganyikans regardless of religious, ethnic or racial affiliation. Thus TANU had both Christians and Muslims members (Sivalon 1992; Smith 1993:100). In some coastal areas, as well as in Tabora and Bukoba, Muslims made up the majority of TANU membership (Said 1998).

According to Van Bergen (1981) and Kiwanuka (1973) many Christians, especially the elite, were not much involved in TANU and the nationalist movement as they were benefiting from the colonial system. Kiwanuka (1973) claimed that churches, especially the Roman Catholic Church, discouraged their members from joining nationalist movements, warning them of the concomitant danger of getting involved in fighting colonialism. Despite such discouragement by the church leaders many Christians did join TANU and contributed significantly to the nationalist movement (Smith 1993:101; Sivalon 1992). Sivalon (1992:20-21) points out that some Catholic church leaders supported TANU policy and sponsored Nyerere's trip to the United Nations in 1957.

Although Muslims constituted a majority in TANU, Mwalimu Julius Kambarage Nyerere, a Christian, was elected as the party's president in 1954. Nevertheless, in 1959 there were attempts by the All Muslim National Union of Tanganyika (AMNUT) to delay independence because of the educational gap between Muslims and Christians. AMNUT feared that Christians would dominate the Muslims, who lagged behind in education (Maghimbi 1992:118). TANU, however, managed to dispute the AMNUT claim, stating that the delay would not be in the interest of Muslims and Tanganyika as a whole. In the event Muslims and Christians together managed to attain independence peacefully in 1961 (Said 2008, 1998; Smith 1993:100).

In 1964 Tanganyika and Zanzibar united to form a new country, the United Republic of Tanzania (URT), and Mwalimu Nyerere became the first president with the then Zanzibar president, Amani Abedi Karume (a Muslim), as vice president.

Relations between Muslims and Christians during the first years of independence were relatively good. On the whole believers of different faiths coexisted peacefully (Smith 1993:102), but did not altogether overcome the religio-centrism which had been cultivated in some places (Njozi 2003:16-17). Van Bergen (1981) reports an event in Bukoba involving Christian and Muslim TANU members. Some Catholic teachers in Bukoba accused the TANU government of favouring Muslims, who were the majority in TANU. Christians felt that Islam was a precondition for becoming a TANU leader (Van Bergen 1981:204), hence there was a mix of politics and religion (Westerlund 1980:92).

This strain intensified during the 1963 district council elections, when 25 Roman Catholic teachers decided to stand as independent candidates against TANU nominees (Van Bergen 1981:204). Most of the independent candidates won at the polls. This created a tense situation between Muslims and Christians in the district, as the Catholic Church ended up being accused of involvement in politics and in funding district council elections. In the same year Nyerere wrote a strong letter to the bishops condemning the churches' involvement in politics (Sivalon 1992:31). The government also barred all public servants from contesting political positions. Those who wanted to run for political posts had to resign from their public service posts first (Van Bergen 1981:204).

In 1967 the government of Tanzania passed the Arusha Declaration that allowed it to nationalise Christian and Muslim schools (Mbogoni 2004). In 1969 all mission schools were nationalised (Njozi 2003:16; Sivalon 1992). The government only spared seminaries. The government had passed a policy aimed at ensuring universal access to education for all who were eligible and firmly believed that this could be accomplished through government run schools. Both Muslims and Christians (priests) were dissatisfied with the decision to nationalise the schools (Said 1998; Van Bergen 1981:205).

Most Christians accused the government of favouring Muslim at the expense of Christian development (Van Bergen 1981; Westerlund 1980:4). At the same time Muslims accused the government of meddling in religion, especially when the East African Muslim Welfare Society (EAMWS) was banned and *Baraza Kuu la Waislamu Tanzania* (BAKWATA)[4] was established in its place in 1968 (Smith 1993:104; Westerlund 1980:95-97; Njozi 2003:19). The government banned EAMWS because it had a pan-Islamic agenda and did not support the government's nationalist policy wholeheartedly (Mfumbusa & Wijsen 2004). Some Muslims feared that BAKWATA was not as autonomous as it should be because of the influence of Christians, who were the majority in government positions (Van Bergen 1981; Njozi 2000).

Still, Nyerere with his *Ujamaa* policy did manage to suppress religio-centrism (*udini*) in the country and maintained a secular government while leaving citizens free to choose their religion and mode of worship. Nyerere himself believed in separating religion from the state. In his book, *Our leadership and the destiny of Tanzania* (1995a:17), he asks: "Is he able to make a distinction between his personal form of religious belief and his position as president of a secular state which respects all religions and upholds religious freedom? Is he able to disagree with his own religious authorities if the national need arises?"

According to Nyerere (1995b:24) those who used religion in politics were politically bankrupt (*wamefilisika*): "Those who are bankrupt in policy in their heads will look for legitimacy. If they won't legitimize their position using their Tanzanian citizenship, and legitimize it on religio-centric grounds, they are people who are bankrupt."[5] Mixing religion and politics was not tolerated under Nyerere's

---

[4] BAKWATA – Baraza kuu la Waislamu Tanzania (lit: Supreme Muslim Council of Tanzania).
[5] Translated from KiSwahili: Watu wote waliofilisika sera kichwani, mtu akisha filisika, anatafuta

leadership, although at the same time he invited religious leaders to play their part in nation building (Westerlund 1980:90; Sivalon 1992:4). Even after his retirement from the presidency he continued to make sure that public offices remained secular, though religious bigotry did persist among some public officials accused of favouring a particular religion at the expense of others. In fact, Nyerere (1968:1) wrote: "Some Government and Party actions were having the effect of encouraging the growth of non-socialist institutions, values, and attitudes." However, some held that Nyerere himself was not innocent of mixing politics and religion (Said 1998; Mbogoni 2004; Sivalon 1992). Although that might not have been attributable to a secret agenda against Muslims, merely by being a Christian Nyerere was closer to Christian religious leaders (especially the bishops and priests) than to other religious leaders.

Nyerere's efforts were geared to establishing a national identity based on the *Ujamaa* spirit of fairness. He was challenged, however, by other peripheral voices which proclaimed and maintained group identities (religious identity, elite identity,[6] etc.), which did not accord with Nyerere's project of building a national identity.

Nevertheless, for years Tanzania enjoyed peaceful coexistence between Muslims and Christians (Kaduma 2004). It is generally agreed that Nyerere contributed greatly by creating an enabling environment in which Muslims and Christians were able to abandon their religious bigotry. As a result Tanzania became a haven of peace to refugees from neighbouring countries fleeing from internal strife. It attracted refugees from various countries: Rwanda, Burundi, and the DRC which border on Tanzania in the west; Uganda and Kenya to the north. These countries had been locked in ethnic and political strife for many years (Wijsen 2004:15).

Although Nyerere is credited with promoting peace in Tanzania, some criticised his approach, especially the *Ujamaa* policy and his religious partiality (Said 1998; Sivalon 1990, 1992; Njozi 2003; Maghimbi 1995). This created simmering tensions that threatened peaceful coexistence (Wijsen & Mfumbusa 2004). Religion contributes a lot to these tensions. Although both Muslims and Christians have contributed to building what is today called Tanzania in peaceful ways (Smith 1993:114), each religion seeks to create its own social identity and estab-

---

uhalali. Kama hawezi kujihalalisha kwa Utanzania...atajihalalisha kwa udini...hawa ni watu waliofilisika (Nyerere 1995b. Nyufa. Mwalimu Nyerere Foundation, Dar es Salaam).

[6] See also Blommaert (1997), who discusses Tanzanian intellectuals' role in the process of nation building.

lish its hegemony, thus threatening the peaceful coexistence both religions have enjoyed for years (Wijsen & Mfumbusa 2004).

Recently there have been struggles between Muslims and Christians for dominance and control of social, cultural and state resources in the country. Some of these conflicts have led to physical violence, as happened during the 1993 Good Friday pork crisis (Mbogoni 2004), the 1998 and 2000 Mwembechai crises (Njozi 2000), and the 2001 Zanzibar riots (Mukandala et al. 2006). These crises call for vigilance and insight into interreligious relations if Tanzania is to maintain the present harmony (Wijsen & Mfumbusa 2004).

Although the constitution of the United Republic of Tanzania provides for freedom of religion, Muslims feel that there are many factors working against their interests. In fact, they believe that there is a conspiracy between Christians and the state to discriminate against them (Smith 1993; Tambila 2006). To them such conspiracy and discrimination stem from the historical development of the country (Smith 1993; Tambila 2006). Many Muslims believe that their participation in the independence struggle has been downgraded, denigrated and ignored by Christians (Musoke 2006:497).[7]

Because of this sense of marginalisation many Muslims in Tanzania suspect there has been an unfair distribution of educational opportunities and positions of power such as those of principal secretaries, commissioners, directors and other public officials (Tambila 2006:217). Musoke (2006:497) maintains that there are individuals and religious groups who claim that in many cases religion is a factor in job placement and promotion. According to this view Muslim-government strife centres on the claim that job opportunities have been, and continue to be, unevenly distributed among the different religious groups (Njozi 2003:17; Musoke 2006:497). These inequalities appear to fan religious tension and conflict between Muslims and Christians (Musoke 2006). Similar sentiments have been expressed by Muslim scholars such as Njozi (2000), Liviga (2006) and Jumbe (1994), who hold that Muslims are considered second-class citizens.

Conversely, Christians have raised concern about Muslims. Malekela (1994:11, cited in Tambila 2006:212), for instance, says that the government of Tanzania favours Muslims to assume positions of power even when they were not properly qualified for those jobs. Other scholars even accused the Mwinyi (Muslim) administration of undue favouritism in job and education opportunities (Tambila 2006). The 2007 USA human rights report on Tanzania notes complaints by

---

[7] This reproach is directed to the first president of Tanzania, the late Mwalimu J.K Nyerere (a Christian), implying that he has a hidden agenda to favour Christians (see also Njozi 2000; Said 1998; Sivalon 1992).

Christian groups that the government tends to give sensitive government positions to Muslims (U.S. Department of State 2007). These misgivings show that Christians are also unhappy about what they construe as deliberate efforts by political incumbents to favour Muslims.

The complaints, however, are more widespread among Muslims, who have continued to object to what they perceive as anti-Muslim behaviour on the part of Christians. This includes allowing the operation of pork butcheries in Muslim dominated neighbourhoods, restrictions on their right to practise open air preaching (*mihadara*)[8] when Christians allegedly obtained such permission without any difficulty. In addition Muslims felt aggrieved that they were denied the right to receive funds from foreign countries (OIC in particular), while their Christian counterparts continued to receive funding from external sources without any suspicion.

1.2. Conceptual design

In this section we explain the conceptual design of our study (Verschuren & Doorewaard 1999:25-108). It comprises the research objective, definition of the problem, research questions, theoretical framework, and key concepts.

Research objective

In the previous section we described a transformation in Tanzanian society and a return of religious rhetoric to the public domain. During the first decades after independence (1962-1985) the dominant discourse in Tanzania was about economic growth (*maendeleo*) and national unity (*umoja*). From 1985 onwards the emphasis has been on liberalisation and consequent pluralisation of society. When Ali Hassan Mwinyi openly spoke about religious diversity and intolerance in 1986 it came as a shock to many (Wijsen & Mfumbusa 2004:16). This was a new way of speaking about religious diversity and tensions between religions, not heard before in Tanzania. In this thesis we study the relation between religious discourse and (the lack of) social cohesion in Tanzania (research object).

---

[8] Muslim open air preaching, locally known as mihadara, started in the mid-1980s after the introduction of the liberalisation policy in Tanzania. Before that speaking about other people's faiths, especially in public, was prohibited. Open air preachers adopt a comparative approach using different scriptures, mainly the Bible and the Qur'an. It was established as a counter measure to Christian crusades, which have been common in the country since the 1970s.

We want to know why and under what conditions religious discourse becomes dominant and whether or not religious diversity threatens national unity and leads to social conflict. In the previous section we spoke about Muslim-Christian relations from a macro sociological (societal) perspective. In this study we start with the micro (situational, interpersonal) level of discourse (focus group discussions), but we are also interested in the dialectical relation between the micro (individual) and the macro (societal) level discourses, and whether or to what extent the mezzo (institutional) level discourse plays a mediating role between the other two discourses.

The dominant approaches in studies of identity and diversity are realism and positivism. Authors write about national, ethnic or religious identities as if identity is based on primordial properties that are shared by members of a group, uniting them and distinguishing them from others (Bourdieu 1991). Consequently national, ethnic or religious identities are exclusive and differences unbridgeable (Huntington 1996). Seen thus, a multicultural society is a tragedy and intercultural communication an illusion. But inter-cultural communication is possible (Wiredu 1996), at least partially, hence this way of looking at and studying identity is inappropriate.

In this book we look for alternative ways of theorising about and studying religious identity and interreligious relations. The main objectives of this research are: (1) to gain insight into the relation between religious discourse and (the lack of) social cohesion (internal objective), and by doing so (2) to contribute to a theory and method of studying interreligious relations (external objective).

Research questions

Earlier we referred to Mazrui's study, *Islam between globalization and counterterrorism* (2006), and the paradox of growing convergence and divergence of religions. In the past two decades various studies have looked into the growing tensions between Muslims and Christians in Tanzania. Whereas some scholars blame the missionary nature of Islam and Christianity and the worldwide growth of extremism in both religions, others see the introduction of multi-party politics and a free market economy as factors exacerbating such tensions.

As noted above, we study social identity transformations through interreligious, particularly Muslim-Christian, relations. We want to know if the rhetoric about the return of religion to the public domain is an appropriate way of speaking about transformations that are taking place in Tanzania. And if this is the case, why and under what conditions people elevate their religious identities above other (e.g. ethnic, national, and economic or gender) identities (Mbogoni 2004:192), and whether or not this leads to social conflict, or the other way round: do existing conflicts in society express themselves in religious rhetoric and vocabulary?

More specifically, the main research questions are: (1) how do Muslims and Christians identify and position themselves and others? (2) What are the socio-cognitive effects of their identification and positioning? Sub-questions relating to question (1) are: (a) how do Muslims and Christians speak about each other? (b) How do Muslims and Christians speak to each other? Sub-questions relating to question (2) are: (a) what are the conditions for understanding/misunderstanding? (b) What are the conditions for cohesion (convergence) or conflict (divergence)?

Theoretical framework

In this thesis we study the relation between religious discourse and (the lack of) social cohesion (the research object) from a practice theory point of view (research perspective), more particularly a theory of communicative practice (Habermas 1984; Bourdieu 1991). So far the dominant paradigm in religious studies has been to study religion as a system of symbols (Geertz 1973) that exists independently of actors, thus *sui generis*. More or less in reaction to this, scholars of religion have brought individual actors to the fore (Asad 1993), or at least the dialectical relation between systems and actors.

To answer the question of how Muslims and Christians achieve convergence, Mazrui and Mazrui (1995, 1998) provide an explanation from the perspective of linguistic pragmatism. They maintain that Muslims and Christians use language (in their case KiSwahili) to create common ground between them. They regard KiSwahili as an ecumenical language, 'ecumenical' being understood in its original Greek meaning of the whole world, not in the later inter-confessional and interreligious sense of the word. Earlier Fabian (1986) described the language as a vehicle for transmitting Christian teachings and Western civilisation. In addition Fabian (1991:34) sees language as contributing to the formation of identity of cultures.

In her "Study of KiSwahili creolization: the case of Dar es Salaam", Bryceson (2009) claims that KiSwahili as a lingua franca facilitated Swahili creolization. According to her the use of KiSwahili by the inhabitants of the coastal areas (Arabs, African, Persians, etc.) fused a culture that later served to identify the coastal people, known as Swahili culture.

Writing about Indonesia,[9] which has the largest Muslim population in the world and lively Muslim-Christian relations, Beatty (1999:27) refers to the language used during ritual meals (*slametan*). By using ambiguous language and playing with words "people of different orientations come together in a single ritual and manufacture consensus or at least the appearance of it". Hallencreutz and Westerlund (2002:3) relate this practice to civil religion, which is used to foster community integration. In Tanzania such civil religion is apparent in the use of the word 'God' in the national anthem and prayers before government and political meetings. These phenomena indicate that religion is central in fostering national cohesion between believers of different faiths in the country.

Blommaert and Verschueren (1991:2) point out that language can act as both a unifying and a divisive factor. They cite the examples of Flemish Belgians and the Dutch, who are unified by the Dutch language, and Serbians and Croatians who are divided by language.

These and other studies look at inter-ethnic or interreligious relations from the perspective of the power of language to make and unmake social groups, and in the process bring about cohesion and conflict (Bourdieu 1991). In his work Pierre Bourdieu proposes a theory aimed at understanding human practice (Rey 2004:331). It can apply to religion and how religion is used and manipulated by believers as a source of capital. Bourdieu uses terms like 'religious field', 'habitus' and 'capital' to further his argument on the "dynamics of the interaction between the individual and social dimension of religion" (Bourdieu 1991; Rey 2004:331). Bourdieu (1977) uses the term 'habitus' variously to describe the system of lasting, dispositions and cognitive structures which individuals use to perceive and act in their social environment. It is also "the system of durable, transposable dispositions which function as the generative basis of structured, objectively unified practices" (Bourdieu 1979:vii). In short, habitus is "a tendency of individuals to behave in a particular way" (Wijsen 2007:20) in the field. According to Bourdieu (1977) and Foucault (1972) a habitus is a product of upbringing and formal education, making it dynamic and structured as well as corporeal (Wijsen 2007:20).

Bourdieu defines 'field' as a network or configuration of objective relations between positions. To him a field is relational because individuals' actions (habitus) are constrained by their positions in the field, thus limiting their freedom. Central to Bourdieu's concept of field is the idea of a struggle for resources (capital) in the field. Bourdieu uses the economic term 'capital' to denote different

---

[9] This project is part of an overall programme which comprised three studies: one case study in Indonesia, another in Tanzania and a comparative study. During this time I had the opportunity to visit Indonesia and share experiences with researchers there and in the Netherlands.

valuable resources (most of them non-economic) which contribute to social relations of power (Bourdieu 1993:73). According to Bourdieu there are many forms of capital in societies, including religious, cultural and economic capital. Individuals are involved in a constant struggle for these forms of capital to acquire what he calls a social relation of power (see Bourdieu & Wacquant 1992:72-98). With regard to religious capital, Bourdieu criticises Weber for ignoring the structures of the religious field, in which the relationship between structures and individual perceptions (religious habitus) are crucial for understanding the sociology of religion. Bourdieu explains that in the religious field there is a constant struggle between orthodoxy and heretical movements, primarily competing for the religious habitus of lay people.

Bourdieu took his original inspiration from Weber's sociology of religion and translated the notion of charisma into capital. Unlike Weber, who saw charisma as a gift from nature, Bourdieu (1984:1) maintains that it is a result of socialisation and education. In his view different cultural environments produce different charismatic leaders. Their differences are also informed by the level of formal education attained (Bourdieu 1984:1).Bourdieu sees charisma as another form of habitus, which is also a product of cultural socialisation and formal education.

Bourdieu's theory of practice is central to our analysis of interreligious relationships, as it furthers understanding of class, power and struggles and consequently affords insight into how people think and apprehend the social world, as well as their reaction (or practice) to others both in and outside the group. This suggests that believers' actions (in our case those of Muslims and Christians) are influenced by their understanding of rational (symbolic power) and practical (resources/capital) behaviour in their immediate environment (field) (Bourdieu 1977:77).

Bourdieu is said to be one of the founding fathers of practice theory, more particularly, of communicative practice. Central to his theory is the concept of symbolic power. Like Karl Marx's false consciousness, symbolic power is exerted in the collaboration between those who exercise power and those who are subordinated to it through non-recognition (false consciousness). As a result symbolic power legitimises the existing order through the "very structure of the field in which belief is produced and reproduced" (Bourdieu 1977:117). Thus, and unlike Marx, imposition of symbolic power becomes non-violent, more of a way of life, justified by its division, recognition, royalty and service. This is particularly so because symbolic power is exercised through the available symbolic capital, resources that only those with access to such capital have a right to exploit and transform into economic capital. Symbolic power is very effective in the religious field where believers struggle for access to religious capital (become true believers). In so doing, they also engage in a process of polarisation and exclusion. Their pursuit of symbolic capital and, eventually, symbolic power legitimises the view that their belief is the *true one* and others are *false beliefs*.

In linguistics one can distinguish scholars who are primarily interested in the language system (*langue*), and those who focus on language use (*parole*), or at least in the interaction between the two. In our research we take linguistic pragmatism as our theoretical framework. In general terms this means that we answer our questions and achieve our objectives from the perspective of a theory of practice, more particularly of communicative practice. In the social sciences practice theories go back to Weber's paradigm shift from 'function' to 'intention' (Weber 1968), and the subsequent debate about 'structure' and 'agency' (Giddens 1991).

Weber has great influence on the communicative theory of practice, especially for theorists who believe that social structures are not the only major determinants of human actions (Weber 1958; Parsons 1968), or of communicative practice for that matter (Wallace & Wolf 1991). Weber's point of departure is that all sciences of human behaviour and culture (religion) are subjective and open to abstraction (Weber 1968; Parsons 1968). Weber's emphasis puts the actor at the centre of empirical analysis and knowledge by accepting a subjective interpretation of events, things, ideas, actions and motives from the point of view of those whose actions are studied (Parsons 1968).

An actor, according to Weber, is an active creature, as opposed to the structuralists' notion of beings responding passively to stimuli from social structures (Weber 1968:3-10). Weber's ideas in our framework imply that a user of language actively participates in the language practice or, to use Wittgenstein's concept, the 'language game' (Wittgenstein 2009), conscious of his/her actions and practices (although there are no guarantees of achieving the intended objectives). The argument is that some actions are not performed properly without uttering words (Austin 1975). Austin (1975:7-8) cites the example of a church wedding, a ritual which involves speaking words like 'I do', or writing on a marriage certificate. In the process language users actively contribute to the construction of their social reality and structures, and vice versa.

In a nutshell, Weber's theory of action marked a shift from the paradigm of social structure and system (macro analysis) to the study of individuals' actions (micro analysis) based on the subjective meaning/interpretation (*verstehen*) attached to particular actions. This was an immense contribution to language studies, which for several decades were influenced mainly by structuralists' ideas, ignoring this crucial factor in the understanding of linguistic practices.

Weber's theory is complemented by the work of Giddens (1984, 1992), especially his structuration theory. In this theory Giddens tries to combine social structure and agency (actor), of course borrowing some ideas from the work of Berger and Luckmann (1966), *The social construction of reality*. Whereas Weber dismissed the idea of structure and its contribution to individual action, Giddens (1984) suggests that the two relate dialectically: "The differences between these perspectives on social science have often been taken to be epistemological, whereas they are in fact also ontological. ... If interpretative sociologies are founded, as it were, upon an imperialism of the subject, functionalism and structuralism propose an imperialism of the social object. One of my principal ambitions in the formulation of structuration theory is to put an end to each of these empire-building endeavours" (Giddens 1984:2).

To Giddens (1984:2) the study of human behaviour and culture should not be restricted to the study of structures and individual actions but should include "*social practices ordered across space and time*". The concept of space is also examined in detail in Pierre Bourdieu's work. To Bourdieu (1989) actors are situated in a particular space according to their membership of a community, which is determined by common interests and/or goals.

Language, as a body of system/structures, provides the speaker (agent/actor) with the means (grammar, vocabulary, etc.) to communicate in a way that others can comprehend. Speakers use the language system to achieve their intended goals (Berger & Luckmann 1966:37). At the same time, the language system gives the speaker a historical background ('knowledgeability') of the speech event(s) and the possible consequences. Thus the language system shapes and constrains speakers by giving them a linguistic compass with which to navigate in language practice (see Berger & Luckmann 1966:37).

The reverse is equally true, because the foregoing in no way suggests that the speaker is always constrained by or confined to the framework of the language system (Berger & Luckmann 1966). Giddens (1984:3) puts it thus: "To be a human being is to be a purposive agent, who both has reasons for his or her activities and is able if asked to elaborate discursively upon those reasons." In other words, Giddens suggests there is room for speakers to deviate (discursively, consciously or unconsciously) from the 'line of conduct' laid down by the system in which they gain their experiences. Berger and Luckmann (1966:52) call this externalisation.

This argument accords with critical discourse analytical explanations (Fairclough 1992:65; Jørgensen & Phillips 2002; Van Dijk, 2008), which maintain that the relationship between the discourse (participant/speaker) and the social structure is dialectical; language use (discourse) contributes to the reproduction and transformation of the social structure, but at the same time social structures shape and constrain the discourse (participants' use of language).

In his book *The theory of communicative action,* Habermas (1984) advances much the same argument as Giddens (1984) and Fairclough (2007). He argues that society evolves and develops through people's communicative action, which is constituted and structured by their social realities and in which those who are unfamiliar with the speakers' worldview will find it difficult to grasp their meaning, thus leading to misunderstanding (see Wallace & Wolf 1991:127). He also considers the role of actors in constructing and reconstructing their own worldview. Habermas (quoted in Wallace & Wolf 1991:128) says: "It is not only a process of reaching understanding; … actors are at the same time taking part in interactions through which they develop, confirm and renew their memberships of social groups and their identities. Communicative actions are not only processes of interpretation in which cultural knowledge is 'tested against the world'; they are at the same time processes of social integration and of socialization."

On the basis of Habermas's ideas we can argue that discourse is an integral part of individuals' lives (e.g. socialisation) and also informs them of what is happening around them. This process is dynamic – open to change and reconstruction. Individuals, on the other hand, are responsible for reshaping and constructing their life world through interaction with others in society.

In his *Language and society* Charles Taylor (1991) presents four points derived from Habermas's study of society from the point of view of language, *The theory of communicative actions.* Firstly, language develops and renews itself in discourse, that is, discourse gives speakers an avenue and an ability to speak in a way that can be understood by others (Taylor 1991:23). Secondly, there is a dialectical (complementary) relationship between structure and practice – as Saussure would say, between *langue* and *parole.* Thus neither can claim to exist in the absence of the other. In other words, structure and practice complement each other (Taylor 1991:24). Also, in speech events speakers are guided by 'background knowledge'. This means that they tend to draw on experience in the existing world, what Taylor (1991:25) calls the "horizons of our implicit know-how and pre-understanding", when making their statements in a discursive event. Lastly, there is the complementarity of 'I' and 'we'. Taylor (1991:2) says, "[We] participate in a common space: our attention, both mine and yours, is focused on the matter in hand: we ignore the fact that this space is produced and maintained at once by speech acts we both use." Besides, a discursive practice contributes to the reproduction of social relations and identities, where the 'I' and 'we' fit in.

Discursive practice also helps to reproduce and maintain the knowledge and belief system of a given society. It informs the ideological and political dimension of that society by either constituting or transforming it. Communicative actions or discursive practices are not merely tools for communicating and understanding, but are the vehicles on which social transformation depends. As Fairclough (2007:63) puts it, "It is a mode of action, one form in which people may act upon the world and especially upon each other, as well as a mode of representation." The idea of transformation becomes clear if the concepts of power, ideology and struggle are included in a discourse. This notion of ideology and power is mentioned only in passing in Habermas's theory of communicative action, which makes it inadequate to explain the social transformation process that could be informed by the discourse.

The question of power and ideology in discourse features prominently in the works of Gramsci (1971) ('hegemony') and Althusser (1971) ('ideology'). Hegemony in Gramsci's usage refers to "a particular form of dominance in which a ruling class legitimates its position and secures the acceptance if not outright support by those below them" (Gramsci 1971). To Gramsci power is maintained, not so much through force or coercion as through the ideology of the dominant class, which is reduced to the level of common sense and/or taken for granted by society. In Tanzania before the 1980s the dominant assumption was that of building a socialist/*Ujamaa* society (Sivalon 1990, 1992; Nyerere 1968; Wijsen 2007:221). Most Tanzanians were made to believe that *Ujamaa* was the only way of achieving societal welfare and that it was to the benefit of everyone (Maghimbi 1995:23). As a matter of fact, Nyerere (1968:2) insists, "we have deliberately decided to grow, as a society, out of our own root [*Ujamaa* path], but in a particular direction and toward a particular kind of objective [having an *Ujamaa* society]". In this way Tanzania became one of the African nations where there was a relatively "harmonious relationship between Christians and Muslims" (Ludwig 2002:216) until the mid-1980s. However, Blommaert (1997:129-144) notes that most of the Tanzanian elite kept a low profile in building *Ujamaa* ideology. Maghimbi (1995) points out, moreover, that *Ujamaa* (especially the *Ujamaa* villages) created an artificial land shortage and consequently lowered agricultural production in the 1970s and 1980s. Maghimbi (1992:119) believes that "the policies and grand plan pursued under the name of *Ujamaa* or African Socialism were a failed conspiracy" (Maghimbi 1992:119).

Whereas Gramsci's conception of hegemony is dialectical, Foucault is deterministic. Foucault (1977:2) believes that power consists in controlling human relations through exclusion. He explains: "Power is mobilized, makes itself everywhere present and visible; it invents new mechanisms, it separates, it mobilizes, it partitions, it constrains" (Foucault 1977:3).

According to Foucault (1977:3) power is not necessarily exercised through force or coercion, simply because it tends to automatically place individuals in different subordinate positions. This constrains them by assigning them various responsibilities in keeping with that position, thus compelling them to act in accordance with the principle(s) of their own subjection (Foucault 1977:3). This is possible because every individual in society has his or her own image of power, which has voices informing him/her of the responsibilities and consequences of failing to comply with the principles of his/her own subjection (Foucault 1978:61).

Actually, according to Nyerere (1968) *Ujamaa* was integral to the freedom of Tanzanians. In other words, accepting *Ujamaa* was tantamount to accepting freedom, hence the title of his book, *Uhuru na Ujamaa* (Freedom and socialism) (Nyerere 1968). *Ujamaa* ideology became the ruling party's ideology (first that of TANU, and later of *Chama cha Mapinduzi*[10] [CCM], the party that led the government after Tanganyika and Zanzibar formed the United Republic in 1964. The ruling and only party in the country was guided by the Arusha Declaration of 1967, which promoted the idea of socialism and self-reliance (Blommaert 1999; Sivalon 1990, 1992). Under this socialist governance the ruling class managed to suppress other ideologies (such as liberalism) to maintain the status quo of *Ujamaa*. The outcome was peaceful coexistence and unity in the country (Ludwig 2002).

In discourse studies Gramsci's hegemony dominates, especially in those that use the critical discourse analysis approach. Fairclough, for instance, uses Gramsci's analysis of Western capitalism and revolutionary praxis (Gramsci 1971) to stress the importance of ideology in the study of discourse and social transformation. According to Fairclough hegemony provides a way of conceptualising change, the evolution of power relations, which allows a particular focus on discursive change as well as "contributing to and being shaped by wider processes of change" (Fairclough 1992:92). Fairclough, like Gramsci, sees hegemony as controlling all spheres of human life, be it economic, social, political, cultural or religious. At the same time he considers hegemony to be dynamic, not static, as it is subject to change and modification. He puts it in a nutshell:

"Hegemony is the power over society as a whole of one of the fundamental economically-defined classes in alliance with other social forces, but it is never achieved more than partially and temporarily, as an 'unstable equilibrium'. Hegemony is about construct-

---

[10] *Chama cha Mapinduzi* means Revolutionary Party.

ing alliances, and integrating rather than simply dominating subordinate classes, through concessions or through ideological means to win their consent. Hegemony is a focus of constant struggle around points of greatest instability between classes and blocs, to construct or sustain or fracture alliances and relations of domination/subordination which takes economic, political and ideological forms" (Fairclough 1992:92).

The concept of struggle is focal in discursive studies, especially when trying to understand the process of social change. For example, the dominance of *Ujamaa* ideology in Tanzania during that period did not mean that there were no other peripheral ideologies that coexisted with it as becomes clear in the Islamic crisis in 1968 (see Njozi 2000:5,204; 2003:18-19). Claiming otherwise is like sailing a dhow against the wind, because there were many ideologies besides *Ujamaa* struggling for attention even under the domineering presence of the state controlled ideology.

In 1985 the then president of Tanzania, the late Mwalimu Nyerere,[11] stepped down and was succeeded by Mwinyi. *Ujamaa* was very soon replaced by a liberal ideology (see Wijsen 2003:134-35), even though it was retained in the constitution as the official ideology. This more liberal approach naturally gave Tanzanians more freedom. In the area of worship many churches and mosques emerged, as well as open air preaching (*mihadara*) (Wijsen & Mfumbusa 2004); economic entrepreneurship and private ownership began to flourish. In fact, economic liberalisation was coupled with political liberalisation, which ushered in multi-party democracy instead of the post-independence one-party *Ujamaa* system.

Thus ideology needs to be seen in terms of a constant struggle to grasp the changes taking place in the discursive process. In other words, in each society there are many ideologies continually struggling for dominance, but only the strongest at a particular point in time can dominate others. Nevertheless the situation remains open to change and reconstruction, for change sometimes comes from within the same ideology as happened in Tanzania with the *Ujamaa* ideology of the ruling CCM party. In fact, Nyerere was also aware of such struggle, evidenced by the statement quoted already that some government and party officials were opposed to *Ujamaa*, its values and attitudes (Nyerere 1968:1; Njozi 2003:17). In a nutshell, struggle is the soul of society and is behind any social transformation.

---

[11] Nyerere, commonly known as Mwalimu, was the first president of Tanganyika and later, after the union between Tanganyika and Zanzibar which formed Tanzania, until 1985, when he voluntarily stepped down and chose Mwinyi as his successor. He was party chairman until 1990 and remained active in local and international politics up to his last days. He was and still is highly respected by the majority, hence acquired the title of father and teacher of the nation.

Parallel to the distinction between syntactics and pragmatics in linguistics, we can distinguish between a systematic and a practical science of religion. Whereas systematic religious studies focuses on the religious symbol system (*parole*), practical religious studies looks at its application by religious practitioners (Klöcker & Tworuschka 2008). The two, however, are interrelated. The symbol system is reproduced through its application (institutionalisation), but the same system can act on the practitioners and influence them.

In this thesis we are not primarily interested in the sources and teachings of religions, but in religious practitioners and their practices, not in structures but in people (Kim 2004:3). So we do not study scriptures (Bible or Qur'an), prophets (Jesus or Muhammad) and the like, but try to determine whether, when, how and for what purpose these symbols are 'used' by believers.

Hannerz (1992:261-267) concludes his *Cultural complexity* with creole language as the root metaphor of what he calls the global ecumene. Just as we discern an interconnectedness between 'standard' and 'pidgin' English, centre and periphery, we see an ongoing struggle between 'pure' and 'lived' religions or, as Bourdieu (1991) puts it, between 'clerical' and 'lay' religion.

In general pragmatist theories are critical of theories that hypothesise about mental realities residing in individual humans. Instead they theorise that identities, attitudes or selves are constructed linguistically (Peräkylä 2005). In this sense we come close to the study of practical classifications (McCutcheon 2007; Bourdieu 1991), and thus to cognitive science.

Social cognitive science owes much to Van Dijk's approach. In his *Discourse and context* Van Dijk (2008) stresses the significance of cognitive processes in discursive events. He says: "[I]t is not the social situation itself that influences the structures of the text and talk, but rather the definition of the relevant properties of the communicative situation by the discourse participants" (Van Dijk 2008:x). Van Dijk, borrowing from socio-cognitive psychology, sees the discursive event as not only controlled by the environment, but also involving "mental construction of the discourse participants" (Van Dijk 2008:57-64).

From the foregoing we conclude that sociology of religion have yet to overcome the dichotomy of classical sociology (of religion) between 'structure' (Durkheim) and 'agency' (Weber), or in linguistic terms, between *langue* and *parole* (De Saussure), language 'competence' and 'performance' (Chomski), and related dichotomies between 'function' and 'meaning', social and human sciences, explanation and interpretation (Flood 1999). Scholars such as Bourdieu (1991) and Giddens (1991) can be credited with trying to overcome these dichotomies by starting from the dialectical relationship between habitus and market, and the process of structuration.

In religious studies there is a similar shift from phenomenological to discursive study of religion (Kippenberg 1983; McCutcheon 1997; Flood 1999; Von Stuckrad 2003; Wijsen 2010). In this book we opt for the latter school of thought or body of knowledge. We start from the *language* model of studying interreligious relations (Panikkar 1978:19-22) and are inspired by the theory of performative speech, or the symbolic power of language to make and unmake groups, a theory which Bourdieu (1991) derives from liturgical language. In our technical design this theoretical premise brings us to the method of critical or socio-cognitive discourse analysis (Blommaert & Verschueren 1991; Fairclough 1992; Van Dijk 2008).

Research concepts

In this book we study religious identity transformations through interreligious, particularly Muslim-Christian, relations. Identity is a widely used but highly controversial concept in the social sciences (Giddens 1991; Antaki & Widdicombe 1998; Kim 2002). This is because it is often defined in terms of intrinsic qualities such as origin, language or colour. Seen thus, people have an identity in the same way that they have a black skin or blue eyes. But in most cases identities are not based on innate properties that can be measured according to objective criteria (Bourdieu 1991:220-228). For example, the identification as Hutu or Tutsi in Rwanda is social rather than natural. In the same way religion is religion because it is placed in a particular narrative context or speech community. Outside that narrative context there is no religion (Asad 1991).

In this study identity is defined as a narrative of the self (Giddens 1991:54). People have not just one identity but multiple identities. Put differently, they are polyphonic selves. They are always involved in a plurality of partly overlapping self-narratives at the same time, while none of these coincide completely with only one society or territory (Van Binsbergen 2003:381). In concrete situations people may choose one narrative of the self out of all possible self-narratives (Hall 1996). Social identity is shared by the members of a group (Tajfel 1978; Tajfel & Turner 1986), but as indicated above, it is fragile, fluid, flexible, not fixed and stable. In this study we use 'social identity' as a blanket term, which includes other identities (e.g. ethnic, national, gender, generational, economic).

Religious identity is only one of the social identities people can have. After more than a hundred years religious studies has not managed to come up with a generally accepted definition of religion. There is disagreement between those who define religion as an autonomous reality, and those who see it as a reflection of something else (e.g. psychic or social processes). Again we assume that definitions of religion are not based on innate properties but are the effect of the scholar's classification system (Asad 1993; McCutcheon 1997). Consequently practices and artefacts are religious because their believers place them in a specific narrative context and distinguish them from other practices or artefacts which are labelled non-religious or secular (Flood 1999:137-141). Put differently, definitions of what is religious and what is not are historical products of discursive processes (Asad 1993:29).

Understanding is defined as a cognitive process aimed at grasping speakers' intentions (Van Dijk 2008: 1-18). Understanding assumes at least partially shared knowledge, a common ground or meeting point. According to the cognitive sciences producers of texts (communicators) always use other 'texts' or 'mental models' stored in their long-term memory. And consumers of texts (interpreters) can only make sense of these texts if they are able to link them to others texts that they have stored in their long-term memory. If they are unable to do so, there is misunderstanding and a breakdown of communication. In everyday life there will always be partial understanding and partial misunderstanding, misunderstanding understanding and understanding misunderstanding (Mall 2000), or working misunderstanding (Tanner & Wijsen 1993).

In this book transformation is defined in terms of conditions, processes and consequences of cultural contact (Burke 2009). If shared knowledge is necessary for understanding, we can conceptualise the conditions for cultural contact in three models. The identity model is based on the assumption that 'we' and the 'others' are basically the same (Wiredu 1996): the 'others' are like 'us'; we are equals. The alterity model is based on the assumption that 'we' and the 'others' are essentially different. The 'others' are not like 'us'. They are strangers, and potential enemies. The analogy model is based on the assumption that there are overlaps between 'us' and 'them'. Human potential is universal. But this does not mean that all people are the same, as they are also products of acculturation and socialisation (Mall 2000).

In regard to processes of cultural contact, scholars distinguish between four strategies of coping with diversity. Some people identify strongly with their own religious culture. After meeting the other they jump back to the familiar. Other people identify with the other's religious culture. They jump over to the other culture and forget about their own. Yet other people identify with no religious culture. They jump beyond them and live in a cultural no-man's land. But most people switch between one culture and another, using the advantages of both (Burke 2009).

With respect to the consequences of long-term cultural contact, scholars distinguish between various models (Burke 2009:79-101). Some hold that there is cultural homogenisation or 'McDonaldization' (Ritzer 1993). People from different cultural backgrounds increasingly think, behave and speak in the same way. According to other scholars there is cultural diversification, or 're-tribalisation' (McLuhan 1962). People define narrow identities and fight holy wars against other 'tribes' (Barber 1995). A third school of thought holds that these narrow identities are not to be interpreted as rivals. They are – to a large extent – local products of the global scene. Hence there is cultural diffusion or 'glocalisation' (Robertson 1995).

In this book we speak about cultural diffusion in terms of 'ecumenisation' and 'creolization' (Hannerz 1992, 2010). In keeping with our discursive or narrative understanding of reality and religion (Ricoeur 1984), we speak about interreligious relations in terms of the translation model, which derives from linguistics. It uses language as a metaphor to study cultural change (Panikkar 1978:19-22). Hannerz (1992) perceives creole languages as metaphor for cultural interconnectedness or a 'global ecumene'. Mazrui and Mazrui (1998:171) refer to the lingua franca of Tanzania, KiSwahili, as an ecumenical language that facilitates "diffusion of Christianity and Islam". In the same vein Bryceson (2009) speaks about "Swahili creolization". When it comes to methods, to be discussed below, this orientation puts us in the tradition of what used to be called ethnography of speech or ethno-science, now linguistic anthropology and discourse analysis (Tyrell, Krech & Knoblauch 1998).

Social cohesion and conflict are defined in terms of convergence or divergence of interests (Bourdieu 1991). Bourdieu perceives society as a pluralistic space made up of more or less autonomous fields (or 'markets') where individuals or groups strive to actualise their interests (make a 'profit') using various resources (forms of 'capital'), partly in coalition and partly in competition with others. Thus inclusion and exclusion almost always go together. As indicated above, Bourdieu is inspired by Weber's sociology of religion. Thus the competition between clerics and lay people for spiritual goods in the religious field would be an apt example of the struggle for hegemony that is going on in other fields.

1.3. Technical design

This section explains and justifies the technical design of this study (Verschuren & Doorewaard 1999:109-207). It describes the research strategy, social settings in which the study was conducted, sampling techniques, methods of data collection, and the process of data analysis, presentation and interpretation. Finally, the section outlines limitations encountered in the course of this study.

Research strategy

The research is based on a single case study. That is to say, we make an in-depth study of Muslim-Christian relations in one particular location, Dar es Salaam. An objective of a case study can be to test, explore or expand theory. In our research we are critical of theories that perceive (religious) identities as fixed and pre-existing (Widdicombe 1998:194). In our view a (religious) identity is shared by members of a (religious) group and distinguishes them from members of other (religious) groups.

The unique characteristics of Dar es Salaam, a multicultural and multi-religious city, made it a perfect case study. Dar es Salaam is a port and the business capital of Tanzania. It is located in the eastern part of the country. In the east it borders on the Indian Ocean. In the north and south it borders on the coastal region, and in the west on the Morogoro region. The city is divided into three administrative municipal councils: Kinondoni, Ilala and Temeke, each in its turn subdivided into divisions, wards, streets/villages and hamlets (*vitongoji*). The following table illustrates the administrative structure in each municipality:

Table 1: Number of divisions, wards, streets, villages and hamlets in the three municipalities of Dar es Salaam

Municipality	Division	Wards	Streets	Villages	Hamlets
Ilala	3	22	65	9	37
Temeke	3	24	97	15	62
Kinondoni	5	27	114	14	14
TOTAL	11	73	276	38	113

Source: Dar es Salaam City Council 2004

According to the 2002 population census the city of Dar es Salaam has an estimated 3 070 060 inhabitants, of whom 1 548 867 are male and 1 521 193 female. Of the three municipalities Kinondoni has the highest population with a total of 1 337 875 inhabitants, followed by Temeke and Ilala with 948 498 and 783 687 inhabitants respectively.

Dar es Salaam is the industrial and commercial centre of Tanzania, home to a multitude of industrial establishments such as pharmaceutical laboratories, breweries, steel and iron works, manufacturers of building materials and soft and hard drinks; tertiary institutions such as universities and polytechnics; and secondary and primary schools.

The major economic activities in Dar es Salaam are internal trade, manufacturing, tourism, transport and communication, urban agriculture, forestry and fishing, mining and quarrying, utility services, construction, and finance and insurance.

The city has a moderate equatorial climate. Generally Dar es Salaam is hot and humid throughout the year with an average temperature of 29°C. There are two main rainy seasons: a short one from October to December and a long one from March to May, with an average rainfall of 1000mm.

KiSwahili is the national and official language in Dar es Salaam and Tanzania in general. English is used sometimes in business and primarily as a language of instruction in secondary and tertiary educational institutions. A mixture of KiSwahili and English (kiswa-English or code switching) is common in an urban setting like Dar es Salaam. Generally the city has diverse ethnic groups, who also speak a variety of vernacular languages. The indigenous ethnic groups in Dar es Salaam are the Wazaramo, Wadengereko and Wakwere. However, at present almost all of the 130 ethnic groups of Tanzania are represented in Dar es Salaam.

Dar es Salaam is also a religious melting pot. Almost all religions and denominations are represented in the city. This aspect was dealt with in the previous sections. Islam, for instance, has been in the city since the 7th century CE, when Arabs made contact with the coastal area. Today Islam is represented by sects such as Ismailiyya, Shia and Sunni. Christianity, on the other hand, was introduced in Tanzania and Dar es Salaam in particular in the 19th century. Christian denominations include Roman Catholic, Evangelical and Pentecostal churches. Other religions in Dar es Salaam are Buddhism, Judaism and traditional religion.

The purposive sampling technique was used to select interviewees in Dar es Salaam city. This study site was selected for three reasons. First, the city made a historical contribution to the spread of Islam and Christianity, as well as the emergence of KiSwahili as a lingua franca. As a result most of these religions have their headquarters in Dar es Salaam. Thus major decisions that have an impact on faith and religious affairs are made in this area. Second, all religions that exist in Tanzania have adherents in Dar es Salaam. Hence it provides a representative sample that yielded a wealth of information on the theme of this study.

Moreover, recent tensions and a resurgence of religious conflict in the country mostly happened in this area. These occurrences are described variously as state versus religious denominations, and intra- and extra-religious tensions and conflict. In the pork incident in April 1993 Muslims in their hundreds destroyed pork butcheries and beer stores at Magomeni in Dar es Salaam, which they claimed defiled their faith.

The pork butchery incident was followed by another dramatic and shocking Muslim-state confrontation, the Mwembechai crisis. This took place in February 1998 (see Njozi 2000). It was triggered by the arrest of the imams of Mtambani, Kibo and Mwenge mosques. They were accused of distributing cassettes and booklets and conducting meetings that ridiculed Christians and their faith. The police then raided the Mwembechai mosque and apprehended sheikh Shaban Magezi. Muslims, enraged by the assault, ran riot. Although the Muslims were in confrontation with the state, the root cause of the confrontation heightened Muslim-Christian tension, attributed to indiscriminate public preaching and attempts to spread both Islam and the Christian faith.

Unlike other regions where there is one dominant religion, Islam and Christianity enjoy almost equal representation (45% each, although there are no official statistics). This has implications, especially when each religion tries to impose its dogma on the community in a bid to establish religious and ideological hegemony and supremacy (Gramsci 1971). All these facts justify the choice of Dar es Salaam as a suitable area for a study of Muslim-Christian relations and interreligious cultural communication and miscommunication, manifesting in violent incidents.

Research sources

As this study focuses on the role of language, the sources were both written and spoken texts: newspapers, pamphlets, brochures, and narrations by informants and respondents. Secondary data came from a review of the existing literature. Primary sources were informants and respondents.

Exploratory research methodology was chosen, principally because of the need to explore a plausible dialectic relationship between language and socio-cognitive effects on Muslim-Christian relations in Tanzania and explain the role of language in intercultural religious communication in the community. This leads to understanding of participants' perspectives with due regard to their social positions and their interest in maintaining and/or changing those positions.

Focus groups discussions were conducted, using gender, religion, age and education as selection criteria. Thus we have Christian, Muslim and mixed groups, each with a male and a female group. These six categories each have four sub-groups: educated and uneducated, young and old. We also conducted individual interviews with some male and female informants. In addition we analysed documents, especially religious brochures, papers and letters, tapes, and newspapers. The researchers attended *mihadara* in Dar es Salaam, where preaching was tape-recorded for research purposes.

(1) Study population

The study population comprised 134 individuals aged 15 to 75, both Muslims and Christians. Apart from involving youth, adults and elderly people of both faiths, attention was paid to gender. Each social category has its own way of communicating and relating with others, hence the need to involve participants from all these groups in order to gain more insight into each category. In fact, participants were more relaxed in the homogenous group than in mixed groups. Since the study was basically qualitative, the sample size was determined by the number of FGDs (focus group discussions) and interviews conducted. Recruitment of participants was terminated on reaching a saturation point.[12]

(2) Selection of research participants

Participants in the FGDs were selected by means of stratified purposive sampling. The criteria were age, sex, education and religion. This facilitated free, homogenous discussion flow, unconstrained by the aforementioned differences. A gatekeeper[13] or participant was approached (local leaders at ward/street/village level) to inform possible participants about the discussions. FGDs comprised three to twelve participants. In all 20 FGDs were conducted involving 120 participants. Table 2 gives the means for participants in terms of religion, gender and age.

Interviewees (key informant interviews) were selected using the purposive sampling technique: individuals who had pertinent information were approached and asked to participate. In all fourteen key informants were interviewed.

---

[12] No additional information was forthcoming from further participants. At this point the information gathered satisfied the needs and demands of the study.

[13] A gatekeeper is a person used to reach informants. Ours were persons well respected by both Muslims and Christians and well-known to all participants. In both Kilakala and Buguruni our gatekeepers were Mtaa Executive Officials (MEO). These are local government employees and therefore religiously neutral.

Research method

Data were collected from both secondary and primary sources. Secondary data came from written and tape-recorded materials. Primary data were collected using a variety of methods such as (a) attending and listening to public speeches, (b) FGDs, and (c) interviews.

(1) Research team

The field research team comprised three individuals who were purposely selected. It comprised a team leader (the author) and two research assistants, namely Faraja Bakari (a Muslim) and Ana Haule (a Christian). The different religious backgrounds of the research assistants minimised biases that could have occurred if the interview were to be conducted by Christian interviewers alone. For the desk work the team leader was assisted by two individuals, Magreth Musomba and Juliet Shibiriti.

(2) Methods of data generation

Document analysis

Various relevant documents were reviewed and studied. These included books, journal articles, chapters of books and papers obtained from different sources such as university libraries, religious bookshops and individual book owners. The internet yielded on-line articles and papers. These documents shed light on discourse(s) in society and facilitated the formulation of research questions used in FGDs and interviews.

Visits to open air religious services (mihadara)

As part of his fieldwork the researcher attended open air services (*mihadara*) conducted in Dar es Salaam. Twelve *mihadara* were visited in Dar es Salaam, six conducted by Muslims and six by Christian groups. These *mihadara* were conducted at Mwembeyanga, Yombo-vituka, Mbagalla Rangi Tatu and Kilakala in Temeke District. The choice of these sites was deliberate, because open air services were regularly conducted in these areas.

The *mihadara* that were visited included only those conducted during the period of fieldwork in Dar es Salaam. The twelve Christian and Muslim *mihadara* were all recorded. In addition a CD bought at a Muslim *mihadara* formed part of the collected primary data.

Tape-recorded and visual materials

In addition to information from written sources, tape-recorded and visual sources were carefully analysed by means of discourse analytical procedures. These materials were obtained from religious bookshops and religious buildings. The assumption was that the language used in these sources would reveal the nature of the discourse and the relationship with other discourses.

Local newspapers that report Muslims' talk about Christians and vice versa were also screened for relevant information. These include *Rai*, *Majira*, *Mwananchi*, *Nipashe*, *The Guardian*, *The Daily News*, *An-Nuur*, *Al-huda* and *Uhuru*. In addition material was gathered from religious sources. These included pastoral letters, religious election manifestos, and religious brochures. The type of discourse in these sources reveals a more complex discourse structure, which in turn reflects social relations in the community as a whole. Speakers or journalists used vocabulary and particular words that were not neutral, thus reflecting their ideological and political leanings.

Focus group discussions (FGDs)

FGDs were the main method of data generation because the study focused on intra- and inter-group relations and communication. FGDs are a useful way of exploring people's norms, values and beliefs. In this study they helped to provide information on how people interact in a group, thus enabling the researcher to examine their attitudes.

In view of the nature of the research problem FGDs were classified according to gender, religion, age and education. This was because individuals feel relaxed to discuss issues with like-minded individuals of their own social group. In such an environment people tend to act naturally and reveal their discursive practices (Fairclough 1995).

Participants were first grouped according to their religions: Christianity and Islam. Then they were combined in a mixed group of Christians and Muslims. This was to establish whether the same discourse(s) that occurred in the separate groups also featured in the mixed group and vice versa. Religious classification was applied to all the social groups (gender, age and educational level).

FGDs were also organised on the basis of gender. As a result the study had male and female FGDs for youngsters, the elderly, businesspeople and workers. The classification was based mainly on religious and cultural values. In the case of Islam males dominated. The purpose of gender stratification was primarily to increase female participation in the study, as they felt free to air and discuss their views in exclusively female FGDs.

There were two age groups: youths and the elderly. Youths were aged between 15 and 24. The elderly were people from 50 years upwards. This classification helped to determine the changing trends in religious discourse between the younger and older generations. The following table illustrates the point.

Table 2: Number of FGDs and participants

	MEN			WOMEN		
	Muslims	Christians	Mixed	Muslims	Christians	Mixed
Elderly I	4	5	9	9	5	5
Elderly group II					6	
Educated youths	6	6	8	4	5	11
Educated youths II			8			
Uneducated youths	4	6	6	5	4	4

This table shows that we had 20 groups of 4 to 11 people each, selected on the basis of gender, age, education and religion. Chapters two, three and four use data from separate Muslim groups (6 FGDs), separate Christian groups (7 FGDs) and mixed groups (7 FGDs). Some groups were so large that we subdivided them into two groups (I and II). This was the case with the Christian elderly female group and the mixed educated male group.

In the FGDs the facilitator(s) followed up on issues emerging from the discussion, because what people speak about, and the way they speak about others, are products of both their cognitive and social environment. FGD participants were selected on the basis of their experience of the Tanzanian local community.

The discussion revolved around topics that could afford insight into the way participants use language to speak about others/other believers. Hence a guiding map was designed with specific topics that were covered in discussions (see appendix 1). Initially all participants were asked to introduce themselves. The researcher and his assistant introduced themselves and explained the objective of the discussion. They also asked the participants for their informed consent to join in the discussion. Then all participants were asked to give their general opinion on their relations with other believers in the community. FGDs were conducted in different social settings. The choice of a venue depended on the preference of the participants in each FGD. In the FGD our main unity of analysis was the social/subject positioning (social relation) and mental model of participants. For example participants positioned as member of the community, as Muslim or Christian, youth or elderly and male or female. Fairclough 1992 cites the educational and medical fields as examples of subject positioning. To Fairclough education discourse particularly that of a class room, position the teacher as a teacher and the student as student (Fairclough 1992:13-15) making this type of discourse different from medical discourse which entail a medical interview involving doctor-patient interaction in a hospital setting (Fairclough1992:17-19, 138-144).

Key informant interviews

Interviews conducted during the study captured information on intercultural communication of religious meanings. Here interactive methods are essential. Hence interviews were a supplementary method to gain information not readily forthcoming in FGDs. Owing to group pressure some individual attitudes may remain hidden or suppressed, but may surface during individual interviews.

In the key informant interviews individual Christians and Muslims as well as politicians were interviewed. These key informants had 'expert' knowledge, that is useful information on their respective religions and how they and other members of that religious group view other religions. A total of 14 key informants were interviewed. These included three members of parliament, five male and six female informants. For the sake of confidentiality the names of key informants are not revealed in the analyses. Instead we use the informants' initials.

(3) Methods of data analysis

The information gathered in the FGDs and key informant interviews were tape-recorded and then transcribed verbatim. For reference purposes the KiSwahili version of all quotations from participants is appended in a footnote. Participants' responses appear in quotation marks. My additions to their responses are in brackets [ ]. Three dots (...) show omissions and/or continuations of the speech.

In analysing text and talk researchers can proceed in two ways. They can focus on the meaning of the language, analysing taxonomies and other classifications. This is what content analysis is about. Or they can analyse the use of language in the construction of social realities (Kvale 2008:103-104). In this research we followed the latter direction and used a socio-cognitive approach to discourse analysis (Van Dijk 2008). Critical discourse analysis – particularly Fairclough's version,[14] which we follow – approaches the text on the following assumptions:

Firstly, discourse is a practice like any other practice. In pragmatic terms, language is not only a way of saying things (informative); it is also a way of doing things (performative) or exercising power (Bourdieu 1991). The only difference from other practices is its linguistic form (Fairclough 1992:71). Thus the first method is the analysis of discourse as linguistic practice, otherwise called 'description' (Fairclough 1989:26).

Also, according to critical discourse analysts, the relation between language and social reality is not direct but occurs via discursive practices. Consequently the second method is to analyse discursive practice or 'interpretation' (Fairclough 1989:26), that is the production, distribution and consumption of texts (Fairclough 1992:71). The discursive practice ('interaction') is crucial, as the dialectic relation between linguistic practice (text) and social practice (context) is based on it.

Lastly, critical discourse analysts assume that the relation between language and social structure is dialectic, primarily because what participants say is shaped by and in turn shapes social structures, either reproducing them or transforming them (Fairclough 1992:72). In other words, critical discourse analysts are interested in the socio-cognitive effects of language – its ideational and interpersonal effects.

On the basis of these assumptions the socio-cognitive approach to critical discourse analysis (CDA) uses three overlapping methods (Fairclough 1992:231): analysis of linguistic, discursive and social practices. Fairclough uses different names for these methods: text, interaction and context analysis, or description, interpretation and explanation (Fairclough 2002:21, 90; 1992:199; Wijsen 2010b:60). In this study linguistic, discursive and social practices are analysed.

Linguistic practice

CDA begins with the analysis of linguistic features of the text (Fairclough 1989:25; 109-139; Fairclough 1992:76-77, 185-194). There are various tools for this purpose, but in our research we use only vocabulary. Fairclough (1992:185-186) explains: "It is sometimes useful for analytic purposes to focus upon a single

---

[14] This study acknowledges the existence of other analytical methods, both within the discourse analysis perspective and in the social sciences generally, but we opted for critical discourse analysis, particularly Fairclough's version of it, as it is better suited to our assumptions and objectives.

General introduction

word" or "culturally salient keywords". The analysis also took into account "alternative wordings and their political and ideological significance" (Fairclough 1992: 77). After all, words are not neutral; there is always a political agenda underlying their use, for instance whether we speak of Palestinians as 'freedom fighters' or 'terrorists'.

This study, therefore, presents religious discourse as reported in various sources such as FGDs, key informant interviews, open air preaching (*mihadara*) and Tanzanian newspapers. We argue that social discourse is tied up with individual experiences in the language game.

In this discourse our focus was on the use of certain words and vocabulary, on the assumption that speakers use certain words and phrases to unmake and make groups. It was discovered, for instance, that some speakers used words with the aim of creating new meanings of social reality. Some words were meant to create a new social identity and for establishing and reconstructing and/or maintaining prevailing social relations. In this regard open air preaching (*mihadara*) was a discursive event constructed in different discursive and social practices.

Discursive practice

In the case of discursive practice Fairclough (2007:78) proposes analysis of the processes of text production, consumption and distribution. When participants produce (communicate) and consume (interpret) text or talk, they draw on members' resources (Fairclough 1989:163) or mental models (Van Dijk 2008:75), stored in their long-term memory (Fairclough 1989:9-10; 24-24). These resources are cognitive in the sense that they are in people's heads; and they are social in the sense that they are socially constructed (Fairclough 1989:24). So the question is: what members' resources or mental models do participants draw on to produce (communicate) or consume (interpret) text?

In order to acquire insight into the production, distribution and consumption of text we analyse the interactions in the FGDs, and correlate them with key informant interviews, *mihadhara* and newspapers. Analysis at this level further considered the intertextuality of the texts. The term 'intertextuality' refers to the productivity of texts, the way they transform earlier texts, restructure and turn them into new conventions (Fairclough 1992:102). This suggests that when speaking people borrow and transform words from other sources or texts to justify their own speech in their social setting. In the FGDs, for example, participants used words from the Bible, the Qur'an and the constitution of Tanzania to justify social relations and identities to which they were referring.

It is important to note that the discursive practices drawn from focus group discussions were already discursive, as they oscillated between formal and informal sources and discussions. In the case of interviews participants had more freedom to speak with minimal control from the interviewer.

Producers of the texts in FGD discourses participated in discussions conducted in Dar es Salaam in 2008. These participants had wide experience of local settings and social structures. This was evident in all the group discussions. Distribution and consumption of the text started with communication and interpretation in FGDs. However, participants were free to discuss and disagree with what other participants said by voicing their own opinions (see chapters two, three and four).

The subject positions of the producers of texts in FGD discourses varied according to the groups taking part. Using the selection criteria mentioned before, the following groups were formed: Muslim female elderly; Muslim female young (uneducated), Muslim female educated, Muslim male elderly, Muslim male young (uneducated), and Muslim male educated. Although the topics were similar, the intensity of the discussions varied.

With regard to intertextuality the text producers in the FGDs and interviews seemed to draw on their experience with Christians and Muslims (see Fairclough 1992:107). For instance, a Muslim participant in an uneducated female group said: "Myself, I have a Christian friend, Rose." Apart from controlling the discourse, she also set the parameters for her own identity ("myself, I have ... ") and defined her position as a friend of a Christian called Rose.

In addition to discourse representation, we observe another intertextual configuration in the form of presuppositions. It is reflected in the use of sentences such as, "I accepted the fact that religion remains faith and not action."[15] The text producer assumes that what she says is already known to consumers of the text (i.e. "religion remains faith"). Faith here can be interpreted as religious belief, such as belief in God or supernatural forces. To her such belief is separable or distinct from community activities and relationships ("not actions"). However, this interpretation was omitted from the text so that her audience would have their own interpretations of religion (because it is assumed to be tacit knowledge) in order that she could remain sincere and/or manipulate the social setting.

Some newspapers actually reflected a mixture of discourses. The sentence, "Everything good belongs to *kafir*" combines socio-economic discourse and religious discourse. Socio-economic discourse is expressed in terms of symbolic/social capital (everything), while religious discourse is expressed in the use

---

[15] Female participant in the Muslim uneducated youth group.

of the word '*kafir*'. In analysing newspaper articles it is also wise to distinguish the animator, the author and the principal of discourse. The animator is the one who makes sounds or marks on paper; the author is the one who puts the words together; and the principal is the one whose position is represented (Fairclough 1992:78).

The producer(s) of the texts in *mihadhara* are preachers. Preachers' utterances reveal different discursive types and genres. These differences in text production also meant that consumption of the text differed because of the diverse social contexts in which the texts were produced. In the *mihadhara* context the intended audiences (consumers) were Muslims and Christians who attended those open air services and those who lived near areas where the services were conducted.[16] In fact, *mihadhara* attract many audiences, especially youths from all walks of life, so consumption of the text could be called collective. However, in some situations the distribution and consumption of *mihadhara* texts became complex, especially when the text appeared in the mass media (newspapers, TV and radio). In that case the text reached a wider audience and drew the attention of more people than texts consumed on the spot by those attending *mihadhara*.

It should be noted that the subject position of open air preachers is that they are considered to have religious knowledge. They have studied both the Bible and the Qur'an. The preachers at *mihadhara* deal with various issues, which are not limited to religion. Besides, their religious doctrines are interpreted to suit that preacher's position.

Producers of texts in *mihadhara* discourse also use a meta-discourse[17] configuration. This was apparent when the preachers used words aimed at distancing themselves from the texts. For example, the producer of the following text starts by referring to the Qur'an, God and Jesus (the Bible): "In the Qur'an God spoke to us Muslims; Jesus gave them a secret..." By uttering those words while citing the authority of the Qur'an, God and Jesus he was not just trying to control the discourse but also restructuring it and creating his own position and that of his audience.

Discursive practice is a necessary step, as it bridges the gap between linguistic and social practice. It tries to illuminate the process in which the text was produced and how it was distributed/received, as well as its interpretation and/or consumption.

---

[16] The use of loudspeakers at mihadara makes the voice and message of the preacher(s) audible to those who live nearby.

[17] Meta-discourse is a form of manifest intertextuality through which text producers distance themselves from the text. See Fairclough 1992:122.

Social practice

Social practice is Fairclough's third dimension of discourse analysis: analysis of the socio-cognitive effects of texts. When participants draw on their cognitive resources they are reproduced (Fairclough 1989:162). Thus social effects are achieved via the members' resources (Fairclough 1989:163). Van Dijk's study of ethnic prejudice shows how stereotypes are reproduced in everyday talk. But they can also be reinterpreted and transformed. So the question is: what are the socio-cognitive effects of what the interviewees say? Do they reproduce the existing order, or transform it?

According to Fairclough (1992) discourse as social practice relates to ideology and power (Fairclough 1992:86). To Fairclough ideology is the construction of a reality that contributes to the production, reproduction and transformation of social relations of domination (Fairclough 1992:87; Jørgensen & Phillips 2002:75). That is, certain uses and forms of language are ideological and serve to establish or sustain relations of domination in a particular discursive practice (Fairclough 1992:87). Fairclough believes that ideologies in all societies are characterised by relations of domination based on class, culture (religion) and gender.

The analysis of social practice as an element of and a tool for social processes begins at the individual and the institutional level (micro and macro levels). Our focus was on the way discourse creates and structures ideology aimed at fomenting conflict and/or unity in society. This is because humans are products of their thinking. What they think is constituted by and constitutes the words they use, their attitudes and social behaviour.

I said in the previous section that a discursive event entails the use of certain words/vocabulary. The use of words like *kafir, haraam*, enemy, friend or relative has both political and ideological implications. According to Bourdieu (1987) producers of texts use these words to include or exclude others in a particular community.

Words like *kafir, haraam* and enemy can be used to position and create new ways of viewing social reality. It signifies and constructs certain forms of reality, which in their turn shape existing social relations and identities. This redefines the relationship between Christians and Muslims. For example, some Muslims regard Christians as their potential enemies. Similarly, some Christians see Muslims as their enemies. Such words convey a symbolic and cultural form of disunity and conflict.

Furthermore, preachers choose their vocabulary – positive and negative – within the struggle for hegemonic power between the two languages. After all, they tend to go for words which they feel communicate particular power relations. The use of Arabic-originated words such as *'kafir'* instead of *'wapagani'* reflects such a desire to capitalise on the power relation between the two languages. Those who use *'kafir'* reproduce a picture with a more divisive impact than *'wapagani'*. Such a word (*kafir*) was/is regarded as defamatory and derogatory by some Christians and state organs. The use of these words has landed some Muslim preachers in trouble, either in conflict with Christians or on the wrong side of the law for inciting hatred. Thus Athuman Mazinge (a Muslim preacher) was arrested for uttering defamatory words which caused chaos between Muslims and Christians in Mwanza region. The incident was reported in *Uhuru* on 8 September 2003. This is the same Mazinge whose words were cited above.

Fairclough also speaks of multi-dimensional perspectives, namely individual (micro), institutional (mezzo) and (macro) dimensions. At the individual level the focus is on participants' views, especially when they speak about their own faith (Wijsen 2010b:61) or their life in the community. At the institutional level they speak as representatives of a particular institution (Wijsen 2010b:67). And in the societal dimension they speak as Tanzanians or representatives of a particular society (Wijsen 2010b:70).

Planning and output

After preliminary investigation into the research topic and approach (September-October 2007), we conducted fieldwork from November 2007 to May 2009, using a cyclic strategy moving back and forth between data generation and data analysis. First we analysed the Muslim groups, transcribing and analysing the interviews with members of these groups. Next we conducted, transcribed and analysed the deliberations of FGDs involving Christians. Finally, the same process was undertaken for the mixed (Muslim-Christian) groups.

In keeping with this outline, the study is structured as follows. After this general introduction we report the outcomes of our analyses of the Muslim groups (chapter 2), the Christian groups (chapter 3) and the mixed group (chapter 4). Our general conclusions follow.

I candidly admit that the scope of a case study is always limited. While we started with the geopolitical theories of Huntington and Mazrui, we studied only one location, Dar es Salaam. Although we acquired in-depth insight into social identity construction in interreligious relations at the grassroots level, we cannot generalise the findings to the whole of Tanzania. Through triangulation, however, we can validate our study by means of case studies conducted by others. Though this study does not seek to be practice-oriented, we nevertheless hope that the acquired insight can be used in the policy making of religious and governmental institutions.

Chapter 2:
How Muslims speak about Christians
'Even a Christian can be my friend."

This chapter analyses the way Muslims in Dar es Salaam speak about Christians. As was explained in the general introduction, we examine language use (discourse) to acquire insight into how Muslims in Tanzania identify and position Christians in relation to themselves, and identify the socio-cognitive effects of their language usage – whether it leads to (mis)understanding and (lack of) social cohesion, and consequently, to socio-religious transformation of the community.

The findings presented in this chapter are from different sources. Focus Group Discussions (FGDs) provided primary data. Six FGDs were conducted with Muslims (male and female), grouped according to age, gender and education. There was a group of uneducated Muslim youths (male); uneducated Muslim youths (female), educated Muslim youths (male), educated Muslim youths (female), elderly Muslims (male) and elderly Muslims (female). Additional sources were six key informant interviews, six Muslim *mihadhara* and local news paper reports.

The total number of participants in the exclusively Muslim FGDs was 31, 14 of whom were male and 17 female. Participants in FGDs were selected purposively according to the clusters mentioned in chapter one. These clusters participated in FGDs comprising four elderly males, nine elderly females, six educated male youths, four educated female youths, four uneducated male youths, and four uneducated female youths. In each FGD the number of participants ranged from four to nine. Participants were selected on the basis of their experience with the local community.

The discussions were conducted in the participants' areas, making it easy for them to take part in the one to three hour sessions. The discussions were conducted in KiSwahili, because all participants were fluent in it and comfortable with this language. The discussions were tape-recorded and transcribed. As explained in the general introduction, the findings were analysed using Fairclough's multi-dimensional and poly-methodical model of critical discourse analysis (CDA) (Fairclough 1992:73-100).

2.1. Analysis of linguistic practice

The first step in CDA is to analyse linguistic practice in (spoken and written) texts. The purpose is to acquire insight of participants' utterances. Fairclough (1992:75) proposes four ways of textual analysis, namely vocabulary, grammar, cohesion and text structure. These four ways cover both the form and meaning potential of the text. The emphasis in this study, however, is on vocabulary. Vocabulary has interpersonal, ideational and textual meaning, and as pragmatist linguists say, the meaning of words is given by their use. Words are not neutral: language users choose words which "signify and construct their social identity, social relations, and knowledge" (Fairclough 1992:76). The purpose is to look at the practice, values and perspectives that vocabulary reflects.

We analyse alternative wording and constantly and systematically compare vocabularies to discover their meaning potential (Fairclough 1992:77; Strauss & Corbin 1990:84). One way of constant and systematic comparison is to turn the vocabulary or words upside down (Strauss & Corbin 1990:84; Fairclough 1992:193) and imagine the direct opposite of the vocabulary used (Strauss & Corbin:84). The reason to study alternative vocabulary is that systematic comparison shows how Muslims use different words/vocabulary to refer to Christians to signify the intended social and ideological relations. It is also a truism that some words and vocabulary have both an exclusive and an inclusive character. Indeed, speakers carefully choose words with the intention of either excluding or including others.

This chapter is thematically arranged according to the themes dealt with in the discussions. The themes that emerged from the data collected included interreligious marriage, *mihadhara*, education, dress, renting accommodation and food, details of which are presented below.

Christians and Christian-Muslim relations
"We live well."

Participants talked about labels that Muslims apply to Christians. A young female in the uneducated group said "we call them *kafirs*, but I do not know what that means".[1] She chose the safer pronoun 'we' rather than 'I' to avoid responsibility and to suggest that the label *kafir* is used even by Muslims who do not know the meaning of the word. But she did agree that Muslims call Christians *kafir*. This was corroborated by a young uneducated Muslim female, who said that parents

---
[1] Tunawaitaga makafiri lakini sijui inamaanisha nini.

called Christians *kafir* when their daughter wanted to marry a Christian: "it is impossible to go to that religion of *kafirs*" and/or "to a *haraam*[2] religion".[3] Although most participants did not use the word '*kafir*', they agreed that Muslims use the name to refer to Christians. In most cases it is used indirectly. According to elderly participants the word can refer to "a person who does not agree with the law of religion and the will of God; this person is a *kafir*". Some elderly women participants explained that this definition of *kafir* also includes Muslims who do not abide by Islamic teachings.

Among the older Muslim women some said that "even a Christian can be my friend"[4] or "friendship does not select".[5] Similar statements were made in other groups with the aim of maintaining existing good relations and civic identity. On the other hand, others in the same group said that "only a Muslim can be my friend, because only she can help me in life and death".[6] Another participant added, "Only a Muslim can be my friend because she can keep secrets."[7] Yet another said, "I don't have to think; a Christian is my enemy."[8] This participant explicitly revealed her religio-centrism. But others reacted to her statement, insisting that "an enemy is a person who does evil to you, and that person can be a Christian and even a fellow Muslim".[9] In fact, one participant in the same group said, "There is a saying, the person who suits you in times of trouble is a friend", adding, "A Muslim who has a bad spirit is not your friend",[10] but "a Christian can do good things for you".[11] Overall, participants were not unanimous on this issue, as illustrated by the disagreements that arose. Most participants considered Christians friends, hence included and embraced them as an integral part of one large society. There was one who considered Christians enemies in a divisive manner, thus identifying more with religion than with society. Others were non-committal, tending to benefit by resources (to use Bourdieu's term) from the political, social and symbolic capital of both sides.

---

[2] Literal English meaning of haraam is 'forbidden'.
[3] Haiwezekani kwenda kwenye ile dini ya makafiri . . . kwenye dini haraam.
[4] Hata mkristo anaweza kuwa rafiki yangu.
[5] Rafiki ni wote wote.
[6] Mimi rafiki yangu ni muislamu kwa sababu yeye ndiye atakayeweza kunimalizia mambo yangu yote; ya uzima na kufa.
[7] Mimi, muislamu ndiye anayeweza kuwa rafiki yangu kwa sababu anaweza kunisitiri.
[8] Mimi sina cha kufikiria, naona mkristo ni adui yangu.
[9] Nitakaye muona adui ni yule anayenifanyia ubaya, na anaweza kuwa mkristo na hata muislamu mwenzako.
[10] Maana hata kuna msemo usemao "Akufaaye kwa dhiki ndiye rafiki" sasa kama ni muislamu ana roho mbaya basi sio rafiki.
[11] Lakini Mkristu anaweza kukufanyia vitu vizuri.

The initial response from participants in all six Muslim groups was that Christian and Muslims live together in peace. Indeed, one of the participants from the uneducated female group said, "We live well without quarrels."[12] Another said, "I live well with Christians. My friend is a Christian and we have never quarrelled."[13] This was corroborated by statements uttered during the discussion with the educated male category, where one participant said, "Muslims and Christians have good cooperation and there is no behaviour creating religious problems here in Buguruni."[14]

The female participant quoted above used a pronoun 'we' to make her statement inclusive. 'We' could include Muslims (*we* Muslims live well with Christians) or could refer to both Muslims and Christians as a community (*we* live well). Whereas this female participant spoke of 'we', others were explicit about the subject identity: "I have a Christian friend", "Muslims and Christians cooperate very well." Participants said, "Muslims and Christians are like children of the same father"; "We live like relatives [*ndugu*]".[15] This is because "in a group of five people two are Muslims and three Christians and all of them may share the same interests".[16]

On the other hand, one participant in the uneducated female group said, "Christians … are not jovial (*hawajachangamka*),"[17] and an elderly female observed, "Christians don't like… they don't like Muslims."[18] This elderly lady explicitly mentioned the subject (Christians), but hesitated to state the object, which eventually she revealed in a second clause ("they don't like Muslims"). An elderly male participant commented that "issues of relationship are spoiled by Christians' use of abusive language".[19] Some Muslim participants felt that Christians use language which destroys amicable relations. The participant called it abusive language.

Nevertheless, in all six groups the expression "we live well" (*tunaishi vizuri*)

---

[12] Tunaishi vizuri tu bila kugombana.
[13] Ninaishi na wakristo vizuri na vile vile rafiki yangu ni mkristo na hatujawahi kugombana.
[14] Waislamu na wakristo Buguruni wana ushirikiano mkubwa wala hamna matatizo ya kujenga udini.
[15] Tunaishi kama ndugu.
[16] Kwenye kikundi cha watu watano, wawili ni Wakristu na watatu ni Waislamu na unawakuta wote wanakuwa na lengo moja.
[17] Wakristu hawajachangamka.
[18] Wakristo hawapendi kabisa, hawawapendi waislamu.
[19] Masuala ya mahusiano yanavurugwa zaidi na wakristo ambao wanatumia lugha ya matusi kwa waislamu.

was repeatedly used by every participant, including ones who later in the discussions had reservations.

Interreligious marriage
"A Christian woman is ready to change her religion."

Participants spoke about interreligious marriages in their community. One educated female youth said she had no problem with changing her religion.[20] This woman said converting to Christianity was not a problem if someone wanted to marry a man from that faith. This was confirmed by an uneducated young female, who said changing one's religion was "just a matter of [personal] agreement between the two"[21] and "falling in love with a Christian".[22] An educated male participant said, "A Christian woman is ready to change her religion if she falls in love with you."[23] Whereas the woman quoted above said she had no problem changing her religion, others preferred to distance themselves from such a stance. All the same, educated male participants indicated that Christian women change their religion once they were engaged to be married to Muslim men. In the elderly female FGD it was stated that "in the past it was difficult to be married to a Christian" because "we avoided Christians.[24] But now it is different because we stay together".[25] This elderly female acted as a representative of a particular group ('we') who avoided Christians. Once again the group was not explicitly mentioned, which left her statement open: did Muslims as a whole avoid Christians, or just Muslim women? According to elderly participants this attitude has changed because "now people are more tolerant. A person will ask you what is wrong with a Christian. Is he not a human being like you? Now why should I run from him?"[26]

Other elderly female participants said that in the past "Christian men pretended to change their religion" just to marry a Muslim girl, but after the marriage they stuck to their religion and attended church.[27] In other words, she was accusing

---

[20] Sina tatizo kubadili dini.
[21] Kubadili dini ni makubaliano tu ya watu wawili.
[22] Kama wanapendana na Mkristu.
[23] Binti wa Kikristu yuko tayari kubadili dini kama amempenda.
[24] Zamani tulikuwa tunawaogopa wakristo.
[25] Sasa hivi ni tofauti kwani tunaweza kukaa wote kwa pamoja.
[26] Mtu anakwambia kwani mkristo ana nani? Si binadamu tu kama wewe? Sasa iweje nimkimbie?
[27] Wanaume wa kikristo walikuwa wanabadili dini kiuongo lakini wakirudi nyumbani anaendelea na Biblia yake kwenda kanisani.

Christian men of being tricksters to whom changing their religion was a strategy to marry a Muslim girl, not genuine conversion to Islam.

Some participants spoke of marriage as an institution which is constituted by and constitutes (Islamic) religious rituals. For example, participants in the educated male youth group said, "There is no marriage between a Christian and a Muslim, but when a Christian converts and becomes a Muslim, then marriage is possible."[28] Another group member added, "There is no marriage of a Muslim and a Christian but rather of a Muslim and a Muslim. If not, these people are committing adultery."[29] To these participants, changing one's religion to either Islam or Christianity makes marriage between people who originally had different faiths possible. This condition of conversion was seen by other participants as a problem; an educated male youth, for example, said that "interreligious marriage is possible, but the problem is religion".[30]

Some educated (male) youths insisted: "We consider a Muslim youth (male) who changes his religion because he wants to marry a Christian girl an infidel [*kafir*]."[31] They said that their "faith does not allow a Muslim to marry"[32] a non-Muslim. Change of religion is regarded as a betrayal of Islam. Thus it was indicated that a Muslim who changes his religion "has betrayed religion" and has "strayed religiously and socially".[33] Changing one's religion is thus regarded as a sin (betrayal) and the person is seen as having banished himself or herself from the religious group, hence the label 'infidel' (*kafir*).

Other educated males explained that "Christian girls often change their religion and convert to Islam so that the couple can have a religious marriage".[34] This was confirmed by another participant, who said, "It is difficult for a Muslim man to change his religion to follow that of a woman, a Christian girl must follow a man."[35] Female participants also confirmed that in interreligious marriages it is more common for Christian women to change their religion than for Mus-

---

[28] Hakuna ndoa ya mkristo na mwislam ila pindi mkristo atakaposlim na kuwa mwislam ndo kunandoa.
[29] Hamna ndoa ya mkristo na mwislam au ndoa ya bomani kuna ndoa ya mwislam na mwislam vinginevyo watu hawa wanazini tu.
[30] Uwezekano upo lakini kuna uzito ambao upo kwenye dini.
[31] Here the word 'kafir' is used to describe Muslims who change their religion in order to marry Christians.
[32] Imani haimruhusu Mwislam kuoa asiye Mwislamu.
[33] Kijana wa kiislamu atakaye badili dini kwaajili ya binti wa kikristo huyo tunamwona kama kafiri hivyo, kwani amesaliti dini hiyo amepotoka kidini na kijamii.
[34] Binti wa Kikristu mara nyingi anabadili dini na kuwa Mwislam ili kufunga ndoa ya kiislamu.
[35] Mwanaume wa kiislam kubadili dini kwenda ya mwanamke ni vigumu, binti wakikristo amfuate mwanaume.

lim men, simply because "a man is the head of the household".³⁶ One educated male youth pointed out: "That is why the law on equal rights has been difficult for Muslims."³⁷ This view was shared by young female participants, who accepted that women readily changed their religion because "children should have their father's religion".³⁸

In fact, some participants said just like Christian women marry Muslim men, some Muslim women converted to Christianity and married Christian men. One elderly female participant said, "I have relatives who married Christians and their marriage was conducted in church."³⁹ The expression 'a marriage conducted in church' signifies a Christian wedding. This is contrary to what the educated male said, but even if a Muslim woman was enticed, she would settle for a civil wedding (*ndoa ya bomani*) rather than change her religion.⁴⁰ Other participants thought this an exaggeration, as they agreed that it was possible for a "Christian girl to convince a Muslim youth to change his religion and become a Christian".⁴¹ It was also mentioned that "some Muslim youths cohabit with non-Muslim women and have children with them"⁴² without having an Islamic wedding.

Participants confirmed that some Muslims opted for civil weddings in which both parties are free to practise their faith. A male uneducated youth said, "My older uncle is a Muslim but married a Christian in a civil wedding and they live in harmony; both continue with their faith; on Friday my uncle goes to mosque, on Sunday my aunt goes to church."⁴³ This participant implies that a civil wedding creates cohesion in interreligious marriages and freedom in the family. It also leaves children "free to choose between their father's and their mother's faith".⁴⁴ The choice of which faith to follow becomes an individual decision. Moreover, it was revealed in all six Muslim FGDs that civil weddings have become popular and participants saw them as an alternative to a religious marriage.

This was described as a change in Tanzanian society, because in the past the

---

36 Mwanaume ni kichwa cha familia.
37 Ndo maana ile sheria ya haki sawa imekuwa ngumu kwa waislam.
38 Watoto watafuata dini ya baba.
39 Mimi nina ndugu aliyeoana na Mkristu na ndoa yao ilifanyika kanisani.
40 Lakini mwanamke wakikristo kama amekupenda yupo tayari kubadili dini lakini kwa mwislam hata kama kuna tamaa imemvuta atakuwa tayari kufunga ndoa bomani lakini sio kubadili dini.
41 Inawezekana binti wa kikristu kumshawishi kijana wa Kiislamu kubadili dini na kuwa Mkristu.
42 Baadhi ya vijana wa Kiislaam wanaishi na wanawake wasio waislam na wamezaa nao watoto.
43 Baba yangu mkubwa ni Mwislam lakini ameoa Mkristu kwa ndoa ya bomani na wanaishi kwa amani, na kila mmoja anaendelea na imani yake. Ijumaa baba mkubwa anaenda mskitini na jumapili shangazi anaenda kanisani.
44 Watoto wanauhuru wa kuchagua imani kati ya ile ya baba au ya mama.

problem was not merely one of intermarriage but of profound suspicion, because "even revealing that you had a [sexual] relationship with a Christian"[45] was a problem. The religious leader "would tell you to offer water"[46] for purification. As a result "interfaith sexual relationships during those times were kept secret".[47] Participants said that in the past there were not many options. For instance, one elderly female participant asked: "What type of marriage will you choose [in such a case]? There were no civil weddings. Whose parent or what religion would you go to in order to get married"?[48]

Although civil weddings and cohabitation are popular, participants said, "Those who stay together with people of a different faith [i.e. are married to non-Muslims] face excommunication."[49] This is because Islam does not recognise civil weddings. In the words of one educated male participant, "in the community people marry, but are like adulterers".[50] This was clarified by another participant in the same group, who said, "Unlike Christians, Muslims don't believe in civil marriages."[51] The participant was speaking of other unions such as traditional and government ceremonies or cohabitation, which are not Islamic marriages.

To most youths, parents and family were the main obstacles to interreligious marriage. As one female youth said, "I have no problem with changing my religion, but the main obstacle is my parents."[52] According to another educated female youth a marriage proposal from a Christian man would be rejected by most Muslim parents. As quoted already, one participant said Muslim parents would turn down such a proposal, saying "it is impossible to go to that *kafir* religion"[53] and/or "to a *haraam* religion"! Parents forbade Muslim girls to marry Christians

---

[45] Licha ya kuolewa yaani hata ikijulikana unamahusiano na mkristo wanakuambia utoe maji.
[46] Wanakuambia utoe maji.
[47] Kama mnauhusiano basi yawe ya siri.
[48] Naona zamani ilikuwa haiwezekani kuolewa na mkristo, mtaoana kwa ndoa ya zipi? Hakukua na ndoa za bomani. Ataolewa kwa baba yake nani? Au kwa dini gani?
[49] Watu wanaoishi pamoja wanatengwa na dini.
[50] Mtaani watu wanaoana lakini ni sawa nakuwa wanazini.
[51] Waislam hawaamini ndoa ya bomani tofauti na wakristo.
[52] Mimi sina tatizo kubabili dini yangu, tatizo ni wazazi.
[53] According to elderly female participants the word 'kafir' refers to "a Swahili person who doesn't have a religion, hence does not go to either the church or mosque. According to them the word 'infidel' (kafir) refers to any person who is not a believer, i.e. someone who is neither a Christian nor a Muslim, or not a faithful believer. However, when discussing intermarriage educated male Muslim youths associated the word 'kafir' with Christianity and Muslim converts to Christianity. In this chapter, therefore, the word 'kafir' refers to non-believers in Islam, including Christians and Muslims who convert to Christianity. A Swahili person in this context is someone who resides in the coastal area and adopts the coastal lifestyle, but does not adhere to the traditional Muslim way of life.

because they considered Christians *kafirs* and Christianity *haraam*. On this point female youths said that their fathers warned them with statements such as "If you change your religion, don't stay in my house."[54] This was corroborated by a participant in the elderly female FGD, who insisted, "I won't allow my child to marry a Christian unless she just decides to go and live there [cohabit]."[55]

According to educated female youths, "it is easier for parents to allow a Muslim youth to marry a Christian female than for a Muslim female to marry a Christian man".[56] As a result Muslim "girls take irrational decisions such as committing suicide by hanging themselves, taking poison or running away from home".[57]

For their part, parents represented by elderly females gave various reasons for objecting to interreligious marriages. One participant in this FGD category said that daughters married to Christians were "not allowed to inherit, bury their parents and practise *eda*[58] when they pass away".[59] Likewise, when the mother passed away the daughter of such a woman would not be allowed to inherit, bury herand/or practise *eda*. According to this participant Islam forbids the faithful from inheriting anything from a non-Muslim. This was confirmed by an educated male youth, who said that "Islamic teaching directs that a child who is born in that situation [intermarriage] will not get approval to inherit resources when a male parent dies". Alternatively, participants said a parent can "give possession of wealth to the child before his death, but this should be done without the knowledge of other children [if any] who are born in wedlock". And "children born in wedlock are not allowed to give resources to their siblings who were born out of wedlock..."[60]

Because of these Islamic codes of conduct some Muslim parents use threatening language such as, "Change your religion, but you should know that I'm not

---

[54] Kama ukibadili dini usikae nyumbani kwangu.
[55] Kwa hiyo hata kama ni mwanangu siwezi kumruhusu labda tu aende wakaishi.
[56] Ni rahisi kwa mzazi kumruhusu mwanaume wa Kiislamu kuoa binti wa Kikristu kuliko mwanamke wa kiislam kuoa mwanaume Mkristu.
[57] Mabinti wanafanya maamuzi ya ajabu ya kujinyonga, kunywa sumu au kutoroka nyumbani.
[58] According to Kamusi ya KiSwahili-kiingereza eda is a period when a woman remains unmarried and in the care of her husband's relatives after his death or a divorce.
[59] Siku akifa haruhusiwi kumrithi, wala kumzika na wala kumkalia eda.
[60] Hivyo kwa minajili ya kiislamu mtoto huyo atakayezaliwa katika mazingira hayo hatapata kibali cha kurithi mali pindi mzazi wa kiume atakapo fariki. (Suala hili linawahusu vijana wa dini ya kiislamu wanaoishi pamoja bila ndoa) Labda tu mtoto huyo arithishwe mali kabla ya mauti ya mzazi wake pasipo kuwahusisha watoto wake wengine walio ndani ya ndoa (kama wapo) kwa wale ambao wamezaliwa ndani ya ndoa hawaruhusiwi kumpa mali (mwenzao aliye nje ya ndoa) isipokuwa kwa sababu za kibinadamu tu.

your mother anymore and that if I pass away, do not attend my burial"[61] to discourage their daughters from getting married to non-Muslims. This non-involvement in their daughter's day-to-day activities was taken by the youths as excommunication/a curse: they said "the whole family will disown you simply because you have a Christian fiancée".[62]

Participants in the FGDs said that intermarriages are also regulated by economics and/or money. One elderly female participant put it succinctly: "We don't choose religion but avarice."[63] If you find a Christian with money, you go with him and thus "currently there are not so many sermons;[64] if, as a mother, you see your son-in-law coming with 2 000 or 5 000 Tanzanian shillings, you see him as a perfect man to stay with your daughter; you advise her to stick to him."[65]

Others, however, saw this attitude as greed, love of money (*uroho wa pesa*). Uneducated male youths said that "high percentages of women nowadays are tricksters … they love someone because of his pocket".[66] This was corroborated by a participant in the educated group: "But if you see a Christian woman married to a Muslim, then there is something that enticed her, which is desire [for money] and if you see a Muslim man converting to Christianity, there is something that has captured him, which is a woman's wealth."[67]

Participants spoke about the government's role in resolving the intermarriage issue. According to male educated participants "the government should get rid of civil weddings" because "it is the government which permitted it", but "now it is causing disputes, especially when it comes to inheritance".[68] This participant preferred religious to secular marriage. To most educated male participants these

---

[61] Badili dini lakini uje mimi sio mama yako tena hata nikifa usije kunizika. (Educated female participant.)
[62] Familia yote watakukataa, kisa umepata mchumba Mkristu.
[63] Hatuchagui dini bali kushiba.
[64] A wealthy person is received or allowed to marry a Muslim without considering his/her religious background and is seen as a blessing to the in-laws because he/she will contribute to the family income.
[65] Lakini enzi hizi hakuna neno sana wewe mwenyewe mama mtu ukiona mkweo anakulete 2,000, 5,000 ndio unaona ni mwanaume wa kukaa na mwanangu unamsihi amshike.
[66] Asilimia kubwa ya wanawake siku hizi ni matapeli… Wanampenda mtu kutokana na mfuko wake.
[67] Ila ukiona mwanamke mkristo kaolewa na mwislam basi kuna kitu kinamvuta ambacho ni tamaa na ukiona mwanaume mwislam kaenda ukristo (kamfata mwanamke) kunakitu kimemteka nacho ni mali za yule mwanamke.
[68] Serikali inabidi ikomeshe ndoa za bomani, kwakuwa yenyewe ndio ilioziruhusu na sasa zinaleta matatizo wakati wa kudai mirathi.

disputes will be resolved by the establishment of *kadhi* courts, because "it will deal with issues of inheritance, marriage and dispute resolution".[69]

Education
"Christians are very advanced in education."

Muslim participants spoke about Christians in relation to education as well. One uneducated male stated that "Christians are very advanced in education compared to Muslims".[70] This participant pictured Christians as having a secular education, which qualifies them for employment in every sector, "that is why everywhere[71] you go you will find many Christians".[72] Another educated participant said that "we Muslims are seen as uneducated".[73] His use of the passive voice, 'are seen', suggests that it is not Muslims who see themselves as uneducated. Indeed, the participant did not specify who sees Muslims as uneducated. Some participants see hope for the current generation, which has access to more educational opportunities. As one elderly participant pointed out, "Present-day children, Muslims, are educated the same as Christians' children."[74]

Educated youths distinguished between Islamic education and secular education. They maintained: "There are two types of education; there is worldly education [*elimu dunia*] and heavenly education [*elimu ahera*]. Worldly education is conducted in classes [secular schools], while heavenly education is obtained at *madras* [Q'uranic schools]."[75] In fact, according to the uneducated male participants the two types of education go together. "In the morning he [the child] goes for primary education at school and in the evening he goes for *madras*."[76] Muslims give heavenly education [*elimu ahera*] "high priority and thus attendance at Q'uranic school is daily".[77]

---

[69] Mahakama ya Kadhi itashughulika na masuala ya mirathi, ndoa na utatuzi wa migogoro.
[70] Wakristu wako mbele sana ukilinganisha na Waislam kwenye swala la elimu.
[71] When stating that "everywhere you go you will find many Christians" the participant was referring to formal employment: Christians are employed in all formal sectors because their secular education is preferred. Thus there are few Muslims in formal employment because they neglect formal (secular) education and prioritise religious education.
[72] Hii ndio sababu popote uendapo utakuta Wakristu ni wengi.
[73] Sisi Waislamu tunaonekana kama hatuna elimu.
[74] Watoto wa sasa hivi wa waislamu ni wasomi sana hali kadhalika na kwa watoto wa kikristo.
[75] Kuna aina mbili za elimu: kuna elimu dunia na elimu ahera. Elimu dunia inatolewa darasani, wakati elimu ahera inapatina madrasa.
[76] Asubuhi mtoto anaenda kupata elimu ya msingi shuleni, na jioni anakwenda Madrasa.
[77] Elimu ya dini inaumuhimu mkubwa ndio maan mahudhurio kwenye madrasa ni kila siku.

Muslim elderly (female) participants said that "Christians don't want Muslims to learn the Qur'an; instead they want them to have Western education [*kizungu*]."[78] Their argument was that formal education leaves no room for Muslim children to attend *madras* and learn the Qur'an, because "the time for tuition conflicts with the time my child is supposed to go to *madras*".[79] However, some have been able to strike a balance between the two. One participant in the elderly group reported that our child "attends extra classes and Arabic too; therefore, there is time for extra classes and time for *madras*."[80] Elderly female participants said they send their children for *madras* because they did not want them to be "roaming around" (*kuzurura*) the streets.

In the past the problem was not merely one of religion but also involved the language or medium of instruction used in school, namely *Kizungu*[81] (English) as opposed to Arabic.[82] The language dilemma, as elderly females put it, made "their fathers forbid" (*baba aliwazuia*) them to attend European schools. Their parents asked, "Will you go to learn Arabic?"[83] But the answer was always no, since *Kizungu* remained the primary language of instruction.

Similarly, in the past "Muslims did not enrol in formal schools because they were afraid to go to Christian colleges, thinking that they will eat pork".[84] This fear has since subsided, as there are "many Muslims who are being educated"[85] in Christian educational institutions and as a result, "now Muslims can study at any school".[86] This was confirmed by an educated female who said, "Currently, in [Christian] seminary schools, Muslims are also allowed to enrol."[87]

Others compared Arabic (religious) education with formal education. They said, "My father enrolled me in school to study Arabic. In the end I studied 2

---

[78] Wakristu hawapendi waislamu wajisifunze Koran badala yake wanataka wajifunze kizungu.
[79] Muda wa tuisheni ni ule ule wa mtoto kwenda madrasa.
[80] Na mimi mwanangu anasoma tuition na kiarabu pia anasoma kwa hiyo kuna muda wa kwenda tuition na ule wa kwenda chuo.
[81] The word 'Kizungu' extends beyond its literal translation (i.e. English) to include all formal education and the European way of life.
[82] The word 'Arabic' is used by different participants to refer to two different things. First it refers to the language (Arabic), and secondly it refers to religion/dini (Islam in this case). The latter is because Islam uses Arabic in prayers and sermons, hence children learn Arabic as their language of worship and to participants there is no demarcation between the language and the prayer/dini.
[83] Utaenda kusoma kiarabu?
[84] Waislamu hawakujiunga na vyuo vya kikristu kwa hofu kwamba watakula nguruwe. (Educated female participant.)
[85] Woga huu kwa sasa umeisha kwani kuna wengi wameelishwa. (Educated female participant.)
[86] Siku hizi waislamu pia wanaenda kwenye zozote. (Educated male participant.)
[87] Kwenye mashule ya seminari hivi sasa hata Waislamu wanaruhusiwa pia kushiriki.

or 3 *juzuu*.⁸⁸ But those who have studied up to form two ... would say I have no education, I only studied religion."⁸⁹ This elderly man observed that in the past religious (Arabic) education had high status. Nowadays secular education has superseded Arabic (religious) education in terms of status. Consequently those who have only studied Arabic are seen as illiterate.

Youths said Christian parents make sure that their children go on to secondary school after passing primary school examinations. As one educated male youth put it, "Both Christians and Muslims appear when results are released... You might find that 40 students have passed, of which seven are Christians and the remaining 33 are Muslims. All those Christians will enrol, but of the Muslims only ten will go on and pass [the final examination]."⁹⁰ This participant was referring to children selected to join secondary schools after passing the primary school leaving examination. His argument was that even when more Muslim children (33) passed their primary school leaving examination than Christians (7), the latter stood a better chance of progressing than the former. Moreover, the participant said only a few Muslim children (10) who passed the examination went on to secondary school. But the participant did not say why they did not go on, let alone why they failed their final examinations (i.e. those who managed to attend secondary school).

Some participants cited "economic position as what makes it difficult for Muslim parents to send their children to school".⁹¹ In other words, "the issue of education no longer relates to religion, but rather to economic status as the pillar for getting education".⁹² According to male youths the main hindrance for some Muslims is their parents' low financial status or income.

Some Muslim youths blamed their parents for the low level of education among Muslims. In the FGD for educated female youths it was indicated that "parents don't like to see their daughters mixing with (male) youths";⁹³ "they don't

---

⁸⁸ According to the TUKI Swahili-English Dictionary, Juzuu is one chapter of the Qur'an.
⁸⁹ Baba yangu alinipeleka shule kusoma Kiarabu na mwisho nilisoma juzuu 2 au 3. Na aliyesoma mpaka darasa la kumi ambaye anaweza kuwa mwanangu ataona sijasoma ila nimezzoma dini tu.
⁹⁰ Katika kufanya mitihani sasa hivi si kama zamani na wanapotoa matokeo sio kwamba wapo wakristo tu hata waislam wapo. Nilichogundua wakristo kwenye swala la kimaisha wapo juu na inapotokea kafaulu huwa ni lazima asome lakini sio kwa waislam unaweza kukuta wamefaulu wanafunzi 40 kati ya hao 7 ndo wakristo na waliobaki 33 ni waislam, hao wakristo wataenda lakini waislam labda 10 ndo wataenda na kufaulu.
⁹¹ Hali ya uchumi ya wazazi ndio kikwazo cha kutopeleka watoto shule.
⁹² Kwenye swala la elimu halihusiani tena na dini bali uchumi ndio nguzo ya kupata hiyo elimu.
⁹³ Wazazi pia wanachangia kwani mzazi wa Kiislamu hataki kumwona binti yake yuko na mvulana labda wamekaa sehemu wanajadili masomo.

want girls to be in discussion groups, particularly when the discussion involves both boys and girls."[94] These participants believed that their parents fail to understand that sometimes boys and girls sit "together to discuss [school] subjects" and not flirtatious or mundane topics. They said that parents should know that these days "education means competition".[95]

Educated male participants noted that Christians are allowed in Muslim schools, but "Christian students have to observe certain laws... For example, all female students are required to wear veils ... and during prayers Christian students are required to remain in class... and Christian students are not allowed to have lunch during the fasting period."[96]

Participants also talked about Christian universities and colleges. One educated male participant said, "Christians have many colleges. First they cooperate, for example, when they want to build a Christian university, they contribute money."[97] This was affirmed by another participant in the same group: "Christians have many universities, more than twenty, while Muslims have one."[98]

One participant in the group followed up by declaring, "The problem is us Muslims, some have money, but they cannot decide to build an Islamic university. Instead our counterparts, the Christians and their organisations, build universities. That is why they have more universities than we have."[99] Another group member said, "Muslims lack understanding [*uelewa mdogo*] when it comes to education – we look at tomorrow, but Christians look further; that is why they are ahead of us in many things."[100]

One participant spoke about Christians' unity. "When Christians have an issue they all gather and become one regardless of their denominations. But we dis-

---

[94] Hawawezi kuwaruhusu waende kujisomea kwenye group discussion hasa za mchanganyiko na wavulana na wasichana.

[95] Wazazi wanatakiwa wajue wakati waliokulia wenyewe ni tofauti na wakati huu ambao elimu ni ushindani.

[96] Mkristo anaruhusiwa kwenda lakini mkristo anapoingia kuna sheria anatakiwa afate mfano wanatakiwa kuvaa mashungi wote, muda wa sala wakasali kwahiyo mkristo muda wa sala atatakiwa kubaki darasani na wakati wa mfungo hatakiwi kula.

[97] Wakristo wanavyuo vingi kwanza wanaushirikiano. Mfano wakristo wakitaka kujenga chuo kikuu cha kikristo anachanga hela.

[98] Wakristo wana vyuo vingi sana zaidi ya 20 lakini waislam wana chuo kimoja.

[99] Tatizo nafikiri ni sisi wenyewe waislam na wengi wao wanapesa lakini wanashindwa kuamua tujenge chuo kikuu cha kiislam badala yake wenzetu wakristo na mashirika ya kikristo wanajitoa kujenga vyuo vikuu ndio maana viko vingi kuliko vya kwetu sisi.

[100] Ninaweza kusema ni uelewa mdogo wa waislam katika swala la elimu, tunaangalia kesho lakini wakristo wanaangalia mbali ndo maana wametupita katika mambo mengi.

criminate – Manzese Muslims versus Buguruni Muslims or Shi'ites versus Sunni Muslims. This causes differences."[101]

The female youth and elderly groups traced the problem of education among Muslims back to colonialism. During this period "all Europeans were Christians and therefore Muslims became very afraid[102] to send their children to school for fear of their being converted to Christianity". One elderly participant recalled her parents saying, "You don't know that it is the Europeans who convert people to Christianity?" Her parents lamented: "You want my child to be a *kafir*? ... Let her go to *madras* instead of studying there."[103] An educated male participant said, "Muslims..., we handicap ourselves when it comes to education, we feel that when we mix with Christians we could be converted and join their religion."[104]

Educated male youths stated that "the government does not prevent Muslims from building colleges and schools, but it is the Muslims who don't have the habit of helping other Muslims"[105] to acquire formal education.

Patterns of consumption and slaughtering meat
"There are foods that Christians eat but Muslims don't."

Meals and their preparation were said to be very important in mixed (i.e. Christian-Muslim) communities. This emerged clearly in all FGDs. In this regard one educated male youth said, "In short, there are foods that Christians eat but Muslims don't eat."[106] Some educated male participants stated that some Christians eat pork secretly in Muslims' environment/homes. Said one participant, "In my opinion, even if Christians use these pork products, they are very secretive. Because you could be staying in the same house, unless you hear a child's name

---

[101] Mfano wakristo wanapokuwa na jambo wanajikusanya wote wanakuwa kitu kimoja bila kujali dhehebu lakini sasa tunajibagua mwislam wa manzese, buguruni au hawa wanaosali shiha au suna kwahiyo hiyo inaleta matabaka. (Educated male participant.)

[102] Wazungu wote ni wakristu kwa hiyo waliogopa kupeleka watoto wao.

[103] Na tulikuwa tunakatazwa na baba zetu kwenda kusoma wao walikuwa wanatuuliza, mnaenda kusoma Kiarabu? Basi ukimjibu Kizungu, yeye anakuambia hapana kwa kuhofia kuwa mkristo. Hamjui wazungu ndio wanawabadili dini? Watu na kuingia kwenye ukristo? Mnataka mtoto wangu awe kafiri bwana, asisome huku aende chuoni akasome madrasa.

[104] Ushirikiano kati ya waislamu na wakristo upo ila waislam wenyewe ndo tunajiweka nyuma katika swala la elimu tunaona tukijichanganya na wakristo tunawezwa kubadilishwa nakuingia dini yao.

[105] Serikali haijawazuia Waislamu kujenga chuo kikuu ila ni sisi waislamu ambao hatuna tabia ya kusaidiana.

[106] Kiufupi, kuna vyakula ambayo Wakristu wanakula lakini Waislamu hawali.

being called, [you don't know] that this is a Christian, they live very secretively."[107] In other words, Christians tended to conceal their religious identity. However, one participant in the elderly male FGD said that "some Muslims eat pork too",[108] even though it is prohibited for Muslims.

Participants agreed that slaughtering of all types of animals for public consumption has to be done by Muslims. An uneducated male youth said: "Muslims won't eat chicken or a cow which was not slaughtered by a Muslim."[109] So far that has been the tradition in Tanzania. If a Muslim goes to a Christian home, s/he must ask who slaughtered the animal/bird. One uneducated male youth said, "If I go to visit a Christian friend and find him eating chicken, and he invites me to the table, I must ask him who slaughtered the chicken, was he a Christian or Muslim? If it was slaughtered by a Christian I will decline."[110] This statement confirmed that Muslims don't eat meat which has not been slaughtered by a fellow Muslim.

Even then not all Muslims are allowed to slaughter animals for domestic and public consumption. This was stated by one young Muslim (male) participant, who explained that although he is a Muslim, he cannot slaughter an animal because he is "not permitted to do so",[111] showing that only qualified Muslims can slaughter.

Some participants said that the Christian faith allows Christians to eat pork because their religion is generally tolerant about it. One participant in the educated male group said, "Their faith allows Christians to eat pork, although some eat it and others don't, but when it comes to Muslims this is a problem because their religion prohibits[112] doing so." This was corroborated by another participant in the same group, who said, "I think the problem is faith. For us Muslims our faith prohibits … pork. Therefore, when we stay with Christians … we respect each other … when a person wants to eat pork he will go and eat it in other places such as a bar."[113] These participants believed that religions regulate and direct believers

---

[107] Kwa mtazamo wangu wakristo hata kama watakuwa wanatumia nyama hizi za nguruwe watakuwa wasiri sana maana utakuta mnaishi labda nyumba moja labda usikie mtoto ameitwa jina ndio utajua huyu mkristo lakini wanaishi kwa siri sana. (Educated male participant.)

[108] Kuna baadhi ya waislamu wanakula nguruwe pia.

[109] Muslim hawezi kula kuku and ng'ombe ambaye hakuchinjwa na Mwislamu.

[110] Kama nikienda kumtembelea rafiki yangu amabye ni Mkristu na nikamkuta anakula kuku, akinikaribisha ni lazima ni muulize nani amechinja, ni Mwislamu au Mkristu. Akisema Mkristu sili.

[111] Mimi siwezi kuchinja, kwa sababu sijaruhusiwa.

[112] Wakristo imani inawaruhusu kula nguruwe ingawa wanaokula ni baadhi si wote kwahiyo linapokuja swala hili kwa upande wa waislam linakuwa tatizo kwasababu dini yao inakataza.

[113] Mimi nadhani tatizo ni imani sisi waislam imani yetu inakataza kula nguruwe kwahiyo tunapokaa na wakristo … tunaheshimiana hata wao wenyewe kama mtu anataka kula nguruwe

regarding the types of food they should or should not eat. For most Christians their faith allows pork. Islam does not.

In the past children were forbidden to attend Christian schools simply because parents were not sure what food their children would eat at school. In the previous section on education I quoted a participant saying that parents "were afraid to enrol in Christian colleges for fear that they will eat pork".[114]

Pork was one reason why Muslim parents used to veto interfaith marriage. An educated Muslim female stated: "A girl who wants to marry a Christian will be asked [by her parents] why she wants to go and eat *haraam* [forbidden] food."[115]

All participants agreed that food, especially pork, is one of the main causes of Muslim-Christian conflict in the area. One elderly male participant said: "This custom of Muslims fearing Christians and Christians fearing Muslims is the result of one animal, namely the honourable pig."[116] Participants said that "this fear [of pork] was there in our forefathers' time and every person in the whole of Tanzania knows that".[117] One educated male participant maintained, "Hatred could arise when a person cooked pork [in a Muslim house] ... because it is not supposed to be done in his household ... and when this become public knowledge that person will be despised in his religion and by other Muslims."[118] This animal "has caused many quarrels"[119] in Muslim-Christian communities.

Participants said it was not just the problem of eating pork but also that of keeping pigs and selling pork in butcheries. In the elderly Muslim FGD there was a complaint that "where we live our neighbours (Christians) keep pigs" when everyone, even the government, "knows and it is written in our books that Muslims don't like dirty things".[120] This alleged insensitivity creates a lot of misunderstanding, especially when "Muslims go to explain that they are unhappy about

---

anaenda kulia kwingine, kama bar. (Educated male participant.)

[114] See Swahili translation in the education section.

[115] See Swahili translation in the interreligious marriage section.

[116] Hii kawaida ya muislamu kumhofia mkristo na mkristo kumhofia muislamu kutokana na mnyama mmoja anayeitwa mheshimiwa nguruwe.

[117] Hofu hii ipo kwanzia kwa wazee wa zamani hadi sasa, na kila mtu anaijua Tanzania nzima.

[118] ... Mwislam kwa hiyo anapokaa ikatokea mtu akapika nguruwe inaweza kutokea hata chuki maana ... haitakiwi iwepo nyumbani kwake kwa maana atadharaulika hata katika dini yake hata kwa Waislam wenzake kama watajua hilo swala.

[119] Imeleta ugomvi sana.

[120] Inafahamika kwa watu na hata Serikalini na kwenye vitabu vyetu waislamu wanasema hivyo kwamba muislamu huwa hapendi vitu vichafu lakini utakuta huko tunakoishi, jirani zetu hawa wakristo wanafuga nguruwe.

the whole affair, and then hostility arises between them".[121] However, the habit of keeping pigs in an area where Muslims live was seen by participants as resulting from "Christians having more money than Muslims, who perhaps do not have any".[122]

Participants in the elderly male FGD said the government was to blame, because "these things happen, but the government is not implementing"[123] its policies: "Even if someone reports it to the police, follow-up is delayed; decisions are not made the same day."[124] One elderly male participant said Muslims who dared to speak about these issues were "branded as instigators who fuel religious hatred between Muslims and Christians".[125] Participants used labels to express complaints about Christians. This participant said they were called 'instigators' of hatred.

According to the participants' understanding keeping animals in the city is "allowed but should not disturb the neighbours and should not lead to uncleanliness [*ukafiri*],[126] and I think the government was supposed to follow up on those things ... But what is happening?"[127] They also complained that pigsties, especially the "smell [emanating from them] does not annoy only Muslims but also some Christians".[128]

Dress
"Christians would go to church to pray wearing short dresses."

With regard to clothing participants said there are no differences in the way believers of the two religions dress. One educated male participant said, "You don't see much difference, because you find a Christian woman wearing *baibui* and a veil (*mtandio*), although they don't wear a long gown (*majuba*)", adding that "cloth-

---

[121] Endapo waislamu wanamwelewesha kwamba yeye hapendi, basi kunakuwa na uhasama kati yao.
[122] Labda hii inatokana na wao kuwa na pesa kidogo, na muislamu labda hana.
[123] Lakini pia, huenda mambo haya yanatendeka kwani serikali nayo haitekelezi.
[124] Na hata mtu akimpeleka mwenzake polisi, ufuatiliaji unakuwa mzito kwani uamuzi hautokei siku ile ile.
[125] Ukiongelea jambo hili unaonekana kwamba muislamu anachonga imani za kidini na hivyo kuleta chuki baina ya waislamu na wakristo.
[126] Ukafir is an adjectival form of kafir. In this context it refers to making a person unclean/unholy, or to dirty a person.
[127] Kwa uelewa wangu mifugo katikati ya mji inaruhusiwa ili mradi isisumbue majirani na wala isitoe kafiri na serilaki nafikiri inafuatilia hivyo vitu. Sasa inakuaje juu ya hali hili!
[128] Huenda inatokana na harufu ambayo haiwakeri tu waislamu ila hata kwa baadhi ya wakristo.

ing is therefore not a criterion for identification".[129] This was confirmed by another group member, who said, "Nowadays it is difficult because you could see a girl wearing trousers, only to find she is a Muslim. For men, they wear robes [*kanzu*], even Christians wear it."[130] Sometimes it is possible to identify a person by the way s/he dresses. In the words of one uneducated male participant, "In the case of clothes sometimes you may distinguish a Christian from a Muslim, especially women."[131]

An educated young female said, "From the very beginning it was a must for Muslims to cover the body before going to the house of God; a Muslim has to cover up."[132] Wearing respectable clothing "is what God wants for young females".[133] Other participants said that "Muslims are taught how to dress, especially young females".[134] However, elderly females said that "the *baibui* we had in the past are different from the ones we have now".[135] This was affirmed by a young female, who stated that "in the past people wore *baibui*[136] but now they wear *juba*".[137] "Even in the past *juba* were there ... but now the Sunni have popularised them."[138]

On the whole participants indicated that the type of clothes that Muslims wore depended on the Muslim calendar and activities of the year. For instance, "during *Ramadan* people [women] wear *madera* but once the month is over they don't wear them".[139] Others "wear *majuba* as a fashion and because they want to please someone",[140] probably their husband or boyfriend. At the same time children of

---

[129] Hakuna tofauti sana maana utakuta mwanamke wa kikristo kava baibui na mtandio ingawa havai majuba yale makubwa, kwa hiyo mavazi sio kigezo sana chakutofautisha huyu ni mwislam au mkristo.
[130] Ila kwa hali ya sasa ni vigumu maana utamkuta msichana kava suruali kumbe ni mwislam. Kwa wanaume wanavaa kanzu lakini hata wakristo nao wanavaa.
[131] Kwa upande mwingine wa mavazi unaweza kumtofautisha Muislamu au Mkristu hasa kwa upande wa wanawake.
[132] Kwa Mwislamu ni lazima ujisitiri, Waislamu tangu mwanzo ni lazima ujisitiri ndio uingine kwenye nyumba ya Mungu.
[133] Kujistiri ndo Mungu anapenda kwa watoto wa kike.
[134] Waislamu wamefundishwa namna ya kujistiri hususani watoto wa kike.
[135] Mabaibui tuliyokuwanayo zamani ni tofauti na ya sasa.
[136] Baibui is a purdan (black garment worn by Muslim women on top of other clothes).
[137] Juba is a loose head veil worn by Sunni Muslim females.
[138] Zamani watu walivaa Mabaibui lakini sasa watu wanavaa juba. Hata zamani majuba yalikuwepo ... ila sasa sunni wameongezea umaarufu.
[139] Kipindi cha ramadhani watu huvaa madera (magauni mapana na mtandio). Lakini mwezi ukiisha watu hawavai tena.
[140] Haya Majuba watu wengine wanavaa kama fashion.

"men who wear trousers that do not reach/touch their heels are mocked by saying that your father is wearing *pedo*[141] nowadays".[142]

Participants also talked about clothing in the past. They said "long ago people had no religion and wore skins or remained naked",[143] but things changed after coming into contact with the outside world and the arrival of religion (i.e. Islam and Christianity). Elderly female participants, referring to their experiences with Christians, said that "we called a Christian's child *mzungu*, because they wore short dresses, which made them look half naked, and they used to boast ... we Muslim children were seen as more traditional/local because of wearing *khanga* or *kaniki*, *vitenge* and *baibui*."[144] "In the past *baibui* was our religious dress and even children had them."[145]

Muslims (especially females) "are not supposed to wear unconventional dress such as trousers and tops."[146] Uneducated male participants advanced many reasons to explain why Muslims have to dress 'appropriately'. They said if young females dressed "inappropriately, men will have sexual desire because of their bodily shape".[147] So if young women wear unconventional dress it "could cause men to be attracted to them".[148] As a result, young uneducated female participants explained, females should "put on veils to avoid putting men into temptation".[149] Similarly, men should cover their bodies properly in order to reduce (female) desire for them.[150]

However, educated male participants declared that even Muslim girls dress inappropriately. One group member said, "There are Muslims who put on *pedo*

---

[141] Pedo (pedal): short trousers that cover the knees. This concept is borrowed from cyclists who roll up their trousers when pedaling. leaving their legs uncovered. The way it is used here is negative, because originally pedo refers to women's shorts.

[142] Lakini watu huwakashfu eti baba yako siku hizi anavaa pedo siku hizi.

[143] Zamani watu hawakuwa na dini na walivaa ngozi au walikaa uchi. (Educated female participant.)

[144] Mtoto wa kikristo tulimwita mzungu kwa ajili ya kuvaa nguo fupi ya kukaa uchi na walikuwa wanaringa. Sisi watoto wa Kiislamu tulionekana wa kienyeji kwa kuvaa khanga au kaniki, vitenge na baibui.

[145] Baibui ndio lilikuwa ndio vazi letu la dini ma hata mtoto mdogo wa kiislamu alishonewa.

[146] Wanawake hawatakiwi kuvaa nguo zisizokuwa za heshima kama suruali na vitopu. (Uneducated female participant.)

[147] Wanawake wakivaa vibaya kutokana na maumbile yao wanaweza kufanya wanaume wapate matamanio.

[148] Wanaume wanaweza kuwatamani. (Elderly female participant.)

[149] Wanaweka ushungi ilikutowaingiza wanaume kwenye majaribu.

[150] Wanaume nao wanatakiwa wavae vizuri ili wanawake wasiwatamani. (Educated male participant.)

though it is not allowed."[151] Another elderly male participant complained, "When you tell a child (female) not to wear trousers, she tells you that you are old-fashioned."[152] This participant attributed such a response from young females to youths who feel that they are "more educated [and hence more up-to-date than their elders], so their religious faith is low".[153] Elderly male participants noted that young females even deceived their parents by wearing respectable dress when leaving their home, only to remove "the dress in the neighbourhood and wear unrespectable ones" once out of their compounds.[154]

Thus clothing remains an issue for both young Christian and Muslim females. This was attested by another elderly male participant, who said, "Tanzanian children are confused, both Muslims and Christians. When they see their peers wearing mini-skirts they also want them."[155] The main difference was that "Christians would go into church to pray in skimpy dresses [mini-skirts], others in tight trousers".[156] "It is like a fashion show in church.... Others wear evening wear meant for clubbing to church, which does not make sense to society and the family ... But we know God does not like that."[157] Uneducated female participants explained that this was not the case with Muslims going to the mosque, because they "cover their bodies (*wanafunika miili yao*)" just like the fathers and sisters in church. According to young female participants "sisters[158] wear respectable dresses".[159] Essentially, a major difference in dress between Muslims and Christians is the way lay believers dress when going to worship.

Funeral ceremonies and practices
"We cooperate with our [Christian neighbours] in the matter of burials."

Participants mentioned funerals as an area where Muslims and Christians cooperate. As one elderly male explained, "It is a truism that we cooperate with our

---

[151] Wapo waislam wanaovaa pedo ingawa hairuhusiwi.
[152] Ukimwambia asivae suruali anakuambia umepitwa na wakati. (Elderly male participant.)
[153] Kutokana na wao kuwa wasomi na hivyo imani kwao imepungua sana.
[154] Na kuna wengine wanatoka nyumbani na nguo za heshima lakini wakifika huko nje kwa majirani wanabadili na kuvaa nyingine zisizo na heshima.
[155] Watoto wa Tanzania wamechanganyikiwa, waislamu kwa wakristo, wakiona mwenzake amevaa kimini na yeye anataka.
[156] Lakini Wakristo anaweza kuingia na kimini kanisani. (Educated female participant.)
[157] Haya mavazi yanakuwa kama kuna maonyesho ya mavazi kanisani mwingine hata mavazi ya klabu anaendea kanisani, inakuwa haileti maana katika jamii na familia zao. Lakini tunajua Mungu hapendezwi. (Educated female participant.)
[158] The sisters referred to are Catholic nuns, who wear a habit and veil.
[159] Masista wanavaa nguo za heshima.

Christian neighbours in issues of burial."[160] This was confirmed by another group member: "We live in the same house. We bury each other."[161] The same sentiments were recorded in other FGDs. One elderly female participant said, "We cooperate, but we don't go to the cemetery or observe the mourning period. That is because our faith doesn't allow Muslims to pay their last respects [to the body of the deceased], it is a sin (*kosa*), and also going to the cemetery is forbidden."[162] Those who dare go to the cemetery are required "to recite the Muslim creed" (*kutoa shahada*). This attitude was confined to religio-centric respondents. It was not universal, since other participants indicated otherwise. For instance, in the uneducated female FGD a participant said, "We cooperate with Christians and we go together to the cemetery."[163] One participant in the same FGD ascribed these cordial relations in rites of passage to good neighbourliness (civic identity and responsibility): "Although our religion does not allow women to go to the cemetery, we do go when it happens to be a Christian funeral. For instance, when your neighbour has been bereaved you have to escort him/her to the cemetery."[164] Another group member added, "Although it is forbidden by our religion for Muslim women to go to the cemetery, we consider the way we have been living together with those people ... we decide to go as well, because religion is in each person's faith."[165] For some participants civic identity is primary, hence the saying, "We go to bury as usual and I remain with my Islamic faith in my soul and they remain with their Christian faith; therefore I won't miss the burial."[166]

Apart from attending the burial, female participants mentioned other areas of cooperation. For example, an elderly participant said, "We cooperate by visiting each other, helping with cooking, sleeping [at the house of the bereaved] and making monetary contributions recorded in a book provided at funerals."[167]

---

[160] Ni kweli tunashirikiana na wenzetu wakristo katika masuala ya vyakula mazishi.
[161] Tunakaa nyumba moja. Tunazikana.
[162] Tunashirikiana, ila kwenda makaburini hatuendi au kulalia matanga, Na hii inatokana na imani yetu Waislamu kwamba kwenda kuaga maiti hatuendi ni kosa na pia kwenda makaburini kuzika nayo haturuhusiwi.
[163] Huwa tunashirikiana na wakristo na tunaenda nao makaburini.
[164] Maana kama umefiwa na jirani yako inabidi umsindikize mpaka kaburini ingawa dini yetu hairihusu wanawake kwenda makaburini lakini sisi tunafanya hivyo panapotokea msiba wa mkristo.
[165] Japokuwa dini inakataza wanawake wa kiislamu kwenda makaburini, lakini sisi tunaangalia jinsi tulivyoishi na wale watu ... Tunaamua nasi twende tu kama kawaida kwani dini ni kila mtu na imani yake.
[166] Na hivyo sisi tunaenda kuzika kama kawaida na ninabaki na imani yangu ya kiislamu katika nafsi na wao wanabaki na imani yao ya kikristo na kwa hiyo mimi siwezi kukosa kwenda kuzika.
[167] Tunashirikiana kwa kutembeleana kupikiana kulala, kisinia (kuchangisha kupitia vitabu).

One educated female participant said, "We cooperate in some chores, for example fetching water, cooking, collecting firewood, washing utensils ... we are like relatives (*ndugu*) who have different faiths."[168] Another duty is to console (*bembeleza*) the bereaved.

An elderly female participant compared past and present practice at funerals. She said, "In the past we buried each other, but there were no contributions (*visima*) ... Also, in the past we did not eat food prepared by Christians ... but nowadays we do."[169] This suggests that society used to be more religio-centric than it is today. Besides, funerals in contemporary society are 'commodified', hence the need for contributions.

Open air preaching
"Christians insult Muslims."

With reference to open air preaching (*mihadhara*), some participants said they chose what messages to listen to and ignored those they considered irrelevant. One uneducated young female participant explained: "I listen to what I like and leave those [messages] I don't like, because other messages such as the teachings on religion and the way a Muslim is supposed to live are relevant. Teachings about putting on a veil and praying bring me nearer to God."[170] In this regard *mihadhara* teach things that "you were not aware of".[171] Therefore "open air preaching is good" and "they are there so you can know more about the faith".[172]

On the other hand, educated female youths said that "*mihadhara* help foment bad relations, because they are divisive even in the mosque".[173] Others said that sometimes these services "have turned into places for ridiculing others and there-

---

[168] Sisi huwa tunashirikiana katika baadhi ya kazi, mfano kuchota maji, kupika, kuchukua kuni, kuosha vyombo mpaka kumpeleka marehemu makaburini, ambapo tunakuwa kama ndugu moja wenye dini tofauti.

[169] Zamani tulikuwa tunazikana kama kawaida lakini mambo ya visima, michango haikuwepo ... Na pia zamani tulikuwa hatuli chakula cha wakristo ... lakini sasa hivi tunakula.

[170] Hivyo huwa nasikiliza yale ninayopenda na kuacha kusikiliza yale ambayo siyapendi. Kutokana na mambo mengine kuwa muhimu kama kufundisha mazingira ya dini, na mamna ambayo muislamu inambidi aishi, hivyo hunifanya niyasikilize. Kufundishwa kufunga ushungi, kuswali, hunisaidia kuniweka karibu na Mungu.

[171] Kupata mambo ambayo uliyo kuwa huyajui.

[172] Mihadhara ni mizuri kwani iko kwa ajili yakujua kuhusu imani.

[173] Mihadhara kuna mahusiano ambayo siyo mazuri, kwa sababu inasababisha hata Msikiti kutengana.

fore cause big rifts in society".[174] One educated female participant said expressively that open air preaching organised by Islamic preachers "often ridicules Christianity, leading to friction and misunderstandings".[175] Other educated male participants countered: "Christians insult Muslims and when the Muslims defend themselves they start fighting with each other."[176] Some elderly male participants identified the main problem with *mihadhara* as the "misuse of doctrine which leads to misunderstanding"[177] between preacher and audience. As a result some angry Christian audiences use their social position to "call the police when a person [preacher] uses phrases such as Jesus is not God, which then causes riots".[178]

One uneducated male participant partly blamed the constitution:, "I think that maybe they [preachers] got permission from the constitution [of Tanzania]; perhaps the constitution allows it."[179] He added, "If I'm not mistaken the constitution allows all individuals to propagate their faith publicly."[180] That was how he explained why the "government allows open air preaching, because open air preaching is part of religion and religion is faith".[181] Another male youth noted that *mihadhara* are allowed to continue because "society benefits (*jamii inafaidika*)" from them. Some youths said that *mihadhara* continued to be conducted because the government was afraid of what would happen if it banned them entirely. In fact, one uneducated male youth said open air preaching has social benefits: "if *mihadhara* had no social benefits they could have been banned."[182]

Other participants complained that Christian *mihadhara* were generally favoured by government and thus could be conducted for a month without being interrupted (*kuguswa*), but Muslim services would be interrupted (*utaguswa*) "on the pretext that we insulted the Christians".[183]

---

[174] Mihadhara imekuwa sehemu za kukashifu wengine na chanzo cha ugomvi mkubwa kwenye jamii.
[175] Dini ya Kiislamu mara nyingi hukashifu dini ya Kikristo na kuleta ugomvi na kutokuelewana.
[176] Wakristu hukashfu Waislamu na Waislamu wakisema wajitetee wanaanza kupigana.
[177] Matumizi mabaya ya misahafu inasababisha kutokuelewana.
[178] Kutumia cheo na ghadhabu zake akaita polisi wanakuja kufanya fujo... anasema Yesu si Mungu.
[179] Lakini nafikiri kwamba huenda ni ruhusa wanayoipata katika katiba kwani huenda pengine katiba inaruhusu.
[180] Ninaposema katiba kama sikosei, inaruhusu kila mtu ana uhuru wa kutangaza imani yake hadharani – kama nitakuwa sikosei.
[181] Ni kweli Serikali inaruhusu mihadhara, kutokana na sababu kwamba mihadhara ni dini na dini ni imani uneducated male.
[182] Mihadhara isingekuwa na maslahi kwa jamii basi wangesha wakatalia isiendelee.
[183] Mhadhara wa kikristo unaweza kukaa hata mwezi usiguswe lakini wakiislam utaguswa na serikali kwakisingizio chakuwa tumetukana. (Educated male participant.)

It was observed that some *mihadhara* preachers used different vocabulary, concepts, or words when responding to questions asked by Christians as opposed to those raised by Muslims. In answering a question from a Christian one open air preacher used the word *'ndugu'*: "Is it true, my comrade (*ndugu*)?" or "What should he do, my *ndugu*?"[184] Here the preacher uses a polite and friendly term with an overt agenda of uniting and creating harmony between Muslims and Christians.[185]

Thus some *mihadhara* preachers deliberately use alternative words (*'pagani'*, *'kafir'*, *'ndugu'*) to either heighten tension or reduce it with their utterances. By and large, just as participants in FGDs spoke about and labelled Christians using words that imply divergence and convergence, so do newspapers and open air preaching discourses. Words such as 'kafir' or 'enemy' lead to divergence and conflict, whereas words like *'ndugu'* or *'rafiki'* foster unity and cohesion

Letting
"Muslims also let accommodation to Christians."

Participants said Muslims and Christians live together in the community as neighbours and some as housemates. One uneducated male participant put it thus: "We have good relations because I rent [a room] in a Christian house and there has been no problem."[186] Educated male participants confirmed that some Muslims rent houses belonging to Christians. The reverse is also true, as one participant in this category explained: "Muslims also let rooms to Christians, but it depends what conditions he sets, whether they are faith based or personal."[187]

This young participant said that renting was regulated by conditions that the landlord laid down for tenants. These conditions could include not cooking pork in the house and dressing 'appropriately'. As one educated male participant put it, "If a Christian accepts the laws of Muslims, such as not eating during Ramadan because it is the fasting period for Muslims, then he can stay; if he won't follow the laws the contract will be nullified … but if they live peacefully with each other, he can stay".[188]

---

[184] Ni kweli ndugu yangu? Tafanya nini ndugu yangu?
[185] When he calls the Christian 'ndugu' the audience can have different interpretations, as ndugu may refer to a relative, comrade or close friend. Nevertheless, it is a polite and accommodative term.
[186] Tunamahusiano mazuri. Mimi mwenyewe nimepanga kwa mkristu na hakuna matatizo.
[187] Wakristo nao wanapangisha waislam inategemea na masharti atakayotoa kama ni ya kiimani au yake binafsi.
[188] Mfano mkristo akikubali sheria za mwislam wakati wa Ramadhan kukaa kwake, kutokula kwa

However, some participants accused Christians of failing to abide by the conditions set by their Muslim landlords. An elderly participant gave the example of her Christian tenant who, despite the conditions she received, "cooked and ate pork" in her "presence while knowing" that she, the landlady, "does not use"[189] pork. As a result of such violations Muslims "don't like letting houses to Christians for fear that the Christians will contravene the conditions agreed upon".[190] This was corroborated by an educated male participant: "It is true that some Muslims don't let houses to Christians, because one Muslim let his rooms to a Christian and gave him conditions, such as not eating pork ... but after paying him one year's rent he violated the condition; that is why some refuse to let houses to Christians."[191]

One educated male participant said that some Christians have adopted Muslim behaviour: "Most of the people who live in Swahili residential areas are Muslims and because Christians have stayed in the area for a long time ... they have adopted our [Muslim] behaviour ... at least they follow our behaviour, that is why we live well together and it is difficult to identify a Christian, unless by his name or you see him going to church on Sunday."[192]

Even so, some educated male participants described a certain ethnic group which traditionally did not let their houses to Christians. "These people from Pemba Island [Pembans], if you are not Muslim they won't let you a room because they will call you a *kafir*."[193] Another group member said, "That issue about Pembans is true. You can be a Muslim but if you don't have a wife ... they will refuse you a house... but for a Christian there is no possibility even if he has a wife."[194] This was confirmed by an educated young female, who said: "You will

---

maana mwislam hali, kama hafuati sheria anavunja ule mkataba lakini kama wanaelewana wataishi vizuri.

[189] Alikuwa anapika na kula nguruwe mbele yangu wakati anajua kwamba mimi situmii.

[190] Hivyo utakuta mtu hataki kumpangisha mkristo kwenye nyumba yake.

[191] Ni kweli wapo waislam hawapangishi wakristo kwa sababu unakuta mwislamu alimpangishia mkristo akampa masharti labda asile nguruwe n.k lakini akishalipa kodi ya mwaka na kuingia ndani masharti anakiuka kwahiyo ndo maana wengine wanakataa kupangishia wakristo.

[192] Maeneo mengi ya uswahilini walio wengi ni waislam na kwa vile wakristo wanakaa sana na sasa wamefata tabia zetu ... angalau wanafuata tabia zetu ndo maana tunaishi vizuri na huwezi tambua huyu mkristo labda kwa jina au umwone jumapili anaenda kanisani. (Educated male participant.)

[193] Hawa watu kutoka kisiwa cha Pemba kama sio Mwislamu hawakupangishi maana watakuita kafiri. (Educated female participant.)

[194] Hilo swala kwa Wapemba ni kweli unaweza ukawa mwislam kama huna mke anakataa kukupa nyumba lakini kwa mkristo ndo kabisa hata kama utakuwa una mke hampi nyumba.

find that Pembans cannot cooperate with Christians."[195] This participant added that Pembans discriminate not only against Christians but sometimes "discriminate even against fellow Muslims and refuse to compromise with them".[196] This was confirmed by an educated male participant who said, "You may be a Muslim but if you're unmarried he won't let you accommodation, but for Christians it is difficult, even if he has a wife he won't let him a room."[197] An educated female participant commented that "generally Pembans never cooperate with others in society".[198] This was corroborated by an educated male participant: "If he has let you a house you might have a funeral but he will open his shop and continue with his business... He differs from his fellow Muslims; he will not even allow a Christian to enter his house."[199]

Nevertheless some Muslims still let their houses to Christians, as one educated male participant described: "Most houses at Buguruni are owned by Muslims ... and Christians are tenants but still live well together [they cooperate]."[200]

Extremists and hardliners
"They use different verses."

Participants also mentioned those who practice *imani kali* (extremists/hardliners) as a source of intrigue and animosity. Indeed, one elderly participant said, "This difference between Muslims and Christians is caused by extremist beliefs (*kiimani kali*)".[201] Another group member attributed the problem to the use of different verses by the extremists: "They use different verses from the ones in the scriptures."[202] "They use these verses to ridicule others, hence the fighting between people of different faiths in society."[203] Participants also lamented the effect

---

[195] Utakuta kuwa hawashirikiani na Wakristu.
[196] Wanabagua hata waislam wenzao.
[197] Unaweza ukawa mwislam kama huna mke anakataa kukupa nyumba lakini kwa mkristo ndo kabisa hata kama utakuwa una mke hampi nyumba.
[198] Kwa ujumla Wapemba hawana ushirikiano katika jamii.
[199] Kama kapangisha kwako unaweza kupata msiba lakini yeye atafungua duka na kuendelea na biashara atasimama hapo na kukuangali tu. Kwa mwislam mwenzake wametofautiana kwa mkristo ndo kabisa hawezi kuingia ndani kwake.
[200] Kwa buguruni nyumba nyingi (wenye nyumba) ni waislam na wapangaji ni wakristo lakini bado wanakuwa na ushirikiano mzuri.
[201] Utofauti huu kati yetu waislamu na wakristo upo katika masuala ya itikadi za kiimani kali.
[202] Hata aya wanazotumia ni tofauti na zilizopo kwenye maandiko.
[203] Wanatumia vifungu kukashifu wengine hvyo kupelekea ugomvi kati ya watu wa dini tofauti. (Educated female participant.)

such religious extremism had within the Islamic faith, saying it has caused rifts even in the mosque.[204]

An uneducated female participant said, "We ordinary believers have no problem."[205] This participant believed that "the religion that discriminates is that of the teachers, sheikhs and priests, not us".[206]

According to Muslim participants the government is also aware of the presence of extremism; hence it allows *mihadhara* to be conducted. In this regard one uneducated male participant observed, "If the government bans *mihadhara*, we might end up with what is happening to our co-religionists in Somalia where there is war."[207] This is because to Muslims "a person who uses a cutlass to defend his faith goes to heaven, because he has stood up for the scriptures".[208]

Conclusion

In the analysis of Muslims' linguistic practice we were particularly interested in the words they used to speak about Christians and about Muslim-Christian relations. In general, Muslims refer to Christians in a friendly, polite manner as relatives (*ndugu*): "we are like children of the same father", brothers and sisters, neighbours, friends/comrades (*ndugu*), and fellows. The sentences were in the active voice. Overall these words describe relations between believers of the two faiths as respectful, good, harmonious and peaceful.

Conversely, there were Muslims who described Christians as infidels (*kafir*), but these sentences were mainly in the passive voice, for example in the context of interreligious marriage and *mihadhara*. The same word was used to describe fellow Muslims who were not faithful to their belief and their values, such as Muslims who change their religion in order to marry ("we see that person as a *kafir*"). In this sense the word '*kafir*' is synonymous with enemy ("a Christian is my enemy").

Some Muslims described Christianity in the passive voice as *haraam*, especially when referring to pork consumption, interreligious marriages and Western (secular) education. The word '*haraam*' was used to describe what Muslims considered to be their religious and moral superiority to Christians by stating that

---

[204] Imesababisha hata ugomvi hata kwenye misikiti na kutengana. (Educated female participant.)
[205] Sisi waumini wa kawaida hatuna matatizo.
[206] Dini inawabagua hawa maustadh mashekhe na mapadri ambao ndio wanaolumabana sio sisi.
[207] Endapo serikali itakataza mihadhara basi itakuwa kama kwa wenzetu Somalia kuliko na vita.
[208] Mtu anayetumia panga kwa ajili ya kutetea imani basi huyo ataenda peponi kwani alisimamia katika maandiko. (Uneducated male participant.)

Muslims do not eat *haraam*; they emphasise religious education, and their style of dress was imitated by Christians.

Thus the main classification noted was not directly in terms of belief or doctrine (apart from the use of the word '*kafir*') but of moral conduct. This is apparent in classifications such as clean/unclean (*haraam*), allowed/forbidden (*halal*), permitted/not permitted, and proper/improper behaviour.

Muslim participants said that in their society there are normal believers and extremists/fanatics. The extremists are both Muslims and Christians, and they are behind both Muslim-Christian and intra-religious conflicts, leading to divisions among and within religions ("the religion that discriminates is that of the teachers, sheikhs and priests"). In the FGDs participants said the problem was not between ordinary Christians and ordinary Muslims, but rather between ordinary believers and their leaders. Religious leaders (Muslim and Christian) are involved in religious conflict. Uneducated female youths said "they are the ones arguing". Relations between Muslims and Christians are seen in terms of discrimination and segregation. In the FGDs participants described Christians as well educated and with higher incomes than Muslims. They used words such as Christians "are on top", "very advanced" and "you find Christians everywhere" to describe their economic status. The participants acknowledged that some Muslims discriminate against not only Christians but also fellow Muslims, specifically citing "people from Pemba".

2.2. Analysis of discursive practice

The second step is to analyse the discursive practice. Analytical questions are: how does this text/discourse relate to other texts/discourses? Is there an order of discourse? As we explained in the general introduction, the underlying assumption is that in producing and consuming texts participants depend heavily on what they know already (cognitions), that is what they have stored in their long-term memory as texts already known to them (inter-textuality). It is assumed, moreover, that some discourses are more influential than others (inter-discursivity). Hence in this section we link the FGDs with discourses referred to in the texts: open air preaching (*mihadhara*), discussions within and between the religions, and debates in parliament. According to Fairclough (1992:71,86) discursive practice connectslinguistic practice (text) with social practice (context).

Religion in the public domain and the media
"God has no business with kafirs."

In the previous section we analysed how Muslims speak about Christians and Muslim- Christian relations. As was explained in the general introduction, it is assumed that the way people label others constitutes and is constituted by a common sense reality reflected in the streets, in newspapers or brochures, open air preaching and on television. As we will see later these classifications serve not only a cognitive but also a social function; they are not only visions of the world but also divisions (Bourdieu 1991).

As noted in the previous section, some Muslims say that Christians are referred to as infidels (*kafir*). That is a common idiom that they pick up from the streets. However, others see this label and other labels as defamatory and leading to problems. On 8 September 2003 the front page headline in *Uhuru* read, "In custody for defaming other religions".[209] The title does not name the subject; even the religious identity of the person in custody is omitted. The journalist writes about a person who was taken into custody for using defamatory language against other religions. 'Other religions' can be any religion: Islam, Hinduism or Christianity. In the article the journalist says that the person used both Bible verses (Christianity) and words considered defamatory by some of the Christians present at that gathering and therefore they decided to call the police, who came and arrested the speaker/defamer.

Some Muslims were against the use of what were seen as words defaming other faiths. They see it as leading to conflict in the community. For example, on Thursday 25 September 2003 the front page of Uhuru reported a speech by the Mufti of the Tanzania Muslim Council, "Mufti rebukes those who defame other religions. He said they are used by foreigners to cause disturbances [*kuvuruga*] in Tanzania".[210]

In An-Nuur (9-15 May 2008) a Muslim journalist also used the word 'kafir': "It is our religious duty to fight against the kafirs and their kafir system."[211] To this journalist the problem is not just the kafirs and what belongs to them but the entire kafir system. Earlier in his article he mentioned the so-called kafir system as follows: "In the 19th century the capitalist system, which is a kafir system,

---

[209] Afungwa kwa kukashifu dini zingine.
[210] Mufti: Wakataeni wanaokashifu dini nyingine. Asema ni wanaotumiwa na watu wan je kuivuruga Tanzania.
[211] Ni jukumu letu la kidini kupigana na makafiri na mfumo wa kikafiri.

challenged the Islamic system...."²¹² The journalist blames the kafirs and their capitalist system and urges Muslims to fight against it. Whereas the journalist referred to capitalism as a kafir system, he did not specify the group identity of the kafirs, leaving it open to different interpretations.

In *The Guardian* of 13 June 2000 journalist Rommel Z. Mauma writes: "[The] Islamic community believes that history has always favoured Westernisation and Christian civilisation vis-à-vis Islamic civilisation." Here the journalist hedges by using "[the] Islamic community believes" to avoid responsibility but at the same time acts as a representative of the Muslim community, which believes that it is disadvantaged in the Westernised world.

Labels such as the ones used in FGDs and newspapers mentioned above are also used by some open air preachers. One Muslim open-air preacher was recorded during our fieldwork as saying, "In the Qur'an God told us Muslims should not to give our secrets to these *kafirs*."²¹³ The preacher uses the word '*kafir*' implicitly assuming that his audience knows the referent but at the same time implying that they are Christians, hence the word '*kafir*' in the statement refers to Christians. In another open air preaching a preacher was recorded uttering the same word when answering questions from a Christian: "It is those *kafirs* who think that the Qur'an is like the Bible."²¹⁴ Apart from using the word '*kafir*', the speaker also placed the Qur'an above the Bible. In his speech he claimed that the "Qur'an is the word of God while the Bible is just individuals' words",²¹⁵ hence lacking authentic truth.

The word '*kafir*' frequently crops up in *mihadhara*. A preacher called Mazinge, for instance, used the word several times when responding to questions from a Christian (Daniel) who attended the service. To the preacher all non-Muslims are *kafir*, as the following utterances reveal: "Normally the *kafirs* never bow in reverence"; "You are a *kafir,* why bow in reverence?"; "God created two samples. He created the *kafir* and Muslims"; "God has no business with *kafirs*"; "Daniel is insane, that is why he converted to *kafir* [Christianity]."²¹⁶ The word '*kafir*' is an impolite name used to distinguish Muslims from non-Muslims. The

---

²¹² Katika karne ya 19 mfumo wa kibepari ambao ni mfumo wa kikafiri, uliupa changamoto mfumo wa kiislamu.
²¹³ Kwenye Korani Mungu katumbia sisi Waislamu kutokutoa siri kwa hawa makafiri.
²¹⁴ Ni hawa makafiri wanaofikiri Korani ni kama Biblia.
²¹⁵ Korani ni neno la Mungu wakati Biblia ni maneno ya watu tu.
²¹⁶ Makafiri huwa hawasujudu. Wewe ni kafiri kwanini usujudu? Mungu aliumba sampuli mbili: Aliumba makafiri na Waislamu. Mungu hana biashara na kafiri. Daniel ni mwehu ndio maana alibadili kuwa kafiri.

way the word is used here sets boundaries between Muslims and non-Muslims, but as we saw earlier it is also applied to Muslims who are not true to their faith.

However, other open air preachers do not use the word 'infidel' (*kafir*) to refer to Christians. One preacher, for example, asked: "Do you want to tell us that all Christians in the world are pagans (*wapagani*)?"[217] This preacher decided not to use the Islamic word *kafir*, but the word that is commonly used by Christians to refer to non-believers, hence the negative connotation is minimal and/or creates common ground. Perhaps this preacher used the word '*wapagani*' in the Christian sense of the word but in the opposite direction. Christians believe that non-Christians are *wapagani*. In the FGDs this word was not used. It is more Christian than Muslim. So the preacher's use of this word was aimed at highlighting differences, using the Christian way of differentiating between the two faiths. But the implication was the same: the only true believers in God were Muslims; the Christians were *wapagani*, non-believers. Hence, one uneducated female participant said, "We should not refer to each other with strange names such as *kafir*", signifying that the word '*kafir*' is foreign to their normal civic vocabulary.[218]

Sacred scriptures and prophets
"Christians call him God but we call him prophet."

As we can see from the analysis of linguistic practice, most key terms and vital themes come from day-to-day conversations, taken from everyday life (e.g. housing, eating/food, clothing, marriage and burial). Similarly, speakers referred to sacred scriptures such as the Qur'an and the Bible as well as the prophets (Muhammad and Jesus) and God to add weight to what they were saying. One uneducated male participant said that the "weakness of women started a long time ago in the time of Adam and Hawa. The scriptures show us that Hawa betrayed Adam."[219].

In the *An-Nuur* issue of 9-15 May 2008 (p. 9) the reporter wrote: "The Qur'an reminds us that [the] Islamic religion was brought by God in order to be above all religions; this does not matter even if the *kafirs* get angry."[220] This reporter refers to the Qur'an to position his utterance in relation to the authority of the holy text and in so doing affirms his argument regarding Islam's superiority to

---

[217] Unataka kutuambia kwamba Wakristu wote duniani na wapagani?
[218] Tusiitane majina ya ajabu mfano kafiri.
[219] Udhaifu wa kina mama umeanza zamani sana toka kipindi cha Adamu na Hawa. Vitabu vinatuonesha kwamba Hawa ndiye aliyemsaliti Adam.
[220] Korani inatukumbusha Waislamu kwamba Mungu alileta Uislamu ili uwe juu ya dini zote; nah ii haijalishi hata makafiri wakichukia.

other religions. Moreover, he opted for an inclusive plural ('all religions') without specifying the subject identity (*kafirs*), hence avoiding taking direct responsibility for his words towards adherents of those other religions [including Christians], who would otherwise have felt offended or ridiculed.

Open air preachers were recorded as alluding to the Qur'an and God to reinforce their arguments. For example, one preacher said, "In the Qur'an God told us that Muslims should not give our secret to these *kafirs*,"[221] adding, "Jesus gave them a secret that I'm Christ and told them not to share it with anybody."[222] In his later statement the preacher quoted indirectly from the Bible (Mt 16:13-20). In this passage Peter confesses that Jesus is the Christ, the Son of the living God (Mt 16:16). Thereupon Jesus told his disciples not to tell anyone that he was the Christ (Mt 16:20).

With reference to *mihadhara*, participants in the FGDs reminded us, "open air preaching is not of today or yesterday; it comes from messengers such as Issa, Jesus and Muhammad who wanted to bring their message."[223] Also speaking about Christians, an elderly female participant reported, "God is one and Jesus is his prophet and Christians call him God; but we call him prophet and Mary, the mother of Jesus, is God's creature."[224] These quotations show that for Muslims Jesus is only a messenger or prophet, but not God incarnate. The Muslims uttering these words were a reminder to Christians that only Muslims are true believers, while implicitly questioning the faith of Christians who allegedly committed an abomination by referring to Jesus as God. To Muslims Jesus is just "God's creature", not God. Another participant in the group affirmed that "we believe Muslims' God is exactly the same as that of Christians".[225] This participant put Muslims and Christians on a par with each other and homogenised the belief of these two faiths.

---

[221] See Swahili version in section on religion in the public domain and media.
[222] Yesu aliwapa siri na kuwataka wasiitoe kwa mtu mwingine kwamba mimi ni Kristu.
[223] Mihadhara haijaanza leo wala jana. Bali zamani toka zama za mitume wetu kina Issa, Yesu Muhamadi na wengineo wote ikiwa na lengo la kuwafikishia ujumbe walengwa. (Uneducated male participant.)
[224] Mungu ni mmoja, na Yesu ni mtume wake. Na pia wakristo wanamwita Mungu na sisi tunamwita Mungu mtume. Na huyo Mariam mama wa Yesu ni kiumbe wa Mungu.
[225] Tunaamini kwamba Mungu wa waislamu ndio huyo huyo wa wakristo kabisa.

Religious feasts
"During eid ceremonies it is difficult to isolate Christians."

In the FGDs participants referred to religious festivals and events and the social implications. Thus they spoke about the companionship between Muslims and Christians during the holy month of Ramadan. One educated male participant said, "During Ramadan it is difficult to know who is a Christian because s/he does not cook and eat until the evening, when Muslims break the fast."[226] This was confirmed by other participants in the group. In fact, another educated male participant said, "Christian students ... are not allowed to eat [lunch] during the period of fasting."

The participants also referred to religious ceremonies where Muslims do not isolate Christians. As another educated participant indicated, "During the *eid* ceremony it is difficult to isolate Christians; this collaboration indicates that religiosity is put aside – there is unity like that of the same family."[227]

Open air preaching
"Open air services (mihadhara) have turned into places for ridiculing others"

On the topic of open air preaching speakers implicitly and explicitly referred to debates among Muslims themselves, between Christians and Muslims, and between religions and government. Most Muslim participants were of the view that open air services are "good" and "help people learn more about their faith".[228] These services serve a religious purpose; they educate believers in their faith and, according to the participants, are not there to make fun of believers of other faiths.

Some educated male participants reminded that the open air services "are not a problem; the trouble is the audience who, because of their lack of knowledge, cause problems. For example, a person gets onto a platform and says Jesus is not God ... therefore another person, due to ignorance, would say he has been defamed/ridiculed."[229] Other participants in this group observed that open air services were misused and as a result they stirred up conflict, contrary to the original

---

[226] Hata mwezi wa ramadhani hutaweza kujua ni mkristo maana nae hapiki chakula na hali mpaka jioni waislam wanapokula.

[227] Katika kusherekea sikukuu ya iddi iliyopita ilikuwa ni vigumu kuwatenga wakristo kwahiyo huu ushirikano unavyoonesha ni kwamba udini umewekwa kwa pembeni kuna umoja kuishi kama familia moja.

[228] Inasaidia watu kujifunza imani yao zaidi.

[229] Mihadhara haina matatizo katika jamii isipokuwa wahusika (hadhira) ndo inakuwa na matatizo kutokana na ufahamu wao mdogo. Mfano mtu anapanda jukwaani anasema Yesu si Mungu kwahiyo mwingine kutokana na ufahamu wake mdogo anasema kakashifiwa.

intention when staging *mihadhara*. As one participant explained, "Open air services have become places for ridiculing others and therefore cause big fights in society."[230]

Elderly male participants remembered that sometimes you hear preachers in Christian open air services saying, "Muhammad is a prostitute and he died of Aids because he had many wives."[231] The use of such strong words in public such as at *mihadhara* is not constructive but creates rifts/divergence in the community that could eventually lead to conflict. This was corroborated by other participants in the group and in other groups as well. For example, in the discussion with educated male participants one participant reminded us, "Christians insult Muslims and when Muslims defend themselves they start fighting with each other."[232] In the same group one participant complained that "Christians' open air services can go on for a whole month without being disrupted, but Muslim ones could be disrupted by the government on the pretext that they contain inflammatory statements."[233] Participants' statements depicted a situation of double standards, in which Muslims are disadvantaged and marginalised more than their Christian counterparts.

It was evident from the discussions that Muslim participants were referring to a discourse that reflects a separation between religion and state: "It is true, the government allows open air preaching, because it is part of religion and religion is faith."[234] Another participant drew upon the constitution of the United Republic of Tanzania (URT) that has granted "permission" (*ruhusu*) for *mihadhara* to take place because of the freedom of worship it guarantees. This participant first said, "They got permission from the constitution," and then realised that perhaps he was not sure, so added the 'perhaps' in the next clause ("perhaps the constitution allows it"[235]) to avoid the responsibility that goes with the original utterance. Implicitly the speaker was referring to a clause in the constitution of the United Republic which reads: "The work of preaching religion, to conduct worship and to spread the faith will be free and a preference of the individual and the administra-

---

[230] See the KiSwahili version in the open air preaching section under linguistic practice.
[231] Mara unasikia Muhamadi alikuwa malaya na kwamba alikufa kwa UKIMWI kwa kuwa alioa wanawake wengi.
[232] See the KiSwahili version in the open air preaching section under linguistic practice.
[233] Mhadhara wa kikristo unaweza kukaa hata mwezi usiguswe lakini wakiislam utaguswa na serikali kwakisingizio chakuwa tumetukana.
[234] Ni kweli Serikali inaruhusu mihadhara, kutokana na sababu kwamba mihadhara ni dini na dini ni imani. (Uneducated male participant.)
[235] KiSwahili version of his statement is provided in the open air preaching section under linguistic practice.

tion of religious communities, outside the authority of the mandate of the state"[236] (URT Constitution 2005:23, article 19:2; [my translation]).

The participants referred to other contexts in defence of *mihadhara*: "If the government banned *mihadhara* we would have war like our friends in Somalia"[237] and "The struggle between the government and the people would reduce the country to one without citizens, and that would not be a nation.[238] War between religions is worse than war between ethnic groups."[239] The participant pictured a possibility of conflict if peripheral voices are silenced by state organs. But the participant suggests that it is an issue between government and religious believers, not between Muslims and Christians.

Politicians and parliamentary discussions on OIC, kadhi courts and education
"Kadhi *courts will deal with issues of inheritance, marriage and disputes.*"

In the FGDs participants mentioned *kadhi* courts, politicians and their discussion of the OIC as key issues in current socio-religious discourse in the country. Educated male Muslims pointed out that "*kadhi* courts will deal with issues of inheritance, marriage and dispute resolution".[240] They explained that "*kadhi* courts have the authority to preside over the rights of Muslims, but those who oppose their introduction are not aware of this".[241] Participants said that *kadhi* courts were primarily a religious issue and that the government should not interfere with their introduction and in the management of Muslim affairs in the country. After all, they insisted, Muslims have a right to have *kadhi* courts, and the government should not be afraid of trouble. As one educated male participant pointed out, "The *kadhi* court has the authority to guarantee justice for Muslims."[242] A key informant also referred to neighbouring countries: "In a country such as Kenya there are *kadhi*

---

[236] Kazi ya kutangaza dini, kufanya ibada na kueneza dini itakuwa ni huru na jambo la hiari la mtu binafsi, na shughuli na uendeshaji wa jumuiya za dini zitakuwa nje ya shughuli za mamlaka ya nchi.
[237] KiSwahili version is provided in section on extremism and hardliners under linguistic practice.
[238] Mapigano kati ya Serikali na watu basi lazima upande mmoja utaisha na hivyo nchi bila watu sio nchi tena.
[239] Vita ya dini ni mbaya kuliko hata ya kikabila.
[240] KiSwahili version of this statement is provided in the interreligious marriage section.
[241] Mahakama ya Kadhi inamamlaka ya kusimamia haki za Waislamu, lakini wanaopinga Kadhi hawajui haya.
[242] Mahakama ya Kadhi inamamlaka ya kuhakikisha kuna haki sawa kwa waislamu.

courts and there are no problems whatsoever. Why we do not have them in Tanzania?"[243]

Another key informant, a member of parliament, underscored the importance of *kadhi* courts for Muslims: "The *kadhi* courts are very important for Muslims ... the question of *kadhi* courts has been there since the beginning of colonialism."[244] *Kadhi* courts were created because there are Muslim cases that cannot be handled adequately in a secular court. In fact, one respondent insisted, "There is enough evidence that the government cannot handle matters concerning Muslims [effectively]. BAKWATA was called to gather the sheikhs to cope with the case."[245] Speaking at a Muslim open air gathering in Dar es Salaam, sheikh Ali Basalehe insisted, "Christians should not fear the *kadhi* court because it has nothing to do with them; it is for Muslims" (*Daily News,* 1 November 2008, p. 3).

However, most educated female participants had different ideas on the establishment of *kadhi* courts in the country. One educated female participant did not support the establishment of *kadhi* courts: "*Kadhi* courts are concerned with inheritance, in which women should only get one third of the husband's property. The remaining property goes to the mosque. If the widow has no sons she does not get any inheritance, because her female children will be married. This leaves the widow with nothing."[246] The main function of *kadhi* courts is to distribute resources. Here, too, educated female Muslim participants appeared reluctant to embrace the introduction of such courts. They explicitly suggested that these courts were likely to benefit males more than females, who can only gain access to assets via the male heir. An educated male participant referred to this fear of gender inequality as a misunderstanding of the function of *kadhi* courts to Muslims, and he insisted, "Those women who are not in favour of the establishment of *kadhi* courts don't understand the meaning of it. For example, it deals with the issue of inheritance; for instance, between a man and woman [on the distribution of assets], the

---

[243] Nchi kama Kenya kuna mahakama ya Kadhi na hakuna matatizo yoyote. Sasa kwa nini Tanzania tunashindwa?

[244] Mahakama ya Kadhi ni muhimu sana kwa waislamu. Na swala la kadhi lilkuwepo tokea mwanzoni mwa enzi za ukoloni.

[245] Kuna ushahidi kwamba serikali haiwezi kukidhi mahitaji ya Waislamu. Kulikuwa na kesi mahakamani ya mwanaume na mwanamke iliendeshwa bila ufumbuzi hakimu akaamua iende kwenye baraza la waislam BAKWATA wakaita mashehe ili waamue kesi.

[246] Suala la Mahakama ya Kadhi kuhusu urithi, kwani wanawake wanatakiwa kupewa theruthi tu ya mali ya mume. Na mali inayobakia hupelekwa msikitini. Kwani kama mjane hana mtoto wa kiume basi hapewi urithi kwa madai watoto wa kike wote wataolewa na hivyo kuachwa mjane na watoto wake akiwa hana kitu.

man must get double the [woman's] inheritance."[247] The use of the active voice in his last statement suggests unequal distribution of resources between men and women.

Another topic of concern to Muslim participants was inequalities in education. They had hoped the situation would improve following the swearing in of a Muslim president (Mwinyi). Indeed, one MP told us in an interview: "Starting with the rule of [president] Mwinyi, Muslims thought they would get opportunities to benefit. But this was not the case, because there were few educated Muslims who were qualified to get the available jobs."[248]

Another MP recalled, "On the issue of education the Muslims themselves are not united. There are those who hold that they were discriminated against by the government, and in their eyes government and Christians are one and the same thing." A similar utterance was made by one educated participant: "The president[249] is a Muslim, but the same president is dominated by Christians. And when a religious issue emerges he is constrained by the constitution."[250] An elderly female participant said the same: "President Kikwete is a Muslim. However, you see who the majority in leadership are? Christians are many!"[251] By mentioning the subject in her last sentence she affirms her arguments about inequality between Muslims and Christians in political leadership, but at the same time shows that there is a Muslim president in a secular government dominated by Christians, hence the inability to get rid of the perceived inequalities.

The debate about Tanzania's OIC membership and the possibility of having *kadhi* courts came up again during the discussion of the budget of the Minister of Foreign Affairs in August 2008, that is, during parliamentary proceedings. The minister said that parliament should consider this issue because there was no harm in the country joining the organisation, which would offer Tanzania many economic benefits. This statement was later reported in all news media in the country,

---

[247] Hao wanawake wanaopinga Kadhi hawajui maana yake ndo maana walikuwa wanalipinga.... Mfano kazi anazofanya nikushughulika na maswala ya mirathi mfano kati ya mwanamke na mwanaume, mwanaume anatakiwa apate mara mbili ya mirathi.

[248] Katika kipindi cha Mwinyi hali ilibadilika maana waislam wengi walifikiri kwa vile Mwinyi ni mwislam basi wangepata nafasi za upendeleo kitu ambacho hakukifanya kwasababu waislam wengi walikuwa si wasomi lakini wachache.

[249] The participant was referring to the current president Jakaya Mrisho Kikwete, who is a Muslim.

[250] Rais ni mwislam lakini lakini rais huyo huyo ametawaliwa na wakristo kwa hiyo likikurupuka swala la dini katiba imembana. (Educated male participant.)

[251] Rais Kikwete ni muislamu. Lakini si unaona viongozi wengi ni akina nani mama? Wengi ni wakristo.

including *Mwanahalisi* of 3-9 September 2008. It was naturally recorded in the parliamentary Hansard of 22 August 2008.

The issue of OIC membership is not new, as one MP reminded the interviewer: "This question has a long history. As you will remember, it started when Zanzibar applied for OIC membership."[252] He added, "It was in 1994 when Zanzibar joined OIC. The Zanzibar government was later forced by the United Republic of Tanzania to withdraw its membership[253], because joining the OIC had to be passed by the government of [the United Republic of] Tanzania."[254] The MP reported that the issue of OIC membership was generally misunderstood and grossly misrepresented: "People judge without proper knowledge." Participants said Christian leaders have "made statements against OIC". Because of Christian opposition on the issue, sheikhs and Muslim leaders sat in Dar es Salaam to answer accusations from bishops (*Mwananchi*, 26 October 2008, pp. 1, 2). *The Daily News* of 1 November 2008 (p. 3) reported: "Muslims were shocked by Bishops' utterances that if the government allowed the debate on OIC and the *kadhi* court to persist in Parliament, it would be jeopardising the country's peace and tranquillity." Participants countered by pointing out, "this was [a result of] prejudice as the OIC deals more with economic issues". To allay what they see as unfounded fears "Muslim leaders insisted that the OIC offers more benefits than harm" (*Daily News*, 1 November 2008, p. 3). This was confirmed by a Muslim key informant who said, "The OIC is there to help poor countries in the world and not [just] Muslims." Furthermore, Dr Said Awaal explained, "OIC gives national development aid ... which could be used to construct roads, bridges, colleges, hospitals and things like that" (*Tazama Tanzania*, 16-22 September 2008, p. 12).

An MP interviewed during field research also sought to clarify issues regarding misgivings about Tanzania's membership of the OIC: "Uganda is a member of the OIC and there are no conflicts; the World Bank and the IMF are also part of it." He added, "Our country has no religion but our citizens have a religion ... In a country such as Uganda three quarters of the population are Christians. In Tanzania we are half Christian and half Muslim." This was corroborated by the *Daily News* of 1 November 2008, which quoted a sheikh Muhammad as saying that there

---

[252] Swala lenyewe ni la muda mrefu sana na swala hili kama unakumbuka lilianza pale Zanzibar walipotaka kujiunga na OIC.

[253] The Constitution of the United Republic of Tanzania provides limited legislative power for the Zanzibar government to enter into international agreements. The Zanzibar government cannot decide on issues that affects the nation. In fact, all international agreements have to be made by the government of United Republic of Tanzania.

[254] Ilikuwa ni mwaka 1994 Zanzibar ilipojiunga na OIC lakini ili lazimishwa na serikali ya Muungano wa Tanzania kujitoa kwani lazima ipitie kwenye serikali ya Jamhuri wa Tanzania.

were clear examples of how neighbouring countries in Africa such as Uganda, Kenya and the DRC have benefited from the OIC (*Daily News,* 1 November 2008, p. 1). The sheikh wondered why it was so difficult for their Christian counterparts to see the significance of the OIC for the country's economic development. He argued that if joining the OIC was a violation of the country's constitution, as has been argued by the bishops of the Christian Council of Tanzania (CCT[255]), then the same constitution had already been violated. The sheikh explained that the Holy See, a Roman Catholic religious entity, established diplomatic representation in Tanzania a long time ago, and Tanzania has representation in the Vatican, the Roman Catholic seat of government. The report was corroborated in *The Citizen* of 1 November 2008 (pp. 1 & 2), quoting a statement by one sheikh Issa: "The OIC and the Vatican (diplomatic representation in Tanzania) are all religious bodies, so why (do Christians) question our decision to join the OIC?"

Other participants preferred the state not to be involved in drawing up the divinity curriculum for schools. They said: "The URT has no religion; therefore, it is not the responsibility of government to prepare the curriculum for Muslim students in different schools in the country" (*Majira,* 29 August 2007, p. 12).

There were other participants, who blamed some political parties and leaders for allegedly instigating conflict in the community by getting involved in religious matters. As one educated male participant pointed out, "Even political parties are involved in conflicts" and "political leaders are involved in religious questions".[256]

Inter-generational, intra-religious and gender conflict
"Those who destroy good relations are the youngsters"

Speaking about the younger generation, elderly male participants said, "Those who destroy good relations are the youngsters, because they have more education."[257] This speaker said that Muslim-Christian relations have become more problematic than ever before because the younger generation has acquired better education. In addition they do not want to know where they come from, let alone familiarise themselves with their tradition. Thus the older generation insisted that the problem lay with the youth, who did not want to obey their elders or learn from them.

---

[255] The Christian Council of Tanzania (CCT) issued a statement countering the Minister of Foreign Affairs's statement on Tanzania's willingness to join the OIC and the establishment of kadhi courts on 24 October 2008, Dar es Salaam.

[256] Hata vyama vya siasa vimejiingiza kwenye vurungu na viongozi wa kisiasa wamejiingiza kwenye maswala ya kidini.

[257] Wanaoharibu mahusiano ni hawa vijana kwa kuwa wamezzoma sana.

One elderly male participant raised the issue of spirit and witchcraft beliefs. He said that according to the youths there is a relationship between witchcraft and education. Thus according to them (youths) "we [elders] have witchcraft beliefs too"[258] ... because we were not well educated",[259] although this was not what he thought himself.

Counter to what the old said about the young, the youths postulated that the older generation was the problem as they were too strict, for example when it came to the issue of marriage. For the younger generation love is the only foundation for a good marriage; for the elders the issue was more complicated; they would prohibit Muslim children marrying Christians, and even disowned them when they went ahead against their wishes.

Another point cited was religious leaders, whom ordinary believers referred to as discriminators. As one young uneducated female participant noted, "The religion that discriminates is that of the teachers, sheikhs and priests, not ours... we, ordinary believers have no problem."[260] They said that as ordinary believers "[we] cannot compete with them as they have more knowledge than we do. We are far behind."[261] This observation made during the young Muslim female FGD was corroborated by a (Christian) MP who underscored the point: "The problem is the leaders."[262]

Religious education versus secular education
"Europeans ... brought secular education."

Muslim participants referred to both worldly education (*elimu dunia*) and heavenly education (*elimu ahera*) as vital in their community. They said in the past worldly (secular) education was known as European education (*elimu ya kizungu*). One participant pointed out that Europeans brought secular education primarily when Europeans (including missionaries) introduced modern education during the colonial era. On their arrival, especially on the coast, the Europeans found Islam had already been established and was providing *elimu ahera*. Arabic was the medium of Islamic religious education. This was what the indigenous people referred to as *elimu ya dini* and/or *Kiarabu* (literally: religious education) provided at *madras*.

---

[258] Sisi wazee uchawi ni chakula yetu na kweli ni wachawi.
[259] Hatujasoma sana.
[260] KiSwahili version is provided in the extremism and hardliner section.
[261] Hatuwezi kulumbana nao maana wanauelewa zaidi yetu. Wametuacha mbali sana.
[262] Tatizo ni viongozi.

Our analysis shows that it was not only Christian faith that Muslims were opposed to but also their educational institutions (Christian education). These Christian institutions challenged the Islamic system, which offered only religious education (*elimu ya dini*). Hence the problem Muslims had to contend with in the past was not only the spread of Christianity in the Muslim domain but also the establishment of secular/Western education threatening to undermine the religious education they were used to.

On this point a Muslim member of parliament explained, "Our first leader, Mwalimu Nyerere, gave Muslims educational opportunities through the nationalisation of seminary schools; I also got the opportunity to study in those schools. This eliminated the big difference between Muslims and Christians. The government provided this opportunity."[263]

Conclusion

In this section we analysed the relationship between the FGDs and the discourses in religious institutions and society at large (e.g. the media and parliament). In producing and consuming texts participants continually borrowed from these sources and, by doing so, they reproduced or transformed them, aspects to be dealt with in the next subsection.

In the FGDs participants said that they lived with Christians harmoniously. Mostly they agreed that they were tolerant of differences and responded to each other accommodatively and politely. Utterances likely to disrupt the existing harmony were immediately silenced by other group participants. For example, when an elderly female participant said, "A Christian is my enemy", others intervened saying "he/she who suits you in time of trouble is a friend".

FGD participants who spoke about Christians linked their responses to the ongoing intra-religious discourse of Muslims (between male and female, young and old, educated and uneducated Muslims), and between Muslims and government. They referred to the prophet Muhammad, the Qur'an, open air preaching, and the bishops whom they accused of ruling the country through indirect mechanisms. They also referred to religious organisations such as the CCT and BAKWATA

---

[263] Kiongozi wetu wa awali Mwalimu Nyerere, alitoa nafasi kwa waislam kusoma, kwa kutaifisha shule za seminari, kwani hata mimi nilipata nafasi ya kusoma kwenye mashule hayo, na pia suala hili liliondoa tofauti kubwa iliyokuwa kati ya waislam na wakristu. Serikali ndio iliyotoa nafasi hii.

and their roles in Tanzanian society. Most participants' utterances could be identified with the moderate brand of Islam, hence situated extremists/radical Islam as peripheral discourse.

The participants also touched on international issues such as Uganda's OIC membership, *kadhi* courts in Kenya, religious wars in Somalia, and diplomatic relations between Tanzania and the Vatican. They referred to the constitution and its effect on religious preaching, to presidents such as Nyerere, Mwinyi and Kikwete and their influence on matters of faith and the attendant problems. It was clear that religious and interreligious debates in the FGDs were linked to national and international debates. On the whole civic discourse dominated religious discourse

The participants said Christians misunderstood them on various issues, such as *kadhi* courts, the OIC and *mihadhara*. Understanding-misunderstanding also featured in the way Muslim participants referred to Christian doctrines and the prophet (Jesus). In speaking about Christianity Muslims tended to phrase stark differences between their religions in terms of evaluative statements such as that Islam is better than Christianity. Misunderstanding was also noted in participants' explanation of the relationship between the government and Christians, and between the government and Muslims. Some participants blamed the government for favouring Christians and discriminating against Muslims. Government's efforts (e.g. nationalisation of schools) were not seen as positive measures to reduce inequality in the country. Moreover, Christian leaders are also blamed for meddling in politics and Muslim affairs (hence the complaints by some religious leaders especially on the issues of the establishment of *kadhi* courts and Tanzania joining the OIC).

2.3. Analysis of social practice

The third level involves the analysis of social practice. As indicated in the general introduction, we are interested in the socio-cognitive effects of language use, ideational and interpersonal changes (i.e. reproduction and/or transformations of subject positions and social relations at this level). This is what Fairclough (1992:119) calls 'explanation' and tracing 'explanatory connections' (Fairclough 1992:72), or linking texts to their social contexts. The main analytical tools are hegemony and ideology.

Everybody has his/her own belief

What participants say constitutes and is constituted by the processes of privatisation and individualisation. They said that nowadays individual believers all have their own convictions. "Everybody has his/her own belief",[264] so they keep to themselves and are self-sufficient. Most participants were of the view that belief is an individual thing which cannot be considered communal or group property: "And this situation is different from the past."[265] This confirmed that pluralisation and diversification are taking place in the community.

Some participants said that individualism started when Ali Hassan Mwinyi took power: "Nyerere always insisted on unity [*umoja*] and that we must resist ethnic or religious discrimination,"[266] it was said. "We must live together as brothers and sisters to maintain peace in our country."[267] But since the Mwinyi administration took over liberalisation and privatisation have led to individualism and diversity, liberty [*rukhsa*]. "Tanzania is a free country, so everybody is free to do whatever he likes,"[268] said one participant. As a result participants identified and positioned themselves primarily as individual believers rather than as representatives of their respective religions. In other words, they spoke for themselves.

I don't have a problem with changing my religion

The way Muslims speak about Christians and Christian-Muslim relations is also linked to democratisation and socio-economic emancipation. This is seen, firstly, in the context of gender relations. In the past Muslim girls were forbidden to be with or talk to Christian men. If a Muslim girl was spotted talking to a Christian man, purification through prayer was required. This has changed. Now young Muslim women decide for themselves. "I don't have a problem with changing my religion,"[269] one participant in the educated Muslim female FGD said; "I can change my religion if I am in love with a Christian,"[270] said another participant in the uneducated Muslim female FGD.

Regardless of category, female Muslim participants agreed that there was still male hegemony. They attributed male chauvinism to the fact that "the man is

---

[264] Kila mtu ana imani yake.
[265] Hali hii ni tofauti na zamani.
[266] Nyerere alisisitiza umoja. Kwa hiyo inatupasa kupinga ubaguzi wa kikabila na kidini.
[267] Ili kuilinda amani ya nchi yetu, ni lazima tuishi kama kaka na dada.
[268] Tanzania ni nchi huru, hivyo kila mmoja anauhuru wa kufanya atakavyo.
[269] KiSwahili version is provided in the interreligious marriage section.
[270] Ibid.

the head"²⁷¹ (uneducated female FGD); "children born will follow their father's religion" (educated female FGD); and "a woman doesn't have religion anywhere she goes"²⁷² (young uneducated female FGD). Female participants generally saw their position as subordinate to that of their male counterparts.

As for inter-generational relations, the youths said that they wanted to decide for themselves, but their parents' influence remained strong and domineering. "The whole family will disown you simply because you have a Christian fiancée," an educated female participant observed. This indicates that some Muslim families position themselves as 'pure' believers, who do not want non-believers such as Christians in their lineage. This has a potential for creating divergence.

There was also evidence of troubled intra-religious relations. Some educated Muslim men said, "A Muslim youth who wants to change his religion because he wants to marry a Christian girl is seen as a *kafir*."²⁷³ This again demonstrates that the word *kafir* is not reserved for Christians but also applies to Muslims who are seen as turncoats. These examples show that young Muslims, both male and female, are victims of religious exclusiveness irrespective of gender and the resultant conflict is inter-generational.

The same applies to the democratisation of intra-religious relations between ordinary believers and their religious leaders. Indeed, as one participant put it, "A discriminatory religion is that of *ustadh*, sheikh and priest (padre). They are the ones who are arguing not us... we ordinary believers have no problem."²⁷⁴ These ordinary believers tried to dissociate themselves from the problematic religious identities their leaders try to create. In contrast to such identity positioning, the participants felt that they "live together like *ndugu*,"²⁷⁵ hence opted for a civic identity which they rated above religious identity.

Religion remains faith, not action

In the course of democratisation another transformation is occurring in Tanzanian society, namely secularisation. In fact, the participants distinguished between religion and society: "I accept that religion remains faith, not action."²⁷⁶ This quotation from a Muslim participant does not tell us immediately what the word 'action'

---

[271] Mwanaume ni kichwa.
[272] Mwanamke hana dini popote tu anakwenda.
[273] KiSwahili version is provided in the interreligious marriage section.
[274] KiSwahili version is provided in the extremism section.
[275] Tunaishi kama ndugu.
[276] Nimekubali ukweli kwamba dini inabaki kuwa imani na sio vitendo.

refers to, but the participant makes a distinction between what religion is (faith) and what it is not (action).

In situations where the distinction between religious and community (secular) affairs is not clear there have been clashes between believers. On 1 September 2008 *Majira* (p. 5) reported that Muslims prevented the launch of a curriculum.[277] The curriculum had not been drawn up by Muslims and as a result they felt that some core principles of Islam had been overlooked. These Muslims believed that the government had overreached itself by interfering in the preparation of a religious education curriculum for pupils and the spread of religion. Their view was that community (secular) affairs should be distinct/separate from religion.

The same distinction was made in the context of social relations. As one participant said, "You can't bring issues of religion home. If you are interested in religions, just go to church or mosque to pray."[278] This was corroborated by another participant in the educated male group: "I myself am a Muslim and I stay with Christians and our relationship is good."[279] He added that "faith is one thing and our relationship in society is another".[280] This participant referred to the separation of religion from day-to-day social relationships (civic identity). That is to say, believers are members of a particular society (civic identity) on the one hand, and on the other are adherents of a particular religion (religious identity). Generally participants concurred that religion and community matters do not go hand in hand, hence the saying "You can't bring religion home."[281] Sometimes participants positioned themselves as members of both Islam and the community.

In the past you knew what a Muslim was

Consequently the participants reproduced the processes of pluralisation and diversification. One elderly male participant said, "In the past you couldn't tell who was a Muslim or who was a Christian, because they were like relatives", but "nowadays you know a Christian or a Muslim and then you may decide what kind of Muslim or Christian the person is".[282] Thus there is religious diversity in Tanzania.

---

[277] Waislamu wazuia ufunguzi wa mtaala.
[278] Kwa sababu mtu hawezi kuleta mambo ya dini ndani, kama unataka dini si unaenda tu kanisani au msikitini kwenda kusali.
[279] Mimi mwenyewe ni mwislam nakaa na wakristo lakini mahusiano yetu ni mazuri.
[280] Linapokuja swala la imani linakuwa ni jambo jingine na mahusiano yetu katika jamii ni jambo jingine.
[281] Huwezi kuleta mambo ya dini nyumbani. (Uneducated female participant.)
[282] Hali hii ni tofauti na zamani kwani hukuweza kumtambua mtu yupi na mwislamu na yupi ni mkristo kwani wote walikuwa ndugu mmoja. Sasa hivi unaweza kumtambua mkristo, mwislamu

Believers identified themselves in different ways, hence have multiple identities rather than just one (Muslim or Christian). Besides, as new "foreign denominations came in"[283] they brought religious transformation and diversified the way believers associated with each other and believers of other faiths.

You cannot tell that a Christian is staying in a particular house

Participants explained that it is difficult to identify a Christian on religious grounds in predominantly Muslim areas, not only during the holy month of Ramadan but also at other times of the year, because of some of the practices that Christians have come to adopt. This participant explained, "Unless you hear a child's name being called you cannot tell that a Christian is staying in a particular house. This is because our households in the Swahili neighbourhood are family friends."[284] These family friends learn to tolerate differences and, where necessary, make social and cultural adjustments. This sketches a picture of social cohesion and homogenization among Muslims and Christians to the extent of regarding each other as friends.

The same participant said such collaboration is regulated by "knowing religious conditions".[285] However, he did not clarify which religious conditions a person needs to know. From the statements of another participant in the group ("s/he does not cook and eat until the evening when Muslims break the fast"[286]) one gathers that by adapting to Muslim religious and cultural ways Christians were able to facilitate the coexistence of believers of the two faiths, hence foster harmony and unity (social cohesion). As for identity, one educated male participant said that the only way to identify a Christian was when s/he went to church on Sunday or walked with a Bible in his/her hand.[287] "But it is difficult to identify who is a Christian and who is a Muslim."[288] In other words, it is difficult to differentiate a Christian from a Muslim in a socially coherent community. Here civic identity is strong and influences religious identity.

---

tena ukajua ni mwislamu wa aina gani au mkristo wa aina gain. Zamani tulijua ni mwislamu wa aina gani au mkristo wa aina gani.

[283] Dini ngeni zilipoingia.
[284] Huwezi kutambua nyumba ya fulani ni mkristo anaishi labda usikie jina la mtoto likiitwa nikwasababu nyumba zetu za uswahilini zinatengeneza 'family friends'.
[285] Mtu kujua masharti ya dini.
[286] Kwasababu hali mpaka jioni Waislamu wanapofungua.
[287] Utaweza fahamu siku ya jumapili akienda kanisani au akiwa na Biblia.
[288] Lakini kwa kukaa huwezi kujua huyu mkristo au mwislam.

We respect each other

Participants identified a process of harmonisation: "When we stay with Christians ... we respect each other... If a person wants to eat pork, he /she will go to eat it in other places such as a bar."[289] Participants spoke of respect between Muslims and Christians, indicating that they try to find common ground and forge unity between the two groups. If Christians eat pork in a bar, unnecessary tension is avoided in the neighbourhood and the result is respect, social cohesion and peaceful coexistence.

In regard to subject position, the participants' statement "we respect each other"[290] suggests that both Muslims and Christians value a shared relationship of mutual respect. Participants indicated that the community has allocated places such as bars where people are free to eat what they like, even food that is considered taboo in a normal neighbourhood. Christians renting Muslim houses or sharing houses with them are not free to eat and/or cook religiously sensitive dishes such as pork so as to promote and sustain harmony in such homes. As one participant put it, "Hatred could arise if a person cooks pork [in a Muslim house], so the tenant may be told that the contract is cancelled and he has to leave [the house]."[291] Afraid of the consequences, some Christians cook and eat pork secretly, as one educated male participant pointed out: "Even if the Christians use these pork products, they are very secretive."[292]

Some families have managed to reach agreement and live in harmony with people of other faiths. As quoted earlier, one participant said, "My older uncle is a Muslim but is married to a Christian through a civil marriage and they live in harmony."[293] Some Christians and Muslims see civil marriages as a meeting point which harmonises their religious differences.

Muslim girls also wear mini-skirts

Other participants constituted and were constituted by the process of homogenisation or unification. They say that it has become difficult to differentiate the be-

---

[289] Tunaheshimiana hata wao wenyewe kama mtu anataka kula nguruwe anaenda kulia kwingine kama bar. (Educated male participant.)

[290] Tunaheshimiana.

[291] Mtu akapika nguruwe inaweza kutokea hata chuki nakumwambia achukue mkataba wake aondoke. (Educated male participant.)

[292] Wakristo hata kama watakuwa wanatumia nyama hizi za nguruwe watakuwa wasiri sana. (Educated male participant.)

[293] The KiSwahili version of this statement is provided in the intermarriage section, linguistic practice.

haviour of a Muslim from that of a Christian, evidenced by the following statement: "We don't know who is a Muslim and who is a Christian."[294] Participants cited current fashions, especially among young Muslim and Christian girls: in the past Christian girls dressed *kizungu* fashion, meaning short dresses, while Muslim girls covered their heads and their bodies in long dresses such as the *baibui* (Arab traditional dress). Generally Muslim women used to cover their heads and wear long, decorous dresses. It was only among Christians that one would spot women wearing short, skimpy dresses and going bare headed. The situation has changed: both Muslim and Christian women wear short dresses and sometimes do not cover their heads, while some Christians cover their heads or wear *baibui* just like Muslim women without necessarily converting to Islam.

But according to another participant, "All religions are against mini-/short skirts."[295] In this respect there is homogenisation of religious and cultural values. This in turn creates common ground between Muslims and Christians. They all speak the same language. Harmonisation is also apparent in eating habits. One participant said, "Nowadays many Muslims eat pork."[296] Here eating pork is less closely associated with a particular religion.

When Christians have an issue, they all gather and become one

"For example, when Christians have an issue they all gather and become one regardless of their denominations. But we discriminate – Manzese versus Buguruni Muslims or Shia versus Sunni. This brings about intra-religious differences."[297] The reference to Christian unity and solidarity has a hint of envy, since the implication is that Muslims lack unity and fail to cooperate effectively. According to this participant the differences make Muslims less united, hence they are unable to settle issues together and discriminate against each other. As for subject position, the participant spoke as a Muslim who is either a victim of discrimination or a culprit discriminating against other Muslims – note the use of 'we' in "we discriminate". According to these participants Muslims lack group identity, unlike their Christian peers who regard themselves as Christians regardless of intra-religious differences.

---

[294] Huwezi kutambua Mwislamu ni yupi na Mkristu ni yupi.
[295] Dini zote zinapinga vimini.
[296] Siku hizi Waislamu wengi wanakula nguruwe.
[297] Mfano wakristo wanapokuwa na jambo wanajikusanya wote wanakuwa kitu kimoja bila kujali dhehebu lakini sasa tunajibagua mwislam wa manzese, buguruni au hawa wanaosali shiha au suna kwahiyo hiyo inaleta matabaka. (Educated male participant.)

Christians don't want Muslims to learn the Qur'an

When speaking about Christians Muslims identified Christianity with religio-centrism, commercialisation and secularisation of formal education. Other sources also show that education has remained a controversial issue in Muslim-Christian relations since the mid-1980s: "Muslims don't have much education."[298] Some participants believe that Christians are favoured in the selection process at institutions of higher learning, hence have access to better positions because of their superior educational qualifications. However, others said that Muslims themselves did not value secular education.

One participant spoke about the way extra tuition[299] competes with *madras* for time. This stems from the prevailing shortage of primary and secondary school teachers in the country, which has necessitated reliance on extra tuition to compensate for the shortfall in regular class teaching, especially in certain subjects. Students seek after-school instruction to be able to cover the material required in the syllabus and prepare effectively for their final national examination. These after-school lessons conflict with the *madras* lessons that are also conducted after school.

Indeed, some Muslim parents interpret the tendency of school children to go for additional tuition after school as sabotage of Islam, because the hours conflict with those of *madras*, hence deny Muslim children an opportunity to learn the Qur'an. In that case Muslim parents have to choose between sending their children for extra tuition to improve their academic performance, or to *madras* to learn the Qur'an.

Participants blame Christians (who allegedly predominate in government offices) for using their offices to sabotage Islam and Muslims by imposing policies which undermine Islam. Other participants differed, arguing that the government and Christians were not responsible for the introduction of extra tuition. They said parents have to strike a balance between time for *madras* and time for extra lessons. As one participant put it, "My child goes for tuition and studies Arabic too; therefore, there is time for both tuition and *madras*."

Extra classes (tuition) are encouraged by both Christian and Muslim parents interested in seeing their children enhance their educational performance. This is part of a transformation in Tanzania which can be described as commodification. Indeed, education is becoming commercialised in the sense that it is seen as a business, a commodity to be sold with the best products competing for the best

---
[298] Waislamu hawajaelimika sana.
[299] The word 'tuition' in Tanzania refers to additional classes after school.

positions. The same trend is seen in other contexts, such as open air preaching which some participants describe as just a business (*ni biashara tu*) for religious preachers to make money and for recipients (customers) to derive some sort of satisfaction from their teachings.

Muslims suspect that Christians interfere in the preparation of the religious curriculum designed for schools under Islamic management. In the previous section we quoted a report in *Majira* (1 September 2008, p. 5): "Muslims prevented the launch of a new curriculum claiming that Christians were involved in its preparation." A similar story appeared in *An-Nuur*, which specifically reported that the curriculum was prepared with aid from Konrad Adenauer Stiftung,[300] which Muslims suspected of being a Christian institution. There was a heated debate on the possibility of balancing worldly education (*elimu dunia*) with heavenly education (*elimu ahera*). Most participants, however, admitted that Christians were not responsible for the dilemma; it was a result of changing times.

Participants' statements also showed that marriage has become a transaction. They noted that formerly a Muslim woman who wanted to marry a Christian was told to go to the mosque to purify herself. Nowadays the reverse applied. For instance, one participant said that given a choice between a poor Muslim and a rich Christian as a husband for a daughter, some Muslim parents would go for the latter, because he would provide security for their daughter. The implication is that marriage is no longer based on religion but on avarice. "It is a selfish hunger for money,"[301] another participant observed. Overall the commodification of society is believed to be a colonial or Western import, which has been appropriated and embraced by Tanzanian society.

The problem is the radical Muslims

From the analyses we infer that there is tension not only between Muslims and Christians but also among Muslims themselves. Apart from the dominant transformation processes of secularisation, democratisation, privatisation and liberalisation, there is a peripheral process of radicalisation: "*waislamu wa siasa kali*", "*ki-itikadi kali*".These radical groups are agitating for Muslim rights, claiming that Muslims have been discriminated against for a long time. As a result some mosques in the country have been taken over by radical groups which want to

---

[300] Konrad Adenauer Stiftung is a German institution. As mentioned already, anything from a Western country is regarded by some Muslims as Christian-oriented.
[301] Uroho wa pesa.

change the running of mosques and teaching of Islam. This is a clear power struggle within Islam, in which some Muslims position themselves as knowledgeable and are regarded by other believers as radicals (*wa siasa kali*).

In recent times there have been struggles among Muslims, which have even threatened the position of the Mufti. The opponents claimed that BAKWATA leaders had been implicated in squandering Muslims' property. On 12 September 2008 *Majira* (p. 4) carried an article on one BAKWATA leader (sheikh Said Mwaipopo) urging Muslims not to listen to radical groups opposing the Mufti. The headline read: "Muslims are advised not to be involved in betraying the Mufti".[302] This radicalisation suggests an ideological struggle between mainstream BAKWATA and other Islamic groups in Tanzania.

What will you learn? Kizungu or Arabic?

The above analysis shows ongoing transformation in the country. So far there have been two major discourses competing for dominance and hegemony: those of Westernisation and Arabisation. These two discourses played a role in the historical formulation of Tanzanian society. Participants indicated that such transformation was particularly evident in the educational sector, where people had to choose between Western-oriented education (*elimu dunia/elimu ya kizungu*) and religiously oriented education (*elimu ya dini/elimu ahera*). Upon completing their studies children of Muslim parents who allowed them to acquire a Western-type education ended up in good positions. Children whose Muslim parents did not send them for a secular education but to *madras* to learn Arabic (*elimu ya dini*) ended up with limited competitiveness when looking for a good position in the public service. As said in a previous section by one elderly male participant: "My father sent me to school to learn Arabic and in the end I studied two to three chapters of the Q'uran." Today people "could see me as uneducated but I have studied religion only".[303] This participant perceives himself as affected by transitions that have changed the status of Arabic education (*elimu ya dini*). Arabic education cannot compete with Western-type education. He added "Someone who has form two, who can be my child, could see me as uneducated!"[304]

However, participants noted that transformations in the educational sector have led many Muslim parents to change their attitude and to value a secular

---

[302] Waislamu washauriwa kutojihusisha na kumsaliti Mufti.
[303] Baba yangu alinipeleka shule kusoma Kiarabu na mwisho nilisoma juzuu 2 au 3. ... ataona sijasoma ila nimezzoma dini tu.
[304] Na aliyesoma mpaka darasa la kumi ambaye anaweza kuwa mwanangu ataona sijasoma!

education in addition to religious education. As a result the majority of Muslim parents send their children for both secular and religious education. More importantly, they no longer simply enrol their children primarily for religious tuition, although there are still those who feel that secular education threatens *elimu ya dini*.

There have been many appeals from Muslim leaders to learn the good things from other religions (including Christians and Christian organisations), especially from their educational institutions. On 13 February 2003, for example, the *Daily News* quoted Dr Abdallah Kigoda (former Minister of Industry and Business, 2000-2005): "The [Muslim] council could copy other religious organisations whose schools are performing very well." Dr Kigoda was addressing the Tanzanian Muslim Council, imploring it to learn from other religious organisations how to operate Muslim schools and improve their students' performance.

Similar views were expressed by the former president of Tanzania, Alhaji Ali Hassan Mwinyi, when opening the World Muslim Council meeting in Dar es Salaam on 7 October 2002 (reported in the Guardian, 8 October 2002). Mwinyi called on Muslims to take education seriously: "Education is your property which got lost many years ago, so when you find it somewhere, please pick it up." Mwinyi was reminding Muslims not to spurn Western-oriented secular education as they did in the past when they focused exclusively on religious education. The expression, 'when you find it somewhere', could also mean that they should not choose schools purely on the basis of religious faith. They could send their children to good schools belonging to other religious institutions.

A similar appeal was made by the first lady, Mama Salma Kikwete, who implored Muslim women to "send your children to school to learn the Qur'an, but worldly education is also important because it helps them to know things and it gives them the capacity to emancipate themselves" (Habari Leo, 23 January 2009, p. 4).

Let us not mix religion and the law of the country

Several participants explicitly or implicitly identified processes of liberalisation and secularisation Tanzania has been experiencing since the mid-1980s. "I say, if we want to collaborate, let us not mix religion and the law of the country,"[305] said one participant. This person cited the pork incident and the destruction of pork butcheries as one of the things that heightened Muslim-Christian tensions.

---

[305] Mimi nasema, kama tunataka kushirikiana, tusichanganye dini na siasa.

The participant elaborated, "At one time our leader Ali Hassan Mwinyi said it is permitted [*ni rukhsa*] to eat whatever one likes. But others came to destroy pork butcheries in Magomeni. Thus, if there is something that you do not eat, do not prevent others from eating it."[306]

The participants suggest that there was a power struggle between the legal discourse and religious discourse. Mwinyi produced legal discourse as a president of the URT adhering to the constitution. But this political and legal discourse was consumed by some Muslims in religious terms. This clearly shows the different subject positions Mwinyi represented. When he said that people are free to eat whatever they liked, he did not speak from his position as a Muslim but from his position of president of the nation. On this issue the speaker (Mwinyi) framed the freedom to eat pork in a legal discourse drawing on the law of the country, not in a religious discourse.

Because Mwinyi did not position himself primarily as a Muslim but as president of the nation, he was no longer, at least to some Muslims, considered trustworthy. Taking into account Bourdieu's insight that language is effective if the speaker is trustworthy and addresses real felt needs (Bourdieu 1991), Mwinyi's speech was not effective and for that reason some Muslims started to attack pork butcheries at Magomeni.

Secular law also provides a way out for inter-faith marriages, where one party might be forced to choose one faith over another. Some participants suggest that this controversial inter-faith marriage problem has to do with a generational conflict in Tanzania, an issue we will address later. We have quoted one who said: "My older uncle is a Muslim but married to a Christian by civil marriage and they have a good relationship; everyone continues with his/her faith; on Friday my uncle goes to the mosque; on Sunday my aunt goes to church."[307] This participant regards a civil marriage, a secular legal obligation, as a means of creating a good relationship and harmony without interfering with the religious beliefs of interreligious couples. Both partners are free to practise their faith within their marriage. In other words, a civil marriage is a win-win situation for both wife and husband.

These examples of civil marriages and consumption preference reveal a situation of legal pluralism in which customary legal (secular) discourse and religious discourse compete for hegemony. Despite this, as the above examples illustrate,

---

[306] Kuna kipindi kiongozi wetu, Rais Mwinyi ni rukhsa kwa mtu yeyote kula anachotaka,. Lakini wengine wakaenda kubomoa mabucha ya nguruwe kule magomeni. Kama kunakitu huwezi kula, usiwazuie wengine kukila. (Educated female participant.)

[307] KiSwahili version of this statement is provided in the interreligious marriage section, linguistic level. (Uneducated male participant.)

secular legal discourse appears to win in the end. But there is also a peripheral discourse struggling for hegemony: that of advocates of *kadhi* courts. This is a fairly recent development that has come about as part of the social transformations taking place in Tanzania.

The state has no religion

Some key informants and participants reproduced the separation of religion and state: "... the government has no religion [is secular] but its citizens have religion."[308] To this participant the government is obliged to safeguard justice and law, and can only do so when there is a clear separation between religion and the state. After all, the president is the representative of the state.

The separation of religion and state arose in the dispute about Tanzania's IOC membership: "Christians have their organisation ... The Vatican embassy is in this country but OIC is rejected,"[309] lamented one educated male participant. Even so, others insisted that the OIC is not a religious but an economic organisation: "The Vatican has been here since Nyerere's era and we have not complained, but the OIC is an economic institution, not a religion."[310] As a result some Muslims warned that Tanzania's failure to join the OIC would be construed as the government bowing to pressure from Christian bishops, who strongly oppose such a move (*The Weekend African*, 1-2 November 2008, p. 1).

Muslims lack economic power

Other participants identified poverty and growing income disparities. One participant said that poverty causes some people to influence others to do things contrary to the expectations of the community. Educated young male participants also questioned the rationale behind the government's refusal to allow Muslims to join organisations that would help lift them from abject poverty and misery. They see the OIC as an organisation offering the country economic benefits, which the government is still reluctant to join. They want the government to speed up the process of joining the OIC, which has benefited other African countries economically. Not surprisingly, *Mwananchi* (1 November 2008, p. 2) carried a headline:

---

[308] Serikali haina dini ... lakini watu wake wana dini. Key informant from University of Dar es Salaam Muslim Student Association (MSAUD).
[309] Wakristo wana umoja wao upo Vatican na ubalozi wao upo hapa nchini lakini OIC imekataliwa.
[310] Vatican ipo hapa toka enzi za Nyerere hatujalalamika chochote lakini taasisi ya OIC ni ya uchumi zaidi kuliko kidini. (Member of Parliament, key informant interview.)

"Muslims insist on Tanzania joining OIC", a story that clearly showed the displeasure of Muslims with the status quo. It quoted one Mzee, a Muslim elder: "Since the government conducted investigations and was pleased that the OIC does not have any negative consequence for the nation but offers economic benefits, we urge it to join the OIC immediately."

This analysis indicates that joining the OIC would benefit both Muslims and Christians. As another participant quoted in the same article, sheikh Ally Basalehe, pointed out, if the money is used for building bridges, "those who benefit are all citizens, Muslims and Christians". The Muslims' position is that the government favours Christians and discriminates against Muslims by denying them access to Muslim organisations such as the OIC.

Conclusion

In general Muslims see belonging to a society as more important than membership of a religion. To them individuals of different faiths must "live together as brothers and sisters", and thus faith must be kept outside social relations, such as renting and living in the same house, marriage, burial ceremonies and friendships. Participants referred to processes of homogenisation, secularisation, unification and convergence. This view tends to be more popular among youths than among elderly participants. According to some elderly participants, however, the youths are stricter because 'they know the faith'.

However, for a few Muslims belonging to a religion is more important than being a member of society. In other words, they value religious identity more than civic identity. These participants want a limitation on interaction between Muslims and Christians. Christians, for instance, should not be allowed to marry Muslim girls, and vice versa. At the same time Muslims should put more emphasis on religious education (*madras*) than secular education ('tuition'). Other participants questioned the logic of these sentiments in the face of changes taking place in Tanzania today. They felt that those championing such views could be considered fanatics/extremists (*wenye siasa kali*).

As Islam teaches humility Muslims generally believe that a Muslim is a person who does the will of God. This is complicated by a few people who manipulate religious scriptures to ridicule other people's faith, thus polarising Muslims into two camps: normal believers, who get along well with Christians and radicals/fanatics/extremists, who instigate interreligious conflict. The latter are a minority, but have enormous influence on the Muslim discourse through open air preaching and in other ways (e.g. style of dress, interpersonal relations with Christians).

The participants reproduced a picture of transformation in Tanzanian society since the 1980s, from Nyerere's unity (*umoja*) to Mwinyi's freedom (*rukhsa*) as a consequence of liberalisation, individualisation and pluralisation. They showed the effects for themselves as individual believers and for their religious institutions. Whereas most FGD participants accepted and then reproduced the consequences, there were a few who regretted these changes and opposed them. They also described the effect of the liberalisation policy, especially the resultant inequalities in education and employment opportunities. On the whole they insisted that Tanzania is a secular state where religion should be relegated to the private domain, and in this sense they reproduced Nyerere's view of society. However, they also positioned themselves as victims of government discrimination, for example by being denied OIC membership and the establishment of *kadhi* courts.

Chapter 3:
How Christians speak about Muslims
"We live well; we live like ndugu."

As explained in the general introduction, the aim of this study is to gain insight into the relation between religious discourse and (the lack of) social cohesion (internal objective), and by doing so to contribute to a theory and method of studying interreligious relations (external objective). In the second chapter we tried to do so by analysing Muslim participants' utterances, which contributed to the ongoing (mis)understanding and (lack of) social cohesion, and consequently the socio-religious transformation of the community. This chapter uses Christians' utterances to gain similar insight, this time from a Christian perspective. We analyse the language Christians use to speak about Muslims to determine whether such utterances afford insight into how Christians in Tanzania construct religious identity and how they position Muslims in relation to themselves.

This chapter presents the findings that were generated through the analysis of the speech of Christian FGD participants and other sources. As in the previous chapter, the main method of data collection was Focus Group Discussions (FGDs). The FGD findings presented in this chapter are from eight FGDs conducted in Dar es Salaam. The total number of participants in the Christian groups was 37, of which 17 were male and 20 female. The FGDs were conducted with five educated females and six educated males. There were also FGDs with eleven elderly females, divided into two groups of five and six participants. In addition we conducted an FGD with five elderly males, as well as two with respectively six and four uneducated male and female youths. As explained in the general introduction, for purposes of triangulation and constant comparison the discursive and social practice sections of the chapter also present findings drawn from other sources, such as six Christian *mihadhara*, eleven key informant interviews and Tanzanian newspapers (e.g. *Majira*, *The Citizen*, *Mwananchi*, *Mtanzania* and *The Guardian*).

As in the preceding chapter, the findings in this chapter were analysed by means of Fairclough's multi-dimensional and polymethodical critical discourse analysis (CDA) (Fairclough 1992:73-100). The chapter is divided into three main sections: linguistic practice, discursive practice and social practice.

3.1. Analysis of linguistic practice

Fairclough (1992:75) proposes four main ways of analysing texts: vocabulary, grammar, cohesion and text structure. For the same reason as in the second chapter, this chapter focuses on vocabulary and syntax to show the modes of action, social structures, social relations and the construction of social identities and subject positions of the speaker and those referred to in the speeches (see Fairclough 1992:63). The meanings attached to the vocabulary are justified through comparison with alternative individual words/vocabulary (see chapter 2). This helps us to understand the forms of social action and social transformation in the community.

The chapter is thematically arranged according to issues that emerged during group discussions. The themes include intermarriage, education, food, borrowing cooking utensils, funerals, clothing, open air preaching, renting houses, income and employment. Our focus was on the social dimension (social condition and effect) of the language used by participants in the discussion groups. Below we give details of the findings and discussions in the groups, starting with Muslim-Christian relations.

Muslims and Muslim-Christian relations
"We live like relatives."

The general response from all participants in the Christian FGDs is summed up by the comment of one of the participants: "We live well; we live like *ndugu*."[1] This was confirmed by another participant in the group: "We live well, we help each other."[2] Another participant said, "In general we live well without any disputes."[3] On Muslim-Christian relations in the country, some said, "The relations between Muslims and Christians in this country are not bad; they are just good."[4] And on neighbourhood relations others said, "In the street you will find Muslims and Christians living in the same house."[5]

Christian participants used various identity labels to speak about Muslims. Apart from the label 'relative' (*ndugu*), they referred to Muslims as 'friends',

---

[1] Tunaishi vizuri... tunakaa kama ndugu. (Uneducated female participant.)
[2] Tunaishi vizuri tunasaidia tatizo likitokea tunajumuika wote na hakuna ubaguzi. (Uneducated female participant.)
[3] Kwa ujumla tunaishi vizuri bila kuwa na migogoro yoyote baina ya wakristu na waislamu. (Educated male participant.)
[4] Mahusiano kati ya wakristo na waislam nchi hii siyo mabaya ni mazuri tu. (Elderly male participant.)
[5] Mtaani huko utakuta mwislam na wakristo wanakaa nyumba moja. (Elderly male participant.)

'neighbours', 'brothers and sisters', 'our fellows', 'house mates', and so on. The labels generally indicated a relatively friendly relationship between Muslims and Christians. Moreover, the use of the plural pronoun 'we' indicated an inclusive statement aimed at maintaining the status quo of friendly relationships and social identity.

However, participants also noted that Christian open air preachers used language which ridiculed Muslims – words such as domesticators of evil spirits (*mfuga majini*), lazy (*mdebwedo*), cousin (*mtoto wa shangazi*), Al Qaeda, and *Mujahidin*, all with negative connotations aimed at deriding Muslims. These names are not neutral. For example, the word 'cousin' (*mtoto wa shangazi*) is both unifying and divisive, in the sense that this is your relative, but a distant one.[6] The label '*Al Qaeda*' links Tanzanian Muslims with terrorist behaviour by some anti-West Muslims in other parts of world, especially in the Middle East. '*Mdebwedo*' suggests laziness and homosexuality, a form of stereotyping.

According to one Christian preacher Muslims used euphemisms and other cooked up phrases to refer to pork in order to hide the fact that they were going to eat it in a pub. He said they used phrases such as "I'm going to see *al-ustaadh*. Yesterday Osama[7] bombed [it was nice meat]; there is a problem with electricity these days..."[8] Other names included '*kitimoto*', '*alhajji*', 'Arab', 'Catholic's goat', 'guest of honour' and '*tigo*'.

Interreligious marriage
"My sister was married to a Muslim."

Findings from the FGDs show that intermarriage is regulated by religious and societal (family) values. As one uneducated female participant put it, "My sister was married to a Muslim, but she did not change her religion."[9] Others in the group also said they could not change their religion to marry a Muslim. One participant insisted, "Myself, I cannot change my religion"[10] to marry a Muslim. But others differed, saying circumstances varied. In fact, one of them said, "A person can change her or his religion because of problems ... and good reasons".[11] And

---

[6] Watoto wa shangazi (ndugu yako lakini baba yake ni mwingine).
[7] Osama refers to the Saudi Arabian who used Islam to incite international terrorist activities and the number one wanted terrorist on the USA list.
[8] Excerpt from a tape-recorded mhadhara conducted by a group called Christian Power in Mbagalla, Dar es Salaam, 2 January 2008.
[9] Dada yangu ameolewa na Mwislamu, lakini hakubadili dini.
[10] Mimi binafsi siwezi kubadili dini.
[11] Inategemea, mtu anaweza kubadili dini kutokana na matatizo ... na sababu maalum.

one participant said explicitly, "I can agree to change my religion"[12] to marry a Muslim. She was supported by another participant in the group, who said, "It is possible to change one's religion and marry if the couple are in love."[13] A woman who already had a child by a Muslim could also change her religion. In this regard one uneducated female participant said, "You find that a person has a child before marriage. She therefore changes her religion to that of the baby's father for the sake of the child."[14]

Changing one's religion was seen by elderly female participants as a recent phenomenon, because "in the past there were [church] regulations; if you allowed your child to become a Muslim, you were excommunicated by the church."[15] Religious values and regulations thus prohibited interreligious marriages. In the discussion Christian participants claimed that Muslim marriages did not last long. This was stated by elderly female participants: "We parents find it difficult to accept these interfaith marriages because of divorces";[16] "Even if we allow our children to change their religion and become Muslims we are not sure if that marriage will last";[17] and "We refuse because our daughters might return home [divorced] after being with the man for so long and having children with him."[18] One elderly female participant added: "Sometimes the marriage hardly lasts two years before it is over.[19] This is what makes us parents object, as he [a Muslim] can marry in the morning and divorce in the evening."[20] Elderly female participants averred that Muslim marriages were different from Christian ones. One participant said, "There are many aspects of Muslim marriages that are different from ours."[21]

Participants said that Islam allows polygamy and Muslims can marry as many as four wives. One elderly participant said, "Christianity insists on one wife un-

---

[12] Mimi nakubali kubadili dini.
[13] Inawezekana, kama wamependana watabadili dini na kuoana. (Uneducated female youth.)
[14] Unakuta mtu kapata mtoto kabla ya ndoa, hivyo inabidi abadili dini na kuwa dini moja na baba wa mtoto kwa ajili ya mtoto.
[15] Zamani kulikuwa na sheria, kanisani, kwamba kama utamruhusu mwanao kuolewa na Mwislamu unatengwa na kanisa.
[16] Na sisi wazazi tunaona ni vigumu kwa ndoa hizi za watu wa dini mbalimbali kwani tunahofia talaka hapo baadaye.
[17] Na hata kama itatokea binti yetu tunamruhusu abadili dini na kuwa muislamu tunahofia kama ndoa hiyo itadumu.
[18] Tunahofia talaka hapo baadaye huku tayari wameishi muda mrefu na kuzaa watoto na hivyo binti yako kuridishwa tena nyumbani kwako.
[19] Maana wanaweza kudumu kwa miaka miwili tu halafu ndoa ikawa imefikia kikomo.
[20] Hapo ndipo sisi wazazi wakristo tunapoleta kikwazo kutokana na haya. Anaoa asubuhi jioni anaacha.
[21] Ndani ya ndoa zao waislamu kuna vipengele vingi sio kama sisi.

til death. But they [Muslims], he marries a first wife and they get property, and then, he marries a second, third, et cetera."[22] Because they are allowed to marry many wives, "when the husband dies property is distributed equally among the wives."[23] This could create problems for the widows. It is contrary to Christian marriages, "in which, when the husband dies, property goes only to the wife and children".[24] These are some of the reasons why Christian parents refuse their daughters' requests to marry Muslim suitors.

Apart from religious values, participants also mentioned personality and individual values as crucial factors in social relationships. They said that Muslims were cruel (*wakatili*), especially for refusing to let their children marry someone from a different faith. They said this was not different even if the father was married to a Christian woman himself; they generally did not want to allow their daughters to marry Christian suitors. As one elderly female, who was married to a Muslim, put it, "... then after this you understand that Muslims are cruel (*wakatili*). Just imagine, we have three children, but he won't allow his daughters to marry a man from his wife's religion."[25] Christians are said to be more flexible than Muslims when it came to interreligious marriages. This was explicitly stated by an uneducated male youth: "When a Christian man wants to marry a Muslim girl there will be a lot of friction which takes a long time to resolve, but this does not happen when it comes to a Muslim man marrying a Christian girl."[26] This indicates that Christians believe Muslims are stricter about allowing interfaith marriages because of their stronger attachment to religious values compared to their Christian counterparts.

Many other participants acknowledged that interfaith marriage is accommodated by some Christians in the community. In fact, one uneducated male youth said, "We cooperate in issues of marriage, meaning a Muslim could marry a Christian girl and a Christian could marry a Muslim girl."[27] Indeed, Christian partici-

---

[22] Mke wa ndoa ni mmoja tu mpaka kufa lakini wao unakuta ameoa mke wa kwanza na kuchuma mali pamoja bado tu ataoa na watatu.
[23] Na [mume] akifa mali zote wanagawia wengine.
[24] Sasa hii kwetu hatuna, tunamume mmoja kwa mke mmoja, umekufa mali ni za mkeo na watoto basi na ndoa ni mmoja tu.
[25] Sasa kutokana na hili ndipo utakapoona ya kuwa waislamu ni wakatili, mpaka mtu umezaa nae watoto watatu bado anashindwa kukubali watoto wake waolewe na dhehebu la mke wake.
[26] Mwanaume wakikristo atapenda kumwoa binti wa kiislamu, msuguano utakuwa mkubwa na huenda ukawa wa muda mrefu tofauti na pale inapotolea mwanaume wa kiislamu akitaka kumwoa binti wa kikristo kwani msuguano huwa si mkubwa.
[27] Ushirikiano upo katika masuala ya kuoleana kwa maana kwamba Mwislamu kuoa binti wa kikristu na Mkristu kuoa binti wa kiislamu.

pants emphasised that marriage is an area where Muslims and Christians cooperate. This shows that flexibility helps to maintain good relationships and social cohesion.

The possibility that one partner in an interreligious marriage would at some point be obliged to change his/her religion for the sake of the other was seen as a major obstacle to interfaith marriages. Making such a choice may be a stumbling block, since "both sides pull in their own favour [i.e. the other partner should be the one to change]".[28] However, some participants indicated that such unions should not be encouraged because "interfaith marriage causes disharmony in the family, especially when some members of the family do not accept their relative marrying someone from a different faith."[29] That is a clear rejection of interfaith marriages.

An educated male youth noted that in most cases the man's family would not accept their son changing his religion, "using a saying that the woman has no religion, she could go anywhere".[30] An uneducated female youth said, "A woman can even be a pagan."[31] This implies that the girl should change her religion and convert to her husband's. The statement that the woman has no choice ('she could go anywhere') reflects the fact that males are dominant and more important in society. Female participants also said that when a Christian girl marries a Muslim the children born of this relationship adopt their father's religion. As one uneducated female participant pointed out, "My sister married a Muslim and she did not change her religion; however, her children followed their father's religion, which is Islam."[32]

Educated male youths said that "when a Christian fiancé is denied permission to marry a Muslim girl, he makes sure that he gets the girl pregnant".[33] This could cause a lot of problems for the girl, especially if there was already friction in the man's family because of fierce opposition to the relationship. An unexpected side-effect of such a scenario is "street children, poverty and economic difficulties for the girl".[34]

---

[28] Masuala haya huleta mvutano kila mmoja akivutia mwenzake ndio abadili dini.
[29] Madhara ya kuoana watu wa imani tofauti huleta mizozo ndani ya familia kwani utakuta baadhi yao hawaafiki ndugu yao aolewe na mtu wa imani tofauti.
[30] Upande wa mwanaume ukitumia kigezo cha mwanammke hana dini, popote tu anakwenda.
[31] Mwanamke anaweza kuwa hata mpagani.
[32] Dada yangu ameolewa na Mwislamu, lakini hakubadili dini. Lakini watoto walifuata dini ya baba yao, ambayo ni Kiislamu.
[33] Endapo mchumba wa kikristu atakataliwa kumuoa binti wa kiislamu anahakikisha anampa mimba.
[34] Ndoa hizi huchangia kuleta watoto wa mitaani, umasikini au hali ngumu kwa watoto wa kike.

Nevertheless, youths said that decisions regarding interreligious marriages can be reconsidered depending on the income of the man's family. By way of explanation one educated male participant said, "A Christian man has difficulty marrying a Muslim girl if he has a low income, but one with a good income can marry a girl without any problems."[35] Another participant chipped in, "Income is [also] a big consideration when a Muslim man wants to marry a Christian girl."[36] "He (the Muslim) has to make good preparations before approaching the Christian's family because Christians are [generally] well off."[37] Here the participant explicitly described Christians as financially better off ("a Muslim has to make good preparation"), hence unwittingly subscribing to the idea of Christians' perceived superiority to Muslims in terms of income distribution. Moreover, the benefits of a good income extend across religions (it serves as a convergence mechanism) and thus regulate interfaith marriages.

In the discussion with educated male youths it was pointed out that some individuals "do not wait to marry a person on the basis of religion, because there is no assurance of getting one from their faith".[38] Therefore "they prefer to marry without attaching much importance to the partner's faith, because their purpose is to start a life and [that does not have] much to do with someone's religion".[39] That, however, depends on the love between the couple. If their decision is "based on true love, there won't be any obstacle for them to get married, because 'love has no eyes or discipline'."[40] Here participants spoke in general terms without placing undue emphasis on any religion, showing that marriage (interfaith or otherwise) has more to do with personal considerations(love and/or starting a life) than religious values (religious teachings on marriage).

Interreligious marriages also depended on the wisdom of the parents. Male youths narrated that "wise parents do not judge their children's courtship on religious grounds. These parents would advise their children to opt for a civil marriage in order to avoid the difficulties that a religious marriage causes for the two

---

[35] Kwa hiyo mvulana wa kikristo hupata ugumu wa kuoa binti wa kiislamu endapo pale uchumi wake utakuwa mbovu, lakini kama uchumi ni mzuri basi ataoa bila wasiwasi.
[36] Uchumi unazingatiwa sana wakati Kijana wa kiislamu anapotaka kumuoa binti wa Kikristu.
[37] Anatakiwa afanye maandalizi mazuri kabla ya kwenda kwenye familia ya kikristu kwa sababu wakristu wanajiweza.
[38] Mtu hawezi kusuburi kuoa au kuolewa na mtu wa imani yake kwani kunaweza usuburi bila mafanikio.
[39] Hivyo mtu anaona ni bora kuoa/kuolewa na mtu wa Imani yeyote na kuangalia zaidi upepo au uelekeo wa maisha na sio dini.
[40] Kama wanapendana kwa dhati basi hakuna litakalokwamisha wao kuoana kwani mapenzi hayana macho wala adabu.

families." "Parents of this type give their children freedom to choose their own religion,"[41] said one participant. This statement, too, is general and inclusive. Parents are placed in one category regardless of their religious identities. By the same token the participant considers a civil marriage a common ground that can enhance social cohesion.

Male youths said that interfaith marriages do not entirely depend on parents' approval but rather on the commitment and love of the couple during courtship. As one Christian male youth pointed out, "Parents are no obstacle in this issue [interreligious marriage] because they would do nothing to separate two individuals who are in love."[42] This was confirmed by an elderly female participant who said, "There is nothing you can do to object to the marriage, because if you do, they [the youths] could commit suicide by taking poison as a result."[43] These statements emphasise the need to respect youth's freedom of choice. Moreover, they show that religion sometimes causes conflict in the family in a different way.

Elderly female participants, however, were against interreligious marriages. They said, "Even today all parents don't accept [interreligious marriages]; it is the youth who insist [on such marriages] and as a result the parent has no choice but to accept [the situation], but this does not mean that parents give them their consent."[44] In other words, the parents are compelled to consent for fear of the worst case scenario: "If they are denied [their right to get married], they take poison."[45] Taking poison reveals the youth's demand for change and desire to be heard by the dominant group (in this case parent).

Education
"Their concentration is more on religion than on education."

In the discussion with elderly females one participant said, "Many Muslims and Christians were educated together."[46] However, many Christian participants also

---

[41] Kwa wazazi wastaarabu hata kama wameshika dini huangalia msimamo wa watoto wao kwani wanaheshimu nakuelewa masuala uchumba. Kwani wanaweza kupendekeza ndoa ya serikalini kuondoa mgongano baina ya watoto wao. Wazazi wa aina hii huwapa uhuru watoto wao.

[42] Na suala hili halina kipingamizi mbele ya wazazi kwani hata wakigoma (Wazazi) hawatowazuia wawili hao waliopendana kuachana.

[43] Hakuna kitu utafanya kupinga ndoa kwa sababu ukipinga matokeo yake wanajiua kwa kunywa sumu.

[44] Mpaka sasa wazazi wote hawakubali isipokuwa vijana wao ndio wanasema ni lazima atakuwa mke au mume wangu hivyo inabidi akubali kutokana na wao kulazimisha lakini sio kwa idhini ya wazazi.

[45] Wakikataliwa, wanakunywa sumu.

[46] Waislamu wengi wamesoma sana na wakristo.

attributed the low level of education of some Muslims to their failure to put more emphasis on secular education. They said that Muslim parents tended to emphasise religious education (*madras*) more than secular education. On this point a male youth said, "Even at the time when I was sent to [secular] school, my friends – Muslims – were going to *madras*."[47] There were also some "Muslim parents [who were] satisfied when their child finished primary school".[48] According to these participants, such parents had no aspiration for their children to acquire further education. One respondent explained: "In the Christian community, even if the child fails primary education, he/she is taken to a private school to get more education."[49] This is one of the reasons "why there are fewer Muslim than Christian students at secondary school."[50] These statements account for existing inequalities as well as the advantage Christians appear to enjoy in terms of educational prospects.

The educated male youth also mentioned polygamy as a reason for some Muslim parents' inability to send their children for further education. "You find that a man has four wives and each wife has her own children; ... as a result he is overburdened with many responsibilities such as children's education, food, clothes, et cetera,"[51] said one participant. This was confirmed by other participants who said, "That tradition of marrying many wives is the cause of all this [problem], because although a parent could manage to pay tuition fees for his children, it is difficult for him to keep up with their educational progress, since they normally would be many, so some children become lazy and play truant; some eventually drop out of school."[52] These statements further account for the situation in which some Muslims end up with less education than they should have, as well as factors that perpetuate such a situation. The same trend was noted by another educated male participant: "Muslims put more emphasis on building mosques. They concentrate

---

[47] Hata kipindi mimi napelekwa shule, marafiki zangu waislamu walikuwa wanaenda madrasa.
[48] Wazazi wa Kiislamu wanaridhika kwa watoto wao kumaliza shule ya msingi tu.
[49] Kwa jamii ya kikristo kwani kuwaendeleza watoto wao kimasomo baada ya kumaliza elimu ya msingi hata katika shule za private endapo mtoto atafeli darasa la saba (7).
[50] Na ndio maana hata mashuleni idadi ya wanafunzi wa kiislamu huwa chini ikilinganisha na idadi ya wakristo.
[51] Unakuta mtu ana wake wanne na kila mke ana watoto wake ... na hivyo mwisho wa siku anajikuta anashindwa kuhudumia familia yake kwani kuna mambo mengi ikiwa ni pamoja kusomesha, chakula, mavazi, nk.
[52] Ile tamaduni ya kuoa wanawake wengi ndio inayoleta hali hii kujitokeza kwani mzazi anaweza kumgaramia mtoto ada ya shule lakini kushindwa kuwa mfuatiliaji wa mwanae katika masomo na hivyo humfanya mtoto awe legelege kwenye masomo na wishowe kuacha shule.

more on religion than on education. As a result they lag behind in development."[53] Christian participants appear to hold Muslims themselves responsible for undermining the chances of furthering their children's education.

These participants believed that the poor education of some Muslims was affecting the development prospects of the whole community. "When we talk of Muslims and Christians, still Muslims will be pushing us backward because of the disparity in education and the economy,"[54] said one educated Christian male participant.

An educated female youth said, "Muslims are also selfish, particularly in their schools because they don't allow Christian children to enrol there."[55] This participant accuses Muslims of religio-centrism. Another participant said when it came to religious subjects, Muslims often stopped Christians from attending; in other words, unlike the other speaker, this one shows that Muslims do allow Christian students to attend Muslim-run schools, but with restrictions. One educated female youth shared her school experience as follows: "I remember when I was at school Muslim children came to the Christian religious class, but we (Christians) were not allowed to go to their religious class,"[56] thus impairing the chances of Christian students to learn about Islam and its teachings.

In the discussion with educated males it was said that missionary schools were the main reason for Christians' numerical educational advantage. They said, "Many Christians were educated in missionary schools."[57] During the colonial period, the participants explained, some Muslims did not send their children to missionary schools, as they feared their children would be forced to eat pork: "This historical phenomenon led Christians to be more advanced in education ... That is why at the time of independence Christians were more educated than Muslims."[58] Furthermore, they explained, "In the past, there was a mistaken belief

---

[53] Waislamu wao wanaendelea na ujenzi wa misikiti na hivyo kuwafanya wazingatie dini kuliko elimu na hivyo kuendelea kubaki nyuma kimaendeleo.
[54] Mimi naona tukizungumzia baina ya waislamu na wakristo, bado mwislamu atakuwa anaturudisha nyuma sana. Kutokana na tofauti iliyopo ya elimu na uchumi.
[55] Kingine hata shule zao wakijenga. Wanaubinafsi. Mtoto wa kikristu haruhusiwi kusoma.
[56] Nakumbuka kipindi kile nasoma shule. Kipindi kile cha dini tulikuwa watoto wa kiislamu wanakuja kwenye vipindi vya kikristu wanasikiliza, lakini sisi hatuwezi kwenda kule.
[57] Wakristu wengi walisoma katika shule za seminari.
[58] Kwa sababu hii ya kihistoria imewafanya wakristo wawe watu wa kuendelea tu. Mpaka wakati wa uhuru wakristo ndio waliokuwa wamezzoma zaidi ukilinganisha na waislam.

[among Muslims] that missionary schools were only for Christians, which was not true."[59]

In the discussion with elderly females one participant actually said, "because they did have schools, mission schools helped them to get educated. ... So, they got education ... which allows them to read books in church."[60]

Dietary patterns and exchange of cooking utensils
"They say pork is haraam, but there are Muslims who normally eat pork."

In the discussions with Christian participants the issue of food frequently was talked about. Participants accused Muslims of being very fussy about food and to comment with disgust in public if they either encountered food prohibited by their religion or suspected they have been 'contaminated' by 'forbidden' foods. One educated male participant said, "in the 1980s my parents and I were staying at Buguruni area in a rented house where we lived with other people who were of a different faith. The problem started when my father came home with pork one day. After eating, I went out with a piece of pork to share with my peers, who also tasted it. One of them was spotted by his mother who later raised a furore between us and the mother of that child. Eventually we decided to move out of the house and went to live in Tabata area."[61]

Christian participants wondered about Muslim's public contempt for pork, particularly since some Muslims were known to eat pork. As one educated male youth put it, "The puzzling thing is that pork is seen as *haraam* but some Muslims themselves eat it."[62] This was confirmed by female educated youths, who said, "They say pork is *haraam*, but there are Muslims who normally eat pork. Some

---

[59] Zamani kulikuwa na dhana [potofu kwamba elimu iliyopatikana katika shule za kimisheni ilikuwepo kwa ajili ya Wakristo tu wakati sio hivyo.

[60] Walikuwa hawana shule ... na mara nyingi shule za mission ndizo zilizowasaidia na wao wakapata kuelimika na wao wakajua shule .... ile elimu ya kujua kusoma kitabu wameipata kwenye makanisa.

[61] Mfano kipindi tunaishi na wazazi wangu kwenye nyumba ya kupanga huko Buguruni katika miaka ya 1980 ambapo tuliishi watu wa imani tofauti. Tafrani ilitokea pale siku baba alipoleta nguruwe, ... na mimi nilipomaliza kula nikatoka na kinyango moja hadi nje na kuwakaribisha wenzangu ambao waliionja. Punde mmoja wao aliporudi nyumbani kwao na kugundulika alikula nyama ile, kwa kweli lilizuka balaa baina yetu na mama wa yule mtoto na kusababisha sisi kuhama ile nyumba nakwenda kuishi Tabata.

[62] Utata uliopo ni kwamba nguruwe anaeonekana kama kuwa haramu huliwa pia na baadhi ya waislamu wenyewe!

of them come from devout Islamic families."⁶³ Uneducated female youths said the same: "At Mwembeyanga, the place where I come from, Muslims eat pork."⁶⁴ To avoid conflict with Muslims some Christians cook pork secretly or do not cook it at all.

Participants said that Muslims insulted Christians when they slaughtered chickens and animals. As an elderly female participant explained, "Although I'm capable of slaughtering a chicken, I always look for a Muslim to slaughter it so we may eat it together;⁶⁵ however, when eating it they still insult Christians by saying that we cannot eat corpses [*kibudu*⁶⁶]. The educated male youth said that Muslims also eat corpses."⁶⁷ Another participant said, "To kill a buffalo they use guns and they eat the corpse which has been killed using a gun. So the issue of *haraam* remains subjective, a matter of faith."⁶⁸

This Muslim monopoly in slaughtering was described by some Christian participants as selfishness. As one educated female youth said, "If a Christian slaughters a chicken, they don't touch it at all. What they like is for a Muslim to do the slaughtering. This is a truism that Muslims are selfish" because they monopolise the social responsibility of slaughtering for public consumption.⁶⁹

The participants said that Muslims did not generally trust food prepared by Christians. In this regard one educated female youth said, "If you invite her [a Muslim] for food, she will ask what it is. If you say it is meat she will say no thank you, thinking that it is pork. If you want things to be okay, cook beans and/or vegetables."⁷⁰ "Even if you give them a glass of water they will not drink it, assuming that it smells of pork."⁷¹ However, "this should not be the case because

---

⁶³ Kama hivyo wenyewe wanavyodai nguruwe ni haramu. Kunawaislamu wengine wanakula nguruwe kama kawaida. Wengine wapo. Watoto waliotoka familia za kiisalamu.
⁶⁴ Mimi nilipotokea huko Mwembeyanga waislamu nao wanakula nguruwe.
⁶⁵ Mimi mwenyewe ninauwezo wa kuchinja kuku lakini kutokana na upendo ambao tuliona mpaka sasa hivi tunawaita watuchinjie tule wote.
⁶⁶ This meant that a chicken slaughtered by a Christian is considered by Muslims to be the same as an unslaughtered carcass (kibudu).
⁶⁷ Wote lakini kumbe wanavyokula wanatutukana, hatuwezi kula kibudu.
⁶⁸ Kumuua nyati wanatumia bunduki na wanakula mzoga ambao umeuliwa kwa kutumia bunduki. Kwa hiyo swala la haraam linabaki kuwa la binafsi, la kiimani.
⁶⁹ Kama akichinja kuku mkristo akichinja wao hawagusi kabisa. Wao wanataka awe amechinja mwislamu lakini kama atachinja mkristu, yaani hawali. Kwa kweli waislamu kwa ubinafsi wanao.
⁷⁰ Ukimkaribisha kwenye chakula atakuuliza umepika chakula gani. Kama umepika nyama anakuambia mie siwezi kula anakwambia inaweza kuwa kitimoto hicho. Labda umpikie maharage, mboga za majani, hapo mtaenda sawa.
⁷¹ Hata kama ukampa maji kwenye glass atajua moja kwa moja hata hii pia inashombo ya nguruwe.

we know that Muslims don't eat pork and we won't dare to give them pork. But they don't have faith [trust] in us. They should have faith [in us]."[72]

This was confirmed by other groups. One elderly female participant said that she has a neighbour who does not eat food cooked by Christians: "Even when you give her food at a funeral ceremony she will throw it away, she will only drink soda"[73] because "she thinks the food contains pork".[74] These statements demonstrate that Christians say that some Muslims are mistrustful and disrespectful towards Christians, who generally speak about themselves as sensitive to Muslims' problems and requirements.

Such attitudes on the part of Muslims were attributed by Christian participants to a lack of trust. One educated female youth lamented, "Christians respect Muslims with regard to the food they take, even at ceremonies you will find that the only foods served are those which can be used by people of all faiths. In my opinion it is the Muslims who do not respect us Christians."[75] This respondent absolves Christians from harbouring any ill intentions when preparing food meant for people of a different faith. Elderly female participants also insisted that they ensured the food they prepared for a Muslim guest did not contain any pork: "We have a wonderful love, because when we have a Muslim guest we do not put pork"[76] on the table.

On the other hand, participants accused Muslims of discriminating against Christians. In the discussion with elderly female participants one of them said "our fellows, the Muslims, discriminate against us".[77] This was confirmed by a young female who said, "Muslims don't allow their children to eat at Christians' homes [on the pretext that they will be fed *haraam*]. This is a result of discrimination that Muslims practise [against us]."[78] On this point elderly female participants mentioned that "nowadays it is difficult to borrow cooking utensils from Muslims; they won't lend them to you. They suspect we will use the utensils for cooking

---

[72] Lakini sio hivyo kama ni mwislamu hali nguruwe huwezi kumlisha nguruwe. Ila tu wao hawana imani. Wanatakiwa waishi kwa imani.
[73] Hata ukimpa chakula wakati wa msiba anakimwaga, atakunywa tu soda.
[74] Atafikiri chakula kina nguruwe.
[75] Wakristo kwa kweli wanawaheshimu waislamu katika maswala ya vyakula kwani hata kwenye sherehe utakuta vyakula vinavyoandaliwa hutumika kwa watu wa imani zote. Waislamu kwa mtazamo wangu ndio naona hawatuheshimu wakristo.
[76] Tuna upendo wa ajabu, kwa sababu wakati kunamgeni hupiki nguruwe.
[77] Wenzetu waislamu wanatubagua sisi.
[78] Hii inatokana na ubaguzi ambapo waislamu hawawaruhusu watoto wao kwenda kula kwa mkristo.

haraam such as pork."[79] So "the main reason for refusing to lend cooking utensils is because we are Christians."[80] "At funerals we don't cook pork; we have never seen anyone cooking pork for a funeral."[81] One elderly female participant stated that "in most places where I go [to borrow cooking utensils] Muslims' responses are always, 'I cannot lend my utensils to Christians because they are *kafir* and they eat pork'."[82] Another elderly female participant added, "They refuse and/or lie that someone has already borrowed the utensils, but all this is because they know that you are a *kafir* and that you will put pork in their utensils."[83]

Christians were worried about the future relationship between Muslims and Christians, as the current discriminatory attitude was being passed on to Muslim children. An educated female youth said, "This attitude [discrimination] is communicated to children and as a result they start making divisions among themselves and they will say 'I won't play with so and so because he is a Christian' and the child will end up playing only with other Muslim children."[84]

Participants said that the foregoing discourse varies from place to place and from individual to individual. One elderly participant used her own experience as an illustration: "I went to ask for cooking utensils at Mgogo's[85] mosque, a sheikh, but if I was to go to Yombo they would not have given me a metal pot."[86]

The mistrust on the part of Muslims is not restricted to Christians borrowing cooking utensils from Muslims; the reverse is also true. As one educated female youth revealed during the discussion, "They say they don't want to use my utensils. If you ask her why, she will say it is because you cook pork. Even if I eat pork, I wash those utensils after cooking."[87] She was reinforcing the point that Muslims

---

[79] Siku hizi ni vigumu kuazima vyombo kwa mwislamu, hawawezi kukuazima, wanahofu kwamba utavitumia kupikia vitu haraamu kama nguruwe.
[80] Sababu kuu ya kutunyima vyombo ni kwa sababu tu wakristo.
[81] Kwa sababu kwenye misiba hatupiki nguruwe. Hatujawahi kumuona yeyote anapika nguruwe kwenye msiba.
[82] Sehemu nyingi mimi ninako kwenda wanasema siwezi nikamwazima mkristo chombo changu kwa maana wao ni makafiri, na wanakula nguruwe.
[83] Na suala ya kuazima vyombo unakuta wanatunyima nakutudanganya kuwa vimeshaazimwa wanajua wewe kafiri utaenda kuweka nyama ya nguruwe kwenye vyombo vyao.
[84] Hii hali ya ubaguzi inapelekwa mpaka kwa watoto na matokeo yake wanaanza kuwa na matabaka miongoni mwao na wanaweza kusema sitacheza na fulani au fulani kwa sababu ni mkristo na mtoto ataishia kucheza na watoto wa kiislamu tu.
[85] Mgogo is a member of the Gogo ethnic group from Dodoma region.
[86] Nilikwenda kuomba vyombo vya msikiti wa mgogo ambaye yeye ni shekhe pale. Lakini ningekuwa huko Yombo wasingenipa hata sufuria, wangeniona mimi ni kafiri.
[87] Wanasema hawawezi kuazima vyombo vyangu. Ukimuuliza kwa nini? Atasema kwa sababu unapika nguruwe. Hata kama ninakura nguruwe lakini huwanaosha vyombo hivyo baada ya

tend to be generally 'uncompromising' when it comes to their principles. For this participant the utensils are clean after being washed; for the Muslim they remain tainted because something forbidden has been cooked in them.

As a way of easing tension Christian participants generally agreed that whenever Muslims guests were around they let them do the slaughtering to avoid unnecessary suspicions and friction. As one elderly female participant pointed out, "I can slaughter my chicken, but for the sake of love I ask a Muslim to do the honours so that we can share the meal."[88]

Death and funeral ceremonies
"Muslims also attend Christian funerals."

All participants confirmed that they have participated in or attended Muslim funerals. This was also reported by one elderly female participant, who said, "When I discovered he is dead, I told them [relatives who happened to be Muslims] to go and report the matter to the police and I volunteered to stay in the room with the deceased, but when the Muslims came they ordered me to leave the room. They asked since when did a woman start staying with a corpse?"[89] Although all Christian participants confirmed that they had been involved in Muslim funerals, they admitted that the involvement was limited. The lady mentioned above indicated that women were not allowed to touch the corpse, let alone lay it out. Those who did so were looked down upon by Muslims and considered ignorant of Islamic values, which forbid women to touch the corpse.

Other participants added that even Muslim females were not allowed to go to the cemetery for burial. "In our comrades' funerals there are principles forbidding women to go to the cemetery,"[90] an educated male participant explained. The participant's omission of the object and his use of a general word instead – 'our comrades' – makes his statement inclusive and open to different interpretations. For instance, in some interpretations one's comrades could be fellow Christians. Moreover, in so doing she maintains politeness and harmony with other members of the group.

---

kupika.

[88] Mimi kuku wangu ninaweza nikamchinja mwenyewe na yeye akaja akala, lakini kwa upendo nisimkwaze naona bora nimwambie yeye (muislamu) aje atuchinjie ili tule wote.

[89] Ikatokea kwamba mtu amekufa na mimi nikawa wa kwanza kugundua hivyo nikawaambia waende Polisi wakaripoti wakati mimi naendelea kukaa na maiti walipokuja waislam wakaniamuru kutoka, nami nikamwambia ukae na maiti, toka lini mwanammke akakaa na maiti?

[90] Kwenye misiba ya wenzetu [waislamu] kuna masharti yanayo wazuia wanawake kwenda makaburini kuzika.

For Christian men the situation is different. "We participate in the funeral regardless of religious differences,"[91] an educated youth said. "When going for burial us Christians join Muslims, to the extent of copying their prayers."[92] This shows that Christian men are accommodative to the extent of saying Muslim prayers.

Elderly female participants said that "Muslims also attend Christian funerals. But they [Muslims] say Christians are buried with their faeces".[93] Such Muslim utterances were regarded by Christian participants as irresponsible and insensitive, hence the lament of an elderly female participant: "I mean they are selfish; they see themselves as better than others; I mean, they believe they know religion better than Christians".[94] Here the participants were making what Bourdieu (1991:220) would call a practical classification, namely superior versus inferior. In other words, Muslims were said to consider themselves to be "better" believers than Christians.

Clothing
"Other Muslims wear normal dress."

Female participants complained about not being allowed to rent houses from Muslims because of the clothes they wear. As one educated female youth explained, "When I was looking for a house to rent, one day I went to a particular house. I liked the house … I was wearing a skirt. The following day I went back to pay the rent. I was wearing trousers. Seeing me in pants, that woman refused to take my money, saying she won't let her house to women like me who wear trousers. Then I realised they had accepted me the previous day because I was wearing a skirt."[95] This participant regarded such treatment by Muslim landlords as discrimination on the basis of gender and religion.

Christians were said to be more permissive in regard to clothing. Participants explained that dress code was one of the conditions that Muslim house owners

---

[91] Tunashirikiana kwenye misiba bila kujali tofauti za kidini.
[92] Tukiwa tunaenda kuzika, sisi, wakristo, tunaungana na waislamu na tunaigiza hadi sala zao.
[93] Waislamu pia wanahudhuria misiba ya wakristu. Lakini wanasema wakristo wanazikwa na vinyesi.
[94] Yaani ni wabinafsi wa kujiona wao ni bora kiliko wengine; yaani wao ndio wanaijua sana dini kuliko mkristo.
[95] Sikumoja nikapelekwa na dalali kwenye nyumba moja… Nilikuwa nimeenda tu nimevaa sketi. Nikaona kile chumba nimeridhika nacho… siku ya pili nilipoenda nikawa nimevaa suruali. Jamani kisa cha kunikatalia nini? Akasema siwezi kupangisha watu kama nyie mmevaa suruali. Nikasema heee kumbe nyie siku ile mlinikubalia kwa sababu nimevaa sketi.

imposed on tenants. Another educated female youth complained, "He said here we don't allow wearing trousers, wearing mini-skirts."[96]

Female youths cited Muslims as saying that "a female's face is not allowed to be left uncovered; it should be covered. As a result some Muslim females put on a *pazia* (face veil)[97] to hide their faces."[98] "But Muslims who dress like that come from the Sunni group only; other Muslims wear normal dress."[99] This participant was explicitly questioning why a Christian woman should be required to wear a face veil when even members of other Muslim sects did not do so.

This also applied to other garbs considered typically Muslim. For example, only Sunni Muslims wear the *baibui,* as other Muslim women tend to wear normal dresses. This was said by the young uneducated female, who insisted, "Sunni Muslims wear those dresses, but other Muslims wear normal dress."[100] These women participants added that "other [Sunni] women put *vipazia* (face veils) over their faces but for the rest they wear normal dresses".[101] Participants said that Muslims who wear face veils were locally labelled as *ninja*[102] or *vipazia*. Some Christians called them *mujahidin*.[103] This latter name refers to hardened freedom fighters, religious extremists or fanatics, especially in the perception of some participants, who considered this form of dress an attempt by these Muslims to distinguish themselves from other Muslims.

Even so, participants observed that some Muslim women failed to dress respectably. Some participants claimed that there were Muslim women who deceived onlookers by wearing *baibui* on the outside while underneath they wore skimpy, indecent clothing. One elderly female participant said, "Even when I was in Zanzibar Muslim females were clever. They put on the *baibui*, but that does not

---

[96] Akasema sasa kuhusu kukaa humu ndani, haturuhusu mtu kuvaa suruali, haturuhusu kuvua kimini.
[97] These Christian participants said that Sunni females wear a curtain over their face. The 'curtain' referred to is a veil or face dress known among Muslims as hijab, which covers the entire face leaving only the eyes exposed (some cover their eyes with a transparent net).
[98] Wanaovaa vipazia ni wale wanaofunika kote na kwenye macho wanaweka kineti. (Uneducated female youth.)
[99] Waislamu suni huvaa mavazi hayo lakini wale wengine huvaa mavazi ya kawaida.
[100] Waislamu suni huvaa mavazi hayo lakini wale wengine huvaa mavazi ya kawaida.
[101] Wengine huvaa 'vipazia' lakini chini huvaa nguo za kawaida.
[102] The word Ninja has its origin in Japanese and Chinese military and spying strategies, which in the 20th century were co-opted by Japanese, Chinese and American movie artists. Participants applied the word to Muslim women wearing face veils, similar to martial artists' disguise in local videos and cinemas.
[103] Majaidina: Ni wale waislamu wanaovaa vipazia (English translation: Mujahidin are Muslims who wear curtains [hijab]).

mean that they dress respectably because underneath they only wore shorts and a blouse. If you undress her you will be surprised at the thing she has put on!"[104] This was confirmed by a young uneducated female who said, "Even among themselves there are those who wear unorthodox dresses ... they wear shorts, trousers and mini-skirts."[105]

Open air preaching (mihadhara)
"Preachers at Muslim mihadhara use very abusive language."

In the discussions some participants said that Muslim open air preachers use insulting language. One elderly female participant noted, "These open air preachers trouble my heart very much and they are big stumbling blocks, because they don't advocate what is written in their book but rather their policy is to insult the Bible and to use invective."[106] Participants charged Muslim preachers with conducting their *mihadhara* in an offensive manner because they deliberately insulted the Bible, Christians and Jesus Christ. This view was confirmed by an educated male youth, "Open air preaching is problematic; the Muslim preachers at these *mihadhara* use very abusive language against Christians."[107] However, other participants acknowledged that the practice of ridiculing other faiths in *mihadhara* was evident in both Muslim and Christian open air preaching. "You find Christian *mihadhara* ridiculing Muslims or Muslims ridiculing Christians,"[108] said one educated male participant.

Some participants said that the preachers who use abusive language "don't reside in the area".[109] This was confirmed by an educated Christian male youth, who said: "Many of the preachers at Muslim *mihadhara* are not residents of the area. For example, you will find a *mhadhara* at Kilakala, but the preachers come

---

[104] Hata wakati nikiwa Zanzibar ambapo wanapenda kuvaa mabaibui yale. Lakini wale ni wajanja sio kusema wanavaa vizuri kwani ndani utamkuta amevaa kipensi tu na kiblauzi, sasa ukimvua ndio utashangaa hicho kitu alichokivaa.

[105] Mbona hata wao wenyewe kuna ambao wanavaa nguo za ajabu ajabu bora hata za wakristo.... lakini vipedo, suruali na vimini wanavaa.

[106] Hii mihadhara ndio inaumiza moyo wangu kweli kweli na ni tatizo kubwa kwani hawa waislamu hawauzi yale yaliyoandikwa kwenye vitabu vyao lakini sera zao ni kuzalilisha Biblia na kutumia mameno ya kashfa.

[107] Mihadhara ina matatizo makubwa. Wahubiri wa mihadhara wa kiislamu hutumia maneno machafu dhidi ya wakristo.

[108] Utaweza kukuta open air preaching ya wakristo ukiwatukaa waislamu au open air preaching ya waislamu kuwatukana wakristu.

[109] Hawaishi maeneo haya.

from outside Kilakala."[110] In other words, these participants believe that outsiders do not care whether they create problems in areas where they do not reside.

The participants described the way Muslim preachers at *mihadhara* gatherings ridicule Christians. "For example, when Christians say Jesus is the Son of God, they defame Christians by saying that he was not born or when they ask who was the father of Jesus. This means they ridicule us and they see us as not right."[111]

By way of clarification an educated female youth insisted that "Muslims should talk about Mohammed and not about other religions".[112] They should learn from Christians who "are [more] knowledgeable than Muslims and this is reflected in their open air preaching, which show goodwill, unlike Muslims who sometimes even kill pigs when they see them around to infuriate the owner who happens to be a Christian."[113] Thus they should learn from Christians, who "conduct their preaching in a normal way, using KiSwahili even a Muslim could understand". [114]

Discussing the origin of *mihadhara*, participants said they started during the presidency of Ali Hassan Mwinyi. One elderly participant said, "Open air preaching started when president Ali Hassan Mwinyi became the national leader. They [Muslims] said now the government is for Muslims, therefore there is freedom to say whatever you like. Then they started to say they don't want pork; they started to insult. But during the Nyerere era this slandering did not happen."[115] This was confirmed by another participant in the same group: "When they saw a fellow Muslim had become president conflict started; during the Nyerere era this did not happen."[116]

---

[110] Ina matatizo makubwa kwa mfano wahadhiri wa mihadhara ya kiislamu mara nyingi huwa si wakazi wa maeneo husika. Mfano utakuta mhadhara unaofanyika Kilakala inakuwa na wahadhiri wa nje ya Kilakala.

[111] Mfano wakristo wanaposema Yesu ni Mwana wa Mungu huwa wanakashfu wanasema Yesu hakuzaliwa au huyo Yesu alizaliwa na nani ina maana wanakashfu na wanaona si haki.

[112] Waislamu waongelee kuhusu Muhamadi na sio dini zingine.

[113] Kwa upande wangu naona wakristo ni waelewa na hivyo mihadhara yao huwa haina lengo baya tofauti na waislamu ambao mara nyingine hudiriki hata kuua nguruwe pindi wawaonapo ili kumkomoa mfugaji huyo ambaye ni mkristo.

[114] Huwa tunaongea tu kawaida, kwa KiSwahili. Hata kama mwislamu yupo ataelewa.

[115] Mihadhara ilikuja baada ya Raisi wa awamu ya pili Rais Ally Hassani Mwinyi kuanza uongozi, wakasema sasa serikali ilikuwa ya waislamu hivyo pana uhuru wakusema wanachotaka, na ndio hapo walipoanza kusema hawataki nguruwe, wakaanza kutukana, lakini wakati wa Nyerere, kashfa hizi hazikuwepo.

[116] Baada ya kuona mwislam mwenzao kawa Rais ndio vurugu iliko anza. Enzi za Nyerere hayakuwepo.

Renting houses
"Before this open air preaching we lived nicely with our Muslim ndugu."

Participants expressed different views on the intricacies of renting houses in neighbourhoods with mixed religions. They said before the open air preaching started Christians used to rent Muslim houses without restrictions.[117] This was narrated by an elderly female participant, who said: "When I came here..., before this open air preaching, we lived nicely with our Muslim *ndugu*. I, for instance, rented a Muslim house and I stayed there for 20 years in the same house."[118] Similarly, some Christians let their houses to Muslims. "In my house I have a Muslim tenant,"[119] said one educated female youth. In all the FGDs participants said that it was common for Muslims to rent rooms in Christian houses and vice versa, because Muslims and Christians regarded each other as *ndugu*. To avoid problems with Muslim tenants some Christian landlords said they refrained from cooking or eating foods that Muslims did not approve of in their houses. This was explained by the educated female youth who happened to own a house and have a Muslim tenant: "I decided not to cook pork in the house (despite it being my house). This is because of her segregated customs; I fear I will disturb her [if I cook pork]. If I want pork, I go out and eat it there."[120]

On the whole Christian participants indicated that they did not have any problem with letting their houses to Muslims. For them the problem lay with the Muslims, who did not want to cooperate with Christian landlords. As one educated female youth explained, "When I let my house to a Muslim, I do it in peace. But while in my house, she becomes divisive. For example, if she wants to give a party for her child she goes back to her family because here there are no Muslims. But when I give a party for my child I invite her and give her an invitation card."[121]

---

[117] The Swahili version of "open air preaching" is in the plural. But, as preaching has no plural in English, we use the singular form to translate it.

[118] Pia nilipokuja hapa miaka ya nyuma pia tulikuwa tunaishi vizuri kabla ya hii mihadhara. Mimi mwenyewe nilipanga kenye nyumba ya mwislam na nimekaa humo kwa muda wa miaka 20.

[119] Kwenye nyumba yangu nina mpangaji Mwislamu.

[120] Sasa tunaishi na muislamu pale kwangu tumempangisha; lakini mimi jinsi ninavyomuona anavyojitengatenga mimi sinunui kitimoto japokuwa nyumba ni yangu. Si nunui kuja kukaanga mle. Naona kama vile na mkera yeye. Kwa hiyo kama nataka kula kiti moto nikale huko pembeni.

[121] Mimi nikimpangisha muislamu na kuwa na amani kabisa. Lakini sasa anapofika pale tena sasa yeye ndio anaanza kunitenga tena mimi. Sasa unakuta kama anataka kufanya sherehe ya mwanae yeye anarudi tena kwao, kwasababu pale hakuna waislamu wenzake. Lakini ukikuta mimi ninasherehe ya mwanangu na mkaribisha na kadi nampa na mwambia njoo.

Even so, some Christian participants were wary of the problems such house sharing could cause even when unintended. One educated male youth said, "Staying in the same house can sometimes lead to disharmony between Muslims and Christians, especially when a Christian decides to eat pork which is considered *haraam* by Muslims. This could create ... problems and fear on the part of the Muslim [i.e. his child could be given *haraam* meat by Christians]."[122]

Some participants said animosity between Muslims and Christians was exacerbated by the introduction of open air preaching. "There was a period when Muslims were discouraged [through *mihadhara*] from renting in Christian houses, because they [Christians] are *kafirs*,"[123] said an educated Christian male youth. This was also noted in the statement of the elderly lady noted above that "Before this open air preaching we lived nicely with our Muslim *ndugu*."[124]

Some participants spoke about Islamic doctrine. "They have certain things which are very awkward. Maybe their doctrine prohibits them,"[125] said one Christian female youth. Some participants spoke about living together as a nation, as Tanzanians with a common identity: "But we are Tanzanians; we are supposed to love each other and cooperate."[126] This participant accused Muslims of generally failing to cooperate with Christians, although this view was not shared by all participants.

After all, despite some fears, Muslims generally live together harmoniously with Christians. Some participants said most Muslims in their area did not own houses. As one participant pointed out, "Here at Kilakala there are more Muslims than Christians, but many Christians live in their own houses while Muslims live in rented houses."[127] This participant ended up alluding to Christians' supposed financial superiority over Muslims, which enables them to afford building houses.

---

[122] Kuishi pamoja kunaweza kuleta mtafaruku kati ya mwislamu na mkristu hasa pale mkristu anapoamua kula nguruwe ambayo ni haraamu kwa mwislamu. Hii inaweza kuleta matatizo na woga kwa upande wa mwislamu kwamba watoto wake wanaweza kulishwa nyama haraam kwa mkristo.
[123] Kuna kipindi waislamu walishawishiwa kutokwenda kupanga kwenye nyumba za wakristo kwa kuwa wao (wakristo) ni makafiri.
[124] Kabla yah ii mihadhara tuliishi vizuri tu na ndugu zetu wakristo.
[125] Wanavitu vyao ambavyo ni vya ajabu; labda vitabu vyao vinawakataza.
[126] Lakini sisi ni Watanzania tunatakiwa kupendana na kushirikiana.
[127] Kwa hapa Kilakala waislamu ni wengi kushinda wakristo, lakini wakristo wengi ndio wanaoishi katika nyumba zao tofauti na waislamu ambao huishi katika nyumba za kupanga.

Superstitious beliefs
"Domesticator of evil spirits."

In the FGDs participants claimed that Muslims were superstitious. Some participants cited personal experiences to support their view. An elderly female participant narrated: "But, when I came to Dar es Salaam in 1979 ... I stayed at Mtoni [street] where the Ndengereko, who are Muslims, live... a [neighbour's] child (boy) got lost."[128] The lady continued, "We searched for him for the first and the second day without success. The child was found in a dam on the third day only after the threat of bringing in the field force [Police Field Force Unit] was used. The child's body had no tongue, no eyes and his private parts were also missing. After the discovery of the missing child the father and mother disappeared the same night ... "[129] This Christian woman spoke about an event which involved Muslim parents who were suspected of practising witchcraft by sacrificing their own son in order to get a promotion at work.

This participant believes that Islam allows the practice of witchcraft, as she continued, "then we saw our Muslim comrades believing a religion which [purportedly] allows the slaughtering of a child for [the superstitious belief of getting a] promotion to high rank!"[130] However, she uses polite words like 'our comrades' to mitigate the negative connotation towards Muslims and in so doing achieves harmony with Muslim believers.

Many other participants called Muslims superstitious."Islamic religion has so many superstitious beliefs – ooh, if a Muslim reads *albadir* [bad omen] it could cause mental instability, or death. If they follow their doctrine, they can harm you, you can wither and die,"[131] said a young Christian female respondent. Her statement confirms the accusation by using the affirmative mode ('can') and reproducing the superstition in Muslims belief; for that reason some Christians call Muslims *wafuga majini* (domesticators of 'evil spirits'), something that many talk about indirectly because it has not been proven.

---

[128] Lakini mimi nilivyokuja Dar es Salaam 1979 ... mimi nilifikia Mtoni ambako wanaishi Wandengereko ... ambao ni waislamu ... Mtoto mmoja alipotea.

[129] Tukamtafuta siku ya kwanza ya pili bila mafanikio. Siku ya tatu anasema analeta field force, ndio sasa mtoto anakwenda kuonekana bwawani. Hana ulimi, macho, sehemu za siri pia hana. Na baada ya kumpata yule mtoto, baba na mama yake ikawabidi watoloke usiku na hawakuonekana tena pale.

[130] Sasa ndio tukaona haya ya waislamu wenzetu ndio dini yenyewe inayoruhusu uchinje mtoto ndio upate cheo!

[131] Dini ya kiislamu ina mambo ya kishirikina sana mara ooh! mtu akisoma albadiri anakuwa kichaa, anakufa... .lakini wao wakitumia msaafu wao, wanaweza kukufanyia ubaya ukakauka.

Employment and job opportunities
"Muslims who own industries discriminate against us."

Participants pointed out that that when it comes to getting employment in Muslim controlled industries and firms, religio-centric Muslims discriminated against them. This was raised by an educated Christian female youth: "I went to ask for a job one day. I did not cover my hair, and as a result I did not get it. They told me there are no jobs."[132] She added, "If the boss is a Muslim, you will not find any Christians working in that office... [133] These Muslims who own industries discriminate against us Christians when [offering] jobs."[134]

This was confirmed by another educated female participant, who said: "There is this Barkhresa, who is well known among the people. My brother, who is a Christian – his name is Robert – went to ask for a casual job. He changed his Christian name and used an Islamic one (Hamisi) and he got the job. The following day, he went back but he could not recall the Muslim name he had used the previous day. He ended up losing the job.[135] Barkhresa, the one who sells water and biscuits, does not employ Christians, neither male nor female."[136] According to this participant some Christians conceal their religious identity when applying for jobs in firms owned by Muslims.

By contrast participants claimed that there was no religio-centrism in firms owned and run by Christians. Individuals in these firms were employed on the strength of their academic and professional qualifications as well as their work experience, not their religion. This view of Christian owned firms was expressed by an educated female youth, who said: "We, on the contrary, don't do things like that. Christian bosses will just look at the person's educational and professional certificates. They don't look at whether you are a Muslim or a Christian. Christians, therefore, are employed because of their qualifications, because we are far ahead in education."[137]

---

[132] Kwa hiyo sasa kuna siku mimi nilienda kuomba kazi pale, sikuwa nimefunga nywele nikakosa. Wakaniambia hakuna kazi.

[133] Kama utakuta boss anakuwa ni mwislamu, hukuti mkristo hata mmoja akiuza pale.

[134] Hawa waislamu wanaomiliki viwanda wanatubagua sisi wakristo kwenye kuomba kazi.

[135] Kuna huyu hapa Bakhresa, watu wote wanamjua, mimi kunamdogo wangu ambaye ni mkristu anaitwa Robert aliwahi kwenda hapo kuomba kazi alibidi ataje jina la kiislamu akapata kazi. Siku ya pili akawa amelisahau jina alilosema. Akakosa kazi. Aliaandika Hamis. Sasa alipokuwa getini akawa ajiuliza hivi jana niliandika jina gani. Akawa amekosa kazi.

[136] Yule Bakhresa anayeuza maji sijui biskuti pale hataki mkristu aombe kazi pale. Hampii. Awe wa kiume au wakike.

[137] Mkristu hatuna ubaguzi. bosi mkristu atakachoangalia tu ni elimu yako (vyeti). Katika Kwa hiyo utakapofika hapo hata angalia wewe ni muislamu au mkristu. Atakuajili tu. Wakristu wengi

Christian participants accused Muslims of idling at home after completing their secondary studies instead of finding something useful to do in the meantime. "An educated Christian who has completed just form four or six and could not get employment would find something to keep him busy and earn an income, but that is not the case with a Muslim, who will be sitting at home without doing anything despite being educated; instead he will be playing *bao*,[138] a tradition of the coastal people."[139] This statement pictured Christians as enterprising [secular] and Muslims as not enterprising, which conformed to the accepted view of Christian superiority.

Because of these assumptions some Christians ridicule Muslims by calling them lazy people (*mdebwedo*). Indeed, one educated male youth noted, "Nowadays Christians have found words with which to ridicule Muslims; they call them *mdebwedo*."[140] The word '*mdebwedo*' means lazy, but it can also mean homosexual/gay, hence reinforcing the derogatory connotation.

Hard liners and extremists
"They may eventually take the law into their own hands"

Christian FGD participants said they lived well with Muslims in their community. As a participant put it, "Since I started staying here, I have never heard of a mosque or a church that has been set ablaze. People live together well without religio-centrism."[141] But they said that they had heard about incidents of religious extremism and fanaticism in other areas. An uneducated male participant explained, "They started fighting among themselves in mosques; you would hear at Magomeni they fought in a certain mosque."[142] According to an educated male participant this showed that "Muslims are divided among themselves. There are those who are pro-BAKWATA and another group which demonstrated when the

---

wameaajiriwa kutokana na elimu yetu sisi tuko juu sana kielimu.

[138] Bao is a board game played on a flat piece of wood.

[139] Vile vile mtu aliyesoma (mkristo) hata kama ameishia kidato cha 4 au 6 na kushindwa kupata ajira basi anauwezo wa kushughulika na kuweza kupata kipato tofauti na muislam ambaye utakuta amekaa tu nyumbani bila kujishughulisha hata kama alisoma badala yake kwa watu wa pwani utakuta anachonga bao.

[140] Sasa hivi wakristo nao wanamaneno yao ambayo ni yakuwakejeli waislamu wanawaita 'mdebwedo'.

[141] Tangu nimeanza kuishi hapa sijawahi kusikia msikiti au kanisa limechomwa moto kwa maana hiyo basi, watu tunaishi vizuri pasipo kujali tofauti zetu za kidini. (Educated male youth.)

[142] Wakaanza wenyewe kwa wenyewe kupigana msikitini mara usikie Magomeni kwenye msikiti gani wamepigana.

American president George Bush arrived for a visit in Tanzania."[143] "We see opposition [*upinzani*] among Muslims themselves. Each group regards itself as better than the other, and thus the other group is considered to have strayed [from the right path]."[144]

Extremism also occurs at an interreligious level, leading to fights between adherents of different faiths. In this regard an elderly participant lamented, "When we say, let us teach them the Bible, they demonstrate, stab [*kuwakata*] and beat up [*kuwachapa*] Christians."[145] Here the participant positioned himself as belonging to a knowledgeable group (of Christians), which wants to spread biblical knowledge. At the same time Muslims are portrayed as individuals who resist by using physical means such as beating and stabbing those who say anything different from what they know already.

Participants said that Muslims were identified by their style of dress. "Those who are very religious, who wear *vipazia* [small face veil/*hijab*] are very bad,"[146] said an uneducated female participant. She did not explain in what way these zealots were bad. She also avoided specifying their religion. But another member of the group identified most zealots as belonging to the Sunni school. She said, "Sunnis are Muslims who have long beards, they don't shave; their trousers never touch the ground."[147] According to another participant, "During Ramadan *walioshika dini* [hardline Muslims] start fasting, and then others follow."[148]

According to some participants religious fanaticism and extremist behaviour "started to emerge when Mwinyi became president".[149] During this time religious "demonstrations started"[150] or were tolerated. In public schools "children were told to wear veils".[151] This was seen by the elderly participants as "undermining

---

[143] Waislamu wenyewe wamegawanyika kati yao kuna hawa BAKWATA na kundi lingine hata kipindi Rais George Bush wa Marekani alipo wasili katika ziara yake nchini Tanzania kundi la waislamu liliandamana kutoafiki ujio wake, wakati BAKWATA hawakuwa na neno juu ya ujio huu.

[144] Hivyo basi waislamu wenyewe kwa wenyewe wanakinzana na hivyo kuwa wapinzani na kila kundi kujiona kuwa bora kuliko jingine na kuona kundi jingine linapotea. (Educated male youth.)

[145] Tukisema tuwafundishe Biblia wao wanaandamana na kuwakata wakristo na kuwachapa.

[146] Wale walioshika dini wanaovaa vipazia ndio wabaya sana.

[147] Suni ni waislamu ambao wanafuga ndevu sana, hawanyoi, suruali hazifiki chini.

[148] Waislamu walioshika dini ambayo kwenye ramadhani ndio wanaoanza wao kufunga ndio wengine wanafuatia.

[149] Baada ya kuingia Mwinyi katika urais nayo ndio ilipoanza. (Elderly female participant.)

[150] Maandamano kuanza. (Elderly female participant.)

[151] Mashuleni watoto wavae vijuba. (Elderly female participant.)

dignity and law and threatening the peace".[152] These elderly participants were surprised at the way "the government is silent".[153] "It could be that they would stand on this table and others on that table and what will happen is an exchange of blows. The government should look into this matter."[154] According to these participants the government should intervene because Christians were also "human and not God"; they "might eventually take the law into their own hands" and so destroy the existing peace[155] in Tanzania, "which is known as a peaceful country."[156]

Conclusion

In this section we analysed linguistic practice in the discourse of Christians, especially with regard to their use of words or labels to refer to Muslims and their view of Christian-Muslim relations. Christians speak about Muslims in a friendly, polite way. Participants, for example, used words such as 'friends', 'brothers' and 'sisters', 'comrades' (*ndugu*), and 'fellows' to refer to Muslims. The polite labels signified a friendly relationship and a desire to opt for a civic identity.

On the other hand participants also classified Muslims impolitely, sometimes even harshly. They said, for instance, that Muslims were polygamists, cruel, selfish, discriminatory, hypocritical, mistrustful, cunning, superstitious and indifferent to education. Muslims were accused of seeing themselves as better than others and of being lazy and intolerant. Other labels used indirectly include *Al Qaeda*, *mujahidins* and *mdebwedo*, all with negative connotations, indicating divisions between Muslims and Christians.

Overall the participants described relations between Muslims and Christians as good, cooperative. Areas where this was possible were interreligious marriages, funerals, good neighbourliness, sharing accommodation and personal friendships. Participants also described some Muslims as religio-centric people who would not compromise on any point for the sake of good relations with Christians. They tended to discriminate against Christians when it came to interreligious marriages, food, letting houses and job opportunities.

The younger generation of Christian respondents emphasised the need for tolerance in interreligious marriages, food sharing and dress. This is understandable,

---

[152] Tunaona kwamba wenzetu wanavunja heshima/sheria na wanahatarisha amani.
[153] Lakini serikali imenyamaza kimya.
[154] Kuna wengine watasimama mwingine meza hii mwingine meza ile kitakachoendelea ni ngumi tu. Serikali iangalie kwa kweli.
[155] Sisi ni wanadamu sio Mungu, tunaweza tukachukua sheria mkononi na hivyo kuvunja amani.
[156] Katika nchi hii ambayo inasemwa kuwa ina amani. (Elderly female participant.)

because the younger generation was brought up in a different environment (at school, work and other places where they had more freedom of choice) where the mixture of values – both religious and cultural – was greater than in their parents' day.

In general and in comparison with Muslim participants, Christians spoke about Muslims more impolitely than Muslims spoke about Christians. They also spoke more about nationalism and the secular state than Muslim did (see chapter two).

3.2. Analysis of discursive practice

The second step is to analyse discursive practice: the production, distribution and consumption of text. As noted in the general introduction, participants draw on other texts stored in their long-term memory when producing and consuming text; that is, they make use of what they already know. In this section we analyse intertextuality and interdiscursivity.

The main focus is on connecting linguistic practice with social practice. We are interested in the sources of the participants' utterances. In other words, when talking about Muslims participants tended to refer to different sources they had come across at some time. In the discussions, for example, participants referred to discourses such as open air preaching, the government, political parties and so on. Participants also referred to people (Mwinyi, Nyerere and Mkapa), prophets (Mohammad and Jesus) as well as sacred books (the Qur'an and the Bible). Their utterances will be triangulated with information from other sources such as local newspapers, open air preaching and key informant interviews.

Superstitions and witchcraft
"I hear from people that they domesticate evil spirits."

In the FGDs participants spoke about Muslim beliefs and accused Muslims of being superstitious. In the previous section we spoke about the Christian lady who narrated a story about Muslim parents who were said to have offered their son in order to get promotion to a higher rank. The same accusation of superstition and witchcraft was put forward by a key informant, who referred to others. "I hear from people that they domesticate evil spirits [*majini*] … one sister [Muslim] once told me that there are two types of *majini*, good and bad ones."[157] The partic-

---

[157] Nasikia kwa watu kuwa wanafuga majini … … ila kuna dada mmoja mwislam alishawahi kuniambia kuna majini ya aina mbili mema na mabaya. (Educated university student.)

ipants' use of the passive voice and indirect expressions indicate that this reality is based on rumour ("I hear from people") and stereotyping of Muslims, not necessarily on irrefutable evidence or fact. The perpetuation of the stereotyping and this rumour generates fear among Christians, hence creates division between Muslims and Christians.

Such stereotyping is exploited by religious opportunists like Christian open air preachers, who make unfounded statements and allegations to suit their nefarious agenda. One Christian preacher alleged, "All those people are sorcerers; all of them are witches."[158] Similar superstitious beliefs are also be attributed to African customs to which many Tanzanians – Christian and Muslim – subscribe. As was described in chapter one, when entering Tanzania, Muslims in general were more tolerant of indigenous beliefs and practices, since they did not come as missionaries but as merchants.

Preachers also attacked Islamic symbols such as the Qur'an by saying, "the Qur'an descended to retard people mentally ... this explains why in a region with many Muslims there are many people who are mentally sick."[159] This was reiterated in another *mhadhara* where the preacher said: "The day before yesterday Muslims read *Kunut* - they call it a destruction prayer – in order to destroy us who are running *mihadhara* here, but we are blessing them instead."[160]

Open air preaching (mihadhara)
"Muslim open air preachers use very abusive language about Christians."

Most participants in Christian FGDs agreed that "open air preaching is problematic, Muslim open air preachers use very abusive language about Christians."[161] An elderly female participant said, "Muslim preachers jeer at and despise the Christian religion."[162] This was confirmed by key informants in their interviews. Indeed, one key informant said, "Those open air preachers ridicule Christianity; one will read the Bible and the other will say, eeh, Jesus did this and you are not doing it. The goal is to ridicule Christians."[163] To most participants open air preachers

---

[158] Excerpt from a tape-recorded mhadhara conducted by a group called Christian Power at Mbagalla, Dar es Salaam on 1 January 2008.
[159] Ibid.
[160] Excerpt from a tape-recorded mhadhara conducted at Mbagalla, Dar es Salaam on 29 December 2007.
[161] Swahili translation is footnoted in open air preaching section.
[162] Wanaichimba na kuidharau dini ya kikristo.
[163] Ile Mihadhara ni ya kutukana dini ya kikristo mwingine atasoma Biblia na mwingine anapokea eeh Yesu alifanya hivi na wao mbona hawafanyi hivi. Kwa hiyo inakuwa ya kutukana wakristo.

foment hatred between Muslims and Christians. "I see *mihadhara* only bring hatred,"[164] said this key informant.

The participants noted that Jesus was focal in Muslims' open air preaching. Preachers at *mihadhara* sometimes used audio-tapes with distorted information on the life and teachings of Jesus to convince members of the audience of the authenticity of their teachings. Such exaggerated, sometimes fabricated information about Jesus annoyed Christian participants. One of them said, "Yesterday I hated it when they brought a tape which said Jesus entered a mosque, while we read in the scriptures that Jesus entered the synagogue and never the mosque."[165]

Participants also reminded each other that Muslims' open air preaching have prompted Christians to launch their own *mihadhara* to counter the challenges of the Muslims. As one key informant put it, "Christians' open air preaching are a response to Muslims, who started these gatherings first. They [Muslims] have ridiculed us until they were tired of defaming the Bible. So we decided to respond by teaching the correct interpretation."[166] Nevertheless, participants admitted that it was difficult for Christians to challenge the Qur'an because "it is written in a language they don't understand".[167] This was confirmed by a key informant who said,[168] "For Christians it will be difficult to challenge the Qur'an because of the language barrier ... therefore there will be nothing or less for Christians to ridicule."[169]

Generally Christian participants noted that open air preaching tended to be negative. They end up causing conflict in the community. This was supported by a key informant who recollected: "They [Muslims] are stirring up trouble because they go around everywhere. I hear the saved [born-again Christians] also have

---

[164] Mhadhara naona unaleta chuki.
[165] Mimi jana nilichukia sana kwani kwenye majira ya saa nne uliletwa mkanda ulioeleza kwamba Yesu aliingia msikitini wakati kwenye maandiko tunasoma kwamba Yesu aliingia kwenye Sinagogi na si msikitini na hivyo kuwafanya watu washangilie ilhali Maneno yale hayakuwa na ukweli wowote. (Educated youth male participant).
[166] Mihadhara ya kikristu ilianzishwa kuwa jibu waislamu ambao ndio walianza mwanzo. Wametukashifu mpaka wakachoka kuikashifu Biblia. Ndio maana tukaona tuwafundishe ukweli wa tafasiri.
[167] Imeandikwa kwenye lugha ambayo hawaielewi.
[168] Njozi (2006:260) admits, "Even today there are very few Islamic publications in KiSwahili". Njozi (2006:255-256) suggests that the use of KiSwahili was "to large extent affected by the adversial relationship between Islam and Christianity" because "the Christian missionaries were initially, strongly opposed to the use of KiSwahili as a medium of instruction in schools on the ground that KiSwahili promoted Islamic values".
[169] Kwa mkristo naona ni vigumu kukosoa Koran kwasababu ya lugha iliyoandikwa mtu mwingine hawezi kuielewa kwahiyo kukashfu kutoka kwa wakristo hapo inakuwa ndogo au chache sana.

their open air preaching which answer those [of Muslims]. It is just chaos. Therefore these [*mihadhara*] are not helping us; we are courting trouble."[170] Another key informant was worried, especially about the language Christian open air preachers used. He reminded the author that, "The Christians are answering. I hear words like ooh, you Muslims, when you die... you wash the person ... I'm afraid of what will happen in the future."[171] This has begun to cause conflict in the community, as this key informant observed: "After teaching them they demonstrated and many people [Christian speakers] were caught and put in cells."[172]

Some key informants also said that most open air preaching, both Christian and Muslim, failed to achieve the intended objectives. Referring to the open air preaching one key informant noted, "Most of the time open air preaching misses the original objective, which is to educate and help build relations with others; ... subsequently the *mihadhara* are used as platforms for argumentation and translating things they don't [even] know."[173] Another key informant confirmed, "Truly, open air preachers should give speeches aimed at educating a person but what happens in these *mihadhara* amounts to slander. If it is a Christian *mhadhara*, then they will be slandering Islam and if it is a Muslim *mhadhara*, then they will be slandering Christianity."[174] He even appealed to the government to ban open air services because they fomented hatred between Muslims and Christians. This also came up in the group discussions. An elderly woman said, "We don't want

---

[170] Mimi naona hawa wanatibua kwa sababu wanazunguka kila mahala. Nasikia pia Walokole nao wana mihadhara ya kuwajibu wao, basi ni vurugu tuu. Kwa hiyo haya kwa kweli hayatusaidii, tanatibua. (Key informant R.)

[171] Ninavyosikia wakristo wameanza kujibu .... Ninasikia kwamba Oh, nyie waislamu mnapokufa mnamuosha mtu ... nahofia mambo kama haya yatakuwaje kwa siku za mbeleni. (Key informant Mzee MT.)

[172] Mihadhara ya kikristo ipo lakini hii imejibiwa baada ya wenyewe kuanza, wamekashifu mpaka wamechoka kuichafua Biblia hivyo na sisi tukaamua kuwajibu kwa kuwafundisha sivyo hivyo wanavyoelewa wao. Baada ya kufundishwa, wao wakaandamana na watu wengi wakashikwa na kuwekwa ndani. (Key informant Ch.)

[173] Mihadhara mara nyingi iko nje ya lengo ingawa maana yake ni kuelimishana, kurekebishana lakini kinaendelea kuwa na ubishani watu wanatafsiri kitu ambacho hakijui. (Key informant M.)

[174] Kwa kweli mihadhara haitoi speech za kumuelimisha mtu isipokuwa kinachoongelewa kwenye mihadhara hiyo ni kashfa. Kama ni mhadhara wa kikristo basi itakuwa anakashifu uislamu na kama ni mhadhara wa kiislamu nao utakashifu ukristo. Kwa hiyo mimi ningeomba serikali iangalie hilo na pengiene ingepiga marufuku Mihadhara hiyo kwa sababu haina maana na haimuelimishi mtu na sana inajenga chuki baina ya upande huu na upande huu kitu ambacho sio kizuri. (Key informant Z.)

open air preaching, we don't want destruction of peace, we want to live like now, loving and supporting each other."[175]

She was supported by other participants, who said, "Open air preaching leads to bad relations in the sense that *mihadhara* are misinterpreted by the people."[176] FGD participants also made reference to the effect of *mihadhara* utterances on contemporary society: "When you insult another fellow (comrade), and s/he happens not to have patience, they could come to blows."[177] That is, it could lead to fighting. The participant used an inclusive, polite word 'comrade', reminding the group members of typical *ujamaa* vocabulary, to maintain the status quo of harmony and peaceful citizenship. And a Christian key informant explained, "It is because our counterparts, the Muslims, are the ones destroying this relationship by thinking that they have more rights than others."[178] The key informant provided another reason for Muslims' attitude towards *mihadhara*: "For example, Muslims remind us that they go to *mihadhara* to defend the Qur'an, which is not correct."[179] It also happened that when Christians want to speak at Muslims' *mihadara* to help them with the correct interpretation of Scripture they start chaos. One elderly participant referred to her son's participation in the open air preaching: "One day my son Joseph went to argue with them. They started throwing sand and stones at him. One of them pulled him away and shouted that you will be killed."[180]

A similar sentiment was repeatedly declared by a Christian open air preacher: "...every day they create chaos in our open air meetings." This preacher quoted the Islamic teaching that "they are instructed by Muhammad: fight the *kafirs* that are near you." According to this Christian preacher "Muslims consider non-Muslims *kafir*". Christian preachers believed that Muslims were instructed by "Muhammad to make Christians their enemy ... Inwardly they are enemies of Christians," he maintained.[181]

Because of such hardline comments key Christian informants feared that *mi-*

---

[175] Sisi bwana hatutaki Mihadhara, hatutaki uvunjwaji wa amani sisi tunataka kuishi kama tulivyo tupendane, tusaidiane.
[176] Mihadhara inapelekea mahusiano mabaya kwa sababu watu wanaitafasiri vibaya.
[177] Kwani wanapokashifu mwenzako na yeye akawa hana subira huwa ndio mwanzo wa ngumi na mapambano.
[178] Wenzetu waislam ndo wanaharibu haya mahusiano maana wanajihesabia haki sana kuliko wengine. (Key informant C.)
[179] Mfano waislam wanasema naenda kuitetea Qur'an wakati sio sahihi. (Key informant C.)
[180] Mwanangu Joseph siku moja kaenda kubishana nao na wakaanza kumtupia mchanga na mawe na mmoja akamvuta akamwambia utauwawa. (Elderly woman.)
[181] Excerpt from a tape-recorded mhadhara conducted by a group called Christian Power in Mbagalla, Dar es Salaam, 1 January 2008.

hadhara on both sides of the spectrum would create further chaos and conflict in the community: "The open air preaching will lead to problems." They remembered that "at the *mihadhara* there is no security; stones are thrown at Christians. This is fighting."[182]

Other participants referred to *mihadhara* positively, insisting that they should not be banned because of their educational nature. As one educated youth reminded, "Open air preaching and crusades I think should continue because they help educate those who don't understand their religion's directives."[183] A key informant said, "*Mihadhara* are good but they should be conducted with respect for the law of the land, which governs open air preaching and demonstrations, especially religious ones",[184] hence "the most important thing is for the government to supervise open air meetings"[185] and ban preachers who ridicule others, such as those of "Simba Ulanga and Mazinge whose open air preaching ridicules other religions ... this should not be condoned."[186]

Participants also referred to the educational level of the audience. One key informant said, "First the people who attend these open air preaching have a low level of education; therefore they misinterpret"[187] the message. Another key informant said that Muslims should use *mihadhara* to encourage their audiences to get more formal education, as Christians do. Speaking for Muslims, the participant pointed out, "We Muslims should go to school and encourage our children to go to school to read because we are backward ... but ... they are pulling themselves back instead of going forward. I think *mihadhara* should be for educating one another."[188]

Referring to Muslim preachers, the participants claimed that the radical preachers were sponsored by foreigners. A Christian key informant said, "I don't

---

[182] Mihadhara hii itatupeleka pabaya. Kwenye mihadhara hakuna ulinzi, wakristo wanatupiwa mawe sasa huu si ugomvi? (Key informant Mzee Ch.)

[183] Mihadhara na mikutano nadhani iendelee kuwepo kwani inasaidia kuelimsha mtu asiye fahamu dini yake ina muongozo gani.

[184] Mihadhara ni mizuri lakini inabidi kuheshimu sheria za nchi zinazosimamia mihadhara na maandamano hasa katika dini. (Key informant Mr Man.)

[185] Suala la msingi ni serikali kusimamia malengo ya mihadhara.

[186] Simba Ulanga na Mazinge wao huiendesha mihadhara kwani hukashifu dini za watu wengine na hivyo hii ndio yenye matatizo na hivyo isiwepo. (Educated male youth.)

[187] Kwanza watu wanaohudhuria hii mihadhara elimu yao ni duni kwahiyo wanatafsiri vibaya. (Key informant Mzee Ch.)

[188] Mimi nilikuwa nafikiria watu wangekuwa wanaongelea habari zao kwamba sisi waislamu tunapaswa kwenda shule na kuwahimiza watoto wetu kwenda shule wasome kwani tumechelewa na hivyo tukimbilie lakini matokeo yake wanazidi kurudishana nyuma badala ya kusonga mbele. Nilikuwa nafikiria kwamba mihadhara iwe ya aina hiyo ya kufundishana.

see them as *wanasiasa kali* [extremists] but as people who are employed to stir up [conflict]."[189] In the same vein an educated male participant said that "the people who conduct these open air services have been commissioned"[190] to do so. He continued by identifying the alleged sponsors of Muslim preachers: "I think the rich Arabs are the ones who employ [the preachers] to do that because they [Arabs] cannot come to do it themselves."[191] This is what FGD participants also referred to, namely that *mihadhara* preachers tended to come from outside the community: "Many of the preachers at Muslim open air services are not resident in the area."[192] This was confirmed in the educated male FGD, where one participant said: "This outside interference involving *mihadhara* issues will discourage Christians from coexisting with Muslims in future."[193]

Repeatedly participants put open air preaching in a business context. An uneducated female youth remembered this worrying trend as follows: "Truly open air preaching is destructive because it does not have the purpose of spreading religion. They [preachers] do business and therefore they propagate many lies ... at the end they say we want [two thousand shillings] ... they will collect about seventy thousand [shillings] for their services. Then they divide the money among themselves. Therefore this is just healing hunger [*kuganga njaa*, survival strategy]!"[194] This was confirmed by an educated male participant: "The people who conduct this open air preaching have been sent [to perform a task with payment in mind]; therefore they conduct *mihadhara* as a business."[195]

Participants claimed that open air services have been turned into political plat-

---

[189] Mimi sioni kwamba wana siasa kali, naona ni kama wameajiriwa ili kuvuruga mambo. (Key informant Mzee x Kilakala.)

[190] Watu wanaoendesha mihadhara huwa wametumwa na hivyo kufanya mihadhara kuwa kama biashara. (Educated male participant.)

[191] Naona ni Waarabu wenye uwezo ndio ambao wamewaajiri wafanye hivyo kwani hawawezi (Waarabu) kuja kufanya hivyo wao wenyewe. (Key informant Mzee x Kilakala.)

[192] Ina matatizo makubwa kwa mfano wahadhiri wa mihadhara ya kiislamu mara nyingi huwa si wakazi wa maeneo husika. Mfano utakuta mhadhara unaofanyika Kilakala inakuwa na wahadhiri wa nje ya Kilakala.

[193] Sababu ambazo zinaweza kufanya wakristo kushindwa kukaa na waislamu kwa miaka ijayo ni hizi external interference ambazo zinahusisha mambo ya mihadhara.

[194] Kwa kweli mihadhara inabomoa kwani unakuta lengo la kutangaza dini halipo, wao wanafanya biashara kwa hiyo uongo unakuwa mwingi ... Utakuta pale wanawachangisha hela hata zikifika 70,000/= halafu wanaenda kugawana kwa hiyo ni kama kuganga njaa.

[195] Watu wanaoendesha mihadhara huwa wametumwa na hivyo kufanya mihadhara kuwa kama biashara.

forms. As a Christian key informant put it, "Now *mihadhara* have become like politics, like opposition parties, and have nothing to do with religion any more."[196]

In the FGDs participants referred to open air preaching and Muslim preachers at these gatherings as the root cause of conflict and unnecessary confrontational arguments in the community. Similar views of open air preaching were aired by key informants and in the preaching of Christian open air preachers. Participants in the FGDs also referred to other social activities and institutions such as the police and crime. Some went so far as to call Muslims criminals. The same accusation was made by Christian open air preachers and key informants.

Gender relations and polygamy
"Islam discriminates against women"

Participants in FGDs referred to gender relations, especially in the context of religious practice. They said that females were subject to gender inequality in Tanzania. They regularly pointed out that the way females dress could either give or deny them access to, for example, housing or employment. "Seeing me in a pair of trousers that woman refused to take my money. She said, 'I won't let my house to a person who wears trousers.'"[197] In similar vein an educated Christian female reminded, "They tend to discriminate against us. For instance, if you go wearing trousers or a mini-skirt they won't allow you to rent [their house]."[198] For these Christian participants refusing to let a woman rent a house because of her dress amounted to gender discrimination.

Most Christian participants also averred that polygamy, which is allowed in Islam, was discrimination against females. A secondary school teacher used the word 'polygamy' when referring to prophet Muhammad's wives and concubines. Similar sentiments were expressed by pastor Godwin Dihigo, citing a verse from the Qur'an: "When you read this [Islamic] verse you realise that Muslim women are linked to plantations … the interpretation of this verse is that the owner of a farm is free to use it as he pleases."[199] Christian participants maintained that Muslim men tended to regard women as inferior to men.

---

[196] Mihadhara kwa sasa imekuwa kama siasa kama vyama vya upinzani na sio dini tena. (Key informant Mzee Ch.)
[197] The KiSwahili translation is footnoted in the house renting section.
[198] Wnatubagua sisi. Kwa mfano ukienda umevaa suruali au kimini hawawezi kukupangisha.
[199] Excerpt from Msema Kweli, 29 July – 4 August 2007, p. 13. Pastor Godwin Dihigo, under the heading "Yanayowatatiza Waislam juu ya Wakristu" (literally: Things which perplex Muslims about Christians).

Christians claimed that Muslim women were discriminated against even in prayers. This was stated by a preacher: "When they are menstruating Muslim women are not supposed to pray or during Ramadan they are not supposed to fast."[200] He also claimed that the Qur'an portrays women as 'stupid'. On the other hand, he defended Christianity: "Today you tell us that women are stupid! Maybe Muslim women and not Christian ones." Here the preacher was trying to remember what he saw as the difference between Muslim and Christian women. To him Christian women were respected, not discriminated against, and treated considerately.

Christians who accused Muslims of discriminating against women with reference to the prophet Mohammad have been perceived as ridiculing Muslims and some were punished for such utterances. On 7 August 2007 *Mtanzania* (p. 3) reported: "A teacher who ridiculed the prophet is suspended."[201] This Christian teacher was working at Usagara Secondary School in Tanga region. He had uttered words referring to prophet Muhammad when teaching in class that "Islam discriminates against women and the prophet Muhammad married four wives and [had] five concubines". Consequently he was suspended from his job, because he was perceived by Muslim students at Usagara as ridiculing prophet Mohammad.

Crime statistics and criminal behaviour
"In the crime files Muslims win."

Referring to crime, participants implicitly and explicitly voiced concern about the high rate of crime and criminal activities in their community. In the educated male group one respondent reported, "I believe Muslims are not tolerant and do bad things."[202] The same was testified at a Christian *mhadhara*, where a preacher told his audience: "...these policemen know; if you go to a police post, in the crime files Muslims win. If you go to court, Muslim cases lead ... These are international statistics"[203] and "this is why we say Muhammad brought the terrorist doctrine... [It] is a person who teaches evil and enmity in society..."[204] Such

---

[200] Excerpt from a tape-recorded mhadhara conducted by Moses Ndimbo at Mwembeyanga, Dar es Salaam, 2007.

[201] Mtanzania, 7 August 2007, p. 3. "Ester Mbussi and Hamisa Maganga; Mwalimu aliyemkashifu mtume asimamishwa (literally: Teacher who ridiculed the Prophet suspended).

[202] Ninaamini kuwa waislamu sio wavimulivu sana, na niwatenda maovu. (Educated male youth.)

[203] Excerpt from a mhadhara at Mwembe Yanga, Dar es Salaam, 27 December 2007.

[204] Excerpt from a tape-recorded mhadhara conducted by a group called Christian Power at Mbagalla, Dar es Salaam, 1 January 2008.

statements could be construed by other believers as insulting Islam and its prophet Muhammad, and hence create disharmony in the community.

BAKWATA, Muslim groups and George Bush's visit to Tanzania
"Muslims are divided among themselves."

Participants referred to the Muslim umbrella organisation known by its KiSwahili acronym, BAKWATA, and its dealings with Muslims. Educated male participants said, "Muslims are divided among themselves; there are those who recognise BAKWATA and another group [that does not]." They remembered that this "other group demonstrated when US president George Bush arrived for his visit to Tanzania, while BAKWATA was not opposed to that visit."[205] They added that "BAKWATA is believed [by a cross section of Muslims] to be a government body; even its schools are not considered Islamic, hence their lack of recognition among Muslims."[206]

God, prophets (Mohammad, Jesus and Moses) and holy books
"Muslims should talk about Mohammad and not speak about other religions."

Participants drew upon religious scriptures such as the Bible and the Qur'an. Referring to the Bible, an educated female participant said, "Using the Bible as a directive, the Old Testament has documented all *haraam* food."[207] The participant then explained the reason for listing all these foods. She also referred to God, Moses and Jesus in her statements: "I think God had a purpose in testing people during Moses' era… When Jesus came all food became *halal*." To her, therefore, "*haraam* [foods] are those which almighty God doesn't like, and not just pork as Muslims believe, while ignoring many *haraam* things which God doesn't like".[208]

---

[205] Waislamu wenyewe wamegawanyika kati yao kuna hawa BAKWATA na kundi lingine hata kipindi Rais George Bush wa Marekani alipo wasili katika ziara yake nchini Tanzania kundi la waislamu liliandamana kutoafiki ujio wake, wakati BAKWATA hawakuwa na neno juu ya ujio huu. (Educated male participant.)

[206] Kundi la BAKWATA linaaminika kuwa ni la kiserikali na hivyo hata shule zao hazionekani kama nizakiislamu, na hivyo kutotambulika mbele ya waislamu. (Educated male participant.)

[207] Kwa kutumia muogozo wa Biblia (Agano la Kale) wameorodhesha v yakula haramu.

[208] Ikiwa nipamoja na nguruwe. Mimi nadhani kuwa Mungu alikuwa na kusudio la kuwajaribu wanadamu kwa kipindi kile cha Musa tunaona baada ya ujio wa Yesu vyakula vyote ni halali. Haramu ni kile ambacho Mwenyezi Mungu hakipendi na sio nguruwe kama waislamu wanavyoamini huku wakisahau mengine mengi ambayo Mungu hayapendi kwa kuwa ni haramu.

Referring to the prophet Mohammad, Christian participants said "Muslims should talk about Mohammad and not speak about other religions."[209] Participants also referred to a discursive incident in Denmark which concerned the prophet Mohammad. They said, "In Denmark they drew a picture of the prophet Mohammad and all Muslims worldwide demonstrated."[210]

Religion and political parties
"CCM is seen as a Christian party and CUF is followed mostly by Muslims."

Participants in FGDs referred to political parties in relation to religion, especially CUF, TLP and CCM. In the discussion with educated male youths they explained that "clashes arise at election time, in which CCM is seen as a Christian party and CUF is followed mostly by Muslims. This division leads to confrontation between the two religions."[211] Here the participant points out that religion and politics mix, believers (Muslims and Christians) being divided politically as well. According to these participants Christians were primarily associated with CCM, whereas Muslims were primarily identified with CUF. The division indicates divergence and conflict.

Participants referred to CUF as a divisive party. One educated female participant claimed, "Look at this party CUF,[212] it is dividing the nation ... I may want to leave CCM and join CUF, but I can't because I see all of them with covered bodies [*wamejitanda*] ... Just watch TV during their demonstrations, you will find that all of them have put on veils ... They are followers of CUF ... This year they could have won the election, but they lost because of religio-centrism. We Christians see that party as religiously inclined."[213] For this party clothing is an identifying criterion, wearing veils and covering the body being associated with

---

[209] Waislamu waongelee habari za Mohamedi na sio kueleza kwamba dini nyingine si kitu.

[210] Kule Denmark walipochora picha ya Mtume Mohamed na waislamu wote wakaandamana duniani. (Educated male participant.)

[211] Utata hutokea kipindi cha uchaguzi ambapo matabaka hutokea. Huwa inaonekana kwamba chama cha CCM huwa ni cha wakristo na CUF inakuwa ya waislmau zaidi, na hivyo huleta upinzani baina ya dini hizi mbili.

[212] CUF is the abbreviation of Civic United Front. It is an opposition party in Tanzania, while CCM stands for Chama Cha Mapinduzi and TLP for Tanzania Labour Party.

[213] Waislamu wanaubaguzi mkubwa ... Kama mimi hapa ningependa kabisa niihame CCM labda niende CUF na siwezi kwenda CUF naona watu wote wamejitanda. Hata ukiangalia kwenye maandamano yao hata kama wewe huendi kwenye maandamano yao wewe angalia kwenye TV utakuta wemepiga ushungi zao ... Ndio wao wanaifuata hiyo CUF ... Hata mwaka huu kingechukua ushindi kimekosa ushindi kwa sababu ya mambo ya udini ... Sisi wakristo ... lakini tunaona kile chama kimenda sana kwenye udini.

being a religio-centric Muslim. In this case clothing implies divergence or social exclusion, as the participant's statement suggests.

Participants constantly reiterated that people should separate religion from politics. A Christian key informant said, "If you join politics, leave religion. If you are a CCM member, leave politics when you go to mosque. Our country will be chaos if politics enters into religion. Because Muslims and Christians are both in CCM, they are both in CUF and in TLP"[214]. In contrast to the participant who sees CCM and CUF as respectively pro-Christian or pro-Muslim, this participant advocates a civic identity which allows Muslims and Christians to be members of the same party (be it CCM, CUF or TLP).

Government and leaders
"Mwalimu Nyerere nationalised schools which belonged to missionaries."

In the discussions participants drew their utterances from both past and present leaders of Tanzania and their handling of issues that have implications for the well-being of people of different faiths. They referred to Mwalimu Nyerere (first president of Tanzania), presidents Ali Hassan Mwinyi, Benjamin Mkapa and Jakaya Kikwete. With reference to Mwalimu Nyerere, participants praised him for maintaining peace and tranquillity in Tanzania on secular lines. Educated male participants remembered: "Mwalimu Nyerere was at the forefront to make sure that peace was not disrupted."[215] However, they noted that since his rule there have been notable transformations, which threaten to undermine the peace Tanzanians enjoy. One participant claimed, "Since 1999 the authorities lack the wisdom and the skills that Nyerere had, hence their failure to solve religious disputes which could wreck peace in Tanzania."[216]

Nyerere was reported as a person who gave all citizens the freedom to choose their own faith. Educated male participants cited this in relation to the current situation. They pointed out, "Everyone is worshipping in his faith, as the late father of

---

[214] Ukiingia kwenye siasa ukiwa umeacha dini. Habari dini siasa acha. Kama wewe ni mwana CCM ukiingia msikitini acha siasa lakini ukiingia siasa kwenye dini katika nchi yetu italeta fujo. Maana kama ni CCM waislamu wapo na wakristo wapo, kama ni CUF waislamu wapo na wakristo wapo, hivyo kwa TLP.

[215] Mwalimu Nyerere alikuwa mstari wa mbele katika kuhakikisha kuwa amani hai toweki.

[216] Utawala wa siku hizi, kuanzia mwaka 1999 hautumii busara kutokana na viongozi wa sasa kuwa na "skills" tofauti ya zile za Nyerere na hivyo kutoweza kutatua migongano ya Kidini ambayo inaweza kuwa chanjo cha kukosa amani Tanzania.

the nation, Mwalimu J.K. Nyerere, said."[217] However, one educated male participant observed, "These two religions will cause complications despite Mwalimu Nyerere having said that everyone should have his own religion."[218]

A Christian key informant referred to Nyerere's efforts to bring about equal educational opportunities for all religions, something that has largely been ignored: "The disturbing thing is their [Muslims'] demands to government. They claim to have been marginalised in education, but they are wrong, because Mwalimu Nyerere nationalised schools which belonged to the missions, schools in which even their leaders, ministers studied, because they had no schools; they had insisted on religious education."[219]

Participants drew upon the colonial period and the historical forces that helped to shape present-day Tanzania. For this participant colonialism introduced secular education to Tanzania. He also refers to Christian missionaries, who pioneered the building of schools and hence the introduction of secular education. According to the participant such outside interference had an impact on Christian-Muslim relations. Before the colonial intervention the people now called Muslims and Christians coexisted peacefully as *ndugu*.

With reference to Nyerere's successors, elderly female participants mentioned president Ali Hassan Mwinyi, especially in connection with what they saw as the origin of open air preaching. They asserted that "open air preaching came after the second president, when president Ali Hassan Mwinyi became leader. They [Muslims] said now the government is for Muslims; therefore there is freedom to say whatever you like. Then they started to say they don't want pork, they started to insult [other religions]." The respondents saw a social transformation from the Nyerere to the Mwinyi era. "During the Nyerere era this slandering preaching did not happen,"[220] one participant observed. This was confirmed in other discussions.

---

[217] Kwa mtazamo wangu naona kila mmoja aabudu katika imani yake kama Hayati Baba wa Taifa Mwalimu J.K.Nyerere alivyosema.

[218] Dini hizi mbili ndio zitakuwa chanzo cha utata hata kama Mwalimu Nyerere alisema kila mmoja awe na dini yake.

[219] Vitu wanavyokera ni madai yao kwa serikali, wanaona kama wanaonewa katika elimu Wakisema hivyo naona hapana kwani Mwalimu Nyerere alitaifisha shule zilizokuwa za mission ambazo hata Viongozi wao wakubwa hata mawaziri walisoma katika shule hizo sababu walikuwa hawana shule za sekondari wala high school kwa kuwa wao wali – insist sana kwenye elimu ya dini. (Key informant Mzee Ch.)

[220] Mihadhara ilikuja baada ya Raisi wa awamu ya pili Rais Ally Hassani Mwinyi kuanza uongozi, wakasema sasa serikali ilikuwa ya waislamu hivyo pana uhuru wakusema wanachotaka, na ndio hapo walipoanza kusema hawataki nguruwe, wakaanza kutukana, lakini wakati wa Nyerere, kashfa hizi hazikuwepo.

However, an elderly female participant thanked Ali Hassan Mwinyi for inviting the Catholic pope to Tanzania: "We thank Ali Hassan Mwinyi, because when he was president he brought the Catholic Church's holy pope, who was able to do his work here in different regions under the president's security."[221]

Regarding president Mkapa, elderly female participants remembered that during his reign interreligious "disputes continued, though on a limited scale; they started fighting among themselves in the mosque. You will hear at Magomeni, they fought in a certain mosque."[222] Mkapa was praised by educated male participants for establishing a special programme for children who had missed primary school because they were over the enrolment age. "Honourable Mkapa came and established education through MEMKWA[223] for children who could not get into primary school to get that education,"[224] they observed. This gave many children of both major religions an opportunity to acquire education they needed to have better prospects.

The OIC, kadhi courts and the constitution
"The kadhi *courts will bring religio-centrism."*

Participants referred to the controversial issues of the OIC and *kadhi* courts. Educated female youths said that "the *kadhi* court will bring religio-centrism"[225] in the country. Similar responses came from different Christians in the community. On 24 September 2008 *Majira* (p. 3) carried a story on a Pentecostal organisation reacting to the *kadhi* and OIC issues. It reported, "Pentecostals reject *kadhi* court, OIC."[226] This is an organisation of bishops representing the Pentecostal churches of Tanzania (PCT), which is officially recognised. The report reads: "Bishops and pastors of the Pentecostal churches in Dar es Salaam requested the government to refrain from putting clause(s) about the kadhi court and the Organisation of the

---

[221] Tunamshukuru Ally Hassani Mwinyi alivyokuwa Raisi alimleta Baba Mtakatifu wa Kanisa Katoliki na akaweza kufanya kazi zake hapa siku zote katika mikoa mbali mbali kwa ulinzi wake Raisi wetu mpaka alipoondoka.

[222] Kipindi cha Mkapa haikukoma lakini ilipungua kidogo, wakaanza wenyewe kwa wenyewe kupigana msikitini mara usikie Magomeni kwenye nsikiti gani wamepigana. (Elderly female participant)

[223] MEMKWA is an abreviation for Mpango wa Elimu kwa Watoto waliokosa elimu ya msingi (English: Special Programme for Children who could not get Primary Education).

[224] Mfano, Mheshimiwa Mkapa alikuja na kuanzisha elimu ya MEMKWA kwa watoto walioshindwa kupata elimu ya msingi na hivyo kuwawezesha kupata elimu.

[225] Mahakama ya kadhi inaleta udini.

[226] Wapentekoste wapinga mahakama ya Kadhi, OIC.

Islamic Conference (OIC) in the constitution." They continued: "Our standpoint is that we are against the inclusion of the kadhi court in the constitution."

Various newspapers reported Christians expressing their misgivings on these issues. *Nipashe*, for example, carried a story entitled "Pentecost rejects kadhi court, OIC".[227] On 30 October 2008 *Nipashe* published an article headed "Bishops prepare grenade against OIC".[228] The first story reported statements by bishops and pastors of the Pentecostal churches in Tanzania (PCT), while the latter reported views of Christian bishops (CCT). Both articles conveyed the same message, rejecting the establishment of *kadhi* courts in Tanzania and opposing any moves to join the OIC. The bishops and the pastors based their rejection on the Christian standpoint. They knew it was their responsibility to speak on behalf of the group they represented.

This was affirmed by the Christian Council of Tanzania (CCT), an officially recognised Christian organisation. On 24 October 2008 the CCT issued a statement entitled "Obstruction of the establishment of *kadhi* court in the country and Tanzania joining the Organisation of the Islamic Conference." This group cited the constitution, claiming that the move was counter to the constitution of the URT (2005), article 19 (2), which stipulates, "Without prejudice to the laws of the United Republic, the profession of religion, worship and propagation of religion shall be a free and a private affair of the individual; and the affairs and management of religious bodies shall not be part of the activities of the state authority."

This was confirmed by another group called "The Bible is the answer" (*Biblia ni Jibu*).[229] In their brochure, "OIC and Tanzania: *Ijue OIC and IAO*" (literal translation: Learn about the OIC and IAO), they report that Muslims' demand to join the OIC and IAO is not new. They pointed out that the issue had been reported in local newspapers since 1999. The implication of this statement is that the nation should not treat the issue as though it was surfacing for the first time.

In the FGDs Christian participants rejected the establishment of *kadhi* courts and opposed Tanzanian membership of the OIC. Christian MPs have also voiced their opposition to any moves to join the OIC or establish *kadhi* courts. Some of them were reported in local newspapers as saying, "The *kadhi* issue is a religious one and it is the Muslims' responsibility to establish it ... without pressurising

---

[227] Nipashe, Thursday 25 September 2008, p. 10. By Futuna Seleman, Pentekoste wapinga Mahakama ya Kadhi, OIC (literally: Pentecost rejects kadhi courts, OIC).

[228] Maaskofu waandaa bomu dhidi ya OIC.

[229] This group was established by some Pentecostal churches as a reaction and challenge to Muslims' mihadhara. They started conducting Christian mihadhara.

parliament to recognise it".²³⁰ In other words, they were saying *kadhi* courts could not be accepted by a secular parliament. "Muslims should establish that in their faith and not inside the government."²³¹ MPs voiced concern in regard to their experience. As members of parliament they represented a constituency (MP-voters relationship). As controller of the government, moreover, they had a duty to oversee government decisions accordingly, in this case not to get involved in what they thought were religious issues (kadhi courts and OIC membership). This was confirmed by a key informant who said, "I think we should look for other institutions such as BAKWATA; they should look at how they can establish [the kadhi court] without involving the government."²³²

Continued Muslim-Christian coexistence
"His faith did not separate him from us"

Despite all these concerns, Christian participants in the FGDs continued to refer to friendly relations and collaboration between Christians and Muslims. This is also reported in newspapers. Privatus Karugendo, a journalist and Catholic priest, hailed cooperation between Muslims and Christians as a value to be cherished in Tanzania.²³³ Karugendo saw such cooperation as a means to what one would call ideal religious coexistence. He cited the example of Amir Chipukizi, who died in Karagwe district in 2008.²³⁴ Karugendo wrote: "Taking into consideration that he was not a Christian [he was a Muslim], his close cooperation with Christians, priests, clergy and bishops, showed that he had something different and important in his heart." This Christian journalist was acknowledging that Muslims do cooperate well with Christians in day-to-day activities. At the wedding of Amir's niece "the reception/ceremony was held in the church hall". It was exceptional for a Muslim to hold a function in a Christian building. After all, most Muslims do not allow their functions to be held in Christian buildings and naturally Amir's relatives had misgivings about it.

---

[230] In Raia Mwema, 3-9 September 2008, p. 16. By Chris Nyamkwembeya: Hoja ya makama ya kadhi isiyumbishe nchi. (literally: Kadhi argument should not sway the country to and fro).

[231] Christopher Ole-Sondeka, MP for Simanjiro, speaking in parliament and reported in Raia Mwema, 3-9 September 2008 by Chris Nyamkwembeya, p. 22.

[232] Nadhani tungetafuta vyombo vingine kama BAKWATA waangalie ni kwa jinsi gani wanaweza kuanzisha jambo hili bila serikali kuliingilia.

[233] Fr Privatus Karugendo was paying tribute to the late Amir Amiri Chipukizi, who died in Karagwe district after interrogation by the Tanzania Revenue Authority (TRA). Amir (a Muslim) was a well-known businessman in the district, region and in the country. Raia Mwema, 29 October 2008, p. 17.

[234] See footnote 559 about Amir Chipukizi.

It was hard enough for other believers to hold a function on Christian premises. As the journalist Karugendo pointed out, "Amir was a Muslim, but his faith did not separate him from us, his *ndugu*[235] who happen to be Christians." The term '*ndugu*' in this context shows the closeness (close enough to be a blood relative) which some Christians maintain with Muslims. All in all this incident demonstrated the harmony and peace that Christians and Muslims enjoy in a mixed society, where they share and experience the same socio-economic conditions (e.g. in marriage).

Conclusion

Participants in the FGDs substantiated their statements from several sources. In the discussions Christian participants preserved group coherence. Nevertheless there were some disagreements on whether or not government should ban open air preaching.

Participants referred to the PCT and CCT, who fiercely objected to Tanzania joining the OIC, and to BAKWATA, the umbrella Muslim body. They also referred to Nyerere and lauded him for nationalising schools in order to create national unity and reduce inequalities, which could have a devastating impact on religions operating in Tanzania. Mwinyi was mentioned for bringing about liberalisation, and also in connection with the emergence of antagonistic *mihadhara*. They mentioned president Kikwete, current president of the country and referred to political parties such as CCM and CUF, which are competing for political power, going so far as to associate them with the dominant religions. They also referred to the constitution, which they claimed was being violated by political leaders. If we analyse the order of discourse, the utterances of Christians clearly indicate that religious discourse is influenced by and influences political discourse. After all, one cannot talk about politics in Tanzania without talking about its effects on the religions, as witness the attempts of some participants to associate CCM primarily with Christianity and CUF with Islam.

Like the Muslim participants in chapter two, Christian participants reproduced a picture which associated the Q'uran with domestication of *jini* (spirit), OIC and kadhi courts with Islamisation, a political party (CUF) with Islam, and Islam with crime. Nevertheless, Christians also used polite and friendly labels to refer to Muslims, giving the impression that they understand them or at least show a will to understand them.

---

[235] The term 'ndugu' was explained in chapter two; here we just mention that it refers to a close friend or comrade.

3.3. Analysis of social practice

Critical discourse analysis at the third level, social practice, focuses on the dialectical relationship between texts/language and social structures (Fairclough, 2007:87). The assumption is that participants' utterances (their discourse/text) have both cognitive and social effects, and are affected by and affects these. In speaking about issues affecting them participants constructed their own social reality by either reproducing or transforming the reality (Fairclough 1992:72). This section analyses the socio-cognitive (ideational and interpersonal) effects of participants' utterances.

"If the boss is a Muslim, you will not find any Christian"

Christian participants positioned themselves as victims of discrimination, especially in the workplace. They claimed that Muslims discriminate against Christians in job allocation by employing only Muslims: "If the boss is a Muslim, you will not find any Christian working at that office."[236] Discrimination also occurred when it came to sharing food. The elderly female participants said, "Muslims don't allow their children to eat in Christian homes."[237] They said that Muslims imposed restrictions on borrowing things such as cooking utensils: "Muslims' responses have always been that I cannot lend my cooking utensils to Christians."[238] Discrimination was also evident in renting houses. Muslim open air preachers persuaded Muslims "not to rent Christians' houses because Christians are *kafir*."[239] All these statements by Christian participants constitute and were constituted by their subject positions as Christians in relation to Muslims. Christian participants position Christians as victims of Muslim discrimination and selfishness. Where they thought Muslims treated Christians unjustly, they position Muslims as discriminators (*wabaguzi*) against Christians.

Discrimination and religio-centrism were also cited as the core of the problems that Christians faced when it came to slaughtering animals. Some Christian open air preachers thought they could remedy the situation by imploring Christians to stop asking Muslims to slaughter poultry and other domesticated animals for them. One preacher told his audience, "Starting today, it is forbidden for a

---

[236] The Swahili translation is footnoted in the employment section of this chapter.
[237] The Swahili translation is footnoted in the dietary pattern section of this chapter.
[238] Ibid.
[239] Kuna kipindi waislamu walishawishiwa kutokwenda kupanga kwenye nyumba za wakristo kwa kuwa wao (wakristo) ni makafiri.

Christian to ask a Muslim to slaughter an animal."[240] He explained the reason why Christians asked Muslims to slaughter animals meant for domestic and public consumption thus: "They (Muslims) say they have a slaughtering god and Christians don't..." There is a power struggle underlying this discourse, more specifically directed to authority to slaughter animals and poultry. Christians questioned the authority over slaughtering animals for public consumption that Muslims have been socially accorded. Utterances by Christian female participants and Christian open air preachers challenged this authority and hegemony. To reverse this trend the preachers urged Christians to start slaughtering animals for public consumption themselves. Muslims view it in the perspective of controlling consumption, since only food classified as not *haraam* can be consumed, and they were the only ones qualified to identify and slaughter beasts for public consumption; otherwise the products would be considered *haraam*.

Open air preaching as business

Some participants related preaching to commercialisation of society. Accordingly they considered "open air preaching to be their [the preachers'] commercial businesses".[241] This development is a product of a process of commodification and commercialisation. Some people in Tanzania, especially preachers, treat religion as a way of earning an income rather than as a primarily spiritual ministry. According to Christians Muslim preachers come from the unemployed group in society; therefore they exploit *mihadhara* as sources of income. The participants claimed that Muslim preachers did not preach for the sake of converting people to Islam but rather to extract money from members of their audience. The participants worried about the repercussions of such a business enterprise. An uneducated female youth, also quoted above, said, "Truly open air preaching is destructive because it does not have the purpose of spreading religion. They [preachers] do business and therefore they propagate many lies... at the end they say we want two thousand shillings ... they will collect about seventy thousand shillings for their services. Then they divide the money amongst themselves. This is just healing hunger [*kuganga njaa,* survival strategy]!"[242] This was confirmed by an educated male participant: "The people who conduct these open air services have been sent

---

[240] Excerpt from a tape-recorded mhadhara conducted by a group called Christian Power at Mbagalla, Dar es Salaam, 2 January 2008.
[241] Mihadhara ni kama biashara zao.
[242] KiSwahili translation is footnoted in the discursive level analysis of the open air preaching section.

to perform a task [with payment in mind]; therefore they conduct *mihadhara* as a business."[243] According to these participants religion is now a commodity like any other. It could be sold (by open air preachers) and bought in the market place (by audiences/believers).

In this respect participants generalised and thought that "for some people open air preaching [has] turned into business just like any other business; they collect money for their transport and other needs."[244] Such an attitude that places individual benefits above those of society is part of the ongoing struggle between individualism and communalism (*ujamaa*), for many years the mainstay of Tanzanian society, in which the former appears to be gaining the upper hand. Many open air preachers conduct *mihadhara* not so much to promote religion or the community as to meet their own needs. This explains why money contributions at *mihadhara* are not passed on to the religious institutions for the benefit of all members but end up in the pockets of the preachers and their assistants.

It is noteworthy that participants' utterances exposed an emerging politicisation of religion. As a key informant observed, "In the past open air preaching was non-existent but now it is growing at an alarming rate. We appeal to government to intervene before it turns out to be like politics. We should not use religion as politics."[245] Another informant said, "Open air preaching is now like politics, like opposition parties, hence no longer religion." This is because "they now get mixed up with other people's religions and therefore cause fights".[246] Participants' statements depicted open air preaching as part and parcel of the political changes in the country which are constituted in the transformation taking place. In 1992 Tanzania changed from a one-party to a multi-party democracy, and this change triggered far-reaching political transformation that did not spare religion. For participants the proliferation of open air preachers as alternative religious authorities – made possible by political liberalisation – inevitably resulted in mixing religion with politics, especially as the self-serving preachers pursue personal gain at whatever cost.

---

[243] KiSwahili translation is footnoted in the discursive level analysis of the open air preaching section.
[244] Mihadhara imegeuka na kuwa kama biashara tu, wanakusanya fedha, kwajili ya nauli na mahitaji yao mengine.
[245] Mihadhara zamani haikuwepo lakini sasa hii imekua speed sana na tunaomba serikali iingilie kati kwani mwisho wake utakuwa kama siasa. Tusitumie dini kuwa kama siasa.
[246] Na Mihadhara kwa sasa imekuwa kama siasa kama vyama vya upinzani na sio dini tena. Kwani wamekuwa wanachanganya na dini za watu wengine na hivyo kunaleta ugomvi.

"This outside interference ... will make Christians not coexist with Muslims in the future"

Participants explained discrimination by identifying foreign interference and negative influences of globalisation on Tanzania. "I think the rich Arabs employ the preachers to do the preaching for the Muslim faith, because they [the Arabs] cannot come to do it themselves."[247] An educated male youth said, "This external interference involving open air preaching issues will make Christians not coexist with Muslims in the future."[248] To these participants open air preaching is a result of influence from Arab countries in the Middle East. Those Muslim preachers get financial and other support from outside Tanzania, the participants insisted, although they did not provide tangible evidence to back up their claims.

Other participants painted a picture of globalisation and its effect on themselves and Tanzanian society as a whole. They cited the furore that ensued following the public display of prophet Muhammad's picture in Denmark, and how the event triggered an unexpected reaction from Muslim communities. They said Muslims worldwide, including those in Tanzania, demonstrated. This shows that there is a connection between Tanzanian Muslims and Muslims elsewhere in the world.

In the first section we cited some global names and labels that Christians used when speaking about Muslims. The label *Al Qaeda* refers to a group of radical Muslims that was headed for many years by one of the world's most wanted terrorists, Osama bin Laden, in Afghanistan. The label *Mujahidin*, used for Muslim women who wear *hijab*, refers to the *Mujahidin* soldiers seen on television news covering their faces with *ninja* masks. By using these foreign terms Christians link local Muslims to international or global events elsewhere in the Muslim world and position them as possible extremists. The negative connotations of the terms do not endear Christians to Muslims. The interconnection between the particular and the universal positions Tanzania as part of the global community. It shows that Tanzania is not an island as it used to be in the socialist era, which had only government controlled news papers and radio stations and no television.

---

[247] Naona ni Waarabu wenye uwezo ndio ambao wamewaajiri wafanye hivyo kwani hawawezi (Waarabu) kuja kufanya hivyo wao wenyewe. (Key informant Mzee x Kilakala.)

[248] Sababu ambazo zinaweza kufanya wakristo kushindwa kukaa na waislamu kwa miaka ijayo ni hizi external interference ambazo zinahusisha mambo ya Mihadhara.

"Both of them dress inappropriately"

When speaking about dress participants explained the existing inter-generational gap in their community, which had led to homogenisation and also served as a meeting point between Muslims and Christians. As one elderly female participant put it, "The issue of clothing is not only of concern to Muslim or Christian children; we are all spoiled."[249] Not surprisingly, style of dress has been a flash point in the resultant inter-generational conflict. Youths tend to adopt new styles of dress, primarily because of their exposure to the internet, television and films where they see different fashion trends in other communities, especially in the West. These new fashions annoy the conservative older generation, who find them offensive to both their taste and the cultural and religious values they grew up with. Thus most elderly female participants said that they did not like the way young females dressed. "As a female," said one elderly female participant, "I would not like to see a young girl dressed in trousers or a mini-skirt with a top which shows her belly button in the presence of her father, brother, grandmother and grandfather."[250] "As a mother, at the church door we ban them from entering the church." "It [the church] is not the place for showing off their bodies and it is not our culture."[251] The woman explained that "this is different from our day, because we used to cover our bodies and as a result men's lust was contained."[252] The elderly participants blamed female youths for not respecting their parents' teachings and advice. They said, "When you come home you find her dressed in a respectable dress, not the dress that they put in their handbags and wear once they are away from home."[253] "If you buy her a long skirt, she will go and shorten it, or when leaving home she wears the long dress but once she is alone she pulls up the skirt so it becomes short."[254]

These statements constitute and are constituted by an inter-generational transformation. That is, in the past young females used to wear what were considered

---

[249] Haya masuala ya mavazi hayana cha mtoto wa muislamu au mtoto wa mkristo ni kwa wote tu wameharibikiwa.
[250] Mimi kama mwanamke nisingependelea kwa msichana akavaa suruali au kimini na kitop ambacho kitovu kiko wazi mbele ya baba kaka, bibi na babu yake.
[251] Kama mama, tunawazuia kuingia kanisani pale mlangoni. Sio sehemu ya miili yao na sio utamaduni wetu.
[252] Tofauti na enzi wetu kwani tulikuwa tunajisitiri na hivyo wanaume kutokuwa na matamanio.
[253] Mtoto akifika nyumbani unamkuta mtoto amevaa nguo za heshima na sio zile ambazo huzificha kwenye kipochi chake.
[254] Wewe unaenda kumnunulia sketi ndefu yeye anaipunguza inakuwa fupi au anatoka nyumbani akiwa amevaa sketi ndefu halafu akifika sehemu fulani anachukua ile sketi anaisogeza juu tumboni ili iwe fupi.

respectable dresses at that time and throughout the generations. This is different from the way present-day young females dress. These statements also refer to social positions, in which regard elderly women felt it was their duty to pass on proper cultural knowledge to the young generation, especially in respect of the dress code. On the other hand, the young generation feels constrained by the teachings of the older generation, hence their rebellious spirit, which frustrates their elders. This development could also be attributed to globalisation, which exposes young children to many cross-cultural influences via television and the internet (now a countrywide source of information and knowledge). They have access to more information and knowledge than the older generation can give them, hence their rebellion and their desire to move with contemporary trends. In fact, the young generation's desire for change ends up challenging existing norms and values. The older generation, on the other hand, wants to maintain the status quo.

"Our president has no religion" and "the government gives us freedom of worship"

Most participants reproduced a process of secularisation and urged for the separation of state and religion: "Therefore our president has no religion and all citizens are free to worship in any religion of their choice."[255] Thus the state (represented here by the president) does not necessarily subscribe to a particular religion at an official level (though at a personal level the situation could be different), but citizens have their religions. These participants position Tanzania as a secular rather than a religious state. They also position and expect top government officials such as the president to embrace secular ideals. The speaker of the statement put herself in the position of the citizens. That is, as citizens they expect to have freedom of worship but also impartial services from the government and its officials, which should serve all Tanzanians without any religious prejudice. On the other hand, there was a subject position of leaders and government/public officials. These leaders are responsible for the wellbeing of the citizens ("the government intervenes when a person breaks the law").[256] This was confirmed by an educated female participant, who said, "In the government there are courts; the judge passes sentences without any regard to religio-centrism."[257]

---

[255] Kwa maana hiyo Raisi wetu hana dini na mwananchi yoyote yuko huru kuabudu dini anayoitaka na serikali ikasimamia pale unapovinja heshima au sheria.
[256] Serikali huingilia pale mtu anapovunja sheria.
[257] Serikalini kunamahakama. Judge anahukumu bila udini.

According to one key informant, "The constitution [of the URT] is very clear on matters of faith and religious issues. The government should not reach a point of getting [directly] involved. They [matters of faith] are heavy, difficult to explain, and beyond our intellectual capabilities."[258] The participant positions the government as secular, and thus, issues of religion are not part of its responsibilities.

The participants reproduced the image of Tanzania as a society in transition particularly in the religious field. One participant said, "When they [Muslims] saw a fellow Muslim had become a president, conflict started; during Nyerere's era this did not happen."[259] Participants said during the presidency of Ali Hassan Mwinyi religion and the state were not clearly separated. As one elderly women participant pointed out, "When Mwinyi became president [religious] demonstrations started; in school children started to wear head veils [*vijuba*]. All these [things] were [occurring] during Mwinyi's reign. Religio-centrism was also introduced in school! Meaning even in the government itself! But the government closed its eyes."[260] These participants praised the Nyerere presidency that ensured a clear separation between religion and state. On the other hand they accused his successor Mwinyi of failing to separate religion from the state. They cited the example of pupils' uniforms as one indication of mixing religion with issues of governance. To them all pupils were supposed to wear the same uniform (headscarves should not be allowed), because public schools were secular.

The Christian respondents also explained that "every time a Muslim president is elected the Muslim community uses the opportunity to pressurise the existing government to further their interests."[261] This positioned Muslims as religio-centrists who use religion to further their interests. President Kikwete succeeded a Christian president, Benjamin W. Mkapa. The Christian participants claimed that the resurgence of the debate on *kadhi* courts and on the OIC happened because the ruling president was a Muslim. The participants' responses suggest that Christian presidents (Nyerere and Mkapa) tend to be more secular than Muslim presidents (Mwinyi and Kikwete).

---

[258] Katiba ipo wazi sana mambo yakiimani au kidini serikali isifike hatua ya kuyaingilia ni mambo mazito hayaelezeki yapo nje ya intelectual abilities zetu.

[259] Baada ya kuona mwislam mwenzao kawa Rais ndio vurugu iliko anza. Enzi za Nyerere hayakuwepo.

[260] Baada ya kuingia Mwinyi katika urais nayo ndio ilipoanza na maandamano kuanza mara mpaka mashuleni watoto wavae vijuba – yote yalikuwa baada ya Mwinyi. Wakaingiza sasa dini hii mpaka mashuleni ina maana mpaka kwenye Serikali yenyewe lakini serikali ilifumbia macho.

[261] Raia Mwema, 3-9 September 2008, p. 22. By Chris Nyamkwembeya. Hoja ya makama ya kadhi isiyumbishe nchi (literally: Kadhi argument should not sway the country to and fro).

Participants rejected calls to establish *kadhi* courts on economic rather than religious grounds (revenue and expenditure). One key informant asked, "That court will be run on whose taxes? People pay taxes, and then you run the *kadhi* court using Christians' taxes?"[262] This issue should not involve the *bunge* (parliament) to the extent of "using taxes of Tanzanians who are not Muslims – those who are Christians".[263] Christians asked who would be responsible for electing the *kadhi*. They wondered whether Muslims would accept a *kadhi* selected by a president who happened to be a Christian. "The question asked was if the president is a Christian, will you [Muslims] accept that a *kafir* [Christian] chooses[264] a *kadhi* for you?" The participant clearly identified two groups of Tanzanians, Christians and Muslims. To him there is not simply one Tanzanian identity but also a Christian identity (Christian money/taxes) and a Muslim identity (Muslim money/taxes). According to him these groups were separate and no group had the right to use another group's money or taxes. Similarly, a president from one group (say Christians) has no right to interfere with another group's affairs (like a Christian president choosing a *kadhi* for Muslims).

One key informant dealt, explicitly and implicitly, with freedom of worship, *kadhi* courts and OIC membership: "The government has given us freedom of worship, but when it starts interfering in religious issues, for example *kadhi* courts … these are difficult issues for government to be involved in."[265] Another participant said, "Any citizen is free to practise any religion of his/her choice."[266] Participants said that *kadhi* courts and OIC membership were religious issues; hence they should be kept in the religious domain. Participants, as citizens, argued that they had a right to be involved in religious issues, whereas the government and its leaders did not have that right. Thus joining the OIC and establishing *kadhi* courts should be the responsibility of believers who are free to worship and/or join any organisation of their choice.

Despite that freedom, citizens must obey the laws of the land and help to maintain order, peace and harmony in the country. The elderly women participants elucidated that they were surprised by the government's reluctance to punish those who broke the law: "We see our fellows breaking the law and endangering the

---

[262] Hiyo mahakama itaendeshwa kwa kodi zakina nani, watu wanalipa kodi utaendesha kadhi kwa kodi ya mkristo?
[263] Kodi za watanzania wengine ambao si waislam ni wakristo.
[264] Swali likawa Rais akiwa mkristo mtakubali kafiri amteue kadhi?
[265] Serikali imetoa uhuru wa kuabudu lakini inapoingia serikali inaanza kuingilia maswala mazima yakiimani mfano maswala ya kadhi … Kwahiyo ni mambo mazito kwa serikali kuyaingilia.
[266] Kila mwananchi anauhuru wa kuabudu dini yeyote anayoipenda.

peace, but the government is silent."[267] Participants urged government to punish those who violated the law in order to maintain peace. Government's failure to act could compel Christians to take the law into their own hands. As an elderly female participant explained, "We are human beings, not God; we can take the law into our own hands and by doing so destroy the peace."[268] The statement again revealed the subject positions of citizens and their leaders. Participants believed that it was the state's responsibility to monitor and supervise religions and religious activities in the country. These activities include open air preaching. One key informant said, "The government should supervise open air preaching, because it has the responsibility of leading the country and power to solve all problems threatening the country."[269]

Some participants accused government of failing to maintain cohesion as it was supposed to by allowing *mihadhara* to continue ridiculing other faiths with impunity. Participants noted that there is a change in the way the state handled religious issues. In the past (under Nyerere's regime) religious issues were confined to religious institutions and ridiculing other faiths was not condoned. Educated male youths, for example, said, "In the past government imposed heavy punishments on those who ridiculed others' faith."[270] This changed under the Mwinyi administration. Open air preaching was allowed and Muslims seized the opportunity (because now the president was a Muslim) to ridicule other faiths. One elderly female participant observed that "when Mwinyi became president, demonstrations started" and that "open air preaching came into being after the second presidency, when president Ali Hassan Mwinyi became the leader. They [Muslims] said now the government is for Muslims; therefore there is freedom to say whatever you like."[271] This was confirmed by educated male youths, who clarified, "This is different today; ridiculing has become the order of the day."[272]

These arguments underscore what participants saw as a shift in government's handling of religious relations. Although the first government under Mwalimu Nyerere accorded citizens freedom of worship, government remained sensitive

---

[267] Lakini tunaona kwamba wenzetu wanavunja heshima / sheria na wanahatarisha amani, lakini serikali imenyamaza kimya.
[268] Lakini sisi ni wanadamu sio Mungu, tunaweza tukachukua sheria mkononi na hivyo kuvuruga amani.
[269] Serikali isimamie mambo ya Mihadhara kwani serikali ndio imechukua jukumu la kuongoza nchi na hivyo kuwa na uwezo wa kutatua matatizo yote yatakayojitokeza ndani ya nchi.
[270] Mfano kwa mihadhara ya zamani serikali ilikuwa inamchukulia hatua yeyote yule ambaye atakae ikashifu imani ya mwenzake.
[271] KiSwahili translation is footnoted in the linguistic section.
[272] Sasa ambapo (kukashifu) inachukuliwa kama ni hali ya kawaida.

to the delicate issue of religion and restricted any activities likely to undermine peace and stability in the country. Restriction of freedom of speech would entail punishing those who deliberately ridiculed other faiths. Under Mwinyi the situation changed. Citizens enjoyed unprecedented freedom of speech as a result of political and economic liberalisation. Religious liberalisation manifested in the proliferation of open air preaching.

There was a close connection between these social situations and the different ways of speaking and ideologies that guided the practices of the two presidents. Whereas Nyerere's government favoured *ujamaa* (socialist) policies and the formation of a Tanzanian identity (unification), Mwinyi's government was more liberal and embraced change (liberalisation) and individualism, hence diversification (pluralism). The latter aspect, according to Christian participants, contributed to the marginalisation of Christians. Nevertheless, judging by participants' responses, Christians have been adapting to these changes, as one educated male youth stressed: "Christians also have their words to ridicule Muslims – they call them *mdebwedo*."[273] This retaliatory approach appears to be divisive, hence promotes divergence rather than social cohesion.

Participants' statements suggested a 'privatisation' of faith: "Everyone is practising his religion as the late father of the nation, Mwalimu J. K. Nyerere, said."[274] To the participants religion is an individual affair, not communal. In taking this position they constitute themselves as individualised believers. Individualism was also cited when participants referred to food, indicating that what one eats remains a private matter. One participant said, "I have a friend, his father is a BAKWATA chairman, but he eats pork. He says his father has his own faith that pork is *haraam* and he has his individual faith that pork is edible."[275] The participant added, "Let us leave religious issues, faith in the care of religious group leaders."[276] Participants spoke of the subject positions of religious leaders vis-à-vis believers. Some insisted that only religious leaders (such as the BAKWATA chairman) should adhere to all religious teachings. Ordinary believers of different faiths (both Muslims and Christians) cannot be barred from day-to-day practices such as eating the same food, including *haraam*, if they so wished.

---

[273] Sasa hivi wakristo nao wanamaneno yao ambayo ni yakuwakejeli waislamu wanawaita 'mdebwedo'.

[274] Kwa mtazamo wangu naona kila mmoja aabudu katika imani yake kama Hayati Baba wa Taifa Mwalimu J.K.Nyerere alivyosema. (Educated male participant).

[275] Kuna rafiki yangu ambaye baba yake ni mwenyekiti wa BAKWATA lakini anakula nguruwe huku akitumia hoja kwamba baba yake ana imani yake kwamba nguruwe ni haramu na yeye ana imani yake kwamba nguruwe analiwa.

[276] Tuyaachie mambo ya kidini, imani yaendelee kulelewa na viongozi wa vikundi vya kidini.

Other participants identified the tension between secularisation and islamisation as an issue that cannot be ignored in present-day Tanzania. One educated male participant said, "My opinion is that the government should convince their [Muslim] sponsors who build their big, expensive mosques to build schools in order to help Muslim youths to get an education, which will make them contribute more to the economy through the education they acquire."[277] This participant claimed that Muslim sponsors built many mosques as part of the islamisation mission. In other words, the participants said Muslims appeared to identify themselves more as Muslims (by building mosques and learning about religion) than as Tanzanians (by getting a secular education). Hence they imply that secularisation should take priority, not islamisation or religio-centrism. In other words, religion should not just be an institution for spiritual development but should also provide believers with secular education. This argument underscores the differences in education. The participant was insinuating that Muslim youths generally were less educated than Christian youths.

Participants reproduced an image of Muslims as resistant to transformation and technologisation. An educated female youth said, "Muslims have to change; they should be in the era of science and technology and do things for the benefit and development of all people."[278] Thus participants were imploring Muslims to respond to the challenge of modernity and technologisation. They suggested that Muslims should abandon some of their traditions that do not conform to science and technology. One educated female participant said, "According to the principles of science and technology all these foods are edible irrespective of one's religious principles."[279] These arguments show that Christian participants positioned themselves as modern, flexible and adaptive. Moreover, they treated social and technological change (civic discourse) as a dominant discourse and religion as a peripheral discourse.

---

[277] Kwa maoni yangu nadhani ni vyema kwa serikali kuwashawishi wafadhili wao (waislmu) ambao huwajengea misikiti mikubwa na ya gharama wawajengee mashule ili kusaidia vijana wa Kiislam kuweza kupata elimu ili kuwakwamua waislamu kiuchumi kupitia elimu watakayoipata shuleni.

[278] Waislamu wabadilike wawe kwenye enzi ya sayansi na teknolojia ili wafanye vitu kwa manufaa na maendeleo ya watu wote.

[279] Kwa misingi ya sayansi na teknolojia vyakula vyote hivi ninaliwa pasipo kuangaliwa misingi ya dini.

"The parents' poor financial situation is the reason..."

When speaking about Muslims Christians introduced various economic, political and social classifications. Economically they distinguished between an advantaged group (mostly Christian) and a largely economically disadvantaged group (mostly Muslim). One participant revealed that the "parents' bad financial situation is the reason behind most Muslims' failure to send their children to ward schools; they only have enough to cover small family expenses."[280] Christian FGD participants positioned themselves as developmentally advanced and their Muslim counterparts as 'backward'. According to participants secular education could help more Muslims have a better life, as "their concentration on religion made them lag behind in development".[281] Here, too, the participant positioned Muslims as religio-centrists and Christians as secularists who took advantage of modernity (development).

Participants highlighted residential differences when speaking about open air preaching. They expounded that open air preachers tended to avoid localities where educated people live, "areas such as Masaki, and Osterbay".[282] Neither did they preach in areas where the majority of the inhabitants were employed. "Open air preaching is taken to people staying in areas with a low education,"[283] explained an educated male participant. These statements imply that residential areas where the educated, the affluent and government leaders lived were spared the disturbances that accompany open air preaching. Areas where poor and uneducated citizens live, on the other hand, were exposed to *mihadhara* and their attendant problems by virtue of their social and residential vulnerability. The following statement by one of the participants confirms this: "In the places where educated people stay open air preaching is limited ... Open air preaching is taken to people staying in poorly educated areas." Indeed, highly educated people are employed and thus "spend most of their working time outside their residential areas".[284] Thus participants argued that "open air preaching annoys those who stay at home",[285]

---

[280] Sababu zinazipelekea waislamu wengi kushindwa kuwapeleka watoto wa shule za kata ni kutokana na hali ya uchumi kuwa mbaya kwani kipato cha mzazi kinakuwa kina kidhi mahitajji madogo madogo ya nyumbani. (Educated male participant.)

[281] Waislamu wao wanaendelea na ujenzi wa misikiti na hivyo kuwafanya wazingatie dini kuliko elimu na hivyo kuendelea kubaki nyuma kimaendeleo.

[282] Kwa hiyo kwa sehemu wanayoishi watu wenye elimu mihadhara huwa ni nadra: maeneo kama Masaki, Osterbay.

[283] Kwa sehemu za watu wenye elimu ya chini ndio wanaopelekewa mihadhara.

[284] Mihadhara inawasumbua wale ambao wanashinda nyumbani.

[285] Mihadhara inawasumbua wale ambao wanashinda nyumbani lakini kwa maeneo kama Masaki, Osterbay huwezi kupata mtu kwani muda mwingi wa kazi wanatumia nje ya makazi yao. Kwa

those who are unemployed because of their poor education. They assumed that the majority of people residing in areas where *mihadhara* are conducted had less education than those in more affluent neighbourhoods that are spared open air preaching (Masaki and Osterbay). To deal with this seemingly intractable problem, some participants suggested: "Special areas for open air preaching or [religious] meetings should be constructed to include areas where government leaders reside, so they will also be subjected to the annoyance that we ordinary citizens with low incomes face."[286] Participants were of the view that government allowed open air preaching to continue because its leaders lived in relative peace away from the noise and trouble associated with *mihadhara*. Their belief was that if government leaders had the taste of *mihadhara*, they would deal with them seriously. In other words, *mihadhara* were also a class issue, that of leaders and citizens, the latter being likely to be affected directly by *mihadhara*. The argument appears to be that leaders do not understand the problems that ordinary citizens face and experience. The statement also reveals another social positioning in the country, namely the economic gap between the leaders, the elite, and ordinary citizens, the poor majority. Participants averred that leaders were financially better off than the majority of ordinary citizens ("we citizens with low incomes").

"An island of peace"

Participants generally identified Tanzania as a peaceful nation, which is borne out by events on the ground and the relative peace the country has enjoyed over the years. To them this peaceful existence is a product of the amicable coexistence between the major religions and because Christians and Muslims regarded one another as *ndugu* (comrades/relatives). As a result they generally treated each other as equals and with respect. This was the main objective of "Mwalimu Julius Nyerere who was at the forefront to ensure that peace is maintained"[287] and also "insisted on unity and elimination of discrimination based on ethnicity, religion and all forms of discrimination"[288] in the country.

---

hiyo kwa sehemu wanayoishi watu wenye elimu Mihadhara huwa ni nadra. Kwa sehemu za watu wenye elimu ya chini ndio wanaopelekewa mihadhara. (Educated male participant.)

[286] Zijengwe sehemu mahususi kwa ajili ya Mihadhara au mikutano ambazo zitahusisha hadi maeneo yanayoishi viongozi wa serikali ili nao waweze kuona kero tunayoipata sisi wananchi wa kipato cha chini.

[287] Mwalimu Nyerere alikuwa mstari wa mbele katika kuhakikisha kuwa amani hai toweki. (Educated male participant.)

[288] Alisisitiza umoja na kuachana na ubaguzi wa kikabila, dini na ubaguzi wote ule. (Educated male participant.)

Participants cited unity (cooperation and unification) of all citizens, regardless of religious affiliation, as a positive factor working in the national interest. They were interested in maintaining Tanzanian identity, hence the statement by an educated female youth: "We are Tanzanians; we are supposed to love each other and cooperate."[289] An elderly female participant said, "This nation should be governed without regard to the president's religion."[290] She continued: "Even if the president is a Christian, Christians should not be arrogant[*kifua mbele*] and see the country as theirs, hence ridicule Muslims. The president rules all [citizens] and stands for all [citizens]."[291] To these participants a president is a unifying national symbol. As such he has to serve all citizens of different faiths without favour. Participants, then, considered national identity as a major cause of national unity and peaceful coexistence. To them a primarily religious identity divided the country and undermined cooperation, love among citizens (Muslim and Christians) and, ultimately, peace. Some participants claimed that many Muslims tended to identify more with their religion than with their nation.

As a result participants were worried about the future stability of the Tanzanian nation. An educated male youth pointed out: "The current leadership lacks the wisdom and skills that Nyerere had. As a result it has become difficult to handle religious problems, which if not solved could cause instability in Tanzania."[292] These problems include *mihadara* and the way they are conducted. The participants strongly believed that unregulated open air preaching can destroy peace in Tanzania: "We don't want open air preaching; we don't want destruction of peace; we want to live like now, loving and supporting each other." To elderly female participants allowing open air preaching to continue threatens the "good things of our Tanzania; which is seen as an island of peace",[293] because "Christian tolerance will end, and hence the destruction of peace".[294] The participants accused the current leadership of failing to unify citizens, hence undermining national identity. As a result, many individuals identified more with their religion(s) than with other

---

[289] Sisi ni Watanzania tunatakiwa tupendane na tushirikiane.
[290] Nchi hii inabidi itawaliwe bila kuangalia raisi ni wadini gani.
[291] Nchi hii inabidi itawaliwe bila kuangalia raisi ni wadini gani. Hata kama Rais ni mkristo, sio wakriso waweke kifua mbele na kuona nchi ni yao na kuwa kkashifu waislamu; hawana ubavu, uwezo wala sauti, hapana, yule Rais anatawala wote na anawasimamia wote.
[292] Utawala wa siku hizi, hautumii busara kutokana na viongozi wa sasa kuwa na "skills" tofauti ya zile za Nyerere na hivyo kutoweza kutatua migongano ya Kidini ambayo inaweza kuwa chanjo cha kukosa amani Tanzania. (Elderly female participant).
[293] Hatuitakii mema Tanzania yetu ambayo inaonekana ni kisima cha amani.
[294] Lakini baadaye huu uvumilivu wa wakristo kwa wenzetu utafika kikomo na hivyo kuvunja amani.

Tanzanians. This, according to participants, could lead to religious conflict and disharmony, especially if Christians also started to identify themselves as Christians first, not as Tanzanians.

The foregoing argument was confirmed by a key informant, who spoke about transformation in terms of national unity. He explained, "Our national unity is not as good as it used to be."[295] He added, "We see fierce debates in parliament and members of parliament forget about their party's ideology and become divided on religious lines."[296] The participant mentioned the 2008 budget session when the minister of foreign affairs, Bernard Member, tabled a bill on the possibility of the URT joining the OIC and the establishment of *kadhi* courts. He claimed that the conflict was a result of "underground Islamic movements"[297] trying to divide Tanzanians on religious lines. These movements allegedly comprised Muslims who wanted to get Tanzania to join the OIC and introduce *kadhi* courts. These issues were explained in the preceding arguments. He said, "I advise Christians to bring national unity. We should spread love. Even if someone calls you a *kafir*, you should see him as a human being."[298] This is because "for Tanzanians national unity is the basic thing that comes before religious selfishness".[299] The participant stressed that national identity brought about unity, whereas religious identity generated diversity and disharmony. An elderly female participant echoed these views: "Let us help our president, let us live in peace and love, and help one another so that the president can do his work smoothly."[300]

"All human beings are equal"

Participant also discussed ecumenism, stating that all religions worshipped but one God. Indeed, one participant revealed, "the God of Muslims and [the God of] Christians are one. It is us human beings who are confused here on earth, because we don't know what constitutes a true religion, since everyone is pulling

---

[295] Kuhusu umoja wakitaifa, kwa jinsi ambavyo nimekuwa nikifuatilia na mambo yanavyo kwenda umoja wakitaifa umekuwa si mzuri kama ulivyokuwa. (UDSM key informant.)
[296] Tunaona mijadala mizito inaenda bungeni na wabunge wanasahau itikadi ya vyama vyao wanagawanyika katika dini. (UDSM key informant.)
[297] Kuwa kuna movement za kichini chini za kiislam. (UDSM key informant.)
[298] Mimi katika kushauri wakristo ili kuleta umoja wakitaifa tuishi kwa upendo hata mtu anapokuita kafir muone bado ni binadamu. (UDSM key informant.)
[299] Kwa Watanzania umoja ni kitu muhimu sana kuliko ubinafsi wa kidini wa mtu.
[300] Tumsaidie Rais wetu tuishi kwa amani upendo na tuishi vizuri tusaidiane kwa nguvu zote ili raisi apate wepesi wa kazi yake. (Elderly female participant.)

on his side."[301] The participants implied that all human beings were equal and that all (Muslims and Christians) worship one God. They referred to homogeneity and inclusiveness, union of faiths and believers, because that would reinforce the peace that Tanzania enjoys.

As a result some participants discussed religious unification, namely having only one religion for all Tanzanians. Some argued against the freedom of worship provided by government for all citizens. One participant in the FGD of educated male youths said, "Instead of being troubled by open air preaching the consensus will be to make all Tanzanians change and have one religion."[302] They said that government should facilitate such unification and control religious issues. As one educated male youth pointed out, "I don't agree that the government should allow every individual to have his/her own religion – it is a big mistake because the world has changed a lot."[303] He continued, "In my opinion it is better for all Tanzanians to have one faith so that we avoid these confrontations,[304] and government should facilitate this."[305] The participants were referring to civic identity. It would mean having one religion for all Tanzanians, so Tanzanians would be able to identify with that religion. What was not specified was what kind of religion, state religion or otherwise, and how a compromise would be reached.

This proposal of a unified religion was not supported by all participants in the group. One said, "Unifying Tanzanians in one religion..., I don't think this will be justice", adding "I think everybody should practise his/her own religion just like the late father of the nation Mwalimu J.K. Nyerere wanted. It is better for everyone to stay in his/her own religion."[306] These statements endorse the process of liberalisation and individualism taking place in the community. The participant thought it unfair to strive for one religion in a nation of such religious diversity; his primary fear was that it would restrict people's inalienable right to practise their own religion. A key informant felt the same way: "If we reach a point of aiming

---

[301] Mungu wa waislamu na wakristo ni mmoja lakini sisi wanadamu tunatapatapa duniani hatujui ni dini ipi ina ukweli kwa sababu kila mtu anavutia kwake.

[302] Kupata suluhisho la kuwafanya Watanzania wabadilike na wawe katika dini moja pasipo kuhangaika na mihadhara.

[303] Lakini siafiki kwamba serikali iache kila mtu awe na dini yake ni kosa kubwa sana kwani sasa dunia inabadilika.

[304] Na kwa mtazamo wangu naona ni bora kwa watanzania wote kuwa na imani moja ili kuepusha hii migongano.

[305] Serikali inaweza kusimamia jambo hili.

[306] Vile vile nadhani suala la kuwaunganisha Watanzania kuwa katika dini/imani moja (kama alivyosema mjumbe aliyetangulia) Sidhani kama ni la haki, kwa mtazamo wangu naona kila mmoja aabudu katika imani yake kama Hayati Baba wa Taifa Mwalimu J.K. Nyerere alivyosema.

for this country to have just one religion, we will be making a big mistake."[307] The solution, most participants reasoned, was for "everyone [to] advertise one's own faith without intruding upon that of others. If you are capitalist, advertise; defend capitalism without intruding on *ujamaa*." These arguments are part of the ongoing liberalisation, diversification and privatisation processes in Tanzania versus the socialist and communalist path that had served society so well. The present processes encourage individualism and competition in all sectors, including the religious sector. Participants' statements also reflect the ongoing ideological struggle in Tanzania between *ujamaa* on the one hand and liberalism/capitalism on the other.

One key informant made a humanistic case. She claimed, "A Muslim is a human being too who needs shelter. Our difference lies in the religions which we inherited. Therefore I see Muslims as my *ndugu* [comrades], that is why I cooperate with them."[308] Here the participant positioned herself as a member of the community, in which both Muslims and Christians live together. For her the choice of a religion is largely predetermined by historical forces that made Tanzania inherit both Islam and Christianity. She therefore identified with the broad community of Tanzania rather than with a narrow Christian community. What emerges from our analysis is that our Christian participants identify with homogenisation in society, whereby some individuals find common ground to compromise with adherents of different faiths in the interest of nation building. This was also apparent in other participants' utterances, such as "We are all human beings created by God, we differ only in denomination."[309]

It should be noted that, while participants were aware of religious differences and ideological struggles ("we differ in denominations, our difference is religion"), to them such differences were secondary to their civic identity, hence the statement: "All human beings are equal and therefore helping each other is very important."[310] This statement refers to a more general identity.

Other participants mentioned unification and national identity, in this case Tanzanian identity. An educated male participant said, "It is important to live as

---

[307] Tukifika hatua yakutaka kubadilisha nchi hii iwe ya dini moja tunakosea sana.
[308] Mwislamu nae ni binadamu anahitaji kupatiwa makazi, tofauti yetu ni dini tulizorithi, kwahiyo mimi nawachukulia waislam kama ndugu zangu ndio maana nashirikiana nao a. (Christian university student.)
[309] Wakati wote ni binadamu tumeumbwa na Mungu ila madhehebu tu ndio tunatofautiana. (Elderly female participant.)
[310] Binadamu wote ni sawa na hivyo kusaidiana ni jambo la muhimu. (Educated youth male participant.)

relatives so that we maintain our country's peace."[311] Educated male participants believed doing so (maintaining peace) would perpetuate the legacy of "Mwalimu Nyerere, who insisted on unity and abandoning discrimination based on ethnicity, religion and any other discrimination".[312] These arguments were very much in line with the political ideology of *ujamaa*. During Nyerere's time everyone was addressed as *ndugu* (comrade), hence all Tanzanians were *ndugu*. This was because Nyerere insisted on national unity in which citizens saw one another as equals, development partners. The participants' use of the term '*ndugu*' is a perpetuation of the *ujamaa* legacy and ideology. By the same token the term represents civic as opposed to religious identity.

Again, participants' statements make it clear that in Tanzania Muslims and Christians are blood relatives who share the same kinship/clanship in terms of Tanzanian nationalism and national ideology. Thus interdenominational differences "won't make us fail to live together because we are *ndugu* and our *koo* [clan] is the same".[313] This axiom was demonstrated in the linguistic subsection, where it was indicated that some participants were either married to Muslims or one of their parents was a Muslim. It shows that Christian-Muslim coexistence was being cemented by social factors such as intermarriage and kinship.

To the participants such coexistence was affected by historical trends in Tanzania. In their words, "If we look back, all of us lived together before the colonialists, who brought education but did not change the fact that we were born in the same clan [*koo*]."[314] This identifies again the introduction of secular education during the colonial and missionary period as one of the factors that shaped present-day Tanzania. Participants also noted that despite their religious differences they have continued living together dynamically, tackling problems that would undermine social cohesion as they continued developing their country. One of the educated participants said, "With regard to Christians and Muslims living together [coexisting] here in Kilakala, it is possible and there has been no conflict between Muslims and Christians about religious issues."[315] Christian-Muslim coexistence was

---

[311] Ni muhimu kuishi kama ndugu ili kuilinda amani ya nchi yetu.
[312] Inatupasa tuishi pamoja kindugu ili kudumisha amani nchini kwetu kwani hata Mwalimu Nyerere alisisitiza umoja na kuachana na ubaguzi wa kikabila, dini na ubaguzi wote ule. (Educated youth male participant.)
[313] Ijapokuwa tofauti hii haifanyi sisi tushindwe kuishi pamoja kwani sisi ni ndugu, na koo zetu ni zile zile. (Educated youth male participant.)
[314] Kwani hata tukirudi nyuma sisi sote tuliishi pamoja tena vizuri tu kabla ya ujio wa Wakoloni waliotuletea elimu lakini na haibadilishi ukweli kwamba wote tulizaliwa katika koo moja. (Educated youth male participant.)
[315] Kuhusiana na suala la wakristo na waislamu kukaa pamoja hapa Kilakala linawezekana na hai-

possible because the founder of Kilakala township, who was a Muslim, "invited both Christians and Muslims to the township without religious discrimination".[316] These participants identify more with their community than with their religious group. They see both Christians and Muslims as community members who cooperate without religio-centrism.

"They demonstrate, mutilate and beat Christians"

Participants voiced concern about extremist and fanatical religious behaviour. Extremism is noted in a statement such as, "They started fighting among themselves in mosques; you would hear at Magomeni, they fought in a certain mosque."[317] Fighting in a mosque is not normal or socially acceptable; the scuffle signified disagreements within the Muslim community. It also exposed struggles within Islam and Muslims in Tanzania. As one participant put it, "Muslims are divided among themselves. There are those who are pro-BAKWATA and another group which demonstrated when the American president George Bush arrived for a visit in Tanzania."[318] "We see *upinzani* [opposition] among Muslims themselves. Each group regards itself as better than the other, and thus the other group is considered to have strayed [from the right path]."[319] This kind of opposition within Islam was regarded by participants as stirring up conflict, not just religious extremism, as this Christian key informant puts it: "I don't see them as *wanasiasa kali* [extremists], but I see them as people who have been employed to stir up things [cause conflict]."[320] The participants lamented that extremist behaviour in Muslim ranks had created boundaries which polarised Muslims into two camps, namely pro-

---

jatokea mtafaruku wowote baina ya Waislamu na wakristo juu ya mambo ya dini. (Educated youth male participant.)

[316] Aliwakaribisha wakristo kwa waislamu bila ubaguzi. Na hivyo kutokana na hii, kwa kweli tunaweza kuishi pamoja bila ubaguzi wa dini. (Key informant Mzee Z.)

[317] Wakaanza wenyewe kwa wenyewe kupigana msikitini mara usikie Magomeni kwenye msikiti gani wamepigana.

[318] Waislamu wenyewe wamegawanyika kati yao kuna hawa BAKWATA na kundi lingine hata kipindi Rais George Bush wa Marekani alipo wasili katika ziara yake nchini Tanzania kundi la waislamu liliandamana kutoafiki ujio wake, wakati BAKWATA hawakuwa na neno juu ya ujio huu.

[319] Hivyo basi waislamu wenyewe kwa wenyewe wanakinzana na hivyo kuwa wapinzani na kila kundi kujiona kuwa bora kuliko jingine na kuona kundi jingine linapotea. (Educated youth male participant.)

[320] Mimi sioni kwamba wana siasa kali, naona ni kama wameajiriwa ili kuvuruga mambo. (Key informant Mzee X at Kilakala.)

BAKWATA (traditional Muslims) and extremists (who demonstrated and fought in the mosque).

In public many extremists were identified by the way they dressed. Women put on (face and head) veils, whereas the men "have long beards" and wore trousers which did "not touch the ground". This group also did some things differently from other Muslims, even during the holy month of Ramadan. They were "the first to start the fasting period" and they did not follow the sighting of the moon in Dar es Salaam. Instead they went by the sighting of the moon in Saudi Arabia, which is always a day earlier than in Tanzania. The participants identified these Muslims as following the Sunni tradition.

The differences between the Sunni and Shiite religious traditions are a result of on-going dynamism and liberalisation in Islam, which gives individuals freedom to practise the brand of religion that suits them. This sometimes leads to conflict between adherents of the two traditions. According to some participants religious extremism also occurred at an interreligious level in demonstrations in the form of fights between Muslim and Christian groups. As one elderly participant explained, "When we say let us teach them the Bible, they demonstrate, mutilate the Christians and beat up [the Christians]."[321] The participant here positioned Christians as victims of Muslim extremist behaviour, namely demonstrations, mutilation of the Bible and beatings; but if no remedial steps are taken to curb this extremism, Christians "may eventually take the law into their own hands, hence destroy peace"[322] "in the country, which is known as a peaceful country".[323]

Conclusion

The analysis of social practice has revealed socio-cognitive effects of language. It supports our premise that when speaking about others participants reproduce their social reality by either maintaining it or changing it. For example, in speaking about and rejecting some Muslims' claims about *kadhi* courts, open air preaching and Tanzania's OIC membership, Christians supported the status quo of Tanzania as a secular state and by doing so they positioned themselves as citizens who embrace the separation of the state and religion more than Muslims.

Most Christian participants positioned themselves as members of society rather than as members of a religion (i.e. Christian identity). This was done by speaking in general terms such as *ndugu* ("I consider Muslims *ndugu*"), relative

---

[321] Tukisema tuwafundishe Biblia wao wanaandamana na kuwakata wakristo na kuwachapa.
[322] Sisi ni wanadamu sio Mungu, tunaweza tukachukua sheria mkononi na hivyo kuvunja amani.
[323] Katika nchi hii ambayo inasemwa kuwa ina amani. (Elderly female participant.)

("we live like relatives"), human being ("a Muslim is also a human being"), and citizen ("we citizens with a low income"). These terms were inclusive and homogenising. The speakers also positioned most Muslims as members of society who compromised well with Christians. Muslims who were identified by Christians as religio-centrists were few. These Muslims were said not to compromise well with Christians.

Most participants projected Christianity as a religion of love; hence a good Christian was one who loved others ("we should spread love"). This attitude meant that Christians were able to compromise well with Muslims and by so doing help to bring about unity and cohesion in their society. Nevertheless things sometimes went wrong and their Christian habitus subjected them to victimisation and abuse at the hands of a few Muslim extremists bent on destroying the peaceful coexistence Muslims and Christians enjoy ("even if someone calls you a *kafir* you should see him as human being"). Extremism and religio-centrism were also noted in some statements by participants and Christian preachers during *mihadhara*. Despite Christians embracing an ideology of love there are other peripheral ideologies struggling for dominance in order to impose change (divergence), and in so doing affect the existing community identity (by creating their Christian [religious] identities) and the cordial Christian-Muslim relationship (leading to disruption of cohesion).

The participants portray Tanzania as a peaceful and united country. This was attributed to the strong foundation laid by the first president Julius Nyerere and other founding fathers who espoused *ujamaa*, which insisted on unity and national cohesion. Participants, however, also depicted Tanzania as an unequal society, in which there are disparities between Muslims and Christians, especially in regard to education and income distribution. The adoption of liberalisation and emergence of individualism reinforced these inequalities, which take on religious overtones. As a result some individuals identify more with religion than with society.

Chapter 4:
How Muslims and Christians speak to each other

"There are things that Muslims see as **haraam** *which are not forbidden for Christians"*

Chapters two and three analysed what Muslims and Christians say about each other. This chapter seeks insight into the interaction between Muslims and Christians in a heterogeneous group: how do they speak to each other? The interaction to be discussed includes not only participants of different faiths (Muslim and Christian) but also fellow believers in the group, and how they construct their religious identities and position themselves in such mixed situations.

As in chapters two and three, the main material to be analysed is the findings from Focus Group Discussions (FGDs). The primary difference from the other chapters is that this chapter uses participants' responses (data) collected in heterogeneous groups (i.e. Muslims and Christians combined) instead of in homogeneous groups (Muslims and Christians separately). In these groups Christians and Muslims were mixed according to gender, age and educational level. In total, seven FGDs were conducted, in which 51 participants took part. There was one group with nine elderly males and another with five elderly females. There were two groups of educated males comprising eight participants each. In addition there were three groups respectively consisting of eleven educated females, six uneducated males and four uneducated females. For triangulation and ongoing comparative purposes the FGD findings were supplemented with information from other sources such as interviews with key informants, newspaper articles, and religious writings and statements.

As explained earlier and demonstrated in chapters two and three, we used the multidimensional and polymethodical model of Norman Fairclough (1992), also known as socio-cognitive or critical discourse analysis (CDA), for analysing our data.

4.1. Analysis of linguistic practice

To analyse linguistic practice Fairclough (1992:75) focuses on vocabulary, grammar, cohesion and text structure, taking into consideration that the text has both ideational and interpersonal (identity and relation) meaning (Fairclough 1992:76).

In each of the aforementioned FGDs a number of topics were discussed. For the purpose of this chapter we select only responses that shed light on participants' utterances about the relationship between Muslims and Christians in a civic situation. Our main question is: how do Muslims and Christians speak to each other in a group? What socio-religious identities and transformations emerge from such interreligious interaction? The focus, therefore, is on the ethos, modality, politeness, turn-taking and topic control[1] of participants in the groups.

Muslim-Christian relations
"The relationship between these two religions is just good"

Speaking about Muslim-Christian relations, a Muslim participant said, "I think that … the relationship between Muslims and Christians has no impact …well… the impact is not that big. We have a good relationship between these two religions … it is good…"[2] Another Muslim in the group said, "For my part, I would say that understanding one another or the relationship between these two religions is just good … as he explained, there are no big differences … on the issue of discrimination … on the discrimination issue or relationship … in short, the relationship is very good."[3] Another Muslim added, "I also find that all communication between Muslims and Christians is good. There is no discrimination between Muslims and Christians."[4]

Christian participants in the group contributed to this discussion. One Christian noted, "Thanks, for my part, I think cooperation in living together is good … but when it comes to employment every individual [group] is independent … For example, you find that a college teacher will have difficulty getting a job in private

---

[1] See Fairclough 1992:137-168.
[2] Mimi nadhani kwamba katika maeneo ninayoishi mahusiano yaliyopo kati ya waislamu na Wakristo hayaathiri na athari ambazo zinakuwa si kubwa. Tuna mahusiano mazuri kati ya dini zote hizi mbili… ni mazuri.
[3] Mimi kwa upande wangu naweza nikasema kwamba maelewano au mahusiano kati ya hizi dini mbili ni mzuri tu kama alivyoeleza hivyo kwamba hazina tofauti kubwa ambazo zinajitokeza katika swala la kubagua. Katika swala la kiubaguzi au mahusiano kwa hivyo kiufupi tu kwamba ni mazuri sana.
[4] Mimi pia naona mawasiliano yote ya kiislamu na kikristo ni mazuri. Hakuna ubaguzi kati ya uislamu na wakristo.

colleges."⁵ Following the Christian's argument, a Muslim participant said, "There is discrimination to some extent. For example, discrimination could happen in employment or jobs at colleges, places where they need believers of that religion. If an Islamic school or college has students who study Islamic theology, those who are associated with teaching Islamic values, who are Muslim, will get the job."⁶ Another Christian said, "I say that the relation is not so good. Sixty percent of it maybe. For the remaining forty percent there is no cooperation."⁷

The first participant started by saying there is no impact, but hesitated ("well...") to further substantiate his argument and then quickly changed his vocabulary, saying that though there was "not that big an impact, we have a good relationship", so his argument suggests a degree of affinity.

His arguments covered a range of vocabulary, namely relationship, no impact, impact not so big and good relationship. In so doing he was setting an agenda for other participants in the discussion. Speaking in so many vocabularies made his argument lack cohesion. This participant opted for a civic ethos by focusing on issues with civic appeal rather than ones in which he personally played a role.

Other Muslim participants did not follow up on the vocabularies raised by the first participant, making the discussion very incoherent. Thus the second educated participant used alternative words such as 'understanding one another'. To him that was what made a good relationship. He also saw differences which he called discrimination; overall, he said there were no big differences, thus achieving both negative and positive politeness.

The third participant again did not pick up on the others but came up with his own vocabulary. He insisted that relationship is about communication, that good relations are achieved through good communication. He said categorically that there is no discrimination between Muslims and Christians.

These participants used various phrases such as 'good relations', 'no discrim-

---

5   Asante, mimi kwa upande wangu naona upande wa kuishi, ushirikiano ni mzuri lakini kwa upande wa ajira kila watu wanajitegemea. Kwa mfano unakuwa mwalimu wa vyuo vya private sasa katika kupata kazi ndio inakuwa tatizo.
6   Suala la ubaguzi nadhani lipo kwa kiasi fulani, kwa mfano kunaweza kutokea ubaguzi katika ajira/kazi katika vyuo maeneo ambayo wanahitajika waumini wa dini hiyo inayohusika kwa mfano. Kama chuo cha kiislamu wa shule ya Kiislam ambayo ina walimu wanaochukua taaluma ya kiislamu, pale watakao kuwa wanapata ajira ni pale watakao kuwa wanahusiana na kufundisha masomo yenye maadili ya kiislamu ambao ni waislamu wenyewe. Haimuidhinishi kumuajira mtu asiye kuwa muiislamu katika chuo ambacho kimetawaliwa kiislamu. (Muslim participant in mixed educated male group I.)
7   Naweza kusema kwamba uhusiano sio mzuri sana unaweza kuwa wa asilimia 60% na hizo 40% naona hakuna ushirikiano. (Christian in mixed educated male group I.)

ination', 'good communication', 'no differences'. In so doing, each participant did not completely dismiss what the previous speaker(s) had said but also did not accept it, hence the use of new or different words.

Apart from the foregoing, another male Muslim in the uneducated group said, "I think ... in the past there was discrimination between Muslims and Christians; now there is cooperation ... During those times I had difficulty mixing with Christians. Now we are all equal." [8] Another Muslim participant in the same group added, "Although I don't have higher education in Islam, I see that this religion does not discriminate against anybody."[9] A Christian participant in the group said, "There are differences; there are things Muslims see as *haraam* which are not so for Christians."[10]

The first participant said cooperation between Muslims and Christians indicated that all are equal, which reflected a civic voice (equality). This was contrary to other participants, who focused on differences. One participant, for instance, talked explicitly about Islam. To him Islam does not discriminate against anybody. On the other hand, the third participant talked about differences between Muslims and Christians. The differences were about things that Muslims see as unclean (*haraam*). However, these unclean (*haraam*) things were not regarded as such by Christians.

Similar statements as those made in educated male group I were uttered in educated male group II. For instance, a Muslim participant in the group said, "There is a good relationship, because we live like *ndugu*."[11] Another Muslim participant agreed, saying that there is "good relationship because there is no religious quarrelling [*malumbano ya kidini*]".[12] A Christian participant also said that "there is a good relationship, because people of different faiths live respecting each other",[13] indicative of civic identity.

As in educated male group I, the discussion in this group seemed to dwell on good relations. Participants used different words for what they saw as the reason for good relations – words such as 'living like *ndugu*'; 'no religious verbal exchange'; and 'respect each other'. Although the words were definitely used in

---

[8] Mimi nadhani hapo zamani kidogo kulikuwa na ubaguzi kati ya waislamu na wakristo lakini kwa sasa umepungua na kuna ushirikiana baina ya Imani hizi mbili. Kipindi kile mimi kuwa na mkristo au kuchanganyikana na mkristo nilikuwa najiona tofauti. Sasa hivi naona wote tuko sawa.
[9] Japo sina elimu ya juu sana katika dini ya kiislamu ila naona dini hii haibagui mtu.
[10] Kuna tofauti kidogo, kuna vitu vingine waislamu anaviona haramu wakati wakristo sio hivyo.
[11] Mahusiano ni mazuri kwani watu tunaishi kama ndugu.
[12] Mahusiano ni mazuri kwani hakuna malumbano ya kidini.
[13] Mahusiano ni mazuri kwani watu waimani tofauti wanaishi kwa kuheshimiana.

the same way, they indicated that participants wanted the group discussion to proceed harmoniously by not directly denying or accepting what was said by other participants.

Participants mentioned labels and names that Muslims and Christians use to refer to each other. One uneducated Christian participant said, "Our comrades/fellow Muslims like very much to call us Christians *kafirs*."[14] This participant started with 'our comrades', which is a friendly, polite word, softening the effect of the word *kafirs*, an impolite name. As one elderly Christian female participant pointed out, "The word *kafir* is not good. It is like being insulted a lot."[15] This is because "the word *kafir* means an argumentative person, who does forbidden things".[16] The participants noted that *kafir* also referred to errant Muslims, hence is not reserved for Christians only. The elderly Muslim female used the passive voice: "If you are a Muslim and you do not follow religious values, you will be called a *kafir*. Thus this word is not only for Christians."[17] Another participant added, "In Islam, if you don't follow Islamic ethics, they will say this is a *kafir*."[18] This was corroborated by a Christian participant in the same group, who said: "This word *kafir*, we all use it; they will call you *kafir* and we also call them *kafirs*. All religions use the word *kafir*."[19] From the participants' statements it was clear that the word is mostly used indirectly, and has become ambiguous, as it can be used to label both Muslims and Christians depending on context and necessity, especially when one wanted to indicate division and/or religio-centrism.

Participants pointed out that Muslims also use the word 'pagans' to refer to Christians.[20] A Christian participant added, "This is because Muslims do not believe Christianity is a religion. They believe there is only one religion, which is Islam, apart from which there are pagans."[21] According to an uneducated female Muslim participant the word 'pagan' is used by Muslims to mean "a person who

---

[14] Wenzetu waislamu wanapenda sana kutuita sisi wakristo makafiri.
[15] Neno kafiri sio nzuri ni kama kukutukana pakubwa sana.
[16] Kwani kwa tafsiri kafiri ni mtu mbishi anayefanya kitu kilichokatazwa. (Christian uneducated male participant.)
[17] Kama ni mwislam na hufuati maadili ya dini utaitwa kafiri lakini sio kwa wakristo tu.
[18] Kunako katika dini yetu ya kiislamu ukiwa hauna maadili yakufata dini ya uislamu watasema huyu ni kafiri.
[19] Hili la ukafiri watu wote tunalitumia wao wanaita kafiri na sisi tunaita kafiri. Dini zote linatumika hili neno kafiri.
[20] Wapagani ni jina ambalo hutumika kwa kumaanisha wakristo. (Muslim uneducated male participant.)
[21] Hii inatokana na sababu kwamba waislamu hawaamini kama ukristo ni dini wanaamini dini iliyopo ni moja tu ambayo ni ya kiislam zaidi ya hapo ni wapagani.

has no religion".²² The expressions "apart from which there are pagans" and "a person who has no religion" are inclusive in the sense that they include not just Christians but other non-believers and believers of other faiths, but in a civic way, hence mitigating the negative reaction of Christian participants.

Christians in the uneducated male group said that the name "Al Qaeda is used for Muslims".²³ However, the participant was not clear why Muslims are called Al Qaeda. This ignorance reduced tension in the group. Another Christian participant in the same group said, "The name 'domesticator of spirit' (*wafuga majini*) is used to denote Muslims".²⁴ Again, the label and name were used indirectly in the passive voice, reporting how people in their civic capacity labelled believers of other faith(s).

Nevertheless, these labels (*kafirs*, *wapagani*, domesticator of spirit, Al Qaeda, etc,) are not neutral; they are used by Christians and Muslims who want to set up boundaries between Muslim and Christian believers or, in the case of *kafir*, between believers and unbelievers.

Employment opportunities
"It is difficult to get a job in private colleges"

With regard to employment, the response of the Christian participant concurred with the statement that there are differences. He said every individual is independent in areas like employment. The participant's statement that it is "difficult to get a job in private colleges" does not reveal the religious identity of the owners of private colleges, so it is not clear which private college he is referring to. It could be any private college, Christian or Muslim.

This did not go unnoticed by some Muslim participants. The comment by the Muslim participant was actually a response to the Christian's statement. He confirmed it by saying that it was indeed difficult for a non-Muslim to get employment at a Muslim-run private college, since he/she will not have 'Islamic values'. Such discrimination was mitigated to some extent, justifying his statement that "discrimination could happen in employment or jobs at colleges, since the nature of that college is tailored for believers of that religion". Again, the identities of the believers and religion were not revealed, so it was not clear whether he was referring to Muslims or Christians. What was clear, however, was that a person's religion can hinder or facilitate getting employment in religiously run colleges.

---

22 Neno mpagani lina maanisha mtu aliyekosa dini.
23 Al-qaeda ni jina ambalo waislamu wanaitwa. (Christian uneducated male participant.)
24 Wafuga Majini ni jina ambalo hutumika kwa waislamu pia.

A participant in educated group I said, "There are very few Muslims at the rank of commanders or district and regional commissioners."[25] Another Muslim participant said, "There is discrimination, for example, in employment there is a discriminatory environment, though this does not affect us much."[26] A Christian participant, responding to the Muslim's argument, said that Christians get employment because "Christians are educated and they occupy higher positions. This is not because of injustice (*dhuluma*) but rather because of historical circumstances. Thus Christians got religion and education when they were at school. Then, after independence, these individuals who had education took over positions from the European colonists and that was because they had education and skills; which is unlike our Muslim fellow citizens who had neither education nor skills."[27]

The Muslim participant spoke about discrimination in employment, but again he hedges his argument with "does not affect". Here the word 'discrimination' is used to describe the fact that there are "few Muslims at the rank of commander and commissioner". The Christian participant's statement has a different word: he uses injustice as an alternative for discrimination. The participant also offers a justification by referring to social transformation in the country. Besides, he said Christians acquired education and skills at mission schools, which gave them job opportunities. The Christian participants' statements indicated that Christian domination in education and their privileged status in the employment sector were not caused by injustice but rather by historical circumstances. In other words, to Christian's participants the apparent inequality between Muslims and Christians had a logical explanation. This maintained the status quo and perpetuated inequality. It is contrary to Muslims' statements, which seemed to challenge the status quo of Christian domination in education and demanded change: "There are few Muslims at the rank of commander ... "[28]

---

[25] Waislamu wachache sana katika ngazi ya makamanda au wakuu wa wilaya na mikoa.
[26] Kuna ubaguzi, mfano katika suala la kikazi kuna mazingira ya ubaguzi japo hauwezi kuathiri sana.
[27] Wakristo wameelimika na wako katika nyazifa kubwa sio kutokana na dhuluma bali ni kutokana na historia kwamba walipata dini na elimu pindi wakiwa shuleni na hivyo kuwa rahisi kwa watu hao kuwapa kipaumbele wenzao wenye historia kama zao, yaani wanawa-consider. Baada ya uhuru watu hawa waliopata elimu walishika nyadhifa za wakoloni wakizungu kutokana na kuwa na elimu pamoja na ujuzi tofauti na wenzetu waislamu ambao hawakuwa na elimu wala ujuzi. (Christian participant in mixed educated male group I.)
[28] Waislamu wachache sana katika ngazi ya makamanda.

Education
"Today a Muslim is educated and a Christian is educated too"

Participants discussed education and its implications for adherents of the two faiths. One uneducated male Muslim said, "Muslims were afraid of their children being converted and becoming Christians if they go there, because all Europeans are Christians."[29] Another Muslim participant said, "I agree with my comrade, Muslims did not like to send their children to school for fear of being converted and becoming Christians; instead they sent them to religious schools for *madras*."[30] This was confirmed by a Christian participant: "In the past [problems associated with] religion targeted Christians because Muslims were afraid of their children being converted to Christianity when they joined those [missionary] schools."[31] Another Muslim participant said, "I see that we Muslims are regarded as having little education ..."[32]

Participants in this group said that in the past education was part of Christianity, hence to get that education one had to change one's religion. This, however, was not corroborated by the Muslimparticipant. The combination of active and passive voice ('I see ... we are regarded') shows disagreement with the idea of Muslims being seen as poorly educated. Unlike the other participant in the group who talked in general terms, this participant specified his Muslim identity and position ('we Muslims'). But he did not specify the identity of those who considered Muslims to be educationally backward. In this way he preserved harmonious group interaction.

Participants in educated male group I said that nowadays Muslims' poor education related not merely to fear of conversion but to the parents' financial circumstances. According to a Muslim participant in the mixed educated male group I, "It is the financial circumstances that we parents face that make us fail to send our children to school."[33] This was confirmed by Christian participants in the group. One of them said: "The focus for individuals is financial. If your family's financial

---

[29] Wazungu wote ni wakristo, kwa hiyo waislamu waliogopa sana wakienda kule watakuwa wanabadilishwa dini na kuwa wakristo.

[30] Namuunga mkono mwenzangu kwamba waislamu walikuwa hawapendi kuwapeleka watoto wao shule kuhofia wao kubadili dini na kuwa wakristo na hivyo kuwapeleka chuoni kusoma Madrasa.

[31] Hapo zamani maswala ya dini yaliwalenga sana wakristo kwani waislamu walihofia kuwa watoto wao kubadili imani na kuwa wakristo pindi watakapo jiunga na shule hizo.

[32] Mimi naona waislamu tunaonekana hatuna elimu sana.

[33] Kutokana na hali ya kiuchumi tulionayo wazazi hivyo kushindwa kupeleka watoto wetu shuleni. Japo sidhani kama kuna ubaguzi wa dini huko shuleni kwani watoto wanachangia madarasa, chumba, na walimu. (Educated Muslim participant, mixed group I.)

position is weak, then you won't get any higher education. In other words, education is not related to religion any more but to money, which enables you to get that education."[34] Because of that, "today [some Muslims] are educated, even the sheikhs in the mosques are educated".[35] A member of the elderly male group said much the same: "Today a Muslim is educated and a Christian is educated too,"[36] which reflects a civic ethos.

Still on education, a Muslim participant said that "religious education is given more emphasis; hence attendance of *madras* is daily..."[37] A Christian participant said, "Most Muslims, especially those who get a bit of education, for example form four, they postpone education and instead become sheikhs in the mosques."[38] A Muslim participant said, "The colonial administration was why most Christians got secular education."[39] A Christian participant said, "Christians are compelled to study more, because even if you want to enter religious administration/leadership you must study at least up to form six."[40] A Muslim participant said, "I support my comrade that Christians' financial advantage is based on the colonial foundation. Muslim communities did not get this opportunity as they continued getting religious education [*elimu ya dini*]."[41]

Participants said that education was generally regulated by income, but conversely, one's educational level determines one's income. Muslim participants also commented on religious education and its implications. They positioned Christians as generally well educated and Muslims as generally less educated. Moreover, participants positioned Muslims as tending to religio-centrism, as they put greater emphasis on religious than on secular education.

---

[34] Watu wanazingatia tu swala la uchumi. Kama familia yako ina uchumi mdogo basi hutopata elimu ya kiwango cha juu. Kwa maneno mengine suala la elimu halihusiani tena na suala la dini bali uchumi ambao ndio nguzo ya wewe kuipata hiyo elimu. (Educated Christian participant, mixed group I.)

[35] Lakini kwa sasa elimu wanayo hata msikitini mashehe nao wanaelimu. (Educated Christian participant, mixed group I.)

[36] Sasa hivi mwislam kasoma mkristo nae kasoma.

[37] Elimu ya dini kwa waislamu inapewa fursa kubwa kwani mahudhurio ya madrasa ni ya kila siku...

[38] Waislamu wengi, hasa wanaopata elimu kidogo mfano ya kidato cha nne huweza kugairi kuendelea na masomo na badala yake huingia msikitini na kuwa mashekhe.

[39] Suala la utawala wa kikoloni ndio chanjo cha wakristo wengi kupata elimu ya dunia.

[40] Wakristo wanalazimika kusoma zaidi kwani hata kama unataka kuingia kwenye uongozi wa dini basi lazima usome zaidi angalau hata kidato cha sita.

[41] Naungana na mwenzangu kwamba suala la uwezo wa kiuchumi kwa wakristo linatokana na msingi wa kikoloni na hivyo jamii za kiislamu hazikupata fursa hii kwani ziliendelea kupata elimu ya dini.

Dietary patterns
"Differences between these two religions are in food"

Discussing the dietary patterns in their community, some participants said the "differences between these two religions were on food issues, because there are foods which are eaten by individuals of one faith, while individuals of the other faith see them as forbidden [*haraam*]".[42] This was confirmed by a Muslim participant who said, "In short, there are foods that Christians eat which are not eaten by Muslims."[43] A Christian participant in the group added, "Food issues bring complications, especially when you are at home eating pork [*kitimoto*] and a Muslim guest arrives… You tell him to wait outside, because some Muslims don't like the smell."[44] A Muslim participant said, "We Muslims don't eat pork and animals like cats, dogs … we eat only *halal* animals." [45] He added, "Christians eat pork, cats, rats and pork is even put in butcheries to be sold." [46]

The participants' utterances indicate that they were in agreement that certain foods were only eaten by Christians, including foods which were forbidden for Muslims. This was seen by some as differences that complicated Christian-Muslim personal relations.

Similar utterances were noted in other FGDs. For example, one elderly Muslim female said, "For a Muslim it is an axiom that we don't eat that animal the pig and the Christian community knows that, so when they have a feast they don't include pork in the menu."[47] The participant started by saying 'we don't eat that animal' without naming it immediately, but it was mentioned subsequently with reference to Christians ("the Christians know that … they don't include pork in the menu").

In the uneducated female FGD a Christian participant said some Muslims also eat pork. In her words, "They are real Muslims, but when you cook pork

---

[42] Masuala ya chakula yanaleta utofauti kati ya dini hizi mbili kwani kuna vyakula ambavyo vinaliwa na watu wa imani moja huku watu wa imani nyingine kuviona haramu.
[43] Kifupi, vipo vyakula ambavyo wakristo wanakula lakini waislamu hawali.
[44] Masuala ya vyakula ndio yanayoleta utata pale unapokuwa kwako huku unakula kitimoto (nguruwe) na akaja mgeni muislamu … labda kwa kumwambia akumgoje nje kwakuwa waislamu wengine hawapendezwi na harufu yake.
[45] Sisi waislamu, nguruwe hatuli na wanyama kama paka, mbwa pia hatuli, bali tunakula wanyama halali.
[46] Wakristo wanakula nguruwe, paka, panya, na ambapo nguruwe huwekwa buchani na kununuliwa.
[47] Kwa mwislam huyo mnyama nguruwe kwakweli sisi hatutumii na jamii ya wakristo wameshaelewa wakiwa na sherehe nguruwe hawaweki.

they rejoice... they eat a lot."[48] Another Christian participant added, "You find a person praying five times,[49] but he eats a lot of pork."[50]

Some participants said that "pork [*kitimoto*] is often consumed at grocery stores or bars and other places but not at home".[51] According to an elderly female Christian, "In Christian homes there are utensils which are not used for food that we eat; there are utensils for visitors, especially when the family knows this is a Muslim ... who is not allowed by his religion to use such things."[52] In her statement this elderly Christian woman avoided the word 'pork', which is generally considered to be disturbing or impolite to Muslims, and instead used words like '*kitimoto*' (KiSwahili slang for pork), 'such things', and so forth. By doing so she maintained harmony and avoided conflict with Muslim participants in the group.

However, an uneducated female Christian participant in the group said, "I think the community and us are complicated, but the Bible doesn't allow a person to eat pork either."[53] She was supported by a Muslim: "I agree that pork is not legitimate in both religions."[54] Hedging words such as 'I think' helped the discussion to flow harmoniously. Moreover, the second statement shows convergence between Muslims and Christians ("pork is not legitimate in both religions"). This also occurred in the elderly female FGD, in which a Christian participant noted that not all Christians ate pork. "I'm a Christian but I don't eat pork," she said. "Not all Christians eat pork. Seventh Day Adventists, for example, don't eat pork. So not all Christians eat pork; just some denominations, but not all denominations."[55] The use of exclusive ('just some denominations') and inclusive ('not all

---

[48] Wale waislamu kabisa lakini ukipika nyama ya nguruwe wanashangilia kama wameona nini sijui na wanakula sana

[49] Pious Muslims are supposed to pray five times a day.

[50] Unakuta pia mtu anaswali swala tano lakini anakula nguruwe sana.

[51] Mara nyingi hicho kitimoto huwa kinaliwa sehemu ambazo ni za starehe kama bar na sehemu zingine lakini sio nyumbani. (Elderly Christian female.)

[52] Kwenye familia ya kikristo ... kunakuwa na vyombo ambavyo havitumiki kwakile chakula tunachokula, kunakuwa na vyombo vya mgeni napengine hata familia inajua huyu ni mwislam ... wanajua hicho kitu haruhusiwi kula katika dini yake.

[53] Nafikiri jamii hata sisi wenyewe ni wagumu lakini Biblia yenyewe hairuhusu mtu ale nyama ya nguruwe.

[54] Mimi naliunga mkono hili kama nilivyosema awali kwamba nguruwe hajahalalishwa katika dini zote mbili.

[55] Hata mimi ni mkristo lakini sili nguruwe. Sio wakristo wote wanakula nguruwe kama wasabato hawali nguruwe kwahiyo sio wakristo wote wanakula nguruwe ni baadhi ya ma Inategemea na mtu aliyemchinja kwani mazingira aliyotumia yanaweza kunizuia mimi kula dhehebu tu yanakula lakini sio madhehebu yote

Christians eat pork') terminology affirmed harmonious group interaction and a civic rather than a religious ethos.

According to one uneducated Muslim male, "Discrimination happens when a Christian decides to keep swine while surrounded by Muslims. This will be seen as discrimination."[56] For this participant keeping pigs amounts to discrimination against Muslims.

Participants discussed the manner in which animals should be slaughtered. An uneducated female said, "Depending on the person who slaughtered the animal, because the condition under which it was killed could prohibit my eating it."[57] This was corroborated in the uneducated male FGD, in which a participant said, "At Christian ceremonies Muslims won't eat a chicken or a cow which was not slaughtered by a Muslim."[58]

However, according to Muslim participants not all Muslims were allowed to slaughter animals or poultry. One uneducated male Muslim declared, "Myself, I don't understand these things because I have not been educated in religion and therefore I cannot slaughter animals or birds because I have not been authorised to do so."[59] This participant believed that slaughtering needs to be done in a particular way and that is why only those familiar with (educated in) religion were allowed to slaughter. For this participant slaughtering is a religious (*dini*) matter.

Female participants said that women were not allowed to slaughter. As one uneducated female Muslim noted, "In our religion a woman is not allowed to slaughter a chicken, but in the religion of our counterparts Christian women do slaughter chickens."[60] This was confirmed by Christian participants in the group: "Aah, I just slaughter! I chop it! The father of the house is not at home, he is at work, should I wait until he returns? I will look in whatever direction and just pull off its head."[61] This Christian participant's use of the direct, active voice shows determination and responsibility, unlike the Muslim utterances which were indirect and passive, hence avoiding responsibility.

---

[56] Ubaguzi unatokea pale mkristo anapoamua kufuga nguruwe wakati amezungukwa na jamii ya waislamu itaonekena kuwa ni ubaguzi.
[57] Inategemea na mtu aliyemchinja kwani mazingira aliyotumia yanaweza kunizuia mimi kula.
[58] Kwenye sherehe za wakristo wenyewe waislamu hawawezi kula kuku au ng.ombe ambayo haijachinjwa na mwislamu.
[59] Mimi mwenyewe siyajui kwani sijasoma dini hiyo na hivyo siwezi kuchinjwa kwani sijahalalishwa.
[60] Kwenye dini yetu, mwanamke haruhusiwi kuchinja kuku lakini dini za wenzetu wakristo mwanamke anachinja kuku.
[61] Ah! Mimi namchinja tu, namkatilia mbali. Baba mtu hayupo kaenda kazini, nitamsubiri mpaka arudi? Mimi popote naangalia navuta tu kichwa.

Participants also discussed alcohol consumption. An uneducated Muslim male said, "At funerals you will find Christians drinking a lot of beer [*wanakandamiza bia*] in contrast to Muslims."⁶² A Christian participant explained, "Personally, I don't see any discrimination. Drinking is not a problem because it is a normal thing ... However, there are some Muslims ... who drink alcohol and become drunk [*kulewa*]."⁶³ This statement was supported by a Muslim participant who said, "Drinking at a funeral is a personal habit and can't lead to problems; these are normal things."⁶⁴ An elderly Christian female said the same: "There are Christians who don't drink beer and Muslims who don't drink beer, but there are some Muslims and Christians who drink beer. I don't see any problem in this ... it is a personal option."⁶⁵ Thus participants ascribed drinking habits to personal (individualised) behaviour and not to religion.

Interreligious marriage
"Muslims have their things and Christians have their things"

Speaking about interreligious marriages, a Christian participantsaid, "To my mind I see Muslims as the ones with problems ... Christians have no problem ... Even if you decide to change your religion it is up to you ... For that reason I don't think there will be understanding between a Christian and Muslims."⁶⁶ This participant sees Christians as more individualised than Muslims. This was not confirmed by the next participant, who said,"I see problems on both sides. I would say it is like a false belief, which we Christians and Muslims have created.

---

62 Pia katika msiba utakuta wakristo ndio "wanakandamiza" bia tofauti na waislamu.
63 Binafsi yangu sioni ubaguzi, suala la kunya vinywaji si tatizo kwani ni mambo ya kawaida...isitoshe kuna baadhi ya waislamu pia ambao ni watoto wa mashekhe nao hunywa pombe na kulewa.
64 Masuala ya kunywa pombe kwenye msiba ni desturi za watu na hivyo haiwezi kuleta matatizo. Ni mambo ya kawaida.
65 Hata wakristo wengine hawanywi bia na waislam hawanywi bia lakini kuna waislam wengine bia wanakunywa na wakristo pia wanakunywa kwahiyo katika vinywaji mimi sioni tatizo mana hilo swala linaenda kwakila mtu ni hiari yake mwenyewe.
66 Mimi kwa upande wangu naona waislamu ndio wenye matatizo kwa sababu hata ukiangalia kwenye familia za kawaida za wakristo inapotokea kwamba binti amepata mchumba, hilo suala la kuoana linakuwa kwenye mkono yake lakini utakuta muislamu akimpata mchumba mkristo lazima kutaleta complain. Wakristo hawana tatizo, hata ukiamu akubadili dini inakuwa juu yako lakini waislamu ndio mwenye tatizo na kwa maana hiyo zidhani kama kutakuwepo na maelewano kati ya mkristo na waislamu.

Muslims have their things and Christians have their things."[67] A Muslim participant said, "I see problems on both sides, for Muslims and Christians, but there are more [problems] for Muslims because a Christian would accept changing her religion in order to marry a Muslim fiancé, but for Muslims it is difficult."[68] Another Muslim participant said, "I'm not far from the others, because I see Muslims as having many problems relating to these *haraam* foods. Because that girl will be asked ... how come you want to eat *haraam* food...? Therefore it will be difficult for the relatives to accept a Muslim changing her religion and becoming a Christian."[69] One Christian participant said, "Problems are on both sides, for example you have a Muslim or a Christian fiancée whom you married at a government office [*bomani*]... When the woman who was a Christian dies ... complications will arise about how the deceased will be buried ... in a Christian or an Islamic way? Everyone will be pulling on his side."[70]

These participants described group interaction and identity creation. The Christian participant established a clear group identity: Muslims have a problem accepting interreligious marriages, Christian don't have this problem. However, this was played down by the second Christian participant, who opted for a civic identity, hence put Muslims and Christians in the same basket (convergence). This is evident in her use of "we, Muslims and Christians" as if these formed one group to which she belongs. The participant also coined an expression ('false belief'), which she considers to create boundaries between Muslims and Christians. She said, "Muslims have their things and Christians have their things." Her argument on the creation of boundaries was evident when it came to interreligious mar-

---

[67] Mimi naona mataatizo yapo katika pande zote mbili, ni seme nikama imani potofu ambazo tumezijenga sisi wakristo na waislamu. Waislamu wana mambo yao na wakristo wana mambo yao.

[68] Mimi naona matatizo yako kote kote kwa waislamu na kwa kwakristo ila kwa waislamu ndio zaidi kwa sababu mkristo anaweza kukubaliwa kubadili dini kwenda uislamu ili akaolewe na mchumba wa kiislamu aliyemtaka, lakini kwa waislamu huwa ni ngumu...

[69] Sikombali sana na wenzangu kwani naona waislamu ndio wenye matatizo sana na yanatokana na vyakula hivi ambavyo havijahalalishwa. Kwani yule binti atakayetaka uolewa na mkristo atauliziwa inakuwaje yeye akale vyakula haramu? Kwa hiyo itakuwa ngumu kwa ndugu kukubali kwa wewe muislamu kubadili dini na kuwa mkristo.

[70] Matatizo yapo pande zote mbili kwa mfano – umepata mchumba muislamu au mkristo na nyie mkakubaliana kufunga ndoa bomani, sasa mkaishi na baadaye yanaweza kutokea matatizo kama msiba sasa unakuta kati ya wazazi au wazazi wa upande mmoja hawakuridhia ndoa hiyo. Siku inatokea mwanamke anakufa na hapo awali mwanaume alikwa muislamu na mwanamke alikuwa mkristo ambaye alibadili dini na kuwa muislamu. Utata unakuja kwenye kuzika kwamba marehemu atazikwa kikristo au kiislamu, kila mtu anavuti upande wake. Mwishowe mnaanza kugombana mara maiti izikwe kiislamu na wengine wanasema izikwe kikristo.

riage. On this issue the Muslim participants said that Muslims find it more difficult accepting interreligious marriages than Christians. The Muslim woman, for instance, toned down her disapproval of the Christian participant by agreeing with her before taking her stand ("but there are more [problems] for Muslims") so that she could maintain a friendly relation with the Christian participant.

Although all participants spoke on the same topic or employed the same discourse (i.e. interreligious marriage), they managed to sandwich in their personal small topics. For example, the first participant mentioned freedom to change one's religion for Christians ("even if you decide to change religion that will be your own responsibility"). The second participant mentioned false belief by Muslims and Christians ("I could say these are like a false belief that we Muslims and Christians have created"). And the third participant referred to *haraam* food. Another Christian participant added civil marriages, parents, death and funerals. Thus some participants' statements pointed to separatism/divisiveness which created boundaries between believers, but there was also convergence, for example when opting for a civil marriage.

Style of dress
"If I see a Christian wearing a **baibui***, in my soul I will just feel happy"*

Participants discussed styles of dress. One uneducated Christian female said, "Although I'm not Muslim, I can wear *hijab*."[71] This was confirmed by another Christian female: "Yes it is true, they wear [the *hijab*] for their own gratification. Myself, I have it and I wear it for my gratification."[72] Another Christian participant said, "I sometimes wear it, but now I have given it to my house helper, because she is a Muslim. But if I want to gratify myself, I wear it."[73] A Muslim participant said, "If I see a Christian wearing a *baibui*, in my soul I will just feel happy with the way she dressed and looked like a Muslim while she is not one."[74]

However, not all types of *baibui* and *hijab* are preferred by Christians. An uneducated Christian female said, "There are those *baibui* which are light and transparent. Therefore, a person can wear a pair of trousers and then put the baibui on

---

[71] Kwa mimi binafsi mimi naweza nikavaa hijabu japokuwa si muislamu.
[72] Ni kweli wapo, wanavaa kwa lengo la kujifurahisha. Mimi mwenyewe ninalo na ninavaa kwa kujifurahisha.
[73] Mimi huwa ninavaa ila kwa sasa ni mempa mfanyakazi wangu kwa kuwa yeye ni muislamu. Lakini nikitaka kujifurahisha ninalivaa.
[74] Mimi nikimuona mkristo amevaa baibui … rohoni nitafurahia tu alivyolivaa na kuonekana kama muislamu ingawa sio muislamu.

top, but what you are wearing underneath is also visible."[75] A Muslim participant in the group said, "You find a person wearing shorts and a blouse and on top she has a *baibui*."[76] She added that there were "different *baibui* fashions, there are thick ones and lighter ones like shawls".[77]

An educated Muslim female said, "I think among Muslims clothing is based on the scriptures. Any Muslim girl or woman is supposed to cover her whole body, leaving just the palms of her hands and eyes to be seen."[78] This was confirmed by another Muslim in the group who said, "Each religion has its own dress code. For Muslims, we are supposed to cover [*kuhifadhi*] the whole body except the face and hands."[79] Uneducated female participants, however, noted that this was practised mainly by a particular group of Muslims. "This is a practice of some but not all Muslims. There are those who cover the whole body; those are Sunnis,"[80] said one of them.

Speaking about Christians, a Muslim in the educated group said, "Christians don't have a special dress code. Some go to church wearing a skirt." One Christian in the group said, "On our side, we go to church wearing skirts and blouses, but I don't think the church would tolerate seeing a Christian going to pray clad in a super mini-skirt or a skimpy top [*kitopu*]."[81] A Christian participant in this group confirmed what the Muslim participant had said, but rejected the notion that they do not have a special dress code, because to her super mini-skirts and skimpy tops are not allowed by the church. This was put slightly different by another Christian in the group who said, "In short, I see there is no [strict] religious dress code, which means a person should just wear his/her clothes, because you don't go to

---

[75] Kuna yale mabaibui ambayo ni mepesi na yanaonesha vazi lililovaliwa ndani. Kwa hiyo mtu unaweza kuvaa suruali yako ndani na juu ukavaa baibui lakini unaonekana kile ulichovaa ndani.
[76] Mtu unamkuta anakipedo, chake na kiblauzi chake na juu ana baibui.
[77] Na siku hizi yapo mabaibui ya fasheni mbali mbali. Kuna mazito, kuna hayo mepesi kama mitandio.
[78] Kwa mimi ninavyoona kwa upande wa waislamu swala la mavazi lipo kwenye maandiko. Msichana au mwanamke wa aina yoyote ile wa kiislamu, anatakiwa aonekane kiganja cha mkono na macho tu alakini kote kulikobakia mwilini kote kuwe kumefunikwa. (Educated female Muslim participant.)
[79] Kila dini ina utaratibu wake wa mavazi kwa waislamu tunatakiwa kuhifadhi mwili wote kasoro uso na mikono lakini mkristo hana mavazi maalum anaweza kwenda kanisani akiwa na sketi.
[80] Huu ni utaratibu kwa baadhi ya waislamu sio wote. Kuna wengine wanavaa kote kote wamejifunika, MASUNI hao.
[81] Kwetu sisi wakristo tunakenda kanisani tukiwa tumevaa sketi na blauzi lakini sidhani kama kanisa litabadili kuona mkristo amekwenda kusali akiwa amevaa kimini kidogo au ki-top.

church naked [wearing skimpy dress]."[82] This affirms that indeed Christians have a dress code but that it is less strict than Muslims' dress code.

An uneducated female participant said some Muslim men also dress differently. She said, "Now ... even men go to mosque in short trousers, unlike others who wear cassocks/robes [*kanzu*] and long trousers when going to mosque. Sunni men put on turbans [*kilemba*] too."[83]

According to some educated females people's style of dress is regulated by religion (*kidini*) and society (*kijamii*). One Christian participant explained, "Socially, I don't think society is ready to see people dressing in a manner that is not respectable."[84] "Similarly, in our families there is no parent who would like to see her daughter's bare shoulders."[85] Therefore, "be it a Muslim or a Christian, this is a cultural issue, that is to wear clothes which show respect for other people".[86]

In the elderly female FGD a participant said, "Today children wear short dresses ... but if you tell them not to wear them, they tell you that you are old and outdated."[87] An elderly participant criticised the way young males dress: "Nowadays boys wear trousers below their waist, but if you tell them, my son, don't dress like that, I don't like it, he will tell you, so mum, how do you want me to wear it? Don't you see that is the way all youths wear their pants these days?"[88] This prompted an elderly participant to say, "The youths' style of dress is the same, there is no religion involved here, as you will find a Christian and a Muslim [dressing the same way]."[89] Participants' statements on youths' style of dress revealed a civic rather than a religious identity.

---

[82] Kwa kifupi mimi naona hakuna utaratibu wa dini unaosema kuwa kila mtu avae mavazi yake, ... kwani huwezi kwenda kanisani ukiwa uchi.
[83] Sasa hao wengine hata mwanaume anaweza uvaa pensi na akaenda nayo msikitini tofauti na waislamu wengine ambao wanavaa kanzu ndefu au suruali ndefu ndio wanenda msikitini. Na wanaume wasuni pia wanavaa vilemba.
[84] Kijamii sidhani kama jamii iko tayari kuwaona watu hawavai mavazi ambayo si ya kiheshima.
[85] Kwenye familia zetu, kwani hakuna mzazi ambaye atakubali kumwona mwanaye anatembea mabega yakiwa wazi.
[86] Niwe muislamu au mkristo suala hili ni la utamaduni kwamba vaa mavazi ambayo yanaleta heshima mbele za watu.
[87] Leo hii watoto wote wanavaa nguo fupi, ukiwambia wanasema we mzee umepitwa na wakati.
[88] Sasa hivi watoto wa kiume wanavaa suruali halafu wanaifungia chini ... sasa ukimwambia mwanangu usivae mvao kama huu mimi sitaki, anakuambia mama sasa unataka nivae aje si unaona vijana wote wanavaa hivyo.
[89] Na hii haina dini maana hapo kuna mkristo na mwislam.

Muslims' and Christians' financial status
"There are poor Christians and poor Muslims"

With regard to income an educated male Muslim in group I said, "There is a financial gap between Muslims and Christians."[90] Another participant claimed, "The financial status of Muslims is low."[91] This was confirmed by a Christian participant, who said, "Christians are the ones with more financial clout than Muslims."[92] He was supported by another Christian: "Christians are on top in the economic sector, since the majority of them are educated compared to the number of educated Muslims, because they put more emphasis on religious education than secular education."[93] However, a Muslim participant in the group said the opposite: "I think it is just a belief; poverty and wealth affect individuals in both religions. You may find a rich Muslim or a poor Christian."[94] His utterance was corroborated by uneducated male participants. For example, a Christian participant said: "Here at Kilakala there are poor [*wachovu*] Christians and poor [*wachovu*] Muslims."[95] His argument was supported by a Muslim participant: "I concur with my comrade that poverty [*uchovu*] is not only for Muslims or Christians but for anyone."[96]

A Muslim participant hedged his statement by using the words 'a gap' (with reference to financial status), but would not specify who had the advantage, thus keeping his point neutral and polite. By contrast all Christian participants were explicit. For example, they said Muslims tended to have low incomes. Other Christian participants indicated that Christians were financially better off ('on top', 'greater financial clout'). Hence they classified Christians as having the upper hand over Muslims financially.

Some Muslim and Christian participants disagreed, maintaining that Christians and Muslims were on an equal footing: "You may find a rich Muslim and a poor Christian." But this Muslim participant, too, started with an ambiguous clause ("I think it is just a belief"), which harmonised his statement with others in the group, since the belief referred to was unclear and therefore open to

---

[90] Suala la uchumi lina gap kati ya waislamu na wakristo.
[91] Uchumi wa waislamu ni kidogo.
[92] Wakristo ndio wenye uwezo mkubwa wa kiuchumi kuliko waislamu.
[93] Wakristo kidogo wako juu katika sekta ya uchumi. Kwa kuwa idadi yao kubwa ni wasomi ikilinganishwa na idadi ya wasomi waislamu … kutokana na wao kufuatilia sana elimu ya dini kuliko elimu dunia.
[94] Mimi naona ni imani tu, umaskini au utajiri unalenga kwa watu wa dini zote mbili. Unaweza kukuta mwislamu tajiri au mkristo maskini.
[95] Hapa Kilakala wapo wachovu wakristo na wachovuwaislamu.
[96] Mimi niko pamoja na mwenzangu kwamba uchovu hauko kwa waislamu au Wakristo, uko kwa yeyote yule.

multiple interpretations. Nevertheless his statement challenged the popular notion of Christians' financial dominance and suggested a homogeneous society, where both Christians and Muslims face hardship depending on prevailing circumstances. Thus the Muslim participant managed to refute the statements of his Christian counterparts.

In terms of discussion control, Muslims and Christians had equal control of the discussion. The Muslim participant first presented a neutral statement, which was not picked up by Christian participants, who were explicit about both their subject and object. Nevertheless the Muslim participant clung to his neutral statement: "I think it is just a belief."

Participants commented on church contributions, which tend to reflect the level of affluence of believers. In the words of a Christian participant "This can be seen in Christians' contributions [*sadaka*] in church on Sunday where you find they contribute something like 200,000 shillings, which is difficult to get in a mosque."[97] Another Christian participant claimed, "That is why padres own good cars and houses while Muslims do not have a good life."[98] To this participant Christian affluence was reflected in their material possessions, such as big cars, houses and contributions in church.

Participants also spoke about organisations which support these religions. An educated Muslim male in group II said, "Muslims are not affluent in life, because Christians have big organisations which further development, while Muslims are denied membership of such organisations." This was confirmed by a Christian participant: "Christians have many progressive organisations in the economic sector. Muslims are prohibited by their policies if they want to join organisations for the purpose of improving their life; hence they fail to get ahead. For example, Zanzibar wanted to join the OIC but was denied this opportunity, so it becomes difficult to get ahead."[99] The participant did not identify who denied Zanzibar IOC membership but used the passive voice to keep his utterance indirect, thereby maintaining group cohesion

The Muslim participant said that Christians were developed because they were allowed to join developmentally oriented organisations. He also said that Muslims

---

[97] Hii inaweza kudhihirika kwenye sadaka za wakristo ambapo unaweza kukuta sadaka za Jumapili kanisani ni kama 200,000/= ambapo kiasi hicho ni shida sana kupatikana misikitini.

[98] Ndio maana mapadri humiliki magari mazuri/ Nyumba na hivyo kwa waislamu huwa hawana maisha mazuri.

[99] Wakristo wanamashirika mengi na yaliyoendelevu katika nyanja za kiuchumi. Waislamu wanabanwa na sera zao pale wanapotaka kujiunga na mashirika ili kujikwamua kiuchumi na hivyo kushindwa kusonga mbele. Mfano ukienda Zanzibar walitaka kujiunga na masuala ya OIC wanakatazwa kwa hiyo inakuwa vigumu kusonga mbele.

were not allowed to join such organisations. According to this participant, it made Muslims less developed than their Christian counterparts. The participant, however, did not disclose the names of organisations that Christians were allowed to join to their benefit. He did not reveal the names of organisations that refused Muslims' OIC membership, nor the reasons why they did this (except the ambiguous phrase ""by their policies"). This reduced the coherence of his utterance.

One Christian participant did touch on the topic of organisations and the economy but, unlike the Muslim participant, he cited their policies as a stumbling block for Muslims seeking membership. He also named one organisation, the OIC, from which Zanzibar was barred.

Mihadhara
"The main objective of mihadhara is to educate"

On some topics, such as in the discussion on *mihadhara*, differences in participants' statements were evident. For example, all Christian participants in educated male mixed group II said open air preaching was destructive. By contrast all Muslim participants supported the idea of holding *mihadhara*.

A Christian participant said, "Among Muslims *mihadhara* are more like business and therefore destructive."[100] Another Christian participant said, "Open air preaching is destructive because preachers use improper ways, although *mihadhara* help to educate people. But the emotional and persuasive language used is a source of problems; hence the main object of educating people ... vanishes."[101] A Muslim participant, on the other hand, said, "All religions' *mihadhara* focus ... aah ... the main objective of *mihadhara* is to educate."[102] This was confirmed by a fellow Muslim: "*Mihadhara* are constructive for both sides, I mean Muslims and Christians are involved."[103] A similar argument was advanced by another Muslim participant, who said, "*Mihadhara* are constructive in both religions regardless

---

[100] Kwa upande wa waislamu mihadhara inalenga zaidi kuwa ya kibiashara na hivyo inabomoa.

[101] Mhadhara inabomoa kutokana na kutumia njia isiyo sahihi japo kuwa mihadhara inasaidia katika kuelimisha lakini lugha ya jazba na yakushawishi watu ndio tatizo kuu. Hivyo kutokana na haya mambo lengo kuu la kuelimisha katika mihadhara hupotea.

[102] Mihadhara ya dini zote inalenga lengo kuu ya mihadhara ni kuelimisha yaani kila mmoja anapata fursa ya kutoa mtazamo wake wa kuwaeleza dini nyingine kile ambacho yeye anakifahamu juu ya imani yao ya Kimungu ikoje.

[103] Mihadhara inajenga, na pande zote mbili yaani waislamu na wakristo zinashirikishwa. Mhadhara wa waislamu hushirikisha wakristo pia na ule wa wakristo hushirikisha waislamu na hivyo inatangaza dini.

of whether they are being conducted outside the mosque or the church."[104] This statement contradicted that of a Christian participant, who said that "*mihadhara* are destructive because each religion opposes the other, using religious books".[105]

From this analysis it is evident that most Christians' statements condemned *mihadhara* as destructive, hence the recurring phrase, "*mihadhara* are destructive", for example "*mihadhara* are destructive because preachers use emotional ... language". The statement by a Christian participant in this group identifies the type of *mihadhara* which are destructive. The participant starts with the words, "among Muslims *mihadhara*...", hence singles out Muslim rather than Christian *mihadhara*. This was contrary to statements by Muslims, which discussed the issue in more general terms without specifying an identity, thus including both Muslim and Christian *mihadhara*. This is evident in comments such as "*mihadhara* are constructive in both religions", "*mihadhara* are constructive for both sides". Such statements supported *mihadhara*. The Muslim participants applied a civic ethos, which saw *mihadhara* as involving both Muslims and Christians (e.g. Muslim *mihadhara* involve Christians and Christian *mihadhara* involve Muslims – and all worship one God).

These verbal trends were noted in all mixed groups with male participants (educated male group I, elderly male and uneducated male groups). The picture was different for all mixed groups with female participants. All participants in the female groups said *mihadhara* were destructive. For example, a Christian participant said: "In *mihadhara* every person pulls on his side ... The truth is that I see these *mihadhara* as making us quarrel [*tugombanisha*]."[106] The participant did not single out any religion, but said every person pulls 'on his side'. She expressed a civic ethos ("making us quarrel"). Her argument was corroborated by another Christian participant, who said, "*Mihadhara* cause quarrels because the person [preacher] does not know the Gospels (New Testament) ... Often the people who preach have not studied these issues ... Those who ridicule [others' faith] are often hooligans [*wahuni*]."[107]

Their arguments were supported by female Muslim participants. For example,

---

[104] Mihadhara inajenga kwa dini zote bila kujali kama iko nje ya misikiti au nje ya kanisa na kushirikisha watu wa imani tofauti.
[105] Mihadhara inabomoa, kwani kila dini inapinga dini nyingine kwa kutumia vitabu vyao vya dini.
[106] Hili la mihadhara kila mtu anavutia kwake ... Kwa kweli mihadhara hii mimi naona inagombanisha.
[107] Mihadhara inagombanisha ni kwamba mtu halijui neno na kama unalijua neno huwezi kugombanisha katika mihadhara kwasababu unalihubiri neno. ... Mara nyingi watu wanaohubiri hivi hawajasomea yale mambo... na mara nyingi hawa wanaokashfu ni wahuni sio wale walioelekea kwenye neno.

one Muslim used much the same words: "I share that view, because these fellows who preach religious things go beyond what is acceptable ... Let's follow religious things and leave hooligan things alone."[108] Another Muslim participant said, "Most of the time *mihadhara* annoy, hurt and disappoint ... because they fail to use good language ... Worse still, they fail to reach out in acivil manner ... They fail to reach those youths who smoke *bhang* [marijuana], who use narcotics ... Instead they preach things which benefit nobody, I mean [things that are] provocative."[109] This was supported by a Christian participant: "Truly, I support that. I advise those who conduct *mihadhara* to study religious issues a bit ... because sometimes they are people from the streets who conduct *mihadhara*, they don't know why they are there."[110]

All participants dwelled on the same topic (*mihadhara*), although they also interjected some new civic topics/discourses such as youth and drug use. Using secular terms such as hooligans (*wahuni*) repeatedly, instead of religious words such as pagan (heathen) or *kafir* (infidels), the participants ended up appealing more to civic than to religious elements. As a result the discussion was very coherent. All participants talked in general terms without mentioning what type of *mihadhara* they were referring to. In doing so, they enhanced politeness and group cohesion.

Extremism and terrorism
"Those Muslims who say five prayers are the ones quarrelling with Christians"

A participant in the uneducated female FGD said, "I myself don't know religion, and how can I argue with a person [on religious issues]?"[111] To this participant "those who know religion are the ones involved in arguments, that is, those who know the holy book [*msahafu*] and the Bible."[112] This was confirmed by a Muslim

---

[108] Sawa maneno kama hayo, maana hawa wenzetu wanaohubiri mambo ya dini wanapita kiwango cha kuhubiri ... Uhubiri tufate mwenendo huu, tufuate mambo ya dini tuache mambo ya kihuni.

[109] Hiyo mihadhara mara nyingi huwa inakera, inaumiza na kusikitisha maana watu wanashindwa kutumia lugha ambayo ni nzuri ... Kibaya zaidi wanashindwa kuifatilia ile jamii ili iweze kuelimika. Mfano, hao vijana wanaovuta bangi, wanaotumia madawa ya kulevya wanashindwa kuwavuta katika dini zao matokeo yake wanahubiri vitu ambavyo havifai kabisa yaani uchochezi.

[110] Kwakweli hata mimi naunga mkono, ninashauri wale wanaotoa mihadhara wawe wamezzoma kidogo mambo ya dini ili wanapotoa neno liwe linatoka kweli kwenye maandiko na lenye maana unakuta saa nyingine ni watu wa mitaani wanaenda kuongoza mihadhara hawajui kilichowapeleka pale ni nini.

[111] Mimi mwenyewe sijui dini nitalumbana na mtu kivipi.

[112] Wanaolumbana ni wale wanaojua dini – wanaojua msahafu na wengine wanaoijua Biblia.

participant: "Those who believe they know religion are the ones arguing, but we who are just Muslims and don't pursue religious issues, we compromise with Christians."[113] Another Muslim participant said, "Those Muslims who say the five prayers are the ones who quarrel with Christians."[114] A Christian participant in the group said, "Like what we said in the beginning, there are those who claim to be Sunni and there are normal ones."[115]

The participant's statement showed that there are Muslims who regard themselves as knowledgeable in matters of faith (enlightened religious leaders) and normal Muslims. Normal Muslims (*wakawaida*) did not engage in heated religious debates and as a result they got on well with Christians. On the other hand, educated (in religious matters) Muslims engaged in religious debates and as a result they did not compromise with Christians. According to participants those schooled in religion belonged to the Sunni tradition.

An uneducated Christian male participant said those who instigate conflict were called Al Qaeda: "They are called by this name because they have long beards, they cut their trousers, they shave their hair and they walk with sticks, they don't wear mourning at funerals."[116] In addition "they are people who initiate chaos and use sticks to beat up people, even in mosques".[117] Educated participants said those who cause interreligious conflict tended to have little education. As one Christian male participant put it, "Those who don't have even a little education are the ones with problems. Lack of education is the cause of these differences which could erode the existing cooperation."[118] However, an uneducated female participant said, "I see *mihadhara* conversations do not bring unity. I don't know if here at Kilakala they have fought, but there are places where they have fought."[119] This was confirmed by an elderly Christian man: "These open air religious preachers

---

[113] Wale wanaojiona wanajua dini ndio wanaolumbana, lakini sisi kama sisi ambao ni waislamu wakawaida tupo tu kwani hatufuatilii mambo ya dini yetu na ndio maana tunaelewana na wakristo.

[114] Wale waislamu wa swala tano ndio wanaogombana na wakristo.

[115] Ni kama tulivyoelekeza mwanzo, kuna hao wengine wanadai ni masuni na hao wa kawaida.

[116] Na wanaitwa jina hili kwa sababu ya wao kufuga ndevu, kukata suruali, kunyoa upara pamoja na kutembea na fimbo, hawavunji matanga kwenye misiba.

[117] Watu ambao wanaweza kuanzisha fujo na kutumia bakora zao kuchapana hata kama ni huko misikitini. (Uneducated Christian male participant.)

[118] Kwa hiyo kwa wale wasio na elimu kidogo ndio wenye tabu kwa hiyo suala la elimu ndio chanzo cha tofauti hizi ambapo inaweza kuleta/kusababisha kuwa na ushikamano mbovu.

[119] Mimi naona maongeze wanayoongea kwenye mhadhara hayaleti umoja sijui kwa hii Kilakala kama walishawahi kupigana, lakini kuna sehemu walishapigana (Uneducated Christian female participant.)

are the ones misleading people and causing chaos in society."[120] He added that these religious preachers cite different scriptures which are not true and end up breeding animosity in society.[121]

An educated Muslim male said, "Islam is humility."[122] To him "all religions don't like wickedness".[123] A Christian participant said, "The important thing is to observe the purpose of religion and not instigate trouble by exploiting existing differences between religions, as this could lead to divisions."[124]

One uneducated Muslim participant said, "In many countries where there are wars, the cause is religion, unlike ours [Tanzania], in which Muslims and Christians live well and if there is conflict, government intervenes because our government is not controlled by [any] religion."[125] On the other hand, an elderly Muslim participant accused the government of being "the one responsible for bringing problems in society andconsequently a flare-up will happen like what happened in the Ivory Coast, Burundi, Rwanda, Congo and other places if the government continues in this style ... because you can't have two children and favour only one of them."[126] This participant added, "It reaches a point when a person doesn't ask for his right but he takes it. Therefore Muslims will wake up and take their rights which they have lost."[127]

Some elderly participants linked religious extremism with poverty; they explained that extremism was facilitated by poverty. As an elderly Muslim male put it, "This is why ... the state of the economy is so crucial, because a person is available to be bought to go and do certain things against other religions."[128] His statement was confirmed by a Christian participant who said, "This relates

---

[120] Kwa sasa hao wanaolingania dini ndio wanaopotosha nakuleta vurugu katika jamii.
[121] Walinganishi wanaleta maandiko ambayo hayapo kwahiyo yananzisha chuki baina ya jamii.
[122] Uislamu ni unyenyekevu.
[123] Dini zote hazipendezwi na maovu.
[124] Cha muhimu ni kuangalia lengo la dini na sio kuchochea tofauti zilizopo baina ya dini ambazo huleta mgawanyiko.
[125] Nchi nyingi zinazopigana chanzo huwa mambo ya dini tofauti na kwetu (Tanzania) ambapo waislamu tunaishi vizuri na wakristo na kama tofauti zinatokea basi Serikali inasimamia kutoa tofauti hizi kwani serikali yetu haiendeshwi kidini.
[126] Serikali ndo imeleta matatizo katika jamii hii na kwa tahadhari kutatokea milipuko kama ilivyotokea Ivory Coast, Burundi, Rwanda, Congo na sehemu nyingine kama serikali itaendelea na mtindo wake unaoufanya sasa hivi maana huwezi kuwa na watoto wawili mmoja unampendelea mwingine unamfanyia.
[127] Huwa inafikia wakati mtu haki yake aombi anachukua. Kwahiyo waislam wataamka nakuchukua haki yao waliyoipoteza.
[128] Ndio maana unakuja kukuta kuna kipindi uchumi unachukua nafasi kubwa ndio maana mtu yupo tayari kununuliwa kwenda kufanya jambo fulani dhidi ya dini fulani.

to poverty, because a person can get something or do something to entice people to destroy our tranquillity."[129] He added, "If you have money, you may set conditions for establishing a religion. There are those who have come and established [brands of] Islam according to personal whims and still claim they are following Holy Scripture."[130]

A Muslim participant in the educated male group said, "This is also a result of these terrorist policies [actually anti-terrorism policies], hence Muslims don't get assistance because they are linked to terrorism."[131] Here the Muslim participant stressed terrorist policies as the factor that made others associate Muslims with terrorism. However, he did not spell out who linked Muslims to terrorism; the organisations from which Muslims ask for assistance were not mentioned. The participant did not say why Muslims were universally linked to terrorism.

Conclusion

At the individual level the analysis of linguistic practice revealed the use of alternative labels such as '*ndugu*', 'friend', 'companion' and 'comrade' to refer to each other and to other believers. These labels were inclusive and indicated homogeneity in the religiously mixed groups. Ultimately group members spoke about themselves and others in civic rather than religio-centric terms. On the other hand, some participants used negative words such as 'Al Qaeda', 'pagan', '*kafir*', '*haraam*' and 'domesticator of evil spirits' that suggested Muslim-Christian divisions and religio-centrism.

Moreover, participants described unfriendly relationships between Muslims and Christians at religious institutions, particularly educational ones. For instance, participants described discrimination at faith-based schools and colleges where an individual from a different faith could have difficulty enrolling children or securing employment ("discrimination happened in employment or jobs at college"). Discrimination of this kind took place at both Muslim and Christian religious institutions, as one participant narrated earlier: "I see problems on both sides. I would say it is like a false belief, which Muslims and Christians have created. Muslims have their things and Christians have their things." Participants said that

---

[129] Linahusiana na umaskini kwa maana kwamba mtu yeyote ni rahisi maana anaweza kupata chochote au kufanya lolote lakushawishi watu ili kuondoa dhana nzima ya utulivu wetu.

[130] Sasa hivi kuwa na hela unaweza kutengeneza mazingira yakuanzisha dini. Kuna wengine wanakuja wanaanzisha uislam katika mipangilio yao nakuona wanafuata maandiko.

[131] Hizi sera za ugaidi nazo zinachangia kwani waislamu hawapati msaada kwani wanahusishwa na ugaidi.

one's chances in life such as a good job depended on the type of education one had access to. Christians' early access to Western/secular education through religious colleges has made them affluent in life.

The government's interference in Muslim affairs was said to cause segregation between Muslims and Christians in the country. For instance, participants mentioned that Muslims were barred by the Tanzanian government from joining Islamic developmental organisations, which makes Muslims lag behind Christians materially ("Muslims are not affluent in life because Christians have big organisations which further development, while Muslims are denied membership of such organisations."). Participants described the government as favouring Christians more than Muslims. As one of them complained, "You cannot have two sons and favour only one of them".

4.2. Analysis of discursive practice

At the level of discursive practice the focus is on the production, consumption and distribution of texts (Fairclough 1992:78). As was explained in the general introduction, in producing and consuming, texts people draw on other texts or 'mental models' stored in their long-term memory (Fairclough 1992:101) such as the constitution, the Bible, the Qur'an and newspapers, and some texts are more influential than others. This is what Fairclough calls intertextuality and interdiscursivity.

As this chapter deals with the analysis of discussions in heterogeneous groups, we repeat what we said in the general introduction about the cognitive process of understanding-misunderstanding. Consumers of texts (interpreters) can only understand the texts produced by others if they are able to link these texts to others texts that they have stored in their long-term memory. If they are unable to do so, there is misunderstanding and a breakdown of communication. In everyday life there will always be 'misunderstanding understanding', or 'understanding misunderstanding' (Mall 2000). This is what Tanner and Wijsen (1993) call 'working misunderstanding'.

Focus group participants
"... Like what my fellow participant said"

In the FGDs participants made (intertextual) references to what their fellow participants had said. This was evident in words such as 'I also support...', 'like what my fellow participant said', 'I'm not far from others' and 'like he said'. These words were uttered by different participants in the group, either in agreement or in disagreement with the statements referred to. For example, in educated male group II one Muslim participant said with reference to a fellow Muslim's statement: "I support my comrade that Christians' financial advantage is based on the colonial foundation."[132] In educated male group I there were two such references. One Muslim participant said, "I support X[133] that all religions encourage good relations."[134] The same participant said, "I concur with Mwalimu X, a Muslim male can marry a Christian girl."[135] In the discussion in the young uneducated female group one Muslim participant referred to a previous discussion with her: "Like we said this morning…"[136] A Christian participant referred to the discussion in the group, "Like we explained earlier…"[137] A Muslim participant cited what others had previously talked about in the group: "Like the others have said…"[138] A participant, who did not concur with the others, used words such as, "I have a different perspective."[139]

The habit of participants to refer to other participants' utterances (intertextuality) was also noted in the educated female mixed group. When discussing the possibility of Muslims and Christians having good relations, a participant referred to other participants using expressions such as "I don't differ with my fellow [Christians]", "I support my fellow (Muslim participant)", "I don't differ much from my fellow [participants]" (two Christians used this expression), and a Muslim said, "I'm not far from what the others have said." Yet another Muslim participant referred to her own earlier statement: "I don't disagree with my earlier explanation." Nevertheless, when participants were in agreement with their fellow believers, they shifted from the plural to the singular pronoun. This happened in the case of statements like "I support my fellow [Muslims]". However, this was very rare. It only happened twice and both times the statements were uttered by Muslims. And when participants' references were very specific they produced utterances such

---

[132] Naungana na mwenzangu kwamba swala a uwezo wa kiuchumi kwa wakristo linatokana na msingi wa kikoloni. (Muslim male in mixed educated male group I.)
[133] His name is withheld for ethical reasons.
[134] Namuunga mukono Iddi wa kuwa dini zote zinachochea uhusiano au mahusiano mazuri. (Muslim male participant in mixed educated male group I.)
[135] Nakubaliana na Mwalimu Chaka muislamu anafunga ndoa na binti wa kikristo. (Muslim male participant in mixed educated male group I.)
[136] Kama tulivyokuambia asubuhi. (Female Muslim participant in uneducated female mixed group.)
[137] Kama tulivyokueleza mwanzo. (Christian female participant in uneducated female mixed group.)
[138] Kama walivyosema wengine (Female Muslim participant in uneducated female mixed group.)
[139] Mimi namtazamo tofauti. (Christian female participant in uneducated female mixed group.)

as, "I don't differ with this sister" and "the same as said by sister B".[140] The intertextuality evident in group interaction was friendly and harmonious. Participants also picked up on discourses already established by other speakers, making the discussion very coherent.

Intertextuality was also evident in the elderly women's mixed group. Phrases such as "it's the same way" (two participants used that), "I see it in the same way", "I walk in the same way"; "truly, I also support her"; "as this woman said". Some participants did not concur with what other participants had just said in the group and they made their stand clear by saying, "It's true but difficult, life is the cause of youth's immorality." This was opposed by another participant, who said, "I oppose what this woman has just said, it is not true." The former statement is more polite than the latter, which is more direct, hence blunt and inelegant. The participant did not disagree with the previous speaker straight away, though her intention was to oppose what the person had said. The use of the words 'this woman' was also rather cold and reflected a negative attitude. The clause, "it is not true" is equally impolite and confrontational. Such utterances promote group divergence rather than harmony.

In the elderly male group, too, direct disapproval (impolite) of other statements was noted. Referring to what the previous (Christian) participant had said, one Muslim participant commented, "I say, it is not true; because in the past individuals showed respect. A Muslim did not stay in a house where Christians stayed."[141] Earlier a Christian participant had said, "In the past the relationship between Muslims and Christians was good."[142] After the Muslim's intervention another Christian participant responded in support of the first Christian: "The opinion that he gave is correct."[143] This identification with other speakers in most case ended up creating group identity. In the mixed group discussions Christian participants tended to support arguments advanced by fellow Christians. Conversely, Muslim participants supported fellow Muslims. This showed that in an interreligious encounter believers tended to draw on member resources shared by fellow believers and in so doing created an intra-religious group identity.

In the uneducated male mixed group there were very few intertextual references. These were made only by Muslim participants, who referred to statements

---

[140] Her name is withheld for ethical reasons.
[141] Mimi nasema si kweli kwasababu kwa miaka ya nyuma watu tulikuwa tunakaa kwa heshima, mwislam alikuwa akiona nyumba hii ina mkristo hakai nyumba ile.
[142] Zamani mahusiano yalikuwa mazuri baina ya waislam na wakristo, walikuwa wakiishi nyumba moja.
[143] Wazo alilolitoa yupo sahihi.

by other Muslim participants. This group's intertextual references took the form of expressions such as "I support my fellow Muslim that Muslims did not like to send their children to school" and "I agree with fellow participants that destitution [*uchovu*] does not affect only Muslims or Christians but anyone".

The youths used relatively more polite expressions than members of the elderly groups. Overall the educated females outstripped other groups in intertextuality. It was noted that Muslims referred to the texts of other participants more often than Christians. Participants also referred intertextually to discourses outside the FGDs, for instance to *mihadhara*, the mass media, government, educational institutions and religious festivals. In addition they cited authoritative texts such as the constitution, the Bible and the Qur'an.

References to politicians, God and prophets
"Muslims believe that Jesus is the son of God"

In the group discussions participants referred to various politicians such as Nyerere, Kikwete and Jumbe. In educated male mixed group I, for instance, one participant mentioned Jumbe: "Even when you look in *bwana* (lord) Jumbe's book, who is a university expert, when he targeted employment statistics, large percentages were Christians."[144]

Others mentioned president Jakaya Kikwete in relation to education prospects. One Christian participant in educated male mixed group I said, "When you find Muslims employed in key positions or anywhere they studied at those Christian-run schools; the example is our president of the United Republic of Tanzania, Jakaya Mrisho Kikwete."[145]

Participants also referred to prophets such as Jesus and his relationship to God. One Muslim participant said, "Muslims believe that Jesus is the son of God born of God's power, that he was a child of the honoured mother, Mama Maryam."[146] In the uneducated mixed group a Muslim participant said, "Some Christians say that Jesus was a Christian, which is not the case, since he was called Issa and not

---

[144] Hata ukiangalia katika kitabu cha Bwana Jumbe ambaye ni mtaalamu wa Chuo Kikuu alilenga katika takwimu za suala la ajira, asilimia kubwa ilikuwa ni wakristo. (Muslim participant in mixed educated male group I.)

[145] Na ukikuta kuna waislamu katika sehemu nyeti au sehemu yoyote katika ajira basi utakuta alisoma katika shule zile za wakristo. Mfano. Ni Rais wetu wa Jamhuri ya Muungano wa Tanzania-Jakaya Mrisho Kikwete. (Muslim participant in mixed educated male group I.)

[146] Muislamu anachoamini ni kwamba Yesu ni mwana wa Mungu amezaliwa kwa uwezo wa Mwenyezi Mungu kwamba kuwa mtoto wa Mama Mtukufu, Mama Mariamu. (Muslim participant in mixed educated male group I.)

Jesus. This Jesus is not a Christian because he entered mosques to pray and he knows the prescribed prayers."[147] The first participant's statement drew on common ground and is therefore inclusive and conducive to homogeneity between Christians and Muslims. The second statement is exclusive, hence creates divergence by positioning Muslims as true believers. This statement also exemplifies a clear misunderstanding of Christianity by some Muslims.

The statement that Jesus was not a Christian also appears in a letter to the state attorney written by Abdul Aziz[148] in 1998 (reproduced in Njozi 2000:146-227). He wrote: "All true Prophets were Muslims, which literally means those who submit/surrender to the one God. Their message was essentially the same – Islam: to call men to worship and submit to one God. Adam was a Muslim; Abraham was a Muslim; Moses was a Muslim; Jesus was a Muslim." The statement proclaimed the universality of Islam and thus positioned Muslims as having a more inclusive religious belief than Christians.

A Muslim participant in the elderly male group put it thus: "The second example was of *bwana* Ibrahim Dibagula in Morogoro. In his teaching he said Jesus is not God but a prophet. He was seen as blaspheming/ridiculing the tenets of Christianity. Then a Morogoro RCO[149] came and sent him to a born again judge[150] who sentenced him to six months in jail."[151] The participant was referring to an incident in Morogoro where a Muslim preacher (Ibrahim Dibagula) was heard uttering words to the effect that Jesus is not God. The participant did not specify who found Dibagula's words blasphemous and a source of ridicule. The participant also mentioned a born again judge sentencing Dibagula, but without identifying him. Some Muslims naturally do not consider D Dibagula's words blasphemous. In his letter to the state attorney in 1998 Abdul Aziz (reproduced in Njozi 2000) insisted: "Neither is it an offence for a Muslim to say that Jesus is not God or God's son, this being an article of Islamic faith that God is one and does not have

---

[147] Kuna wakristo wengine wanasema kwamba Yesu ni mkristo lakini sio hivyo, bali yeye anaitwa Issa na sio Yesu. Yesu huyu sio mkristo kwani anaingia msikitini kusali na anazifahamu hatua za kusali. (Muslim participant in uneducated male mixed group.)

[148] Abdul Aziz is a Tanzanian Muslim who in 1998 submitted a letter to the Tanzania State Attorney, Dar es Salaam with a title "Submission to the Attorney General of Tanzania in the mishandling of the issues of Muslim preaching by the CCM government". 15th May.

[149] Regional Crime Officer (RCO).

[150] In Tanzanian structures RCOs don't appoint judges. Judges are appointed by the court registrar or the chief justice.

[151] Mfano wa pili ni Morogoro wa bwana Ibrahim Dibagula katika mafundisho yake akasema Yesu si Mungu lakini ni mtume akaonekana amekashifu akaja RCO wa Morogoro akampeleka kwa hakimu mlokole, yule bwana akahukumiwa kifungo cha miezi 6. (Muslim elderly male participant in mixed group I.)

equals, partners, or sons.... The bottom line is that what is blasphemy in Christianity is not blasphemy in Islam and vice versa."

This author of the open letter reproduced a picture of misunderstanding-understanding between Muslims and Christians as a cause for conflict between the two faiths, because "what is blasphemy in Christianity is not blasphemy in Islam and vice versa". This is where disharmony and conflict germinate.

Mass media
"I have heard, maybe from the mass media..."

Participants drew on news reports in the mass media and their role in nation building, especially in promoting freedom of expression. One participant said, "I have heard, maybe from the mass media, that some people talk about the employment issue in the government; the employment ratio in government differs to some extent... "[152] The participant's statement shows that the media provide a platform on which people can air their grievances, also in regard to employment.

This was confirmed by another participant, who said that "in the past people didn't talk about discrimination, unlike now when we have media such as newspapers/magazines in which people from different places talk about it."[153] Mass media have increased freedom of expression and allow different people to speak about civic problems such as religious discrimination. These participants were very general and inclusive in their discussions, hence took a civic rather than a religious position.

Religious festivals and ceremonies
"That is why Muslims make noice..."

Participants referred to religious festivals and ceremonies such as Ramadan, Christmas, Muslim Fridays and Christian Sundays. Speaking about Ramadan, one participant said, "During fasting, during Ramadan which is one of the pillars of Islam, a Muslim may receive *futari*[154] from a non-Muslim person without spiritual

---

[152] Nimepata kuyasikia labda kwenye vyombo vya habari kama baadhi ya watu kutafsiri suala la ajira serikali uwiano uliopo wa ajira katika serikali kidogo unatofautiana. (Muslim participant in educated male mixed group.)

[153] Miaka iliyopita watu walishindwa kuzungumzia suala hili la ubaguzi tofauti na sasa ambapo kuna vyombo vya habari kama majarida na watu kutoka maeneo mbalimbali kuishi huu kuliongelea. (Muslim participant in educated male mixed group.)

[154] Literal translation: food eaten to break a fast.

effect."¹⁵⁵ This shows that there are common grounds which Muslims and Christians share irrespective of religious differences and which bring cohesion in the community.

Another Muslim participant in the elderly male FGD referred to an event during the holy month of Ramadan. He said, "Look at the 2000 elections in Pemba. Many Muslims were in the opposition party. As a result police were sent during the Ramadan fast; they did bad things to the citizens, there are some whose property was destroyed, some who were raped, killed... this creates a bad image. Why is the government harassing people?"¹⁵⁶ The participant first referred to many Muslims being members of the opposition party without revealing the name of the party. He also used the passive voice (e.g. "police were sent") without revealing the subject to make his statement inclusive and thus promote harmony with Christians in the group. He also mentioned bad things being done to citizens, which again was inclusive and did not divide the citizens according to their religions (Muslims versus Christians). He made this statement as though there were no religious divisions among citizens. In the last sentence he questions why the government is harassing people. This statement is non-committal on the religious identity of the people concerned. It does not reveal their religious identity, but the participant was explicit about the conflict between the government and some religious believers on Pemba Island.

A Muslim participant¹⁵⁷ in the elderly group reminded his fellow participants of weekends: "That is why Muslims make a noise [*piga kelele*]; all the time we are ill-treated. For example, weekends are rest days for Christians and the government adopted [this] ... this is a Christian system; therefore we Muslims are complaining: why don't we rest on Fridays? If this system continues we won't understand one another in the future."¹⁵⁸ The participant compared the Muslim and

---

[155] Mfano katika kipindi cha mfungo kipindi cha Ramadhani ambao ndio moja ya nguzo tano katika dini ya kiislamu, Muislamu wanaweza kupokea futari ya mtu asiye mwislamu pasipo madhara yoyote kiroho. (Muslim participant in mixed educated male group I.)

[156] Angalia uchaguzi wa mwaka 2000 kule Pemba waislam wengi ni chama cha upinzani matokeo yake wakapelekewa askari wakati wa mfungo wa ramadhani wakawafanya vibaya wananchi wapo walioharibiwa mali zao, kubakwa, kuuawa... hili linaleta sura mbaya kwanini serikali iwaonee watu wengine.

[157] This participant reproduced the same utterance (repeated wording) whenever given opportunity to speak. This shows that peripheral voices are struggling to emerge in the public domain whenever possibilities arise.

[158] Ndo maana waislam wanapiga kelele siku zote sisi tunaonewa. Mfano siku ya jumapili ni siku ya mapumziko kwa wakristo na serikali nayo imefuata inapumzika mfano mabenki na sehemu nyingine hazifunguliwi na jumamosi pia, sasa huo ni mfumo wa wakristo kwahiyo waislam tunalalamika mbona ijumaa hatupumziki, mfumo huu ukiendelea huko mbele hatutaelewana.

Christian days of worship. Christians worship during weekends when government offices are closed. But Muslims have to work on Fridays, which is their day for worship. To him the government follows a Christian system, something that could become a flash point in the future. As for positioning and ethos, the participant positioned himself as a defender of Muslims against a Christian system ("if this system continues we won't understand one another in the future"). He adopted the ethos of a Muslim believer representing other Muslims in the mixed group, evidenced by the comment "therefore we Muslims are complaining". His statement, however, was neither followed up by other participants in the group nor mentioned by participants in other groups.

This same participant referred to New Year festivities. He reminded, "Look at the New Year's festival; this is a Christian feast, but the president, who heads a nonreligious government, makes a speech during this festival. We are saying this is improper; it is the Christians' festival. He should leave it to pastors, padres and bishops to deliver their speeches."[159] To the speaker the president and his government are nonreligious; hence have no part in religious matters. But in terms of this speaker's contribution to the discourse the participant maintained his position as a Muslim representative. And his repeated phrases such as "ill-treated", "make a noise", "make complaints" make him an advocate of religio-centric discourse. At the same time his strongly worded utterances reveal that peripheral voices exist side by side with the dominant ideology of unity and cohesion.

In reaction to his statements one Christian participant said, "I think what he has been talking [about] … was based on a viewpoint. That is why we said that religious issues are very sensitive and it is a mistake to intrude in a matter of faith or religion."[160] This participant's statement was reconciliatory and inclusive at the same time, evidenced by the use of pronouns such as 'we' which do not specify group identity, making the statement open and unclear. The 'we' could mean anything; it could refer to Christians in the group, or Christians in general, or all participants (both Muslims and Christians). This also applies to the clause "was based on a viewpoint". Again the 'viewpoint' was left open, as the participant

---

(Elderly male Muslim.)

[159] Jambo lingine, angalia sikukuu za mwaka mpya hii ni ya kikristo Rais ambae anaongoza serikali isiyokuwa na dini anahutubia sikukuu hii. Hilo nalo tunasema halifai ni sikukuu ya wakristo awaachie wachungaji, mapadre, maaskofu watoe hotuba zao. (Elderly male Muslim.)

[160] Mimi nafikiri aliyokuwa anaongea hapa ameongea kutokana na mtazamo ndo maana tukaseme swala la dini ni nyeti sana na kuingilia imani ya dini ni nyeti. (Christian participant in elderly male mixed group.)

appeared to have opted for a civic identity, thus enhancing group cohesion and harmony.

Some participants mentioned ongoing collaboration in religious festivals. A Muslim participant in educated male group II said, "Muslims are also involved in Christian religious festivals."[161] The participant's statement is inclusive and strives for social cohesion and unity.

Government and its institutions
"The government is the one creating problems in this society"

Participants in the FGDs referred to the government and some of its organs such as the police. The Muslim participant quoted above, speaking about the Christian dominated calendar in Tanzania, said: "The government is the one creating problems in this society and if it continues in this style, there will be explosions like what happened in Ivory Coast, Burundi, Rwanda and Congo, because you can't have two children and favour only one of them … this is not accepted; that is why Muslims make a noise [*piga kelele*]. All the time we are ill-treated".[162] The participant's repetition of words and expressions (over-wording) revealed religiocentrism and also reflected peripheral voices demanding change in society. The participant accused the government of favouring one group. His last clause clearly states which group is not favoured. As Muslims are being ill-treated, they have a right to complain ("Muslims make a noise"). The participant also refers to crises ("explosions") that happened in other countries (Ivory Coast, Burundi, Rwanda, Congo) as a consequence of failure to act responsively and timely. The explicit warning portrays extremism, an attitude that breeds conflict and disharmony. Here again, the participant repeatedly (over-wording) uses expressions such as "Muslims make a noise" to remind other participants of his point about being ill treated.

Muslim participants referred to a memorandum of understanding that government had purportedly signed with the church. As one participant explained, "Another thing is the memorandum of understanding which the government signed with the churches. I mean, the government supports the churches, especially on

---

[161] Mfano katika sherehe za kidini kama ni za wakristo basi waislamu nao wanashirikishwa. (Muslim participant in mixed educated male group I.)

[162] Serikali ndo imeleta matatizo katika jamii hii na kwa taadhari kutatokea milipuko kama ilivyotokea Ivory Coast, Burundi, Rwanda, Congo na sehemu nyingine kama serikali itaendelea na mtindo wake … maana huwezi kuwa na watoto wawili mmoja unampendelea mwingine unamfanyia jambo … hili halikubaliki ndo maana waislam wanapiga kelele, siku zote sisi tunaonewa. (Elderly male Muslim.)

educational issues. Muslims make a noise [*piga kelele*] about education, we are left behind; we are ill-treated [*tunaonewa*]."[163] The participant mentioned both the subject and object of the memorandum of understanding, that is, government and the churches were signatories. He also refers to being left behind in education and hence being ill-treated. The participant again assumes the role of a Muslim believer speaking on behalf of 'ill-treated' Muslims. He does not specify, however, who is ill-treating Muslims, the churches or the government – or both?

This kind of statement has been reported in recent local newspapers, quoting some Muslim leaders expressing the same sentiment. *The Citizen* of 3 July 2009 quoted a statement by the Tanzanian mufti on behalf of the Tanzanian Muslim council, BAKWATA, saying: "Muslims are not treated fairly in this country: why should we keep on demanding what is our right for over 20 years and still there is no indication that the government is listening?" The mufti continued: "Is this country governed by Christians? Why are they treating Muslims as second-class citizens of this country?" In the first statement, the mufti asserts that Muslims were not treated fairly and the government was not listening to their grievances. Later he rhetorically implied that the country was being governed by Christians and that Muslims were treated as second-class citizens. The mufti adopted the ethos of a religious leader representing a group of believers (Muslims). Aware of another religious group (the Christians), which is allegedly 'closer' or listened to by the government ("Is this country governed by Christians?"), he makes a serious statement to force the government to intervene and avoid a situation in which Muslim felt they were being treated as second-class citizens by their own government in their own country.

Moreover, Christian participants in the elderly male mixed groups drew on Muslims' complaints in the discussions. One of them said, "In the past we talked about this, that the government contributes through state organs to oppress Muslims, but we were looking at who is the top leader. People said the president is a Christian, but when president Mwinyi came into power *mihadhara* were conducted and riots [*vurugu*] were happening." Unlike the Muslim participant quoted immediately before him, this Christian participant spoke in inclusive terms. The words 'we' or 'people' could include both Muslim and Christian participants in the group or Muslims and Christians in society.

The participant revealed neither the identity of the state organs which oppressed Muslims nor the name of the Christian president. Instead he mentioned

---

[163] Kingine kinaitwa "Memorandum of understanding" serikali ilitia saini na makanisa yaani serikali isaidie makanisa hususani kuhusu swala la elimu hapo ndo waislam wanapiga kelele kuhusu swala la elimu tumeachwa nyuma tunaonewa. (Elderly male Muslim.)

the president who succeeded the Christian president, namely Mwinyi. Mwinyi was president of the second government. The first government was headed by Mwalimu Julius Nyerere. The participant's statement suggests that before Mwinyi people were looking at the president and associating the alleged 'oppression' of Muslims with his Christian religious identity. To this participant the president's religion was not an important factor in addressing or understanding complaints from religious groups.

Newspapers also quoted statements by Christian religious leaders speaking about the government and religion. On 23 February 2009 *Nipashe* quoted Polycarp cardinal Pengo, the Catholic archbishop of Dar es Salaam archdiocese, as saying, "The discussion aimed at securing the aims of one side could cost the nation dearly when peace disappears."[164] The bishop does not say exactly on which (religious) 'side' the discussion was being conducted, nor does he say which faith or who conducted the discussion with that side. Thus the bishop avoided responsibility and confrontation with those (government/Muslims/Christians) referred to in the statement.

Some participants referred to employment opportunities in the public service. As one male participant in educated group I noted, "The police force has released job statistics on district, regional and national commanders. If you look at that book, the biggest percentage is our Christian fellow citizens."[165] This Muslim participant refers to high positions in the police force, which he asserts were occupied by Christians. The use of the phrase 'our Christian fellow citizens' shows that Muslims try to be polite and friendly when they speak about or refer to Christians.

One participant in the elderly male group referred to police involvement in religious issues. He cited the Mwembechai riots of 1998 when "there was a *mhadhara* full of people, both Muslims and Christians. Then a parish priest passed by … he went to the police saying he had heard Jesus being insulted. Police came and created chaos, killing people who were not guilty, simply because padre Lumbano complained that Jesus had been insulted."[166] The participant did not mention the identity of those who conducted that *mhadhara*, but he said that it was attended by both Muslims and Christians. He did name the one who felt offended (padre

---

[164] Majadiliano yenye lengo la kufanikisha upande mmoja (wa dini), inaweza kusababisha hasara kwa taifa endapo amani itatoweka. Nipashe, 23 February 2009.

[165] Jeshi la polisi limetoa takwimu kwa vituo kuanzia wilaya na mikoa na makamanda wao kitaifa. Kile kitabu ukiangalia asilimia kubwa ni wenzetu wakristo. (Educated male Muslim.)

[166] Mfano Mwembechai mwaka 1998 kulikuwa na mhadhara kulijaa sana watu waislam na wakristo mara akapita paroko akasikia mahubiri yale akageuza akaenda polisi akasema amesikia Yesu anatukanwa polisi wakaja pale nakufanya fujo nakuua watu pasipo hatia kisa padre Lumbano kasema Yesu katukanwa. (Elderly Muslim participant.)

Lumbano) by the alleged insult. This padre happened to be just a passerby and not a member of the audience.

Educational institutions
"In Islamic schools Christians are also allowed"

Participants said that educational institutions – both private (especially religious owned) and public, such as primary and secondary schools as well as tertiary institutions – affect the welfare of Muslims and Christians and their interreligious relationship. One Muslim participant said, "There is a problem with education provided at religious schools. You will find that Christian-run schools have regulations [which say] that [in order] to study there [at these institutions] the person should leave Islam, in one way or another. This is not the case in Islamic schools which do not set such regulations for Christian students. What they care about is that a student is at school for educational purposes and nothing else."[167] This differed from what other Muslim participants said, namely that "Christians are allowed in Islamic schools, but in small numbers as they have to respect Islamic values".[168] In other words, there are restrictions on the admission of Christian students to Islamic schools.

This was observable in *An-Nuur* of 9-15 May 2009, page 10, where two Islamic teachers' colleges (Ubungo Islamic Teachers' College, Dar es Salaam and Kirinjiko Islamic Teachers' College, Kilimanjaro) advertised training open only to Muslims. The same favouritism was seen in *An-Nuur* of 8-14 May 2008, page 10, advertising for the opening of form five education at various Islamic Propagation Centre institutions, but only for qualified Muslims. The advert reads, "These are Muslim schools, therefore applicants should be Muslims who are ready to adhere to Islamic values." The advertisement creates clear boundaries between Muslims and non-Muslims, but also between real Muslims and Muslims who don't follow an Islamic way of life. This showed that Muslims are also divided among themselves. There are those who adhere to Islamic values and those who don't.

---

[167] Tatizo katika elimu hasa kama shule ni za kidini, unakuta shule za kikristo zinamasharti kwamba ili mtu asome shuleni hapo inabidi auvue uislamu kwa namna moja au nyingine tofauti na shule za dini ya kiislamu ambazo hazina masharti kwa wanafunzi wa kikristo. Wanachojali ni mwanafunzi amekwenda shuleni kwa minajili ya elimu na si vinginevyo. (Muslim participant in mixed educated male group I.)

[168] Katika shule za kiislamu wakristo pia wanaruhusiwa japo wachache kwa sababu wanaweza kuheshimu maadili ya kiislamu. (Muslim participant in mixed educated male group I.)

Kadhi courts and OIC
"They wanted to join the OIC but they were refused"

Participants drew on discourses related to Tanzania's OIC membership. A Christian participant said, "For example, Zanzibar wanted to join the OIC but was barred, so it becomes difficult to get ahead."[169] The participant made a general but sympathetic statement about Zanzibaris, who were denied the opportunity to join the OIC. By speaking in such general terms the participant positioned the OIC as a national issue, thus reducing its religious implications.

The OIC issue was referred to by another participant in the elderly group. This Muslim participant said, "Bishop Kilaini said that the OIC is not allowed here, but the OIC is an Islamic organisation which supports all countries. Good examples are Mozambique, Rwanda ... [which] get assistance [from the OIC]... [And the] USA has also joined ... then why is Tanzania refusing to join? There is a secret movement which made the bishop say [what he said]."[170] This participant depicted a struggle for hegemony between Muslims and Christians in religious discourse. The confrontation also indicates divisions in society and the strong drive among some Muslim Tanzanians to change the status quo and let Tanzania join the OIC.

Other participants referred to the controversial matter of the introduction of *kadhi* courts. A Muslim participant in the elderly male group said, "Muslims want the *kadhi* court reinstated and the other side objects, saying why they should allow this to happen. The Muslims feel they are being denied their right."[171] Again the participant mentions the 'other side' without specifying its identity. This is a polite way to avoid mentioning the groups in question, especially in an FGD in which their members are represented.

The debate on *kadhi* courts has been carried on in parliament and occupies space in local newspapers. Thus we get headlines like "Muslims up with court" (*Mahakama ya Kadhi Waislamu wacharuka*);[172] "the *kadhi* court saga: CCM in overnight vigil tabling BAKWATA" (*Sakata la Mahakama ya Kadhi:*

---

[169] Mfano ukienda Zanzibar walitaka kujiunga na masuala ya OIC wanakatazwa kwa hiyo inakuwa vigumu kusonga mbele.

[170] Askofu Kilaini alisema OIC haikubaliki hapa lakini OIC ni taasisi ya kiislam inayosaidia nchi zote mfano mzuri Msumbiji, Rwanda zimepata msaada Mmarekani nae kaingia kwanini Tanzania inakataa kujiunga kuna ajenda ya siri mpaka Askofu kusema. (Muslim participant in elderly male group.)

[171] Waislamu wanataka kadhi irudishwe na upande wa pili wanapinga kuwa itakuwaje, waislam wanaona hawatendewi haki. (Muslim participant in elderly group.)

[172] Majira, Wednesday 1 July 2009, a daily newspaper.

CCM yakesha kuijadili BAKWATA);[173] "Mufti stands firm on *kadhi* court" (*Mufti achachamalia Mahakama ya Kadhi*);[174] "BAKWATA: no courts, no votes for CCM".[175] Clearly a religious issue has been politicised and it is used as a weapon primarily for political gain.

Conclusion

The analysis of discursive practice demonstrates that participants' contributions to FGDs drew on reports in the mass media, happenings in religious institutions such as BAKWATA, and Holy Scriptures, as well as the participants' daily lives and activities. This discussion also demonstrates that religious issues tend to be influenced by local (e.g. political) discourse and global discourse (e.g. joining the OIC, as in the case of the USA, Rwanda and Mozambique).

Interventions in the group were friendly and polite (e.g. prevarications such as 'it is just a belief'), in order to avoid provoking negative responses from other participants. In so doing they affirmed an identity as discussion group member rather than standing out as representatives of their respective religions.

They speak about Muslim-Christian relations in terms of 'discrimination' and 'cooperation'. They say that there is 'good communication' between Muslims and Christians, and 'no differences'. However they also say that there is 'discrimination to some extent', for example in job opportunities. According to some Muslims, Christians are allowed (by the government) to join Christian (international) organisations, but Muslims are not allowed to enter Islamic (international) organisations such as the OIC. Therefore Christians are better off. Muslims 'fail to get ahead' because they are restricted from joining organisations that could help them develop.

In the mixed groups understanding-misunderstanding was noted in participants' statements. Muslim participants in different groups associated Christians with the government ("The government supports the churches especially on educational issues. That is why we are making a noise"), and with the CCM political party ("no votes for CCM"). Christians, on the other hand, felt the government was mixing religion with politics ("When president Mwinyi came into power *mihadhara* were conducted and riots [*vurugu*] were happening").

This indicated a communication breakdown between participants who reproduce the dominant discourse about the separation of religion and politics and

---

[173] Majira, Monday 6 July 2009, a daily newspaper.
[174] Habari Leo, 4 July 2009. Habari za Kitaifa, published weekly on Saturday
[175] The Citizen, 3 July 2009 08:00:00, BAKWATA: no courts, no votes for CCM.

the participants who reproduce a peripheral discourse about the government and Muslim and Christian believers. Blommaert and Verschueren (1991:5) explain: "If communication breaks down during such encounters ... the communication failure is either naively blamed on deficient language competence on the part of the minority member or – and this is the more common case – on the minority member's attitudes, abilities, personality, or intelligence, as they were perceived through his interactive behavior during encounter." Presupposing that the communication breakdown in this case was not due to language competence, it was due to a clash between minority and majority voices.

4.3. Analysis of social practice

As was explained in the general introduction, at the level of social practice Fairclough (2007:86) analyses ideological and hegemonic relations in texts/discourse, and socio-cognitive effects of what participants say. The assumption is that discourse is never neutral. Participants' language is constituted by and constitutes a particular social reality, including social positions and social relations. In other words, their usage of language is aimed at constructing and reconstructing existing social reality by either reproducing or reshaping it.

"We live like ndugu"

In the discussions participants uttered words which reproduced an image of creolization and coexistence rather than conflict in Tanzania. For example, in mixed educated male group II one Muslim participant said that "the [Christian-Muslim] relationship is good because we live like *ndugu,* that is why even here we have people of different faiths; we are mixed."[176] This was confirmed by Christians in the same group, who said, "I think it is possible for Muslims and Christians to live together and they can also be friends. A good example is me; I have Muslim friends and we play together without any discrimination, and everyone continues with his religious practices."[177] Another Christian participant in mixed educated

---

[176] Mahusiano ni mazuri kwani watu tunaishi kama ndugu na ndio maana hata hapa tumekuja watu waimani tofauti yaani tumechanganyika. (Muslim participant mixed educated male group II.)

[177] Upande wangu naona inawezekana kwa waislamu na wakristo kuishi pamoja na vilevile watu hawa huweza kuwa marafiki. Mfano mzuri ni mimi mwenyewe ambaye nina marafiki wa dini ya kiislamu na tunacheza pamoja, na hivyo hakuna ubaguzi huku kila mmoja akiendelea na taratibu zake za dini. (Christian participant mixed educated male group II.)

male group II said, "There is no problem in our relationship and we live nicely."[178] These participants' discourses affirmed a good relationship between Muslims and Christians, suggesting co-existence of Muslim and Christian cultures. This is evident in statements like, "we are mixed". It reflects unification and harmony, in which people of different faiths discuss and share ideas amicably in a group. A clear indication of creolization was the participants' use of terms *pagan* and *kafir*. This was also evident in the *mihadhara* context where preachers used these terms interchangeably. Another example of creolization was the use of the word 'mosque' equating it with a synagogue. Muslims said, "Jesus entered a mosque".

Participants' statements constituted and were constituted by the process of religious individualisation and privatisation. Christian participants, for example, stated that everyone continues with "his religious practices", indicating that faith was a private and/or individual issue, which should not interfere with group interests or personal relationships, as one participant emphasised: "I have Muslim friends and we play together without any discrimination."

By using these words participants sought to maintain existing relations, which made coexistence possible. These participants adopted a civic ethos, which allowed civic members to talk and made "it possible for Muslims and Christians to live together" in harmony like *ndugu*. The same spirit was apparent in other groups, with participants generally using polite terms, sensitive to the feelings of other group members. The educated male quoted earlier (see analysis of linguistic practice) said, "I think that … relations between Muslims and Christians have no impact … well … the impact is not that big. We have good relations between these two religions." The text reflects a sudden change when the participant observes the group's composition (mixed Muslim and Christian) so as to maintain cordial ties and rapport between Muslim and Christian participants; as a result he shifted his position from overly negative to positive. This was also noted by other participants in the same group.

In educated male group II a Muslim participant said, "Where I live I do not think relations between Muslims and Christians have [any] negative effects, and if there are any they tend to be minimal … On the whole, we have good relations between these two religions … they [relations] are good."[179] The participant first wanted to link up with the status quo of good relations ("don't have [any] negative

---

[178] Mahusiano hayana shida na kwamba tunaishi vizuri. (Christian participant mixed educated male group II.)

[179] Mimi nadhani kwamba katika maeneo ninayoishi mahusiano yaliyopo kati ya waislamu na Wakristo hayaathiri na athari ambazo zinakuwa si kubwa Tuna mahusiano mazuri kati ya dini zote hizi mbili… ni mazuri… (Muslim participant mixed educated male group II.)

effects"), which mitigated what he wanted to say later, an admission that that there were some negative effects. But after realising the challenge his assertion posed to the good relationship, he did a U-turn and emphasised that relations "are good" after all. His vacillation exposes the ideological struggle in the discourse that challenges the status quo of good relations. This was evident in the Muslim participant's statement that "there is discrimination to some extent" and that of the Christian participant, who said "but on the side of employment every individual is independent". These examples suggest discrimination and individualism.

The same may be said of some participants' utterances which dared challenge the status quo of good relations. For example, in the mixed educated group I a Christian participant said, "I say that the relationship is not so good. Sixty percent of it maybe [is good]. For the remaining forty percent there is no cooperation."[180] Compared with the statements quoted above, this one is relatively critical of the dominant discourse about good relations between Muslims and Christians. It challenges the status quo. He positions himself as someone who understands the struggle in Muslim-Christian relations. By using the sixty, forty percent figure he confirms that good relations dominate bad ones and he clarifies what is "not so good", namely "no cooperation".

In the general response section the Christian participant also described this struggle. He maintained that Muslims and Christians cooperate in civic activities, "but on the side of employment every individual [group] is independent". Employment is seen as something distinct from the common good; it has been privatised, so each religious group has to strive on its own to secure jobs. Nevertheless members could continue living together despite these apparent differences. There are also restrictions imposed on a particular group: "He will have difficulty getting a job in private colleges." The participant used the general term ("individual") and did not specify the identity of the private colleges, leaving the term open to many interpretations. That way he could maintain courtesy and avoid confrontation with other participants. Of course, the implication is that privatisation and individualisation in society mean that some private colleges – regardless of religious affiliation – have set exclusive conditions, hence the accent on individual initiative ("every individual is independent") as opposed to group initiative.

In all FGDs participants used expressions such as "we live like *ndugu*". Similar words were uttered by a Muslim participant in the uneducated group, who

---

[180] Naweza kusema kwamba uhusiano sio mzuri sana unaweza kuwa wa asilimia 60% na hizo 40% naona hakuna ushirikiano. (Christian participant mixed educated male group I.)

said "Even in houses we live with Christians as *ndugu* and in peace."[181] In this utterance Christians are considered relatives. The words suggest harmonious interaction and relations. Participants attributed such harmonious interaction to the transformation some people have undergone. One participant said, "During those times I had difficult mixing with Christians. Now we are all equal." This is a development in Muslim-Christian relations.

"Although I'm not Muslim I can wear hijab"

Participants identified ongoing creolization taking place in the country, especially in dress styles. An uneducated Christian female said, "Although I'm not a Muslim I can wear *hijab*."[182] Another Christian female said, "Yes, it is true, they wear [it] for their own gratification. Myself, I have and I wear [it] for my gratification."[183] Another Christian said, "I sometimes wear [the *hijab*], but now I have given it to my house helper, because she is a Muslim. But if I want to gratify [myself], I wear it."[184] A Muslim participant in the group responded, "If I see a Christian wearing a *baibui*, in my soul I will just feel happy with the way she is dressed and looks like a Muslim while she is not one."[185] The participants' statements made it clear that some typical Muslim garments also appealed to Christians. In this respect clothing is facilitating the process of cultural creolization. Thus it is no longer taken for granted that certain clothing indicates a particular faith, as harmonisation and homogenisation of dress are making the borders of group identities fluid ("she dressed and looked like a Muslim while she is not one"; "although I'm not Muslim I can wear *hijab*").

"At Mwembechai in 1998 there was a mhadhara full of people, both Muslims and Christians"

Some Muslim participants' utterances challenged the status quo and hinted at oppression and victimisation. An example is the statement by an elderly Muslim

---

[181] Na hata majumbani tunakoishi kwa kuchanganyika na wakristo pia kama ndugu na kwa amani. (Muslim participant mixed uneducated male group.)
[182] Kwa mimi binafsi mimi naweza nikaaa hijabu japokuwa si muislamu.
[183] Ni kweli wapo, wanavaa kwa lengo la kujifurahisha. Mimi mwenyewe ninalo na ninavaa kwa kujifurahisha.
[184] Mimi huwa ninavaa ila kwa sasa ni mempa mfanyakazi wangu kwa kuwa yeye ni muislamu. Lakini nikitaka kujifurahisha ninalivaa.
[185] Mimi nikimuona mkristo amevaa baibui ... rohoni nitafurahia tu alivyolivaa na kuonekana kama muislamu ingawa sio muislamu.

participant: "At Mwembechai in 1998 there was a *mhadhara* full of people, both Muslims and Christians. Then a parish priest passed by … He went to the police saying that he heard Jesus being insulted. Police came and created chaos, killing people who were not guilty, simply because padre Lumbano said Jesus had been insulted."[186] Although other participants in the group did not pick up on this topic, the participant referred to a situation which, according to his version, exposed police brutality against harmless civilians.

The *mhadhara*, we are told, was full of people, both Muslims and Christians, who, according to the participant, were innocent. In this case both Muslims and Christians were victims of police brutality and repression. Moreover, the participant's statement shows that there were people (a Christian religious leader) who were favoured (listened to) by the police. From the participant's point of view, this applies to padre Lumbano (simply because he said Jesus had been insulted). Because of such alleged favouritism normal citizens, Muslims and Christians, became victims of the situation (killing people who were not guilty). By speaking in general terms the participant made his statement inclusive, hence minimised its negative impact on Christian participants. Their non-response to his statement supports this view.

"Muslims are not treated fairly in this country"

Participants in the FGDs also reproduced discourses about injustice and discrimination against believers. In the elderly male FGD one Muslim participant said that "we [Muslims] are left behind; we are ill-treated (*tunaonewa*)." The participant positioned himself as a Muslim who was being discriminated against ("we are left behind"). This, according to the speaker, was unfair and unjust ("ill-treated"). The participant tactfully absolved the Christians by placing the blame for injustice to Muslims squarely on the shoulders of government ("the government supports the churches especially on educational issues"). In this way the speaker avoided alienating the Christian participants, hence facilitated group cohesion. By saying that government offered support to churches – but allegedly not to Muslims – the participant was accusing the government of discriminating against Muslims.

---

[186] Mfano Mwembechai mwaka 1998 kulikuwa na mhadhara kulijaa sana watu waislam na wakristo mara akapita paroko akasikia mahubiri yale akageuza akaenda polisi akasema amesikia Yesu anatukanwa polisi wakaja pale nakufanya fujo nakuua watu pasipo hatia kisa padre Lumbano kasema Yesu katukanwa. (Elderly Muslim participant)

The Tanzanian mufti raised similar concerns about supposed unfairness and injustice or discrimination directed against Muslims.[187] The mufti, quoted already in the discursive practice section, said: "Muslims are not treated fairly in this country: why should we keep on demanding what is our right for over 20 years?" The mufti also asked, "Why are they treating Muslims as second-class citizens of this country?" Going through the mufti's statements we find apportionment of blame, highlighting the alleged unfairness/injustice and discrimination against Muslims. The mufti accused government of not listening ("still there is no indication that the government is listening") to their grievances. At the same time he associated the government's reluctance to respond to Muslims' pleas with alleged Christian machinations ("Is this country governed by Christians?"). Listening only to Christians was seen by the mufti as discrimination and "treating Muslims as second-class citizens". According to the mufti Muslims have been victimised both by government's failure to respond to their demands, and by Christians who influenced government decisions.

A Christian participant in the elderly group said, "In the past we talked about this, that the government contributes through state organs to oppress Muslims, but we were looking at the top leader. People said the president is a Christian, but when president Mwinyi came into power *mihadhara* were conducted and riots [*vurugu*] were happening." This statement was a response to the Muslim's argument about the government's alleged unfair treatment of Muslims. Instead of saying that Muslims had been talking, the speaker decided to use the plural pronoun 'we', which is more inclusive and in that sense affirmed group harmony and identity. Moreover, according to this participant 'we' indicates the position of citizens who look at government's responsibilities or actions (e.g. oppression) and government officials (e.g. the president) vis-à-vis citizens or a particular group (e.g. Muslims). The president and the government are supposed to be secular, but the participant suspects foul play ("when president Mwinyi got into power *mihadhara* were conducted and riots [*vurugu*] were happening"). Other participants, however, did not explicitly accuse government of religious bias. This point was made by an uneducated Muslim male, who said, "If there are conflicts, the government intervenes because our government is not operated by religion."

"Those who know religion are the ones involved in arguments"

Participants identified cases of extremism, terrorism and fanaticism. One female in the uneducated group said, "Those who know religion are the ones involved

---
[187] The Citizen, 3 July 2009.

in arguments – those who know the holy book [*msahafu*] and others who know the Bible."[188] This statement was confirmed by another Muslim participant in the group, who noted, "Those who consider themselves to know religion [better] [fanatics] are the ones arguing, but us who are just Muslims, we are not fanatics, that is why we compromise with Christians."[189] Another Muslim participant said, "Those Muslims who say the five prayers are the ones who quarrel with Christians."[190] A Christian participant in the group said, "Like what we [were] told in the beginning, there are those who claim to be Sunni and the normal ones."[191]

These group participants' way of discussing the issue showed that they were trying to strike a compromise or establish convergence between Muslims and Christians, so participants of both faiths could share the same discourse without antagonism. The participants agreed that within the Muslim community there were fanatics ("those who know religion", "those who say the five prayers", "those who claim to be Sunni") and "normal Muslims". Participants in this group positioned themselves as normal Muslims, and thus could sit in the same group with Christians ("that is why we compromise with Christians"). According to them Muslim fanatics did not compromise with Christians because they were "involved in arguments".

Some Muslims said these fanatics were found in both religions – "those who know the holy book [*msahafu*] [Muslims] and others who know the Bible [Christians]". But to other participants fanatics were mostly Muslims ("those Muslims who say the five prayers", "those who claim to be Sunni").

According to the uneducated Christian male participant religious fanaticism and extremism were directed not just against Christians, but sometimes also against Muslims. After all, Muslim fanatics or extremists "initiate chaos and use sticks to beat [others] even in the mosques".[192] According to this participant the effect of extremism and fanaticism among Muslims was evident in the chaos and use of weapons during fights in mosques, supposedly too holy for such uncouth and wicked actions.

Some elderly participants said religious extremism was promoted by poverty. As one elderly Muslim man noted, "This is why… the state of the economy is so

---

[188] Wanaolumbana ni wale wanaojua dini – wanaojua msahafu na wengine wanaoijua Biblia.
[189] Wale wanaojiona wanajua dini ndio wanaolumbana, lakini sisi kama sisi ambao ni waislamu tupo tu kwani hatufuatilii mambo ya dini yetu na ndio maana tunaelewana na wakristo.
[190] Wale waislamu wa swala tano ndio wanaogombana na wakristo.
[191] Ni kama tulivyoelekeza mwanzo, kuna hao wengine wanadai ni masuni na hao wa kawaida.
[192] Watu ambao wanaweza kuanzisha fujo na kutumia bakora zao kuchapana hata kama ni huko misikitini. (Christian uneducated male participant.)

crucial, because a person is ready to be bought to go and do certain things against other religions."[193] A Christian participant concurred: "This is related to poverty, because a person can get something or do something to entice people to destroy our tranquillity."[194] He added, "If you have money, you may set conditions for establishing a religion. There are those who have come and established [brands of] Islam according to personal whims."[195] Here again elderly participants reached consensus on the causes of extremism. They believe that religious followers can be bought to fan religious conflict and in so doing disrupt the country's tranquillity. At the same time religions have been commodified, enabling rich people to establish denominations and/or influence religious actions. According to the participants this was possible because of poverty, since poor people are easily enticed (bought) to cause conflict. Moreover, to most participants *mihadhara* have become 'business' to preachers who use them as their source of income and care less about the consequences of their utterances to the community.

Some participants positioned Muslims as the main perpetrators of terrorism. In fact, one Muslim participant in the educated male group said, "This is also a result of these terrorist policies [actually anti-terrorism policies]; hence Muslims don't get assistance because they are linked to terrorism.[196] The effect of such association with terrorism is lack of assistance. Thus innocent Muslims become victims of (anti-)terrorist policies.

Participants reproduced an image of peaceful coexistence of Muslims and Christians in Tanzania, unlike in other countries where religion has caused strife. One uneducated Muslim participant said, "Religion is the cause of war in many countries where there are wars, unlike ours [Tanzania] in which Muslims and Christians live together well."[197] The participant argued that the peaceful coexistence of Muslims and Christians prevented the outbreak of religious war. An elderly Muslim participant cautioned that civil strife could happen in Tanzania if

---

[193] Ndio maana unakuja kukuta kuna kipindi uchumi unachukua nafasi kubwa ndio maana mtu yupo tayari kununuliwa kwenda kufanya jambo fulani dhidi ya dini fulani.

[194] Linahusiana na umaskini kwa maana kwamba mtu yeyote ni rahisi maana anaweza kupata chochote au kufanya lolote lakushawishi watu ili kuondoa dhana nzima ya utulivu wetu.

[195] Sasa hivi kuwa na hela unaweza kutengeneza mazingira yakuanzisha dini. Kuna wengine wanakuja wanaanzisha uislam katika mipangilio yao nakuona wanafuata maandiko.

[196] Hizi sera za ugaidi nazo zinachangia kwani waislamu hawapati msaada kwani wanahusishwa na ugaidi.

[197] Nchi nyingi zinazopigana chanzo huwa mambo ya dini tofauti na kwetu (Tanzania) ambapo waislamu tunaishi vizuri na wakristo na kama tofauti zinatokea basi Serikali inasimamia kutoa tofauti hizi kwani serikali yetu haiendeshwi kidini.

the government continued favouring one religion ("because you can't have two children and only favour one"). [198]

The participant used the two children as a metaphor for Christians and Muslims, with the government as the parent (father/mother). The speaker, who accused the government of discriminating against Muslims (the other child) cautioned that such maltreatment could lead to conflict because "it reaches a point when a person doesn't ask for his right but he takes it. Therefore Muslims will wake up and take their rights which they have lost."[199] In other words, if the government failed to act and institute remedial measures, Muslims could take their rights through whatever means ("it reaches a point when a person doesn't ask for his right but he takes it"). This statement challenges the comfort zone of good Muslim-Christian relations evident in this group and emphasised by other participants, who used expressions such as "we live well" or "we live like *ndugu*". More explicitly, the participant's position identifies him as a Muslim who knows (has true consciousness) and wants other participants in the group to recognise it.

Conclusion

By using labels like *ndugu*, friends and fellow/comrade participants' reproduced a picture of mutual harmonious, good and cooperative relations, but also labels constituted by and constituting a discriminatory and unjust relationship (ill-treated, second-class citizens, etc.). For example, in the FGDs participants attempted to maintain good and harmonious ties, in which both Muslims and Christians chose words and statements carefully to avoid antagonising other participants. Impolite words and statements were indirect and phrased in general or plural terms so as to maintain good relations in the groups, but at the same time posing challenges or exposing struggles in the discourse.

Evidently at lower or group level individuals find ways to compromise by concealing their religious identity, emphasising their civic identity of 'living well' with people of different faiths. At the community level participants reproduced several forms of creolization as in the use of terms like pagan/kafir, Jesus entering mosques and so forth.

---

[198] Serikali ndo imeleta matatizo katika jamii hii na kwa tahadhari kutatokea milipuko kama ilivyotokea Ivory Coast, Burundi, Rwanda, Congo na sehemu nyingine kama serikali itaendelea na mtindo wake unaoufanya sasa hivi maana huwezi kuwa na watoto wawili mmoja unampendelea mwingine unamfanyia tofauti.

[199] Huwa inafikia wakati mtu haki yake aombi anachukua. Kwahiyo waislam wataamka nakuchukua haki yao waliyoipoteza.

However, participants also, albeit indirectly and mostly in the plural, referred to favouritism, discrimination and injustice, which they claimed were rife in their society. Most Muslim participants alleged that Muslims were victims of discrimination and injustice, while their counterparts, the Christians, were favoured. Some Muslim participants said that government favoured Christians through their church affiliated organisations, especially by supporting their educational institutions. According to one Muslim participant this could cause misunderstanding and/or conflict between Muslims and Christians and threaten the peaceful coexistence of believers.

In addition participants identified poverty as a facilitator of religious extremism and consequently a threat to the peace and tranquillity that Muslims, Christians and other Tanzanians enjoy. The participants justified this by explaining that religion has become commodified, so poor believers could be bought by the rich to carry out their nefarious agenda of instigating conflict between Muslims and Christians.

In general participants revealed that the mixing of religion and politics was not tolerated and thus government officials were expected to be impartial in discharging their responsibility without religious prejudice. On the other hand, religion as an institution must play its part in nation building and the enhancement of peace, which included teaching its believers to be good citizen and not to stir up religiocentrism.

Participants demonstrated that coexistence is possible and thus people have managed to find ways to compromise through respect and sharing of members' resources with other believers in the community. Evidently coexistence in this society is facilitated by creolization, evident in utterances (e.g. the use of the word *wapagani* instead of *kafir*) and/or in practices (e.g. Christians dressing in I), and so forth. However, conflicts arise when believers feel neglected, marginalised or unfavoured. As one participant put it, "you can't have two children and favour only one of them." In most cases conflict is not between Muslims and Christians but rather between believers (Muslims/Christians) and state organs (e.g. the police).

Chapter 5:
Muslim-Christian relations in Tanzania
"Islam is humility"; "Christianity is love"

In the general introduction we said that this thesis sets out to answer two questions: (1) How do Muslims and Christians identify and position themselves and others? and (2) what are the socio-cognitive effects of their identification and positioning? The background to these questions is that scholars noted growing religio-centrism (*udini*) in Tanzania (Wijsen 2003; Tambila 2006), or a return of religion to the public domain, whereas in the socialist era (*Ujamaa*) the trend was to excise religion from the public domain. In this study we wanted to determine if the rhetoric about the return of religion to the public domain is an appropriate way of speaking about transformations that are taking place in Tanzania, and if so, why and under what conditions people elevate religious identity above other (ethnic/national) identities.

If the elevation of religious identity above other identities is in fact happening, this is the opposite of the dominant or usual picture of coexistence and mixing religions in Tanzania. Hallencreutz and Westerlund (2002:3) refer to this mixing as 'civil religion'. From a linguistic perspective, scholars prefer to speak about creolization (Bryceson 2009; Hannerz 1992:2010). From the literature we took three concepts describing trends in multicultural and multireligious societies, namely homogenisation (McDonaldization), diversification, differentiation, re-tribalisation, creolization (ecumenisation) and diffusion. We dealt with these issues in chapters two, three and four, using the socio-cognitive approach of Critical Discourse Analysis (CDA). The main objectives of our research were: (1) to gain insight into the relation between religious discourse and (the lack of) social cohesion (internal objective), and by doing so (2) to contribute to a theory and method of studying interreligious relations (external objective).

The main focus of this chapter is the contribution to theory on interreligious relations and the method of studying these. The conclusions after the various sections in the preceding chapters have already laid the foundation for this endeavour. Findings in chapters two, three and four came from different sources, such as FGDs, interviews with key informants, local newspaper reports and open air preaching (*mihadhara*). In chapter two, for instance, we analysed information from six separate Muslim focus group discussions, six recordings of Muslim open air services, local newspaper reports, and five interviews with key Muslim informants. Likewise, chapter three analysed information from seven separate Christian FGDs, local newspaper reports and six recordings of Christian open air preaching. Last but not least, chapter four analysed information from seven mixed [Muslims and Christians together] FGDs and local newspaper reports.

5.1. Conclusions regarding social identity construction

Chapters two, three and four analysed in three stages (description, interpretation, explanation) and at three levels (individual, institutional, societal) discourses regarding the transformation of socio-religious identities through Christian-Muslim relations in Tanzania. They used data generated by FGDs and other written (newspapers) or spoken (open air praching) sources in Dar es Salaam. This section provides general conclusions with respect to social identity transformation and discusses the information presented in earlier chapters.

At an individual or interpersonal level most Muslims and Christians indicated that belonging to society was more important than belonging to a religion. This preference showed that they inclined towards a civic rather than a religious identity. Participants (with a few exceptions) said they can be friends with adherents of other faiths. They used polite, respectful words when communicating with such people and thus were inclusive rather than exclusive, egalitarian rather than hierarchical, and communitarian rather than individualistic (Wijsen 2007:242). Reconciliatory terms such as friend, fellow (or fellow Christian, Muslim, participant) and relative/comrade (*ndugu*) are common, resulting in harmonious interaction with others in the group. This is reflected in their attitudes towards marriage, burials and other ceremonies. They are generally ready to tolerate interreligious marriages; they send their children to schools run by another religion, and so forth.

This is not merely because Muslims and Christians in Tanzania are peace-loving people (Smith 1993:95) more than Muslims and Christians in other countries where conflicts occur. Muslims and Christians in Tanzania want to coexist because of the perpetuation of *ujamaa* ideology (Wijsen & Ndaluka 2012). The word '*ndugu*' was a common salutation in Nyerere's *ujamaa* era. *Ujamaa* propagated egalitarianism which permitted different faiths, races and ethnic groups to coexist in the same society, as we noted in the introduction. This included the nationalisation of religious schools, village-isation, introducing KiSwahili as a national language, mixing of people with different ethnic and religious backgrounds. Consequently it weakened affiliation to a particular religion or ethnic group.

Ujamaa, the dominant ideology, continues to play a crucial role in this community, as it insists on people living together on equal terms and encourages communal ownership of public resources. Thus *ujamaa* ideology is a members' resource (Van Dijk 2008) stored in long-term memory that participants draw on when they produce (communicate) or consume (interpret) texts. Even after the institution of economic and political liberalisation in the 1980s participants continued to treat each other with respect (*u-ndugu*, brotherhood), perpetuating the *ujamaa* spirit. This shows that Nyerere's speech on *Ujamaa* was effective and has been stored in people's memories and is reproduced in perpetual social cohesion.

In the discussions, some participants said that they had migrated to Dar es Salaam from other parts of the country. On arrival they were received by inhabitants of the city, the majority of whom were Muslims. Participants in Temeke district mentioned the late Mzee Kilakala, a Muslim leader and administrator of the area, as a key figure in welcoming upcountry migrants, many of whom were Christians.

The multicultural nature of the Dar es Salaam city and the metropolitan necessitated an attitude of compromise and coexistence, facilitated by the use of KiSwahili. Bryceson (2009; Hannerz 1992, 2010) calls this mingling of diverse traditions and cultural experience creolization of cultures. In our FGDs participant spoke about youths "dressing the same way" and Muslims' use of the Christian word *pagan* to refer to Christians and Christians' use of the Islamic word *kafir* to refer to Muslims. Since the first millennium CE Dar es Salaam has been a city of strangers: first traders from Arabia and Persia, who named the city Dar es Salaam (haven of peace), and later on migrants from upcountry who moved there to earn a living. Regardless of their origin, inhabitants of Dar es Salaam were concerned with "the 'creation' and continual affirmation of an 'urban culture' ... which depended on strong social cohesion" (Bryceson 2009:3).

Ujamaa ideology, the lifeblood of the country's socio-economic development for many years, also promoted the process of KiSwahilisation (Mazrui & Mazrui 1998:95). This process absorbed Dar es Salaam inhabitants' linguistic diversity and bridged their cultural differences, which otherwise might have divided them racially, religiously and ethnically. Thus *ujamaa* and KiSwahilisation facilitated communication and unification among people from different linguistic and religious backgrounds. For example, during the *ujamaa* period all individuals/citizens, including their leaders, were saluted as comrade (*ndugu*). In the FGDs participants used and consistently affirmed the KiSwahili term *ndugu* when referring to other believers. This shows that *Ujamaa* voices and ethos continue to influence interpersonal relations and identities in Tanzanian society.

This thesis confirms Mazrui and Mazrui's (1998:171) statement that KiSwahili is an ecumenical language in Tanzania. Indeed, participants used KiSwahili terms such as *ndugu* (comrade), *rafiki* (friend), *wenzetu* (fellows) and *watoto wa baba mmoja* (children of the same father/relative). A word search revealed that in the mixed group participants used the word *rafiki* 41 times, *wenzetu* 21 times and *ndugu* 23 times. In the Muslims only group the word '*ndugu*' featured 7 times, *rafiki* 19 times and *wenzetu* 16 times. In the Christian group 16 incidences of *rafiki* were counted, while *wenzetu* and *ndugu* occurred 28 and 5 times respectively. This confirms strong social affiliation and enhances friendly, harmonious relations (social cohesion).

Arabic/Islamic terms were also used by some participants, primarily to convey religio-centric sentiments. A word search revealed 34 instances of the word *kafir* and 13 of *haraam* in mixed groups; 8 of *haraam* and 23 of *kafir* in the Muslims only group; and 23 of *haraam* and 17 of *kafir* in the Christians only group. All these words, however, were used indirectly in order to avoid conflict with members who belong to other faith(s) and by doing so, to establish and maintain good relations with them. In open air preaching shifts to Islamic/Arabic and English terms were common. Islamic/Arabic terms were often used in Muslim *mihadara*. Christian preachers, on the other hand, tended to mix KiSwahili and English terms. It was also common for Muslim preachers to use Christian terms such as *wapagani* (pagans) and for Christian preachers to use the term *kafir*. This code-switching and mixing (Blommaert & Verschueren 1991:6) showed that Muslim preachers reproduced an Islamised/Arabised position, while Christian preachers positioned themselves as Westernised. The various orientations (Arabisation/Islamisation and Westernisation) showed divergence and served to elevate a particular position (religious identity).

Peaceful coexistence at an interpersonal level is also a reflection of creolization, depending on the place of residence and dominant religion in that area. This is in line with Burke's (2009:112-115) concept of creolization and cultural orientations. For example, after meeting believers of other faiths people picked and used aspects that were beneficial to them. In the discussion a participant said, "Most people who live in Swahili neighbourhoods are Muslims and because Christians have stayed in those areas for a long time ... they have adopted our [Muslim] behaviour ... at least, they follow our behaviour, that is why we live well and it is difficult to distinguish a Christian [from a Muslim] except by his name or if you see him going to church on Sunday." Another participant said, "I had a Christian friend, Rose, we went to a church, and she made something like a cross for me. While they were praying, I was just sitting there. I attend many Christian events because most of my friends happen to be Christians."[1] This indicates that individuals imitated the behaviour (habitus) of the dominant (in this case religious) group and reserved or concealed their religious identity, at least temporarily, for the purpose of sustaining harmonious relationships.

Some Muslims and Christians, however, followed a hard line. They associated more strongly with their religious than with their civic identity. These individuals regard other believers as 'enemies' or 'infidels', and as a result they never consort with them: they never rent houses from, eat with or marry members of other faiths. Thus, apart from the discourse on 'peaceful coexistence' (Hannerz 1992) we also noted a 'clash of civilizations' (Huntington 1996) discourse, as described in the general introduction. It attests the struggle between dominant and peripheral voices in society, only some of the latter are submerged. As one participant put it, "That is why we make noise"; and "we are ill-treated". In such a statement the participant voices his anger and in the process peripheral voices (i.e. religiocentrism) find their way into the public sphere. These voices reflect an ethos of social divergence and disharmony.

In some situations peripheral voices also reproduce and constitute ethnoreligio-centrism rather than inter-religiosity. Participants, for instance, accused Pemba Muslims of being uncompromising, not only towards Christians but also towards fellow Muslims who did not belong to their ethnic group. According to participants these Muslims from Pemba in the Zanzibar archipelago inclined more strongly towards their ethnic than towards a civic or religious identity. Arguably this group has not creolised with Swahili culture, which stresses social cohesion and coexistence.

Most participants believe religion is used by opportunists to politicise religious sentiments with the aim of promoting discrimination, inequality and religiocentrism among ordinary believers. Our participants related this religious struggle to developments in party political discourse. In the words of one participant, "It is like what you see between CCM and CUF."[2] Some of these religious opportunists decide to take the law into their own hands. These include a few Muslims mentioned by participants in the FGDs, who walk with sticks, stir up conflict and invade mosques to unseat the leaders; and the actions of open air preachers (Christian and Muslim) who are financed by those with sinister motives to instigate hatred between Muslims and Christians. Thus the motivation behind these

---

[1] Nilikuwa na rafiki yangu mkristo, Rose tukaenda naye kanisani akanisfungia vitu mfano msalaba. Mimi mle kanisani nilikuwepo tu wao wakawa wanasali . . . . mimi huhudhuria mambo ya wakristo kutokana na marafiki zangu wengi kuwa wakristo. (Uneducated Muslim female.)

[2] Yaani ni kama unavyoona CCM na CUF. (Christian female in uneducated mixed group.)

movements is economic rather than religious, the objective being to attain hegemonic power rather than to promote faith. Our participants explained this in terms of economic discourse namely as commodification/commercialisation ("are like businesses") and privatisation ("everyone has his/her own faith") of religion.

At the institutional level both Islam and Christianity seek to promote peace. As one participant pointed out, "Both religions don't like wicked things." A Muslim participant said, "Islam is humility." Another Muslim said that "Islam ... does not discriminate against anybody". Moreover, an elderly Christian woman said, "Christianity is love." Hence the main issue is not Muslim-Christian relations, because "all worship one God", but the relationship between government officials (politicians) and adherents of these faiths, or religion and state. It is also between ordinary believers (who represent everyday religion) and their religious leaders (who represent official religion). These dichotomies are very pertinent to the problems these two major religions in Tanzania face in trying to forge unity and interreligious harmony. The picture that is consistently reproduced is that in their experience peace and love are central to both Muslims and Christians. The only problem is that Muslims and Christians have created 'a false belief' which makes them discriminate against each other. As one participant said, "Muslims have their things and Christians have their things"; and. this seems to apply particularly to educational institutions.

The Qur'an mentions Christians as people of the book who can be friends with Muslims. It also recognises Jesus (Issa) and his mother Mary (Maryam). In our FGDs a Muslim participant said, "God is one and Jesus is his prophet and Christians call him God, but we call him prophet and Mary, the mother of Jesus, is God's creature." This quotation shows that Muslims and Christians have things in common, which they can exploit to promote or further enhance interreligious communication. That happens when people take advantage of positive factors (i.e. deploy members' resources) and avoid positioning others according to their own (mis)understanding, which makes them focus on differences even when there are commonalities they can work on. Hence we get statements such as, "Muslims and Christians are different and we are used to that"; [3] "each religion has its own people ... religion is faith and each has his/her own faith".[4] Despite such remarks interreligious communication still continues among Muslims and Christians on the ground. As one female Muslim participant stressed, "For us, in this street, we

---

[3] Wakristo na waislamu ni tofauti kama tulivyozoea. (Uneducated female Muslim in the mixed group.)
[4] Dini ni imani na kila mtu anaimani yake. (Uneducated female Christian in the mixed group.)

see it as normal, you can be a Christian or a Muslim; we are all equal."[5] This statement signifies that Muslims and Christians generally believe that they belong to the same society, and this reality overrides membership of a religion or an esoteric community.

As noted above, lack of cohesion does not derive from scriptures but results from (mis)interpretation of these scriptures by different actors, and from the power struggle between them. These interpretations and misinterpretations tend to generate either understanding (positive) or misunderstanding (negative) between Muslim and Christian believers. In Tanzania Jesus' divinity is focal in religious discourse and the issue that caused, at least initially, the Mwembechai killings (Njozi 2000: 31). Whereas Christians believe that Jesus is (the son of) God, Muslims claim that Jesus is not (the son of) God, but accept Jesus (Issa) as God's prophet. Moreover, Muslims position Jesus as a Muslim. To them Muslims are all those "who submit/surrender to the One God", who do the will of God (Aziz, in Njozi 2000:159).

Misunderstandings emanate from lack of mental models that Muslims and Christians share and draw on to enhance interreligious communication. And, as we noted in the introduction, these mental models are generated in educational institutions (Bourdieu 1994). Failure to do so condemns many believers to the age-old pattern of stereotyping others by manipulating their religious symbolic resources (Bourdieu 1991) such as the Bible, Qur'an and the 'prophets' (Jesus and Muhammad). Thereby they create boundaries between true believers and infidels/heathens, normal believers and fanatics/extremists: they end up presenting or treating the other religion as a false belief. The Mwembechai chaos and the Dibagula case, to mention only two instances, exemplify this lack of resources to bridge members' knowledge gap. Some religious leaders and a few individuals romanticised these events to expand their sphere of influence and attract new 'customers' (believers) from the other faith, without adopting any meaningful strategy to initiate interreligious communication that could clear up misunderstanding.

An example was the Mwembechai chaos, the topic of Njozi's book, *The Mwembechai killings and the political future of Tanzania* (2002). Njozi politicised this case and attributed it to religion and state relations, arguing strongly that the state favors Christians more than Muslims, which reflected interreligious sentiments. However, our participants felt otherwise. None of the participants in the separate Muslim FGDs mentioned the matter, indicating that many Muslims

---

[5] Kwetu sisi hapa mtaani kwetu tunajionea sawa tu, uwe mkristo au mwislamu, wote ni sawa. (Uneducated female participant.)

saw it as peripheral. In the six mixed groups only one elderly male[6] referred to the Mwembechai riots, but did not relate them directly to Christians in general. Other participants in the group neither picked up on the matter nor mentioned it in their discussions. This response showed that, unlike Njozi (2002) and other sympathisers, many Muslims considered the Mwembechai killings as something outside or peripheral to the religious discourse. This finding is in line with Tambila's (2006:60) survey which reported that 84% of the respondents said they had not heard of religious conflicts; 12% of the respondents in the survey reported to have heard of religious conflicts, which generally gives the picture that religious conflict was a peripheral voice normally unheard by the majority.

As the struggle to expand their spheres of influence continues, some religious opportunists (extremists/fanatics) propagate religio-centrism by stressing the psychological and social needs of believers (both Muslims and Christians) to defend their faith by whatever means. Individuals start to strongly identify with their religion and see believers of other faiths as rivals. In the FGDs one participant said, "The difference is that those are Christians and we are Muslims, thus Christians are not Muslims."[7] Such an exclusive way of looking at other believers creates boundaries ('others are not like us').

The resultant negative portrayal or treatment of both Christianity and Islam by these radical groups shapes and influences existing and future Muslim-Christian relations and undermines the long-standing spirit of coexistence in Tanzania, as it sows divisive religio-centrism. The inevitable consequence is to divide believers and ultimately weaken social cohesion.

However, most participants in the FGDs portrayed Tanzania as a secular society. One participant said, "You cannot bring up religious issues at home." Religion was portrayed as something personal that cannot be mixed with social relationships. Tolerance of intermarriage, dietary patterns and dress codes was emphasised by the younger generation, possibly because they are growing up in an environment where a mixture of cultural values (creolization) is the norm and operates in even higher spheres (school, work and home). They also have more freedom of choice than the older generation. On the other hand, the older generation saw the younger generation as the cause of interreligious problems because

---

[6] After the FGD we learned that this participant taught religion at a religious schools in Ilala, Dar es Salaam, and was therefore informed on religio-politics. Other participants may have recognised the sensitivity of the matter and refrained from discussing it in order to maintain group harmony.

[7] Utofauti upo, kwamba wale ni wakristo na sisi waislamu na hivyo wakristo sio waislamu. (Uneducated Muslim female.)

they were more educated and extreme (they consider older people outdated and uneducated). The older generation referred to their past experiences as more flexible because they were not educated, hence did not know much about their faith. This generated a habitus (Bourdieu 1984) which furthered social harmony and avoided interfaith conflict.

When we speak about socio-religious transformation in Tanzania, the fact that there are peripheral voices is not new. During the *ujamaa* era there were also peripheral voices but they were suppressed, did not come to the fore. The flow of information (e.g. media, schools) was government controlled. What is new in the *rukhsa* (liberalisation) era is that these peripheral voices are allowed to be heard and express themselves in the public domain.

Globalisation plays a crucial role in the socio-religious transformation of Tanzania, since communication media such as television, videos and the internet influence the youth's conduct and ways of relating to others. Youths were critical of Arab funding for the construction of mosques instead of educational institutions such as universities, which benefit them far more. This manifested a shift from a religio-centric attitude intent on gaining religious education to a secular one seeking access to secular resources (e.g. formal education and employment opportunities). In this regard globalisation has helped to homogenise the youths' manner of shaping their identities and interpersonal relationships. In other words, globalisation has necessitated convergence of (Muslim and Christian) cultures, which in turn makes it possible to establish harmonious civil relations at the societal level. As we have seen before, the older generation consider that the younger generation creates problems in the community because they have access to formal education.

Huntington (1996:1) introduced the notion of a 'clash of civilisations'. In fact, most participants demonstrated that more homogenisation than divergence was taking place in Tanzania. Contrary to what Huntington (1996) said, this confirms Ali Mazrui's (2006: 224-232) observations on convergence of Islam and Christianity quoted in the general introduction. For example, on the issue of interreligious marriages participants demonstrated that believers opt for civil marriages and continue practising their different faiths side by side, whereas others change their religion, not for religious reasons but as a way of striking a compromise socially and in so doing avoid family conflict.

This finding confirms Tambila's (2006:59) findings which covered 839 participants. In his survey Tambila discovered that 80% of participants indicated a good relationship between Muslims and Christians, as opposed to only 3.7% who thought there were disharmonious relations between Muslims and Christians.

Whereas Tambila's data were based on a quantitative approach, our study used a qualitative approach, looking at the data from the perspective of social constructivism. Statistical research intends to give a picture of reality. Our study shows how reality comes about through discourse.

Nevertheless globalisation has connected believers via internet and television, which inform them of events in other parts of the world. In the FGDs it was clear that Tanzanian Muslims spoke more about occurrences outside the country, especially those pertaining to Muslim issues, than their Christian counterparts. This was the case with the American wars in Iraq and Afghanistan, the war on terrorism, and the Palestinian question. To express their concerns a section of Muslims demonstrated during George W. Bush's visit to Tanzania in 2008.

It was equally clear from participants' views that religious discourse was influenced by political discourse. Thus Muslim-Christian relations are confused with religion-state relations. Both Muslims and Christians preferred a secular scenario, in which there was separation of religion and state. Most participants noted that under the first post-independence government the state was completely separate from religion. They said president Nyerere did not mix religion with politics, and that party policies should not be based on any religion. So they reproduced the dominant image of Nyerere and *ujamaa* that we also found in the literature (see general introduction, 1.3). The participants observed that this was not the case with subsequent governments. For instance, religious issues such as OIC membership and the establishment of *kadhi* courts were discussed in parliament (a secular organ), consequently dividing members of parliament along religious lines (Muslim versus Christian MPs). Some political parties also tended to be associated with a particular religion. Thus some participants associated the CCM with Christianity and the CUF mainly with Islam. This showed that religion and politics/state were being mixed and religion was being reproduced in political party ideologies.

Participants confirmed that politico-religious transformation had been going on in Tanzania since independence. After independence (1961-1984) Nyerere advocated national unity and a Tanzanian identity. This helped citizens to coexist as *ndugu*. They had freedom of worship ("everyone should have their own religion"), but the government remained secular. Participants noted that there was a clear separation between state and religion during this period. They said Nyerere nationalised missionary schools so that Muslim and Christian children could have equal access to education. Indeed, as one participant put it, "Mwalimu Nyerere nationalised schools which belonged to missions in which even their big leaders, even ministers studied." This is in line with the premises of Mbogoni (2004) and

Mushi and Mukandala (2006) that nationalisation of religious schools and hospitals was aimed at bringing about equity and unity between Muslims and Christians, thus overcoming existing inequalities in education that gave Christians the upper hand (Mushi & Mukandala 2006:534). In the same vein most Christian participants believed that these inequalities were a result of historical circumstances (establishment of secular education by Christian missionaries during the British colonial period), while most Muslim participants reproduced a picture of government discrimination against Muslims.

Before World War I the German colonial administration employed Muslims in different colonial and administrative posts – as clerks, translators, police, civil servants and civil administrators, the Jumbes and Akidas (Smith 1993:96). The Germans employed mainly Muslims because they could read and write Arabic. Muslims were therefore privileged because they were considered more educated than other Africans, who were illiterate (Smith 1993:97). At that time Christians did not yet have the upper hand.

The situation changed in the post-World War I period, when Britain was mandated by the League of Nations to oversee Tanganyika as its protectorate. The British administration favoured secular education and used Roman instead of Arabic script, which entailed shifting from Arabised to Westernised education. As indicated in previous chapters, Muslims generally tend to associate the Western system closely with Christianity. Therefore the change from the Arabic (or Islamised) script to the Western script was viewed with suspicion by Muslims, who equated it with a shift from Islam to Christianity (Smith 1993:98). Gradually the hitherto privileged Muslims lost their grip on government opportunities and resources. Under the British those with secular (Western) education, who knew how to read and write the Roman script (Smith 1993:98), got priority; these generally turned out to be Christians.

In the discussions some participants noted the role of missionaries in helping Christians to gain the upper hand. As the participants observed, missionary activities, to use Marx's concept, were the material condition that facilitated Christians' rise to the top. Mission schools provided the secular knowledge and skills the colonial administration needed. In the post-independence era the vacant posts previously held by colonial administrators were filled by those with such skills and knowledge. This was explained in the FGDs, where participants said that early Christian converts and a few Muslims who dared to attend mission schools held high ranking posts after independence due to their privileged status.

After independence the first government under Nyerere tried to address the educational imbalances (through nationalisation of schools in terms of *ujamaa* ideology) by creating educational opportunities for all Tanzanians regardless of religious affiliation. Njozi (2000), who is a prolific advocate of Muslims' rights in Tanzania, praises Nyerere's *ujamaa* as the only ideology capable of addressing such inequalities. He writes:

"Since Tanzania has, especially beginning with President Mwinyi's era, abandoned socialism, the only ideology capable of guaranteeing economic progress, freedom and justice to all; many poor people are psychologically frustrated as a result of the economic miseries they experience under liberalisation. Left with no hope for the future in this world, these poor souls turn to religion for solace and for hope at least in the world to come. Because of their deep-seated economic frustrations and their ignorance, this group can easily be manipulated to divert its fury from the real enemy which is capitalism to a racial, ethnic or religious 'other'. And this is precisely what is happening in Tanzania" (Njozi 2000:16).

After 1985, when Mwinyi took over leadership, a group of Muslim religious opportunists exploited the idea that inequalities in education and employment opportunities were a result of calculated Christian discrimination against Muslims through government policies, because Christians occupied important positions in government, hence could affect changes in their favour and victimise Muslims. This idea was supported by some Muslim participants in the FGDs. One elderly Muslim said, "That is why we say we are ill-treated", a religio-centric view representing peripheral voices which also positioned Tanzania as a divided society. One needs to understand this when it comes to social, political and religious transformations in Tanzania.

After Nyerere *ujamaa* was replaced by economic liberalisation and political pluralism, as Njozi (2000:16) explains. One of the tenets of liberalisation policy is competition. By its very nature competition does not do justice to the weak; only the strongest survive in the market place. In the case of Tanzania, liberalisation widened the gap between haves and have-nots that persisted in spite of *ujamaa* policies. As most participants pointed out, both Muslims and Christians were affected ("there are educated Christians and educated Muslims", "there are poor Christians and rich Muslims").[8] However, Muslim religious opportunists and some politicians tend to associate inequalities and discrimination with Christians. This contradicts the FGD participants' view that these inequalities and discrimination are in the first place grounded in historical and material conditions. Whatever one thinks about school nationalisation, indeed during *ujamaa* era (nationalisation) education institutions were used to bring social cohesion, while the cur-

---

[8] Kuna wasomi wakristu na wasomi waislam; kuna wakristu masikini na waislamu matajiri.

rent liberalisation era (*rukhsa*) has brought divergence and educational institutions play a major role in facilitating these developments.

Overall the discussion revealed that Christians speak about Muslims in different ways, and vice versa. Both sides demonstrated that the realisation of peace or cohesion/harmonious relations is 'something' desired at a societal level, which also confirms the participants' inclination towards a civic rather than a religious identity. Religious identity tends to come to the fore when there are unsolved differences in the civic identity.[9] These differences only surface when, at the political level, there are fewer efforts and lack of a clear ideology to address the social problems that cause unequal distribution of resources/capital. As a result some individuals feel deprived and start looking to their religious and/or ethnic groups for answers. The consequence is a divided, disunited society prone to conflict and disharmony. In other words, people elevate their religious identities over other identities (see general introduction, 2.3) when they feel marginalised, ill-treated or disregarded. This is in harmony with Bourdieu (1991b). Religion is a resource to serve people's needs, in competition or in collaboration with others, and this can be both intra- and interreligious, for example normal/moderate Muslims and Christians identified Tanzania as a secular country and collaborate to maintain peace but normal and radical Muslims/Christians compete over the same issue. The result of this struggle and competition is conflict and/or lack of social cohesion.

This dichotomy shows on the one hand hat there are peace-loving and open-minded people striving for cohesion, and on the other hand that things go wrong (lack of cohesion) if people's needs are not adequately addressed, This is exactly what Nyerere did in the past by formulating an ideology of national unity, *ujamaa* and nationalising educational institutions (Wijsen & Mfumbusa 2002:324) and by doing so developed a shared knowledge between Muslims and Christians. To some Muslims Tanzania is a Christian dominated country and Muslims are at best tolerated and/or regarded as second-class citizens. Understanding this relationship calls for a multi-dimensional approach. FGD participants, for instance, said that religious meetings (*mihadhara*) and marriage have become commercialised or politicised, thus mixing religion with politics or economic interests (Mushi & Mukandala 2006:534).

---

[9] See Foucault's order of discourse (Foucault 1972:43-53), where he uses criminal behaviour to demonstrate the order of discourses such as psychiatric, medical, judicial (i.e. the police, prison, etc.) and social discourse (the family, sexual behaviour, etc.).

5.2. Conclusions on the theory underlying CDA

Key concepts in the theory underlying CDA are power, power relations, identity creation and ideology (ideological struggle). Theorists have used CDA to gain insight into the way power is constructed, constituted and distributed in society. Michel Foucault (1977:3) suggested that power is exercised in binary divisions and branding and is not coercive. And Bourdieu (1991: 220) said, "Practical classifications are always subordinated to practical functions and oriented towards the production of social effects". As was shown in our analysis, participants applied dichotomies such as ordinary faithful versus religious leaders, normal believers versus religious extremists, clean versus unclean (*haraam*) residents, *kafirs* versus true believers, lazy (*mdebwedo*) versus hardworking Tanzanians, and respectable versus not respectable people. These classifications were used either to include or exclude believers of other faiths; in so doing they facilitate social cohesion or conflict in the society.

This kind of classification (disciplinary partitioning, Foucault 1977:2) facilitates and sanctions the existence of some individuals' power over others in society. In the FGDs and interviews participants showed that when believers elevated their religious identities above, say, national or civic identities they were considered to be radical (*wenye siasa kali*), extremists and outside the rule of law, hence not normal (*siyo wa kawaida*). This shows that power is exercised by labelling and classifying individuals as abnormal (Foucault 1977:3) or outside the desired order, hence through a process of abnormalisation (Blommaert & Verschueren 1998:122), which is indicative of an ideological explanation of the meaning of the situation and the dominant voice of "We Tanzanians are a tolerant/unified people".

When members of a group experience that their interests are disregarded, their reaction is expressed in anger ("we are ill-treated", "a Christian is my enemy"). They believe that society is treating them as second-class citizens, while the other group is favoured by government ("is the country governed by Christians?"). For example, one Muslim participant declared, "Muslims will wake up and fight for their rights." This implies that favouritism is the root cause of radicalism, as one participant claimed, "a father cannot have two children and favour one of them". Peripheral voices have been superseded or appear to have been silenced in the *ujamaa* period and emerged in the *rukhsa* era as we noted above.

Like Foucault, Gramsci (1971:12) sees the ideological struggle for dominance as non-coercive. Hegemony and power are attained through consent rather than the use of force (Fairclough 2001:332). That is to say, the hegemony of the dominant voice (say, Christians) was achieved by winning the consent of the majority in society. Thus a Christian, Julius K. Nyerere, was freely elected as TANU chairperson and first president of Tanganyika, later Tanzania, by both Muslims and Christians despite the Muslim majority in TANU during that period (Smith 1993:100-101).

In our FGDs and interviews as well as content analyses of newspaper reports there was a tendency to reproduce a Christian repressive mechanism, also evident in Christian participants' negative reaction to Muslims and their plight. Muslim participants, on the other hand, were less critical of Christians. However, in the long run this repressive mechanism could have negative consequences for inter-religious coexistence. This is what Blommaert and Verschueren (1991:5) call a communication breakdown as a result of passive rather than real discrimination. As things stand, the dominant group (Christians) is (allegedly) to blame for the peripheral (Muslim) group's failures or misfortunes. Christian participants claimed Muslims were illiterate because they preferred religious to secular education; they also charged Muslims with not wanting work and accused them of being troublemakers (extremists/radicals). All these negative statements showed that Christian participants were frustrated with Muslims for failing to live up to their part of the bargain. On the other hand, some Muslims positioned themselves as second-class citizens or victims of Christian discrimination and/or machinations. Their main opponent is the government and not necessarily Christians, although they maintain that government is dominated by Christians. Sivalon (1990:119), for example, commented that Nyerere, being a Roman Catholic, was close to Catholic priests and bishops, and consequently his government was pro-Christian and anti-Islam.

Following Gramsci, Bourdieu (1987) adds that the dominant class perpetuates its hegemonic domination through 'instruments of domination', entrenching the dynamics of false consciousness (misrecognition/recognition) which legitimises social inequalities. In his explanation of the effect of false consciousness on the dominated class, Bourdieu writes:

"The dominant culture contributes to the real integration of the dominant class (by facilitating the communication between its members and by distinguishing them from other classes); it also contributes to the fictitious integration of society as a whole, and thus to the apathy of the dominated classes; and finally, it contributes to legitimating the established order by establishing distinctions (hierarchies) and legitimating these distinctions" (Bourdieu 1990b:167).

In our FGDs most Muslim and Christian participants confirmed that Muslims generally had low levels of education and suffered from income disparities as a result of historical circumstances which made them reluctant to enrol for 'secular missionary education'. Over the years this has affected their access to professional and other opportunities that require both academic and professional qualifications. Since the majority of Muslims did not have secular education, literacy (one symbolic production) was used by the dominant class as an instrument of domination.

As mentioned in chapter one, Bourdieu (1990b) uses concepts such as field, habitus, profit and capital to gain more insight into pluralistic society. In the FGDs participants indicated that, at a societal level, Muslims and Christians live relatively homogeneously ("we live like *ndugu*") but operated in separate fields, a reflection of modern pluralistic society. For example, participants said: "We Muslims don't eat pork", "I have a Christian friend", "we live in the same house", and "my sister is married to a Christian". All these statements illustrate that Tanzania is a melting pot and/or pluralistic society in which, despite diversities, citizens find converging points where both play in the same field through friendship or interreligious marriage.

In the religious field Muslim and Christian believers contend for religious capital. In the FGDs a participant said that slaughtering domestic animals and poultry was conducted by Muslims ("I always look for a Muslim to slaughter a chicken", "if a Christian slaughters a chicken, they [Muslims] won't touch it at all"), hence slaughtering is religious capital monopolised by Muslims. Some Christian participants objected to this monopoly (hegemony) ("What they like is for a Muslim to slaughter. This is why we say Muslims are selfish"). Some Christians have even started slaughtering themselves to redress the situation. An uneducated Christian female in the mixed group said, "Aah, I just slaughter! I chop it! ... I look in whatever direction and just pull off its head." This shows that Muslims and Christians are constantly struggling for socio-religious capital.

The struggle is partly explained by the fact that Muslims and Christians have different fields, which inform their habitus (disposition or behaviour). As was shown above, religious institutions seem to be less influential than educational institutions although some of the educational institutions are faith based. We learn from Bourdieu (1984) that there is a link between a person's *habitus* and his/her formal education. On the one hand, Muslims are told in the mosques to behave and act in certain (religious) ways, such as not eating meat that has not been slaughtered by a fellow Muslim because it is unclean (*haraam*). Muslims' *habitus* positions them to behave in a manner that would control a particular form of socio-religious capital in a religious field. On the other hand Christians, through their faith based educational institutions, are also disposed to behave in certain secular ways.

As we learned from the participants, at least until recently some Muslims favoured religious education (*madras*) whereas Christians favoured secular education ('*kusoma kizungu*'). As a result a struggle for resources is bound to happen when believers of the two religions aspire to control the same socio-religious capital, which would allow one party to acquire power and prestige in society (Bourdieu 1990b; Rey 2004:332). Employment (Mushi 2006:427) is just one of the many forms of capital that both Muslims and Christians aspire to control, and as we have seen from participants' responses there is an indirect link between job opportunities and religion. It is not because of the Christian faith that Christians got employment, but because they were better educated through their faith based educational institutions. Muslims who joined these Christian based educational institutions have better jobs too (Mushi 2006:427-428).

Bourdieu claims that members of the same class will have a homogeneous habitus. Rey (2004:335) correctly points out, "Agents from the same class have relatively homogeneous habitus because they undergo similar formative experiences, such as family structure, quality and degree of education and form of religion." Like Bourdieu, Rey (2004) maintains that habitus is shaped and strongly influenced by the class identity of the agents, in our case Muslims/Christians and/or a social class, for example, leadership. In the FGDs participants said, "The religion that discriminates is that of the teachers, sheikhs and priests, not us".

Often these boundaries between fields (e.g. between religion and the economy) have become fluid, hence there could be what our participants described as identity crossover and multiple identities.[10] Individuals could be Muslim or Christian, members of the community or village/street, and (Tanzanian) citizens. In our FGDs participants positioned themselves as Muslim or Christian, which gave them access to religious capital. At the same time they positioned themselves as members of the community or street, which made them benefit from the cultural and social capital available in the community (*tunazikana, tunaoana, watoto wetu wanacheza pamoja*). Similarly, participants positioned themselves as citizens, hence assumed national identity ("our country in a haven of peace"). Using this category, they could exploit national and political capital. The boundary separating one identity from another is very porous and depends on the form of capital that a person wants to exploit. In other words, the habitus of agents in a particular class is not always homogeneous, because individuals or agents in the same class may have different interests (polyphonic voices) and means of exploiting forms of capital from other fields (code switching/mixing).

---

[10] See Fairclough 1992:69 on the shift of discourse boundaries and boundaries between subject positions. He sees boundaries between discourse and subject positions as dynamic, subject to context and power relations.

Bourdieu (1971) claims that capital can be is transferred from one field to another. This makes that particular form of social capital more important than others. In the FGDs participants considered Christians to be (generally) more educated than their Muslim counterparts. Thus they could invest more educational capital in the professional field (employment opportunities, etc.), in economic production and in political power. It can also be transferred to private fields such as marriage. Indeed, as one elderly female Muslim put it, "We don't choose religion but avarice. If you find a Christian with money, you go with him." Given these circumstances, educated Christians are able to exploit several forms of capital in different fields to legitimise their privileged positions and dominance in society. This is reinforced and justified via religion and its institutions, especially educational institutions such as schools, universities, et cetera. As one participant noted, "Christians have more than twenty universities." This reflects Christians' mode of symbolic expression (Bourdieu 1971:315), that of a secular lifestyle. On the other hand participants noted that Muslims placed much more emphasis on religious than on secular symbols. For example, they covered their bodies when going to mosque, a Muslim has to slaughter animals for public consumption, and they prioritise *madras* at the expense of secular education. These actions inform Muslims' mode of symbolic expression (i.e. their lifestyle), which is regulated by Islamic values, implying religious dominance.

From this discussion it is evident that the struggle for religious capital between Muslims and Christians cuts across many practical classifications (Bourdieu 1971) and/or series of polar oppositions: between rich believers and poor believers, educated and uneducated believers, clean and unclean worshippers, and so forth. There is also the popular view that Christians have the upper hand, so these aspects end up dividing society along Muslim-Christian lines or between true believers and non-believers (*kafirs*), each camp vying to control and safeguard its interests in the religious field.

As was shown in the introduction there are two types of charisma:[11] inborn charisma (a person is naturally born charismatic) and socially or personally cultivated charisma. Sometimes the two qualities may coexist in one person. Weber believed that religion is a source of the dynamics of social transformation, so that a charismatic religious leader acts as a catalyst for these changes (Weber 1968:19). The charismatic leader "must appeal to some source of accepted moral author-

---

[11] According to Weber (1968:25), charisma is a power conceived by analogy that may be harnessed in the service of human beings, just as the naturalistic power of a spirit can be harnessed. Whoever possesses the power of charisma to employ the proper means is even stronger than a god, whom he can compel to do his will.

ity", says Weber (1968:15 19-20; see also Rey 1998:346). After Nyerere, who qualified as charismatic leader, political and religious leaders seem to have lacked this moral authority. Although some participants said that open air preachers were just "healing hunger", which means that they just do business and cause problems instead of solving them, other participants said the open air preachers educate people. Irrespective of one's interpretation of open air preachers, the fact is that open air preaching continues to be conducted and to attract audiences. By challenging and criticising political, religious and legal institutions they seem to appeal to moral authority and give voice to the voiceless. By doing so, they seem to fill the vacuum left by political and religious leaders in the community. Drawing on their experience of Dar es Salaam society, they use everyday language but rely heavily on their religious ideologies to shape and communicate their message. Their utterances are founded on religious symbols such as the Bible, the Qur'an and the prophets (Jesus and Muhammad). In fact, the utterances of open air preachers demonstrate the dialectic relation between discourse and socio-religious transformation. On the one hand, open air preachers were able to practise as such because of the liberalisation process that was going on in the country, triggered by President Mwinyi's word *'rukhsa'* (permitted). On the other hand they were also catalysts of this liberalisation process and became part of the process by challenging the dominant status of the mainstream religion. In so doing they were seen as stirring up lack of cohesion, as participants said that "too much freedom brings chaos".

Open air preachers radically appropriate religious symbols such as Jesus and Muhammad and employ "comparative religious study" (see Abdul Aziz, reproduced in Njozi 2000: 161) rhetoric by comparing the Bible and the Qur'an, using these authoritative sources as foundations for their appeal. Muslim open air preachers, for instance, constantly cited the Bible and Jesus to strengthen their arguments. One preacher said "Jesus (Issa) was a Muslim" and "The Bible says...". By using and manipulating Christian symbols (the Bible and the church's head, the messiah) the preachers managed to respond to the ideological and religious needs of their audiences and convey the message that Muslims are on the right track (true believers). Christian preachers for their part used the Qur'an, a Muslim symbol, to show how Muslims have strayed. This, as affirmed by participants in the FGDs, shows that the two religions, via their open air preaching, were constantly competing for religious capital and believers, who are the consumers of religious messages.

Clearly some *mihadhara* preachers distinguished themselves from other believers by setting up boundaries and assuming the position of good believers who will not mix with nonbelievers (*kafirs*). The impact of such charismatic authority was shown in participants' utterances. Some Muslim and Christian participants said that open air preaching persuaded people in their communities to stop letting their houses to tenants of a different faith; others refused to lend or borrow utensils from *kafirs*/pagans, let alone eat with adherents of a different faith.

Open air preachers have also challenged the status of religious institutions. Whereas in the past religious authorities were priests or sheikhs, the emergence of open air preachers represents a radical shift in the hierarchy of religious institutions. In chapter three the mufti of Tanzania was quoted as appealing to Muslims not to listen to those who instigate divisions (referring to Muslim open air preachers); we also cited the scandalous incident in which padre Lumbano claimed that Jesus was insulted by open air preachers at Mwembechai. The former illustrates the intra-religious struggle for control of production, accumulation and legitimacy of religious authority (capital) between open air preachers and the orthodox hierarchy (the sheikhs), seen by Muslims as having legitimate authority (capital) over religious belief and perceptions (habitus). The latter example represents an inter-religious struggle for religious capital between Muslim preachers and Christian religious leaders; often these challenges were not received well by the orthodox hierarchy which, in its turn, resisted the new movements. This is what happened when padre Lumbano reported the matter to the police, who then used force to break up the meeting.

Evidence from our participants' shows that this struggle is not confined to *mihadara* but extends to relations between ordinary believers and their religious leaders. Ordinary believers see their religious leaders as the cause of interreligious conflict/disharmony. A female Muslim participant said, "The religion that discriminates is that of the teachers, sheikhs and priests, not us." "We ordinary believers have no problem." In their view religious leaders mix religion with politics and turn religion into a commodity that can be bought or used as a business to generate profit.

This struggle for the souls of believers and religious power is not limited to the interreligious field (Muslims versus Christians), but is also intra-religious. Participants mentioned Muslims who used sticks to fight other Muslims in the mosque, a development which threatened the hegemony that orthodox leaders (sheikhs and priests) once commanded or enjoyed because of their religious positions and functions. As a result orthodox leaders invoked the state's coercive power (see Gramsci 1971:12) to threaten or discipline the group propagating a new ideology, so as to restore order or preserve the status quo. According to Gramsci (1971:23) this shows a "complete separation between the intellectuals (clergy or sheikhs) and the people". The clergy/sheikhs (orthodox religious leaders) and open air preachers use the same religious scriptures, but offer different interpretations.

Suffice to note here that open air preachers use the religious field by radically exploiting its symbols to accord with believers' habitus and so fill the existing ideological vacuum. Thus they capitalise on the socio-religious transformation: liberalisation (*rukhsa*) opens up space for preachers to practise, but in the process they serve as catalysts of the ongoing socio-religious transformation. This illustrates the dialectics between language (speaking about) and transformation in Tanzanian society.

What is more important here is that religion appeals to the ideological sentiments of marginalised people in society, using religious symbols to fill the gap left by *ujamaa* ideology. Through interaction (e.g. open air preaching) in the religious field religion is elevated to the public domain, exploiting the believers' lay religious habitus, and thus affecting their attitudes by giving them a sense of identity that differentiates them from other believers. One participant said that open air preaching persuaded some individuals in the community to avoid consorting with adherents of other faiths. As a result they refused to employ them, rent their houses, lend/borrow their utensils, or eat food prepared by them simply because they see them as enemies, unclean or non-believers (*kafirs*).

Here again we need to go beyond Bourdieu's pluralism and adopt a polyphonic approach. In postmodern society religious issues are multiple and diverse (Hannerz 1992). They are not limited to relations between Muslims, Christians and/or other religions, or Muslims and Muslims, or Christians and Christians. In our study participants bemoaned the fact that religion has been commercialised ("it is like a business") and politicised ("it is like a political party"). The study of such diverse relations needs a multi-perspective and poly-methodic approach.

This thesis links the materialist and idealist approaches of CDA to interpret religious discourse in Tanzania. We argue that the two (material conditions and religious discourse) interact dialectically and thus complement each other (e.g. *mihadara* are often conducted in low income areas). At the same time we have to be alert to the complexity of postmodernity and adopt a multi-perspective and poly-methodic approach in studying religion and interreligious relations.

The theory underlying CDA is based on linguistic pragmatism assuming that language is performative. Analysing the power of language to make and unmake social groups, and consequently to create cohesion or conflict, Nyerere's *ujamaa* rhetoric is an interesting case. Whatever one thinks about the effect of his rhetoric in the economic arena (Maghimbi 1995), it did have an effect in the political arena. More than forty years after the introduction of *ujamaa* people still speak about it. As we observed in the FGDs, *ujamaa* sentiments and statements are used to orient people's lives and to generate behaviour, avoiding conflict and maintaining harmony. Nyerere's rhetoric more or less confirms what Bourdieu (1991:107-116) said about the conditions for the effectiveness of speech. The person must be considered to be trustworthy and he/she must address issues that are recognised as real.

5.3. Conclusions regarding the method of CDA

Fairclough (1992:71) argues that linguistic practice (text) constitutes and is constituted by social practice (context), in terms of both social conditions and effects, through discursive practice (interaction). Unlike Fairclough, Van Dijk (2008) maintains that linguistic practice (text) is conducted via mental models, hence has socio-cognitive effects. This thesis has demonstrated, by analysing participants' utterances, that Fairclough's and Van Dijk's models are complementary and offer a theoretical and methodological approach to discourse analysis, looking beyond the discourse to gain insight into the socio-cognitive effects of language. This includes understanding how social context influences participants' way of speaking (Van Dijk 2008) and the other way round, that is how participants' speech influences the social context. In our discussions participants spoke about other believers in terms of an axiom that 'Tanzanians are peaceful people who coexist well'. By using polite words and the passive voice and by speaking indirectly (also suppressing or silencing peripheral voices) they reaffirmed and constituted the status quo of peaceful, harmonious coexistence, thus emphasising civic as opposed to religious identity. This confirms that the socio-cognitive effect of language is reflected in individual attitudes.

Scholars of religion have been searching for years for empirical methods of studying religions. Some opted for scientific methods such as experiments, neurological and quantitative (statistical) methods, which would guarantee *objectivity*. Others said there is no such thing as an objective situation (Van Dijk 2008:119), because, as Bourdieu (1999:617) puts it, "True submission to the data requires an act of construction based on practical mastery of the social logic by which these data are constructed." This thesis concurs with Bourdieu that objectivity is attainable, but only via conscious subjectivism (Bourdieu 1990b:124). CDA does just that. It moves beyond the subjectivism/objectivism divide and, instead, benefits from these two approaches.[12]

---

[12] Wijsen et al. (2010d:5) is optimistic that CDA can bridge the gap between interpretation and

Validity in CDA is achieved through an inter- and intra-disciplinary approach (Fairclough 2001:230). Fairclough (1992:193) proposes a comparative approach; Van Dijk (2008) speaks of 'variation'. However, Fairclough's work does not demonstrate or describe comparison systematically (Wijsen 2010c). Strauss and Corbin (1998) suggest the use of ongoing comparison in which data sources and knowledge are constantly compared. In this thesis constant comparative analysis was achieved through triangulation of data sources; different data were collected from different sources such as FGDs, interviews with key informants and analysis of newspapers reports, religious letters and documents, as well as open air preaching. Utterances by participants in the FGDs were compared with information from other sources to enhance the validity of the findings.

In terms of reliability, this was a case study which should be understood in relation to the contexts of participants and the data sources. However, the findings and discussions do not claim to be representative beyond the discourse in which the data were collected, as explicated by Wijsen et al. (2010d:4): "[T]he reliability of representation is a complicated issue that has to do with the distinction between science and ideology; and between the discursive and non-discursive." Human practice can be influenced by different contexts and circumstances.

As mentioned already, in Tanzania language (KiSwahili) has played a vital role in society, first as a unifying instrument, and second as a medium of communication between the two major religions in the country (Islam and Christianity), making it an ecumenical language (Mazrui & Mazrui 1998). Since language is so important for understanding social processes, this thesis argues that CDA could be a method of religious studies committed to the analysis of social changes, identities, power struggles, relationships, interreligious communication, and the production of new theories. CDA as an analytical method needs to be improved through further research to make it more applicable and reliable in religious studies. By means of CDA this thesis seeks to show that language indeed has a socio-cognitive effect. We demonstrate this through our participants' utterances, especially the socio-religious transformation on the ideational and relational levels.

As was shown in the introduction (theoretical framework, par. 2.3), theorists such as Giddens (1984) and Bourdieu (1977) have long moved with and beyond classical thinkers such as Durkheim, Weber and Marx, and have concluded that analysis of information should be conducted at the level of both the individual agents (micro) and societal structures (macro), as the two complement each other

---

explanation. (The paper was read at the 20th International Conference of the International Association for the History of Religions, held in Toronto, Canada in 15-12 August 2010.)

(Fairclough 1992:85-86; Hannerz 1992:10-16). This is based on the premise that individual actions, which include manner of speaking, on the one hand are shaped or constituted by structures. On the other hand, individual actions (language) constitute or shape social structures. This is in accordance with Giddens' concept of duality of structure (Giddens 1981, 1991). Giddens had already overcome the dichotomy between agency and structure.

In harmony with the process of individualisation, there has been a tendency in the social sciences to down-play the role of the institutional or mezzo level in the analysis of individual actions, as is the case in rational choice theories. The mezzo level (institutions) has been regarded as mere elements whose role is to inform and perpetuate the social structure (macro level). This thesis argues that the mezzo level plays an independent role as a unit of analysis. That is to say, individual actions do not entail the dualism of agent (Weber) and structures (Durkheim), but some actions are moulded at the mezzo level. Institutions inform and influence individual actions and decisions. For example, young participants in our FGDs said that individuals have the freedom to choose their marriage partners (participants say that youths "can marry if they are in love"), that social structures allow them to marry (e.g. the law of the country which makes civil marriage possible), but that marriage also depends on the willingness of family members to accept it ("I have no problem marrying a Christian but the problem is the parents").

In itself our argument that institutions serve as an independent unit of analysis is not new. Berger and Luckmann, with their influential study of the *Social construction of reality* (1966), must be credited with initiating a trend in the social sciences which came to be known as 'new institutionalism'. As noted in the introduction, Foucault (1972) and Bourdieu (1984) in particular showed the influence of educational institutions in shaping people's *habitus* or disposition of behaviour.

In his study *Distinction: a social critique of the judgement of taste* (1984) Pierre Bourdieu, who in his inaugural lecture as professor at the Collège de France defined sociology classically as the "science of institutions" (Bourdieu 1990a:177) observes that "cultural needs are the product of upbringing and education" (Bourdieu 1984:466). Bourdieu saw the family and the school as important institutions influencing the socialisation and development of the person.

In addition to Bourdieu (1984:466) our study shows that the family has become less influential in shaping individual's behaviour, but that the influence of schools remains very strong. Various interviewees said that belief ["everyone has his/her own faith", "you cannot bring up religious issues at home"], dress code ["children wear short dresses … but if you tell them … they tell you that you are old and outdated"], marriage ["they [people of different faiths] can marry if they are in love"] and food ["he has his individual faith that pork is edible"] have become private affairs and that parents lost influence on their children. In this sense there is a massive individualisation and thus de-institutionalisation going on in Tanzania. However, this seems not to apply to educational institutions.

This can be illustrated on the basis of two advertisements from two different newspapers. The first was in *An-Nuur* of 28 November to 4 December 2008, page 10. The second was taken from *Habari Njema* of 22-28 July 2007, page 2. Both newspapers are owned by religious institutions, *An-Nuur* by Tanzania Muslim Professional Association and *Habari Njema* by a Christian group.

The TAMPRO advert specifies who are supposed to apply for admission to their institution by stating, "*walengwa ni waislamu wanawake na wanaume ...*" ("the target is Muslim women and men"). The Baptist advert is open to everyone, regardless of creed. The discrepancy in educational levels between Muslims and Christians has prompted some Muslim institutions to employ positive discrimination strategies aimed at benefiting primarily the Muslim population, because Western education (qualifications for employment and affluence) was introduced late into Muslims population. The advert gives a discursive dimension aimed at restructuring formal educational institutions and the practice of education in a religious dimension (Fairclough 1992:69, 207-208).

Some Muslim participants said that in the past their parents did not send their children to Christian schools for fear of the Christian faith but because of their fear of secular education (fear to learn *kizungu*). In the past becoming a Christian meant to learn (*kusoma*) and a Christian was known as literate (*musomi*). As we noted in the introduction, under the German colonial administration the situation was reversed. Coastal people, hence Muslims, were regarded as literate, whereas upcountry people (mostly adherents of indigenous religions) were not. The Germans preferred to employ coastal people (i.e. Muslims) in their administration because they were literate (Mbogoni 2004).

To the extent that there is a power struggle between Muslims and Christians, the focus is on education, both in explaining why Muslims' are considered second class citizens (e.g. imbalance in job opportunities), as well as explaining why relationships between Muslims and Christians continue to be good (e.g. interreligious marriage is no problem if the partner is well educated and therefore has a high income). Elders said that the youth are stricter because they are better educated.

Earlier we noted that Tanzanians are not better than people in other countries where there are conflicts between Muslims and Christians. It was largely due to deliberate policies of the Tanzanian government during the *ujamaa* era that Muslim-Christian relations are relatively harmonious. Introduction of KiSwahili as lingua franca and nationalisation of schools created a common ground or shared knowledge (e.g. mental models) that facilitated understanding and convergence between Muslims and Christians. Seen from this perspective, the policy to liberalise schools, which is quite understandable for financial reasons, contributed to growing divergence between Muslims and Christians. On the other hand, creolization goes, on as we saw with words such as *ndugu*. *Shukran* and *asalaam aleykum* are Arabic words, but are integrated into KiSwahili and are wide-spread. This shows that people create shared meaning and thus that there is re-institutionalisation.

Speaking about the method of critical discourse analysis, Fairclough (1992) showed that classroom communication constituted and was constituted by images ('mental models') of what good education is and by the social positions of students and teachers in the context of the commercialisation and democratisation of education. The advantage of his model is that Fairclough (1992:72) combined three dimensions (levels) of analysis (micro, mezzo and macro) with three methods (stages) of analysis, which he derives from linguistics, micro and macro sociology. What this study has shown is that his method can be applied fruitfully to the communication between believers of different faiths (e.g. Muslims and Christians) as well as between believers within one and the same faith (e.g. communication, or lack of communication, between ordinary believers and religious officials).

Epilogue

The study of religion and interreligious relations may be considered rare in Tanzania, especially at the University of Dar es Salaam, where I trained as a sociologist of religion and my present workplace. Religion was considered to be outside the public domain and hence not of interest to a public university. The study of religion was confined to theological schools or seminaries. It is only recently that a Department of Philosophy and Religion was established, yet in 2011, the year in which the University of Dar es Salaam celebrates its 50th anniversary, religion and the study of religion are still regarded as sensitive matters to be addressed and handled with care. This did not dampen my determination and interest in a study of religion and interreligious relations, knowing that such a study will contribute to the understanding of Muslim-Christian relations in Tanzania, where religious discourse has resurfaced in the public domain.

Having a background in sociology, registering for a PhD project at the Faculty of Religious Studies of Radboud University Nijmegen was a challenge I had to face. To me religious studies was a new field with its own traditions and terminology, which I had not been exposed to before. I had to struggle to learn some of the terms used in this academic discipline. During my two years of fieldwork religious issues were central in the newspapers, parliament, religious preaching and politics. This made my study a very interesting one and I was increasingly fascinated by religious rhetoric in Tanzania. I collected much information from the participants and from the media and focused my analysis on this.

Although my sociological studies had exposed me to the work of Gramsci, Althusser and classical sociologists in the debate about micro (actor) and macro (structure) levels of analysis, what was again new to me was the focus on linguistic and cognitive anthropology. Scholars such as Blommaert (1999) and Fabian (1966) have made socio-linguistic analyses of the use of KiSwahili in various contexts, showing a close link between communication, cognition and culture. I came to understand that language is not only informative about a culture and society, but also performative. By reproducing and transforming language people construct their social reality.

As I embarked on data analysis, I opted for critical discourse analysis as a method. Lacking a background in linguistics, this posed a challenge. Reading scholars with a socio-cognitive approach such as Blommaert and Verschueren

(1998), Fairclough (1992) and Van Dijk (2008), I was encouraged and decided to choose Fairclough's CDA approach. Since CDA is still in its infancy in religious studies and sociology of religion, my contribution is very useful. In other disciplines, however, CDA has proved to be a useful method of data analysis, particularly in studies of relationships, identity creation and ideological struggle in discourse. This study has demonstrated that CDA also helps to gain insight into the socio-cognitive effects of language use in interreligious studies.

Researching Muslim-Christian relations in a country like Tanzania, popularly known as a haven of peace (Smith 1993; Blommaert 1997; Ludwig 2002:216; Wijsen & Mfumbusa 2004) where Muslims and Christians coexist peacefully, needed careful selection of a place and a method for such a case study. I learned from the CDA approach that interreligious understanding is only attained if individuals draw from the same pool of resources (mental models). The opposite is also true: misunderstandings arise when members lack these shared resources. This reminded me afresh of the importance of education, demonstrated by Bourdieu (1984), Fairclough (1992) and Foucault (1977). It is through education that people learn to classify and acquire mental models. However, as I pointed out, this is a case study at micro level. In view of the nature of this approach, it should be used for further research in religious studies. A broader study using a bigger sample and more methods of data collection should be conducted to test the arguments this thesis has advanced and to examine a wider spectrum of interreligious relations. Such a study should aim to contribute to a multi-perspective and poly-methodical approach to interreligious studies.

At my Department of Sociology and Anthropology, University of Dar es Salaam this study has opened a window on studies of religion. Currently the department is planning to establish a research centre on socio-cultural and religious issues. The aim is to coordinate and stimulate research and studies of this area. As I reflect on the long journey of writing this thesis it makes me feel content and I appreciate the rich experience and knowledge which I gained from my participants and from the literature on the subject. It is my hope that after it has been defended more people will share my experience and in doing so enhance knowledge.

Bibliography

Abushouk, A. 2006. Globalization and Muslim identity: challenges and prospects. *The Muslim World* 96, July.

Allport, G. 1973. The religious context of prejudice. In Beit-Hallahmi, B. (ed.). *Research in religious behaviour. Selected readings.* Wadsworth, Berkeley: University of California Press.

Althusser, L. 1971. Ideology and ideological state apparatuses. In Althusser, L. (ed.). *Lenin and philosophy and other essays.* New York: Monthly Review Press.

Ammah, R. 2007. Christian-Muslim relations in contemporary sub-Saharan Africa. *Islam and Christian-Muslim Relations* 18 (2), 139-153.

Antaki, C. & Widdicombe, S. (eds). 1998. *Identities in talk.* London: Sage.

Asad, T. 1993. *Genealogies of religion. Discipline and reasons for power in Christianity and Islam.* Baltimore, MD: John Hopkins University Press.

Austin, J. 1975. *How to do things in words.* 2nd edition by Urson, J. & Sbisa, M. (eds). Cambridge: Harvard University Press.

Barber, B. 1995. *Jihad vs. McWorld.* New York: Ballantine.

Beatty, A. 1999. *Varieties of Javanese religion. An anthropological account.* Cambridge: Cambridge University Press.

Berger, P. & Luckmann, Th. 1966. *The social construction of reality.* Harmondsworth: Penguin.

Biernatzki, W. 1991. *Roots of acceptance. The intercultural communication of religious meanings.* Rome: Pontifical Gregorian University.

Blommaert, J. & Verschueren, J. 1991. Intercultural and international communication: introduction. In Blommaert, J & Verschueren, J (eds). *The pragmatics of intercultural and international communication.* Amsterdam: Benjamins.

Blommaert, J. 1997. The slow shift in orthodoxy: (re)formulations of integration in Belgium. *Pragmatics* 7 (4), 499-518.

Blommaert, J. 1999. *State ideology and language in Tanzania.* Cologne: Rüdiger Köppe.

Blommaert, J. 1991. How much culture is there in intercultural communication? In Blommaert, J & Verschueren, J (eds). *The pragmatics of intercultural and international communication;* Amsterdam: Benjamins.

Blommaert, J. 2005. *Discourse. Key topics in sociolinguistics.* Cambridge: Cambridge University Press.

Blommaert, J. & Verschueren, J. 1998. *Debating diversity. Analysing the discourse of tolerance.* London, New York: Routledge.

Borsboom, A. & Jespers, F. (eds). 2003. *Identity and religion. A multidisciplinary approach.* Saarbrücken: Verlag für Entwicklungspolitik.

Bourdieu, P. 1971. Intellectual field and creative project. In Young, M. (ed.) *Knowledge and control: new directions for the sociology of education.* London: Collier Macmillan.

Bourdieu, P. 1977. *Outline of a theory of practice.* Cambridge: Cambridge University Press.

Bourdieu, P. 1979. *Algeria 1960.* Cambridge: Cambridge University Press.

Bourdieu, P. 1984. *Distinction: a social critique of the judgement of taste.* Cambridge: Harvard University Press.

Bourdieu, P. 1987. Legitimation and structured interest in Weber's sociology of religion. In Whimster, S. & Lash. S. (eds). *Max Weber, rationality, and modernity.,* London: Allen & Unwin, pp. 126-131.

Bourdieu, P. 1987. What makes a social class? On the theoretical and practical existence of groups. *Berkeley Journal of Sociology* 32, 1-18.

Bourdieu, P. 1989. Social space and symbolic power. *Sociology Theory* 7(1), 14-25.

Bourdieu, P. 1990a. *In other words. Essays towards reflexive sociology.* Stanford CA: Stanford University Press.

Bourdieu, P. 1990b. *The logic of practice.* Stanford: Stanford University Press.

Bourdieu, P. 1991a. *Language and symbolic power.* Cambridge: Polity Press.

Bourdieu, P. 1991b. The genesis and structure of the religious field. In *Comparative Social Research: Religious institutions*, vol. 13, edited by Graig Calhoun. Greenwich CN: JAI Press, pp. 1-44.

Bourdieu, P. 1993. *The field of cultural production.* New York: Columbia University Press.

Bourdieu, P. 1999. Understanding. In Bourdieu, P., Ferguson, P., Emmanuel, S., Johnson, J., & Waryn, S. Trans. Ferguson, P., Emmanuel, S., Johnson, J. & Shoggy, T. Waryn. *The weight of the world: social suffering in contemporary society.* Cambridge: Polity Press.

Bourdieu, P. & Wacquant, L. 1992. *An invitation to reflexive sociology.* Chicago: University of Chicago Press.

Bryceson, D. 2009. Swahili creolization: the case of Dar es Salaam. In Cohen, R. & Toninato, P. (eds). *The creolization reader: studies in mixed identities and cultures.* London: Routledge, pp. 364-375.

Burke, P. 2009. *Cultural hybridity.* Cambridge: Polity Press.

Burton, R. 1987. *First footsteps in East Africa or, an exploration of Harar.* 2 vols. Edited by Isabel Burton. New York: Dover.

Dar es Salaam City Council. 2004. *Socio-economic regional profile.* Dar es Salaam: Dar es Salaam City Council.

Davie, G. 2007. *The sociology of religion.* London: Sage.

De Vere Allen, J. 1993. *Swahili origins: Swahili culture and the Shungwaya phenomenon.* London: Currey.

Evans, I. 1929. *The British in tropical Africa: an historical outline.* London: Cambridge University Press.

Fabian, J. 1986. *Language and colonial power: the appropriation of Swahili in the former Belgian Kongo.* Cambridge: Cambridge University Press.

Bibliography

Fabian, J. 1991. Accident and method in the study of intercultural communication: colonial description of Swahili in the former Belgian Congo. In Blommaert, J. & Verschueren, J. (eds). *The pragmatics of intercultural and international communication.* Amsterdam: Benjamins.

Fairclough, N. 1989. *Language and power.* London: Longman.

Fairclough, N. 1992. *Discourse and social change.* Cambridge: Polity Press.

Fairclough, N. 1995. *Critical discourse analysis.* Boston: Addison Wesley.

Fairclough, N. 2001. Discourse of new labour: Critical Discourse Analysis. In Wetherell, M, Stephanie Taylor, Simeon Yates. *Discourse as data: a guide for analysis.* London: Sage, pp 229-266.

Fairclough, N. (ed.). 2007. *Discourse and contemporary social change.* Bern: Lang.

Festinger, L. 1957. *A theory of cognitive dissonance.* Evanston: Row & Peterson.

Flood, G. 1999. *Beyond phenomenology. Rethinking the study of religion.* London, New York: Cassell.

Foucault, M. 1972. *The archaeology of knowledge.* London: Tavistock.

Foucault, M.1977. *Discipline and punish. The birth of the prison,* vol. 3. *Panopticism.* Translated by Alan Sheridan. London: Land.

Foucault, M. 1978. *The history of sexuality*, vol. 1, *An introduction.* Translated by Robert Hurley. New York: Pantheon.

Gadamer, H. 1975. *Truth and method.* 2nd revised ed. New York: Continuum.

Geertz, C. 1973. *The interpretation of culture.* New York: Basic.

Giddens, A. 1981. *A contemporary critique of historical materialism.* London: Macmillan Press.

Giddens, A. 1984. *The constitution of society; outline of the theory of structuration.* Berkeley, Los Angeles: University of California Press.

Giddens, A. 1991. *Modernity and self-identity. Self and identity in the late modern age.* Cambridge: Polity Press.

Giddens, A. 2009. *Sociology.* 6th revised ed. Cambridge: Polity Press.

Gramsci, A. 1971. *Selection from the Prison Notebooks.* Edited and translated by Hoare, Q. & Smith, G. London: Lawrence & Wishart.

Green, M. 2003. *The priest, witches and power: popular Christianity after mission in southern Tanzania.* London: Cambridge University Press.

Habermas, J. 1984. *The theory of communicative action, reason and the rationalization of society,* vol. 1. Cambridge: Polity Press.

Hall, S. 1996. Who needs "identity"? In Hall, S. & Du Gay, P. (eds). *Questions of cultural identity.* London: University of Chicago Press, pp. 114-119.

Hallencreutz, C. & Westerlund, D. 2002. Introduction: anti-secularist policies of religion. In Westerlund, D. (ed.). *Questioning the secular state: the worldwide resurgence of religion in politics.* London: Hurst, pp. 1-23.

Hamilton, M. 2009. *The sociology of religion,* 2nd ed. London, New York: Routledge.

Hannerz, U. 1992. *Cultural complexity. Studies in the social organization of meaning.* New York: Columbia University Press.

Hansen, H. & Twaddle, M. (eds). 1995. *Religion and politics in East Africa: the period since independence*. London: Currey.

Hasu, P. 2006. World Bank and heavenly bank in poverty and prosperity: the case of Tanzanian Faith Gospel. In *Review of African Political Economy*, ROAPE 110 (33), Sept., pp. 679-692.

Heather, N. 2000. *Religious language and critical discourse analysis*. Oxford, Bern, Berlin: Lang.

Henschel, J. 2000. *Listen to the story of the tombs: Bagamoyo Mission 1870-1930*. Ruvuma: Peramiho.

Hermans, H. & Kempen, H. 1993. *The dialogical self. Meaning as movement*. San Diego: Academic Press.

Hüsken, F. & De Jonge, H. 2002. Violence and the new order. In Hüsken, F. & De Jonge, H. (eds). *Violence and vengeance. Discontent and conflict in new order Indonesia*, Saarbrücken: Verlag für Entwicklungspolitik, pp. 1-10.

Huntington, S. 1996. *The clash of civilizations and the remaking of the world order*. New York: Simon & Schuster.

Jørgensen, M. & Phillips, L. 2002. *Discourse analysis as theory and method*. London: Sage.

Jumbe, A. 1994. *The partnership: Tanganyika Zanzibar union, 30 turbulent years*. Dar es Salaam: Amana.

Kaduma, I. 2004. *Maadili ya Taifa na Hatma ya Tanzania; Enzi kwa Mwalimu Julius K. Nyerere*. Dar es Salaam: Vuga Press.

Kim, C. 2004. *Islam among the Swahili in East Africa*. Nairobi: Paulines Africa.

Kim, M. 2002. *Non-Western perspectives on human communication*. Thousand Oaks: Sage.

Kincaid, D. 1987. *Communication theory*. San Diego CAL: Academic Press.

Kippenberg, H. 1983. Diskursive Religionswissenschaft. In Gladigow, B. & Kippenberg, H. (eds). *Neue Ansätze in der Religionswissenschaft*. Kösel-Verlag München.

Kippenberg, H. & Von Stuckrad, K. 2003. *Einführung in die Religionswissenschaft. Gegenstände und Begriffe*. München: Neck

Kittler, G. D. 1957. *The White Fathers*. New York: Harper.

Kiwanuka, M. 1973. The politics of Islam in Bukoba district. Political Science Paper 7 (a), dissertation. Dar es Salaam: University of Dar es Salaam.

Klöcker, M. & Tworushka, U. 2008. *Praktische Religionswissenschaft*. Köln: Böhlau.

Krieger, D. 1991. *The new universalism. Foundations for a global theology*. Maryknoll NY: Orbis.

Kvale, S. 2008. *Doing interviews*. Los Angeles: Sage.

Levtzion, N. & Pouwels, R. eds. 2000. *The history of Islam in Africa*. Athens. Ohio University Press.

Lewis, I. (ed.). 1980. *Islam in tropical Africa*. 2nd ed. London: Hutchinson.

Liviga, A. & Tumbo-Masabo, Z. 2006. Muslims in Tanzania: quest for equal footing. In Mukandala, R., Othman, S., Mushi, S., & Ndumbaro, L. (eds). *Justice, rights and worship: religion and politics in Tanzania*. Dar es Salaam: E&D, pp. 129-164.

Bibliography

Liviga, A. 2006. Religion and governance in Tanzania: the pre-liberalisation period. In Mukandala, R., Othman, S., Mushi, S., & Ndumbaro, L. (eds). *Justice, rights and worship: religion and politics in Tanzania.* Dar es Salaam: E&D, pp. 320-333.

Locke, T. 2004. *Critical discourse analysis.* London: Continuum.

Lodhi, A. & Westerlund, D. 1999. Tanzania. In Westerlund, D. & Svanberg, I. (eds). *Islam outside the Arab world.* Richmond: Curton Press, pp. 97-110.

Ludwig, F. 2002. After *ujamaa*: is religious revivalism a threat to Tanzania's stability? In Westerlund, D. (ed.). *Questioning the secular state: the worldwide resurgence of religion in politics.* London: Hurst, pp. 216-236.

Magesa, L. 2010. *African religion in the communication debate: from intolerance to co-existence.* Berlin: LIT.

Maghimbi, S. 1992. One-party aggrandisement in Tanzania. In Hunter, J & Lombard, C (eds). *Multi-party democracy, civil society and economic transformation in Southern Africa.* Windhoek: Southern African Universities, Social Science Conference, pp. 113-130.

Maghimbi, S. 1995. The rise and fall of Nyerere's populism (*ujamaa*). In Foster, P & Maghimbi, S. (eds). *The Tanzanian peasantry: further studies.* Aldershot: Avebury Ashgate, pp. 23-36.

Malekela, G. 1994. Education and democratization in Tanzania. *Basic Education Forum* 4, January.

Mall, R. 2000. *Intercultural philosophy.* New York: Oxford University Press.

Martin, B. 1977. The spread of Islam. In Martin, P & O'Meara, P. (eds). *Africa.* Indiana: Bloomington University Press, pp. 98-113.

Maurer, J. 2002. Playing or juggling with words? In Hüsken, F. & De Jonge, H. (eds). *Violence and vengeance. Discontent and conflict in new order Indonesia*, Saarbrücken: Verlag für Entwicklungspolitik, pp. 31-51.

Mazrui, A. & Mazrui, A. 1995. *Swahili state and society. The political economy of an African language.* Nairobi: Currey.

Mazrui, A. & Mazrui, A. 1998. *The power of Babel.* Oxford: Currey. Mazrui, A. 2006. *Islam between globalization and counter-terrorism.* Oxford: Currey.

Mbogoni, L. 2004. *The cross versus the crescent: religion and politics in Tanzania from the 1880's to the 1990's.* Dar es Salaam: Mkuki na Nyota.

McCutcheon, R. 1997. *Manufacturing religion. The discourse on sui generis religion and the politics of nostalgia.* New York, Oxford: Oxford University Press.

McCutcheon, R. 2007. *Studying religion. An introduction.* London, Oakville: Equinox.

McLuhan, M. 1962. *The Gutenberg galaxy. The making of typographic man.* Toronto: University of Toronto Press.

Meyer, B. 1995. *Translating the devil. An African appropriation of pietist Protestantism.* Amsterdam: University of Amsterdam.

Morgan, D. 1997. *Focus groups as qualitative research.* 2nd ed. London: Sage

Mukandala, R. 2006. Introduction. In Mukandala, R., Othman, S., Mushi, S. & Ndumbaro, L. (eds). *Justice, rights and worship: religion and politics in Tanzania.* Dar es Salaam: E&D, pp. 1-17.

Mukandala, R., Othman, S., Mushi, S., & Ndumbaro, L. (eds). 2006. *Justice, rights and worship: religion and politics in Tanzania.* Dar es Salaam: E&D.

Mushi, P. 2006. Religion and provision of education and employment in Tanzania. In Mukandala, R., Othman, S., Mushi, S., & Ndumbaro, L. (eds). *Justice, rights and worship: religion and politics in Tanzania.* Dar es Salaam: E&D, pp. 534-541.

Mushi, S. & Mukandala, R. 2006. Religion and plural politics in Tanzania. In Mukandala, R., Othman, S., Mushi, S., & Ndumbaro, L. (eds). *Justice, rights and worship: religion and politics in Tanzania.* Dar es Salaam: E&D, pp. 534-541.

Musoke, K. 2006. The relationship between religion and employment in Tanzania. In Mukandala, R., Othman, S., Mushi, S., & Ndumbaro, L. (eds). *Justice, rights and worship: religion and politics in Tanzania*, Dar es Salaam: E&D, pp. 496-513.

Mwakimambo, H. 2007. Christian-Muslim relations in Kenya: a catalogue of events and meanings. *Islam and Christian-Muslim Relations* 18 (2), April, 287-307.

Njozi, H. 2000. *The Mwembechai killings and the political future of Tanzania.* Ottawa: Globalink.

Njozi, H. 2003. *Muslims and the state in Tanzania.* Dar es Salaam: Dar es Salaam University Muslim Trusteeship.

Njozi, H. 2006. Islam, the KiSwahili language and integration in East Africa. A. Kasosi & S. Ünay (eds). *Proceedings of the International Symposium on Islamic Civilization in Eastern Africa.* Istanbul: Research Centre for Islamic History, Art and Culture.

Nolan, F. 1977. Christianity in Unyamwezi, 1878-1928. PhD thesis, University of Cambridge.

Nolan, F. 1978. *Mission to the Great Lakes: the White Fathers in western Tanzania (1878-1978).* Tabora: T.M.P.

Nyerere, J. 1968. *Freedom and socialism.* London: Oxford University Press.

Nyerere, J.1995a. *Our leadership and the destiny of Tanzania.* Harare: African Publishing Group.

Nyerere, J. 1995b. *Nyufa.* Dar es Salaam: Mwalimu Nyerere Foundation.

Pambe, I. 1980. Christianity and meaning. In *Pastoral Orientation Service* 4(6), pp. 21-27.

Panikkar, R. 1975. *Intra-religious communication.* New York: Paulist Press.

Parsons, T. (ed). 1968. *Max Weber: the theory of social and economic organization.* New York: Free Press.

Peräkylä, A. 2005. Analyzing text and talk. In Denzin, N. & Lincoln, Y. (eds). *The Sage handbook of qualitative research.* Thousand Oaks: Sage.

Pouwels, R. 1987. *Horn and crescent: cultural change and traditional Islam on the East African coast 800-1900.* Cambridge: Cambridge University Press.

Rebel, H. 1989. Cultural hegemony and class experience: a critical reading of recent ethnological-historical approaches. *American Ethnologist* 16 (1), Feb., 117-136.

Rey, T. 1998. The virgin Mary and revolution in Saint-Dominique: the charism of Romaine-la-Prophétesse. *Journal of Historical Sociology* 11 (3), September.

Rey, T. 2004. Marketing the goods of salvation: Bourdieu on religion. *Religion* 34, 331-343. www.elsevier.com/locate/religion.

Ricoeur, P. 1976. *Interpretation theory: discourse and the surplus of meaning.* Fort Worth: Texas Christian University Press.

Ricoeur, P. 1984. *Time and narrative.* Translated by Blamey, K. & Pellauer, D. Chicago: University of Chicago Press.

Rigby, P. 1980. Sociological factors in the contact of the Gogo of central Tanzania with Islam. In Lewis, I. (ed.). *Islam in tropical Africa,* 2nd ed. London: Hutchinson.

Ritzer, G. 1993. *The McDonaldization of society. An investigation into the changing character of contemporary social life.* Thousand Oaks, CA: Pine Forge Press.

Robertson, R. 1995. Glocalization. Time-space and homogeneity-heterogeneity. In Lahs, S. & Robertson, R. (eds). *Global modernities.* London: Sage, pp. 25-44.

Rukyaa, J. 2007. Muslim-Christian relations in Tanzania with particular focus on the relationship between religious instruction and prejudice. *Islam and Christian-Muslim Relations* 18 (2), April, pp. 187-204.

Rupper, G. 1988. *Pugu hadi Peramiho: Miaka 100 ya Wamissionar Wabenedikitini katika Tanzania; Historian na Simulizi.* Ndanda-Peramiho: Benedictine Publications.

Said, M. 1998. *Abdulwahi Sykes (1924-1968): the untold story of the Muslim struggle against British colonialism in Tanganyika.* London: Minerva Press.

Schulte, N. & Samuel, H. 2004. Introduction: Indonesia after Suharto: rethinking analytical categories. In H. Samuel & H. Schulte Nordholt (eds), *Indonesia in transition,* Yogyakarta: Pustaka Pelajar.

Sivalon, J. 1990. Roman Catholicism and the definition of Tanzanian socialism 1953-1985: an analysis of the social ministry of the Roman Catholic Church in Tanzania. PhD dissertation, Toronto: University of St Michael's College.

Sivalon, J. 1992. *Kanisa Katoliki na Siasa ya Tanzania Bara 1953 hadi 1985.* Peramiho: Benedictine Publications Ndanda.

Smith, P. 1993. Some elements for understanding Muslim-Christian relations in Tanzania. In Konrad-Adenauer Stiftung. *Islam in Africa south of the Sahara. Internationale Zusammenarbeit, working papers,* October, pp. 95-116.

Spear, T. & Kimambo, I. (eds). 1999. *East African expressions of Christianity.* Dar Es Salaam: Mkuki na Nyota.

Strauss, G. & Corbin, J. 1998. *Basics of qualitative research. Grounded theory. Procedures and techniques.* Newbury Park: Sage.

Sukidi, M. 2006. Max Weber's remarks on Islam: the Protestant ethic among Muslim puritans. *Islam and Christian-Muslim Relations* 17 (2), April, pp. 195-205.

Sumner, W. 1906. *Folkways. A study of the sociological importance of usages, manners, customs and morals.* Boston, New York: Ginn.

Sundermeier, Th. 2003. Aspects of interreligious hermeneutics. In Frederiks, M., Dijkstra, M. & Houtepen, A. (eds). *Towards an intercultural theology.* Zoetermeer: Boekencentrum, pp. 48-53.

Tajfel, H. 1978. Social categorization. In H. Tajfel (ed.). *Differentiation between groups.* London: Academic Press.Tajfel, H. & Turner, J. 1986. The social identity theory of intergroup behaviour. In Worchel, S. & Austin, W. (eds). *Psychology of intergroup relations,* Chicago: Nelson-Hall, pp. 7-24.

Tambila, K. 2006. Interreligious relations in Tanzania. In Mukandala, R., Othman, S., Mushi, S. & Ndumbaro, L. (eds). *Justice, rights and worship: religion and politics in Tanzania.* Dar es Salaam: E&D, pp. 57-72.

Tanner, R. & Wijsen, F. 1993. Christianity in Usukuma. A working misunderstanding. In *Neue Zeitschrift für Missionswissenschaft* 49 (3), 177-193.

Tanzania National Bureau of Statistics. 1973. *Tanzania National Demographic Survey.* Dar es Salaam, National Bureau of Statistics.

Taylor, C. 1991. Language and society. In Honneth, A. & Joas, H.(eds). *Communicative action: essays on Jürgen Habermas's theory of communicative action.* Cambridge: MIT Press, pp. 23-35.

Taylor, C. 1991. The dialogical self. In Hiley, D. (ed.). *The interpretive turn: philosophy, science, and culture.* Ithaca: Cornell University Press, pp. 304-314.

Taylor, D. & Moghaddam, F. 1994. *Theories on intergroup relations. International social psychological perspectives.* Westport, Connecticut, London: Praeger.

Thomas, S. 2005. *The global resurgence of religion and the transformation of international relations.* New York: Palgrave McMillan.

Tworushka, U. 2008. Praktische Religionswissenschaft. In Klöcker, M. & Tworushka,U. *Praktische Religionswissenschaft*, Köln: Böhlau.

Tyrell, H., Krech, V. & Knoblauch (Hrsg.), H. 1998. *Religion als Kommunikation.* Würzburg: Ergon Verlag.

United Republic of Tanzania (URT). 2005. *The constitution of the United Republic of Tanzania of the year 1977.* Dar es Salaam: President's Office.

U.S. Department of State. (2007). *Human Rights Report: Tanzania.* Bureau of Democracy, Human Rights, and Labor, Washington, DC.

Valkenberg, W. & Wijsen, F. (eds). 1997. *The polemical dialogue. Research into dialogue, truth and truthfulness.* Saarbrücken: Verlag für Entwicklungspolitik.

Van Bergen, J. 1981. *Development and religion in Tanzania: sociological sounding and Christian participation in rural transformation.* Christian Literature Society, Madras and Inter-University Institute for Missiological and Ecumenical Research,Leiden.

Van Binsbergen, W. 2003. *Intercultural encounters. African and anthropological lessons towards a philosophy of interculturality.* Münster: LIT Verlag.

Van Bruinessen, M. 2004. Post-Soeharto Muslim engagements with civil society and democratization. In Samuel, H. & Schulte Nordholt, H. (eds), *Indonesia in transition.* Yogyakarta: Pustaka Pelajar.

Van Dijk, T. 1987. *Communicating racism. Ethnic prejudice in thought and talk.* Newbury Park: Sage.

Van Dijk, T. 2008. *Discourse and context. A sociocognitive approach.* Cambridge: Cambridge University Press.

Van Meijl, T. & Driessen, H. 2003. Multiple identifications and the self. Introduction. Focaal. *European Journal of Anthropology* 42, pp. 17-29.

Verschueren, J., Ostman, J. & Blommaert, J. (eds). 1995. *Handbook of pragmatics.* Amsterdam, Philadelphia: Benjamins.

Verschuren, P. &. Doorewaard, H. 1999. *Designing a research project.* Utrecht: LEMMA.

Bibliography

Versteijnen, F. 1991. *The Catholic mission of Bagamoyo*. Saarbrücken: Zuber & COD.

Von Stuckrad, K. 2003. Discursive study of religion. From states of mind to communication and action. *Method and Theory in the Study of Religion* 15, pp. 255-271.

Wallace, R. & Wolf, A. 1991. *Contemporary sociological theory; continuing the classical tradition,* 3rd ed. Englewood Cliffs, Nijmegen: Prentice-Hall.

Weber, M. 1958. *Essays in sociology*. Translated & edited by Gerth, H & Mills, C.W. New York: Oxford University Press.

Weber, M. 1968. *Charisma and institution building. Selected papers*. Translated and edited by Eisenstadt, S. Chicago, London: University of Chicago Press.

Welbourn, F. 1965. *East African Christians*. London: Oxford University Press.

Wester, V. & Peters, J. 2004. *Kwalitatieve analyse. Uitgangspunten en procedures*. Bussum: Coutinho.

Westerlund, D. 1980. Freedom of religion under socialist rule in Tanzania, 1961-1977. *Journal of Church and State*, pp. 87-103.

Whitely, W. 1971. *Maisha ya Hamed bin Muhammed el Murjebi: Kwa maneno yake Mwenyewe*. East Africa Literature Bureau, Dar es Salaam

Widdicombe, S. 1998. Identity as an analyst's and a participant's resource. In C. Antaki & S. Widdicombe (eds). *Identities in talk*. Thousand Oaks: Sage, 191-206.

Wierzbicka, A. 2006. The concept of dialogue in cross-linguistic and cross-cultural perspective. In *Discourse Studies* 8, pp. 675-703.

Wijsen, F. 1997. "Strive in competition for good deeds." Christians and Muslims in Tanzania. *Studies in Interreligious Dialogue* 7 (2), pp. 158-176.

Wijsen, F. 2000. Inculturation or syncretism. Popular Christianity in East Africa. In A. Kalliath (ed.), *Pilgrims in dialogue*. Bangalore: Dharmaram, pp. 247-285.

Wijsen, F. 2002. "When two elephants fight the grass gets hurt". Muslim-Christian relationships in upcountry Tanzania. In Wijsen, F. & Nissen, P. (eds), *'Mission is a must'*. Amsterdam, New York: Rodopi, pp. 235-248.

Wijsen, F. 2003. Religionism in Tanzania. In A. Borsboom & F. Jespers (eds), *Religion and identity*, Saarbrücken: Verlag für Entwicklungspolitik, pp. 121-137.

Wijsen, F. 2007. *Seeds of conflict in a haven of peace. From religious studies to interreligious studies in Africa*. Amsterdam, New York: Rodopi.

Wijsen, F. 2010. Discourse analysis in religious studies: the case of interreligious worship in Friesland. In *Anthropos. International Review of Anthropology and Linguistics* 105, pp. 1-15.

Wijsen, F. & Mfumbusa, B. 2002. Seeds of conflict. Christian-Muslim relationships in Tanzania, In Gort, J., Jansen, H. & Vroom, H. (eds), *Religion, conflict and reconciliation,* Amsterdam, New York: Rodopi, pp. 316-326.

Wijsen, F. & Mfumbusa, B. 2004. *Seeds of conflict. Religious tensions in Tanzania*. Nairobi: Pauline Publications Africa.

Wijsen, F., & Tanner, R. 2008. The limitation of an ecumenical language. The case of Ki-Swahili. In *Anthropos. International Review of Anthropology and Linguistics* 103, pp. 549-554.

Wijsen, F. & Nicolay, C. 2010. Interreligious worship in Friesland: a discourse analytical approach. *Studies in interreligious dialogue* 20 (1), pp. 58-77.

Wijsen, F. & Marcos, S. (eds). 2010. *Indigenous voices in the sustainability discourse: spirituality and the struggle for a better quality of life*. Münster: LIT.

Wijsen, F., Ndaluka, T. & Suhadi, C. 2010. "There are radical Muslims and normal Muslims". An analysis of the discourse on Islamic extremism. Paper read at the 20th World Congress of the International Association for the History of Religion, Toronto 15-12 August, 2010.

Wijsen, F., T. Ndaluka, 2012. Ujamaa Still Alive. A Sign of Hope for Africa? In A. J. Bwangatto (ed.), *Africa is not destined to die: Signs of Hope and Renewal*, Nairobi, Paulines Publications.

Wiredu, K. 1996. *Cultural universals and particulars. An African perspective*. Bloomington, Indianapolis: Indiana University Press.

Wittgenstein, L. 2009. *Philosophical investigations*. 4th ed. revised by Hacker, P. & Schulte, J. Malden, MA: Wiley-Blackwell.

Appendix
Discussion guide/topics

1. Relation between Muslims and Christians in general:

Probing question: How would you describe relations between Muslims and Christians in your area?

2. Relations of power, privilege and justice:

Probing question: What is your opinion about relations of power, privilege and justice between Muslims and Christians? How are power, privilege and justice distributed (in education, employment, etc.)?

3. Gender relations between men and women (interreligious marriage, divorce, dress codes):

Probing question: Are gender relations based on personal interpretation or on religious teachings?

4. Family and neighbourhood relations:

Probing question: How are community relations created? Who creates them? Are the relations religiously based? How do people relate with others of a different faith in the neighbourhood? How do they label believers of other faiths (naming)?

5. Coexistence:

Probing question: Is it possible to live together? Is everybody the same? (Probe on issue of trust.)

6. Causes of conflict:

Probing question: In your opinion, what causes conflict between Muslims and Christians?

7. Perception of open air preaching (*mihadhara*):

Probe whether faith gets stronger or is destroyed through *mihadhara*. Is open air preaching helpful?

Summary

This thesis studies the relationship between Muslims and Christians in Tanzania, more particularly social identity transformations through interreligious relations at individual (micro), institutional (mezzo) and societal (macro) levels. Until recently Tanzania has been regarded as a harmonious country where peaceful coexistence between Muslims and Christians was possible. Since the early 1990s, however, scholars have noted growing religio-centrism (*udini*) in Tanzania (Ludwig; Tambila; Wijsen) or the return of religion to the public domain. In this study we wanted to determine if the rhetoric about the return of religion to the public domain is an appropriate way of speaking about the transformations taking place in Tanzania. And if so, why and under what conditions do people elevate their religious identity above other (e.g. ethnic, national) identities? The main objectives of this research are to gain insight into the relation between religious discourse and (lack of) social cohesion (internal objective), and to contribute to a theory and method of studying interreligious relations (external objective).

The study looked at social identity transformation from the perspective of a theory of communicative practice and used Norman Fairclough's multidimensional and polymethodical model of critical or socio-cognitive discourse analysis to describe, interpret and explain the data. This gave us insight into how believers (Muslims and Christians) in Tanzania identify and position themselves in relation to other believers; how they draw on cognitive resources or mental models to produce (communicate) and consume (interpret) text and talk; and how they try to reproduce or transform the existing order by the way they speak about it. More particularly, we analysed socio-cognitive effects of language usage, that is whether participants' language use leads to (mis)understanding and (lack of) social cohesion in the community.

Data for this study were generated through Focus Group Discussions. Twenty-four FGDs were conducted in Dar es Salaam, Tanzania. In total, 134 participants were selected on the basis of religion, gender, age and education. Participants were first grouped according to their religion. There were groups of only Christians, groups of only Muslims and mixed groups of Christians and Muslims. Moreover, groups were organised on the basis of gender, age and profession. Consequently there were male and female groups of youngsters, male and female groups of elders, male and female groups of businesspeople and male and female groups of workers. Additional data were collected from 14 key informants, 12 open air preachers and local newspapers such as *Rai, Majira, Mwananchi, Nipashe, The Guardian, The Daily News, An-Nuur, Al-huda* and *Uhuru*. In addition, religious brochures and pamphlets were collected and analysed.

The thesis has five chapters. In the first chapter we outline the historical background to religion and interreligious relations in Tanzania and introduce the conceptual and technical design of the study. In chapters two, three and four we present and analyse the data for the Muslim groups, the Christian groups and the mixed groups respectively. In each of these chapters, using Norman Fairclough's model, we analyse the linguistic, discursive and social practice at micro (individual), mezzo (institutional) and macro (societal) level, focusing on mental models, subject positions and social relations. Chapter five draws conclusions with respect to social identity transformation in Tanzania, the theory of critical discourse analysis and the method of critical discourse analysis.

Data analysis revealed processes of socio-religious transformation in Tanzania. These transformations were expressed in terms of diversification, homogenisation and diffusion or creolization. Findings showed that there is quite a lot of individualisation and privatisation in the country and that de-institutionalisation has become a dominant trend. However, educational institutions have remained relatively strong and influence other institutions such as the family. Educational institutions have been the main cause of divergence between Muslims and Christians in Tanzania. Those who got a Western, and thus secular education in mainly Christian schools and colleges were able to get good jobs, send their children to school, allow their children to marry people of a different faith, compromise with others, and so forth.

This study also shows that despite a resurfacing of religion in the public domain, there is still strong social cohesion between Muslims and Christian. The dominant discourse that Muslims and Christians are children of the same father, comrades (*ndugu*), friends, fellows, et cetera is maintained. This shows that Nyerere's *ujamaa* rhetoric on national unity was reproduced as a mental model to enhance social cohesion and avoid conflict. There were also peripheral voices of those, mainly Muslims, who said that they are second class citizens in their country and ill-treated by their government. In themselves these voices are not new. They were also heard shortly after independence, but were suppressed during the socialist (*ujamaa*) era. What is new in the liberalist (*rukhsa*) era is that these voices are free to express themselves openly. This is what triggered the rhetoric of a resurgence of religion. Believers elevate their religious voices above other (e.g. ethnic, national) voices (as a Muslim informant said, "this is why we make noise") if

Summary

they feel that they are marginalised or that one religion is favoured above other religions (as another Muslim informant said, "A father cannot have two children and favour one of them").

In analysing religious discourse in Tanzania we assumed that language is performative and thus makes and unmakes social groups (Bourdieu; Blommaert; Van Dijk). Whereas KiSwahili as a lingua franca creates a common ground for Muslims and Christians, and thus can be considered an ecumenical language (Mazrui & Mazrui) we also noted the inclusion of English and Arabic words and phrases, which cause 'understanding misunderstanding' or 'understanding understanding' (Wijsen & Tanner). More particularly we noted an imbalance in open air preaching. Whereas the Bible was brought to Tanzania in German, French or English and was translated into KiSwahili and made available on a large scale, this applies less to the Qur'an. As one informant said, "For Christians it is difficult to challenge the Qur'an because of the language barrier." Nevertheless, whereas some informants saw open air preaching as a form of business or entertainment, it continues to attract audiences and remains popular. Open air preachers seem to challenge the political, economic, legal and religious domain and by doing so fill the vacuum left by charismatic leaders such as Nyerere.

In the introduction we explain that Norman Fairclough distinguishes perspectives (micro, mezzo, macro), methods (description, interpretation, explanation) and units (mental models, subjects positions, social relations) of analysis. On the methodological level Fairclough claims that discursive practice (or interaction) mediates between linguistic practice (or text) and social practice (or context). On the level of perspectives scholars of discourse analysis have claimed that most discourse analysis takes place at micro and macro level. In their analyses the relation between micro and macro level is not clear. After analysing religious discourses in Tanzania we add to Fairclough's model that the institutional (mezzo) level mediates between the individual (micro) and societal (macro) levels. Educational institutions in particular constitute the mental models which people use to produce (communicate) and consume (interpret) texts and talk.

Curriculum Vitae

Thomas Joseph Ndaluka holds a BA and MA in Sociology and has got an additional master training in Public Health. He has been working in the Department of Sociology and Anthropology, University of Dar es Salaam since 2000, first as a teaching assistant and since 2003 as an Assistant Lecturer. He teaches and works on issues related to the relationship between society and religion, social theory and methodology and poverty. Apart from working at University of Dar es Salaam, he is a part time lecturer at the Institute of Finance Management in Tanzania. Here, he teaches sociology courses for postgraduate diploma and undergraduate students. In addition, he has also worked as a part time lecturer at the Open University of Tanzania in 2007-2009. In 2009, he taught a course on 'discourse analysis as a qualitative analytical tool' to CODESRIA participants at the University of Dar es Salaam.

Apart from 10 years of teaching at the University of Dar es Salaam, Thomas Joseph Ndaluka conducted various research projects with the university, the government and private institutions in community related issues. Since 2007, he was engaged in a research project on 'Religious discourse, social cohesion and conflict in Tanzania'. This research involved two years field work with a focus on Dar es Salaam. Dissemination of research findings from this project was done at international seminars at the University of Dar es Salaam in Tanzania and Gadjah Mada University, Indonesia, in 2009. He also presented the project findings at a CERES Summer School, Radboud University Nijmegen, The Netherlands, in 2009. From this project and a sister project in Indonesia, two joint articles have been written and submitted for publication namely, 'There are radical Muslims and normal Muslims. An analysis of the discourse on Islamic extremism' and '*Ujamaa* is still alive. A sign of hope for Africa'. In 2001 Thomas Joseph Ndaluka was involved in desk research for a project on 'Democracy and religion in Tanzania'.

In 2008, Thomas Joseph Ndaluka worked for the Ministry of Health and Social Welfare: Department of Social Welfare and Family Health International, to develop the National Quality Standards for Care to Most Vulnerable Children, Tanzania. In 2011, he was also involved in a Baseline Survey on Artisanal and Small Scale Mining Activities and Preparation for an Artisanal and Small Scale Mining Data Base, under the Ministry of Energy and Minerals in Tanzania. Other works that he conducted are in the areas of culture, society, religion, health and environment.

Interreligious Studies
edited by Prof. Dr. Frans Wijsen and Dr. Jorge E. Castillo Guerra (Radboud University, Nijmegen)

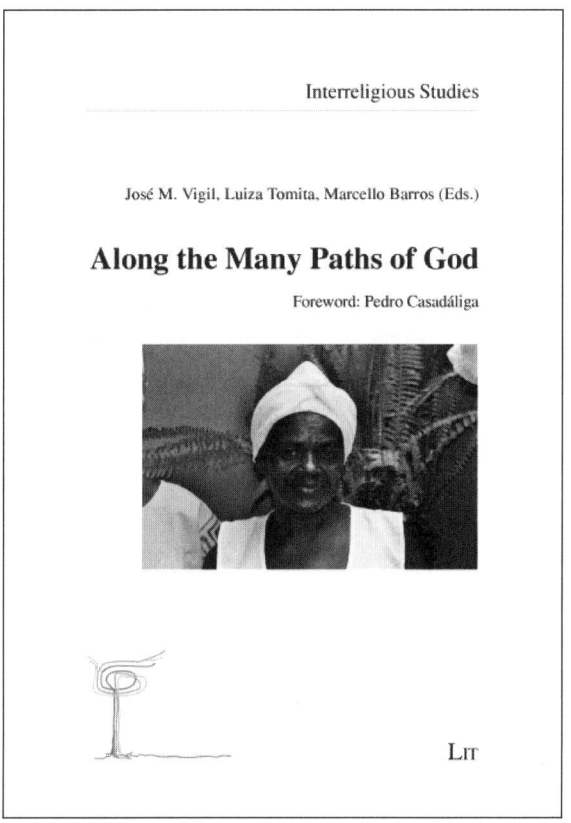

José M. Vigil; Luiza Tomita; Marcello Barros (Eds.)
Along the Many Paths of God
Foreword: Pedro Casadáliga
Latin American theology is associated with liberation, basic Christian communities, primacy of praxis and option for the poor. The present volume shows that Latin American theologians added new themes to the previous ones: religious pluralism, inter-religious dialogue and macro-ecumenism. It is the fruti of a programme of the Theological Commission of the Ecumenical Association of Third World Theologians (EATWOT) in Latin America, to work out a liberating theology of religions.
Bd. 1, 2008, 288 S., 29,90 €, br., ISBN 978-3-8258-1520-2

LIT Verlag Berlin – Münster – Wien – Zürich – London
Auslieferung Deutschland / Österreich / Schweiz: siehe Impressumsseite

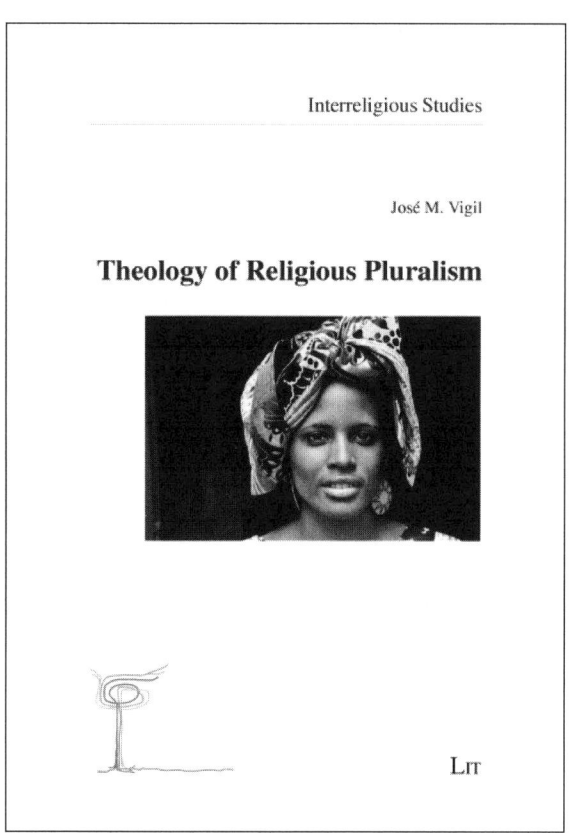

José M. Vigil
Theology of Religious Pluralism
This book offers a theology of religious pluralism. It was conceived and developed in Latin America from the perspective of liberation theology. One of the issues at play in the liberation of humanity is the world's ability to accept religious pluralism, and Latin American theology does not want to be silent on this topic. Born out of Latin American spirituality, this theology of religious pluralism is a liberating theology. It may be the first Latin American book that seeks to express something complete and systematic on this topic from the perspective of this continent and that of liberation theology.
Bd. 2, 2008, 360 S., 34,90 €, br., ISBN 978-3-8258-1519-6

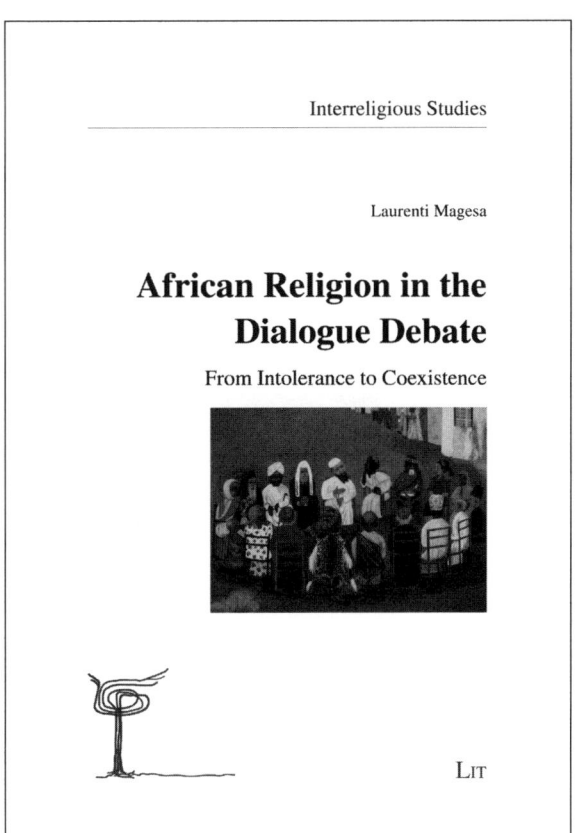

Laurenti Magesa
African Religion in the Dialogue Debate
From Intolerance to Coexistence
Dialogue between African Religion and other world religions has, regrettably, been a much neglected area in formal religious discourse in Africa to date. Moreover, up to now, the imperative of dialogue in the process of evangelism figures only peripherally – if at all – in the study of African Christian Theology. This book is probably the first deliberate, extensive and well-argued attempt by an African theologian to fill this unfortunate lacuna. How can Christian and African spiritualities interact with and enrich each other on the basis of mutual respect, without – as has historically been the case – the one necessarily seeking to eradicate the other? This is the fundamental question of dialogue discussed in the pages of this book.
Bd. 3, 2010, 208 S., 19,90 €, br., ISBN 978-3-643-90018-0

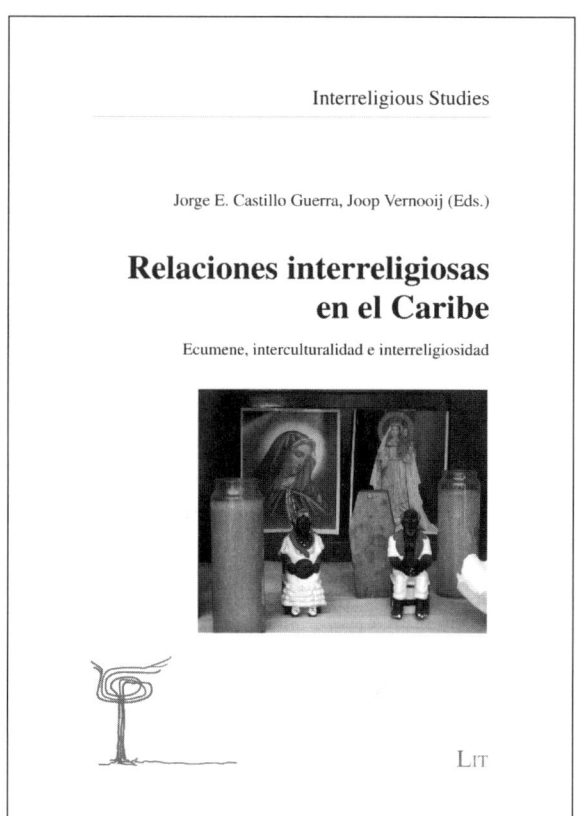

Jorge E. Castillo Guerra; Joop Vernooij (Eds.)
Relaciones interreligiosas en el Caribe
Ecumene, interculturalidad e interreligiosidad
Una investigación del campo religioso en el Caribe – de la que la presente publicación es una muestra muy valiosa – no sólo es urgente para rescatar el valor de la diversidad religiosa y espiritual, sino para «devolver» a sus pobladores algo de la riqueza apropiada por los poderes coloniales y neocoloniales. Además, puede dar un impulso decisivo para investigaciones parecidas en América Central y Sudamérica, tanto en países con fuerte presencia de religiones afrodescendientes (Brasil, Colombia, Ecuador) como indígenas originarias (Guatemala, México, Panamá, Ecuador, Perú, Bolivia). (...) En la presente publicación, se ha optado por un abordaje integral y sobre todo empírico del campo religioso en el Caribe. Se intenta articular los diálogos intercultural, ecuménico e interreligioso, partiendo desde la religiosidad popular, y no desde unos parámetros de tipo ideal o doctrinales (teológicos). Se trata, ante todo, de un intento de «fenomenología» religiosa que incluye aportes antropológicos, sociológicos y comparatísticos, complementados por enfoques más pastorales y eclesiológicos. La riqueza fenomenológica constituye una base muy valiosa y sólida para futuras investigaciones y reflexiones de tipo teológico, misionológico y hasta filosófico.
Josef Estermann
Bd. 4, 2010, 200 S., 19,90 €, br., ISBN 978-3-643-90021-0

LIT Verlag Berlin – Münster – Wien – Zürich – London
Auslieferung Deutschland / Österreich / Schweiz: siehe Impressumsseite